PROTECTION AND EMPIRE

For five centuries protection has provided a basic currency for organising relations among polities. Protection underpinned sprawling tributary systems, permeated networks of long-distance trade, reinforced claims of royal authority in distant colonies, and structured treaties. Empires made routine use of protection as they extended their influence, projecting authority over old and new subjects, forcing weaker parties to pay them for safe conduct and, sometimes, paying for it themselves. The result was a fluid politics that absorbed both the powerful and the weak while giving rise to institutions and jurisdictional arrangements with broad geographic scope and influence. This volume brings together leading scholars to trace the long history of protection across empires in Asia, Africa, Australasia, Europe and the Americas. Employing a global lens, it offers an innovative way of understanding the formation and growth of empires and uncovers new dimensions of the relation of empires to regional and global order.

Lauren Benton is Nelson Tyrone Jr Professor of History and Professor of Law at Vanderbilt University, Tennessee. She is a comparative and world historian whose research focuses on law in European empires, the history of international law and Atlantic world history.

Adam Clulow is Senior Lecturer at Monash University, Victoria. He is a global historian whose work focuses especially on European interaction with Tokugawa Japan and the maritime history of early modern Asia.

Bain Attwood is Professor of History at Monash University, Victoria. He has published extensively in the history of settler colonialism.

Protection and Empire

A GLOBAL HISTORY

Edited by

LAUREN BENTON

Vanderbilt University, Tennessee

ADAM CLULOW

Monash University, Victoria

BAIN ATTWOOD

Monash University, Victoria

CAMBRIDGE
UNIVERSITY PRESS

CAMBRIDGE
UNIVERSITY PRESS

University Printing House, Cambridge CB2 8BS, United Kingdom

One Liberty Plaza, 20th Floor, New York, NY 10006, USA

477 Williamstown Road, Port Melbourne, VIC 3207, Australia

314-321, 3rd Floor, Plot 3, Splendor Forum, Jasola District Centre, New Delhi - 110025, India

79 Anson Road, #06-04/06, Singapore 079906

Cambridge University Press is part of the University of Cambridge.

It furthers the University's mission by disseminating knowledge in the pursuit of
education, learning and research at the highest international levels of excellence.

www.cambridge.org
Information on this title: www.cambridge.org/9781108405966
DOI: 10.1017/9781108283595

First published 2018
First paperback edition 2018

A catalogue record for this publication is available from the British Library

Library of Congress Cataloging in Publication data
NAMES: Benton, Lauren A., 1956– | Clulow, Adam. | Attwood, Bain.
TITLE: Protection and empire : a global history / edited by Lauren Benton, Vanderbilt
    University, Tennessee, Adam Clulow, Monash University, Victoria, Bain Attwood,
    Monash University, Victoria.
DESCRIPTION: New York, NY : Cambridge University Press, 2017.
IDENTIFIERS: LCCN 2017024131| ISBN 9781108417860 (hardback) | ISBN 9781108405966
    (paperback)
SUBJECTS: LCSH: Responsibility to protect (International law) | Security, International. | Human
    security. | Imperialism–History. | Imperialism–Philosophy. | BISAC: LAW / International.
CLASSIFICATION: LCC JZ6369 .P74 2017 | DDC 355/.033–dc23 LC record available
    at https://lccn.loc.gov/2017024131

ISBN 978-1-108-41786-0 Hardback
ISBN 978-1-108-40596-6 Paperback

Contents

List of Maps

Notes on Contributors

Ahmad Amara is a postdoctoral fellow at the Center for the Study of Multiculturalism and Diversity, Hebrew University. He has held an international advocacy fellowship at Harvard Law School's Human Rights Program and is the author of several articles and book chapters. He was awarded his PhD by New York University.

Bain Attwood is Professor of History at Monash University. He is the author of several books, including *The Making of the Aborigines* (1989), *Rights for Aborigines* (2003), *Telling the Truth about Aboriginal History* (2005) and *Possession: Batman's Treaty and the Matter of History* (2009).

Lauren Benton is Nelson O. Tyrone Jr Professor of History and Professor of Law at Vanderbilt University. Her books include *Rage for Order: The British Empire and the Origins of International Law, 1800–1850*, co-authored with Lisa Ford (2016), *A Search for Sovereignty: Law and Geography in European Empires, 1400–1900* (2010), and *Law and Colonial Cultures: Legal Regimes in World History, 1400–1900* (2002).

Annabel Brett is Reader in the History of Political Thought at the University of Cambridge and Fellow of Gonville and Caius College, Cambridge. She is the author of *Liberty, Right and Nature: Individual Rights in Later Scholastic Thought* (1997), and *Changes of State: Nature and the Limits of the City in Early Modern Natural Law* (2011), and co-editor with Jim Tully of *Rethinking the Foundations of Modern Political Thought* (2006).

Adam Clulow is Senior Lecturer at Monash University. He is the author of *The Company and the Shogun: The Dutch Encounter with Tokugawa Japan* (2014) and articles in the *American Historical Review*, the *Journal of World History*, *Monumenta Nipponica* and other journals. He is the editor of *Statecraft and Spectacle in East Asia* (2010, 2013).

Barnaby Crowcroft has studied at the London School of Economics and Yale University and is currently completing a PhD in the Department of History at Harvard University. His dissertation research has been supported by the Social Science Research Council, the Krupp Family Foundation and the John Clive Memorial Fund. He is the author of articles in publications including the *Historical Journal* and *The Times Literary Supplement*.

Lisa Ford is Associate Professor of History at the University of New South Wales. She is the author of *Settler Sovereignty: Jurisdiction and Indigenous People in America and Australia, 1788–1836* (2010), and the co-author with Lauren Benton of *Rage for Order: The British Empire and the Origins of International Law, 1800–1850* (2016). She is the co-editor with Tim Rowse of *Between Indigenous and Settler Governance* (2013).

Karen B. Graubart is Associate Professor of Latin American History at the University of Notre Dame. She is the author of *With Our Labor and Sweat: Indigenous Women and the Formation of Colonial Society in Peru, 1550–1700* (2007) as well as articles in journals including *Hispanic American Historical Review*, *Colonial Latin American Review* and *Slavery and Abolition*.

David L. Howell is Professor of Japanese History at Harvard University. He is the author of *Capitalism from Within: Economy, Society and the State in a Japanese Fishery* (1995) and *Geographies of Identity in Nineteenth-Century Japan* (2005), and the editor of the *Harvard Journal of Asiatic Studies*.

Moses E. Ochonu is Cornelius Vanderbilt Professor of African History at Vanderbilt University. He is the author of *Colonial Meltdown: Northern Nigeria in the Great Depression* (2009), *Africa in Fragments: Essays on Nigeria, Africa, and Global Africanity* (2014), and *Colonialism by Proxy: Hausa Imperial Agents and Middle Belt Consciousness in Nigeria* (2014).

Gabriel de Avilez Rocha is Assistant Professor of History at Drexel University. His book manuscript, Empire from the Commons: Making Colonial Archipelagos in the Early Atlantic, examines how popular struggles over shared property and collective resources contributed to the formation of the Portuguese and Spanish empires in the sixteenth century. He was awarded his PhD by New York University.

Luca Scholz is a Mellon Fellow at Stanford University. He has held visiting scholarships at the University of Saint Andrews and Columbia University, and a lectureship at the Free University of Berlin. He is the author of several book chapters. He was awarded his PhD by the European University Institute.

Philip J. Stern is Sally Dalton Robinson Associate Professor of History at Duke University. He is the author of *The Company-State: Corporate Sovereignty and the Early Modern Foundations of the British Empire in India* (2011) as well as co-editor with Carl Wennerlind of *Mercantilism Reimagined: Political Economy in Early Modern Britain and its Empire* (2014).

Inge Van Hulle is Assistant Professor in Legal History at Tilburg University. She has held a visiting fellowship at the Cambridge Lauterpacht Centre for International Law, and has published several journal articles. She was awarded her PhD by the University of Leuven in Belgium.

Acknowledgements

Many of the chapters in this volume began life as papers for a workshop on protection and empire that was held at Harvard University in April 2016, for which the Harvard Australian Studies Committee, Monash University and Vanderbilt University provided the funding, the Department of History at Harvard University supplied the venue, and Mary McConnell, Nick McGregor and Ann Kaufman did most of the organisational work. We are indebted to all these institutions and people. We also wish to thank all the participants and chairs and especially Professor David Armitage and Professor Charles Maier, who acted as commentators for the workshop.

The Geheimes Staatsarchiv Preußischer Kulturbesitz gave permission to reproduce the map that accompanies Luca Scholz's chapter, and the Başbakanlik (Government) Ottoman Archives granted permission to use the map that appears in Ahmad Amara's chapter. We thank Helen McFarlane of Monash University for preparing the latter map for publication.

Part of Lauren Benton and Adam Clulow's chapter appeared in the *Journal of Global History* and is reprinted here with the consent of that journal.

At Cambridge University Press, Finola O'Sullivan lent her utmost support to this volume from the beginning.

Finally, our families deserve thanks for putting up with our absences and our absent-mindedness as we worked together on this volume.

Introduction: The Long, Strange History of Protection

LAUREN BENTON AND ADAM CLULOW

In a dizzying array of forms and fonts, every passport begins the same way. The opening page exhorts governments of all nations to provide protection for the holder when travelling in foreign territories.[1] Although seldom noted and even less frequently read, these words carry power: they convey the right to call on consular assistance, and they establish a legal basis for government action in support of sojourning citizens.

Such words offer a glimpse into a long, shared history of protection.[2] Protection underpinned sprawling tributary systems, permeated networks of long-distance trade, reinforced claims of royal authority in distant colonies and structured treaties. Empires made routine use of the notion of protection as they extended their influence, projecting authority over old and new subjects, forcing weaker parties to pay them for safe conduct and sometimes paying for it themselves. Smaller political communities, including those nestled inside empires, leaned on ideas of protection as they negotiated their status in relation to more powerful neighbours and would-be conquerors. The result was a fluid politics of protection that absorbed both the powerful and the weak while giving rise to institutions and jurisdictional arrangements with broad geographic scope and influence.

If protection arrangements served only to guide relations across political communities, they would be of enormous significance in world history. But promises of protection did much more. Protection as a framework for inter-polity relations developed in dynamic tension with protection as a way of describing power *within* political communities. It lent legitimacy to sovereigns and to their delegates and agents, who pledged to shelter subjects and dependants from poverty and harm as well as the exercise of arbitrary justice. In this way, diverse rulers used the language of protection both to promote internal order and to project power beyond their borders.

Protection travelled well. Indeed, the strategic value of what has been called 'protection talk' lay in its capacity to spark analogies across very different political settings.[3] In this environment there was value in vagueness. References to protection flourished especially in zones of ambiguous control, and the imprecision of the term made definite legal status and responsibility elusive, permitting multiple interpretations to co-exist at the same time. The blurring of 'inside' and 'outside' dimensions of protection meant that it was often unclear who was protecting whom or what was the exact nature of the relationship between the protector and the protected individual, group, vessel or polity. Practices of protection were in this sense like other kinds of cultural practice: there was ample scope for improvisation, virtuosity and false steps, and participants had a tendency to represent vaguely understood routines as firm rules of conduct when it suited them to do so.

Despite its ubiquitous nature and clear importance in world history, scholars have only just begun to take the measure of protection as both fluid doctrine and flexible practice. One effort belongs to historians of international law and order. Looking backward from the twentieth-century emergence of the Responsibility to Protect – the doctrine guiding interventions by sovereign states inside other states in order to protect endangered groups – they have sought its origins in shifting meanings of protection in political thought and diplomatic practice over several centuries.[4] Another strand in the study of protection has analysed the jurisdictional politics surrounding efforts to protect special classes: examples include claims by the Catholic Church to protect 'miserable peoples', the creation of a special class of Indian protectors in the Spanish Empire, and the proliferation of offices of protection for slaves, Aborigines and other vulnerable subjects in European empires.[5] A third set of works on protection has focused on its relation to violence. By definition the extension of protection was a promise of shelter from harm, and on the other side of that promise lay the possibility of real physical danger. Military or naval power allowed the collection of protection payments of various kinds, including payments to forestall attack by the protectors, a practice that generated sprawling, mafia-like 'protection rackets'.[6]

The chapters in this volume build on these approaches to the study of protection while opening up new ways of writing its history. Our shared starting point is a basic premise: protection, though present across an array of political communities, held particular significance in the politics of empires. As vast, composite polities, empires were not just large states but also systems of states in which 'inside' and 'outside' references to protection overlapped and recombined.[7] Imperial agents and their interlocutors touted protection as a framework for interpolity relations, a strategy for rule and, at times, a justification for rebellion. This reliance on protection in turn shaped institutions and ideas with long-lasting influence and even the capacity to shift the character of vast regional and global regimes. Just as historians have placed empires at the centre of world history, the contributors to this volume situate protection at the heart of the study of empires.[8]

We know the outlines of much of this story. Protection arrangements linked to tribute were common to early empires, from China to Rome, and conquests across Central Asia and the Middle East depended on promises to protect the lives, property and religion of invaded communities upon their submission.[9] In medieval Europe royal promises of protection helped to structure composite monarchies, and the Church insisted on its special standing to protect vulnerable subjects.[10] If such dynamics were already present, the early modern period witnessed an acceleration and expansion of the uses of protection. As long-distance trade and cross-polity interactions intensified, global empires came routinely to cite protection in constructing fluid networks of alliances and in efforts to consolidate control over territory. In the nineteenth century, particularly in some British crown colonies and in settler colonies like New South Wales, protection claims pervaded the daily business of government and led eventually to the formation of specialised institutions to protect native peoples. On the peripheries of empire, colonial officials asserted that they were acting to protect persecuted foreigners when they annexed territories under rulers they defined as despotic overlords.[11]

The imperial promise to protect old and new subjects shaped inter-imperial and international projects of protection still later. The creation of formally designated protectorates and protected states in the late nineteenth and early twentieth centuries again placed protection at the heart of the international order. In the late twentieth century, debates about the extent of states' obligations to intervene in other sovereign states to prevent atrocities crystallised in the Responsibility to Protect doctrine.[12] Imperial strains of protection talk persisted in this doctrine, and they continue to recur within international law.[13]

Contributions to this volume deepen our understanding of the phases and transitions of this history while also generating new findings and questions about protection and empires. The volume's broad geographic scope spanning Asia, Africa, the Middle East, Europe and the Americas reminds us that although protection was central to European empires Europeans did not invent the idea of protection or export it via European imperial ventures. As Ahmad Amara shows in his chapter, Ottoman officials and subjects referred to their empire as *memalik-i mahruse-i şahane* or 'the well-protected domains of His Imperial Majesty' while networks of protection and tribute acted to extend Ottoman influence far beyond imperial borders.[14] In Southeast Asia protection formed a vital commodity of cross-polity exchange and found its way into treaties and informal pacts distributed across the region. In the Chinese Empire protection and the promise thereof featured in a sprawling tributary system that allowed distant states to petition for protection against foreign incursions.[15] Rather than introducing something new, Europeans found that protection arrangements could facilitate their entrée into other societies. Our own contribution to this volume describes the process by which transitions from alliance-making to conquest operated within fluid arrangements of protection. The same arrangements made possible the continued existence over long periods of important regional formations that we call 'interpolity zones'.[16]

Protection could provide a mechanism capable of facilitating peaceful interactions among polities. It could also spark violence. In this volume, Gabriel Rocha shows that in the region stretching from southern Portugal and Spain along the coast of West Africa and encompassing the Azores and the Canary Islands, French and Iberian captains relied on protection gambits like convoys to stake tenuous claims over resources and commandeer the booty collected through plunder. Rocha's story is not the usual one of Iberian 'expansion' and European 'rivalry'; rather the exercise of protection encouraged violence by projecting and sustaining the logic of plunder and raiding.

Where it was deployed across the early modern world, protection generated areas of patchy or overlapping control, some on distant imperial fringes but others in congested arteries of transport and trade. In his chapter, Luca Scholz shows that mobility in the fragmented political landscape of the Holy Roman Empire depended on a consistent but imprecise notion that sojourners could carry protection with them. Riverine regions hosted sharp jurisdictional conflicts as merchants, their sponsors and strings of polities along rivers negotiated the safe conduct of travellers, resulting in unevenly configured claims to dominion over riverine space. In a contrasting case, Karen Graubart reveals that the Spanish empire's promise to protect Indians in the New World – a promise initially unconnected to geographic constraints – gave rise in at least one place to a walled enclosure of protected people. The politics of protection in these and other cases shaped the multiform legal geography of early modern empires.

Continuities and discontinuities in the discourse of protection open a promising theme in the history of political thought and legal culture. Annabel Brett reveals that the language of 'protect' and 'protector', though muted in the sixteenth century, became a louder refrain in the fraught context of civil war in seventeenth-century England. Discussions about the king's rights and responsibilities repeatedly deployed 'the protection card', to use Brett's evocative phrase, and the slippage between protection as a function of the sovereign's power and protection as a corollary of the sovereign's justice – might and right – was politically charged and generative. Brett's account disturbs the neat story others have told about the Hobbesian origins of a necessary link between protection and sovereignty that international intervention would disturb in later centuries. In his contribution Philip Stern argues that the layered qualities of political and legal ordering in England and its empire depended on refrains about the legitimacy of the corporation, a form encompassing not just overseas companies but also other combinations of association and authority in fragmented political orders. At home and abroad, overseas corporations toggled between their overlapping roles as protecting and protected enterprise, in the process generating what Stern describes as a cacophony of claims.

In their attention to the presence of multiple permutations, studies of protection and the construction of colonial governance undermine assumptions about the smooth development from European ideas about Leviathan to more recent models of state sovereignty. Bain Attwood's novel reading of the Treaty of Waitangi challenges a long-standing tendency for historians to highlight the dominant strand of imperial thinking or policy about protection rather than recognising the presence of multiple registers of 'protection talk', each available to be combined and recombined.[17] Analysing British claims to New Zealand from 1800 to 1840, Attwood shows that a wide range of actors – entrepreneurs, traders, missionaries, politicians, officials, settlers, colonisation companies, missionary societies, indigenous people and others – invested considerable political capital in protection arrangements, in an untidy process that pulled British subjects into the state's jurisdiction.

By the mid-point of nineteenth century, as we learn from Lisa Ford's chapter, multiple schemes for protection were circulating, available for modification and impressment in very different contexts. Offers of protection through the extension of jurisdiction, a strategy deployed by colonial authorities in New South Wales, echoed the widely circulating rhetoric of abolition while at the same time sounding local variations. In practice the process put in place a 'cut-rate model of protection' that tasked a handful of officials with overseeing vast spaces and exposed the contradictions of imperial authority. Ultimately, the promise of treating all people equally under the law eroded the intellectual buttress for special protection for some classes of people.

Just as the politics of protection constituted the authority of colonial governments, references to protection also coursed through relations between imperial governments and local elites. Several chapters in this volume examine the layered sovereignty of empires as the counterpart to replicating practices of protection. Ahmed Amara establishes the salience of protection inside the Ottoman Empire, then traces the way Bedouins, as subjects of Ottoman protection, also positioned themselves successfully as the protectors of Ottoman borders. Moses Ochonu uncovers a protective system in West Africa that was 'replicable'. Examining political arrangements in Nigeria, he shows how British colonial officials enfranchised Muslim Hausa sub-protectors in a position over their 'pagan' apprentices. This system would yield unexpected results when British colonial officials had to intervene to protect a range of groups from the practices of the very authorities that they had themselves placed in power.

If a focus on protection prompts a reassessment of imperial conquest, expansion and consolidation, it also sheds new light on later transitions, from the nineteenth-century rise of international law to the twentieth-century end of empire. Inge Van Hulle corrects the usual story of the emergence of protectorates in the nineteenth century as a European invention of the late nineteenth century. In her original account, layered colonial politics in the Gold Coast gave rise to a form of 'protectorate' avant la lettre. The shift in perspective facilitates broader arguments about the imperial origins of international law.[18] Focusing on the collapse of the protectorate system in the twentieth century, Barnaby Crowcroft shows how in a series of unlikely alliances imperial or colonial officials, nationalist champions and local leaders sought either to brush aside decades of improvisation as meaningless fictions or to give substance to claims of protection. Examining the British West African territory of the Gold Coast, he demonstrates how the language of protection offered a mechanism for the leaders of the Northern Territories to place an unexpected roadblock in front of the planned British withdrawal.

Protection arrangements and their systemic change developed simultaneously inside and across multiple empires, and our perspective allows us to recast the international order as still in part an inter-imperial construct. David Howell explains that first Tokugawa and then Meiji officials became increasingly interested in deploying protection as a way of securing an uncertain frontier. Japanese claims to nurture and protect the Ainu were presented in direct opposition to real or imagined Russian designs. For a magistrate in charge of shogunal policy in Hokkaido, the local Ainu population had to be protected in order to ward off Russian incursions that aimed to use false displays of benevolence and charity to extend European influence. This chapter and other contributions shift our gaze away from the usual benchmarks of European diplomacy and writings about international law to the imperial and inter-imperial practice of protection and its deep consequences for regional and global configurations of power.

The chapters in this volume catalogue the multiplicity of meanings attached to protection: it could signify a relationship between the church or sovereign and vulnerable peoples, refer to guarantees of safe conduct through provision of passes and licences, constitute an arrangement for alliance and mutual security or represent a corollary to divided or layered sovereignty. The array of meanings and contexts is so vast, one has to ask: to what extent does the sheer variety of forms of protection present a problem for historians? Can a chameleon concept be analytically precise? Put another way, is it possible to write a global history of protection?

Certainly, we will grant that protection is difficult to pin down. Within the confines of a particular encounter, meanings of protection could swing between weightily substantial and airily vague. At times, claims to protection seemed to be empty rhetoric, little more than an irrelevant promise observed by neither side; in other cases it signalled seemingly irrevocable pacts, so firm that any hint of rupture could trigger commitments to go to war. Equally, though protection talk sometimes came accompanied by clear-cut guarantees of safety, we should not assume that, even when couched in the strongest possible terms, it automatically translated into actual security. Safe-conduct passes meant something up until the moment they failed to work, when protected parties were left clutching worthless documents, their goods and sometimes lives placed at risk by the very agents supposedly bound to aid them. How to make sense of such a chimeric phenomenon?

Despite these flickering qualities, protection arrangements could open up real spaces for security, and their absence could spell disaster. Protection was, in other words, more than cheap talk. Weaker polities and merchant diasporas came back again and again to protection precisely because it served a genuine purpose in a dangerous world, and they avidly sought out multiple protectors or worked to pile up protective arrangements. Even when imperial conquerors simply gestured at protection to install legitimate rule, its promise held political possibilities. The 'vice-regal ghetto' where Indians found a space for indigenous law enabled the preservation of lives and property, hardly an inconsequential outcome for those inside the circle of protection. The rhetoric of protection facilitated rounds of maritime raiding but also sheltered vulnerable merchants from waves of violence and produced a regulatory order for the seas in a bewildering but widely recognised array of pass systems. As a rationale for small wars, arguments about protection appealed to despotic imperial agents and colonial officials, even as some subject populations deployed the same protection language as a shield. Consider the example of early nineteenth-century Ceylon, where the British paired a discourse about extending the protection of British law with the plan of annexing the Kingdom of Kandy.[19]

Such combinations of inside and outside protection, and of protection talk and actual institutions, were anything but random. We find some repeating and generalisable historical processes and patterns, some with significance for periodisation in world history. The exercise of protection of subjects by imperial powers ('inside' protection) served to thrust imperial influence into new territories and realms ('outside' protection). Security arrangements between two polities ('outside' protection) often transitioned into claims of political dominance and the extension of rule ('inside' protection). This multiform ambiguity lent protection its appeal and injected an element of instability into any imperial or inter-imperial order built around this framework. But it also constituted a series of interconnected regional and global regimes and made them visible and resilient. Centred on empires and inter-imperial relations across a long phase of global interactions, such fledgling regulatory orders spanned periods that historians sometimes divide into early modern and modern phases. The same processes conditioned the rise of international law and decolonisation in the nineteenth and twentieth centuries.

Its usefulness and mutability allowed protection in its various forms to serve as a touchstone for arrangements of power from the early modern period to the twentieth century. Protective regimes helped to regulate interpolity relations, giving clear shape to expectations about interactions across political, legal and cultural divides. Like passports, such regimes facilitated movement, framed commercial interactions and generated translatable political terms. Their history offers a new way of characterising the cultural politics of empires and, as these chapters show, of narrating the history of the world.

NOTES

1 Although we make no claim to have conducted an exhaustive survey of passports, this formulation is standard across a vast range of these documents.

2 Lauren Benton and Adam Clulow, 'Legal Encounters and the Origins of Global Law', in Jerry H. Bentley et al. (eds), *Cambridge History of the World, Volume 6, Part 2*, Cambridge University Press, Cambridge, 2015, pp. 50–79.

3 For a general discussion of 'protection talk', see Lauren Benton and Lisa Ford, *Rage for Order: The British Empire and the Origins of International Law, 1800–1850*, Harvard University Press, Cambridge, MA, 2016, Chapter 4.

4 Anne Orford, *International Authority and the Responsibility to Protect*, Cambridge University Press, Cambridge, 2011; Luke Glanville, *Sovereignty and the Responsibility to Protect: A New History*, University of Chicago Press, Chicago, 2014.

5 Alan Lester and Fae Dussart, *Colonization and the Origins of Humanitarian Governance: Protecting Aborigines Across the Nineteenth-Century British Empire*, Cambridge University Press, Cambridge, 2014; Alan Lester and Fae Dussart, 'Trajectories of

Protection: Protectorates of Aborigines in early 19th Century Australia and Aotearoa New Zealand', *New Zealand Geographer*, vol. 64, no. 3, 2008, pp. 205–20; R. Jovita Baber, 'Law, Land, and Legal Rhetoric in Colonial New Spain: A Look at the Changing Rhetoric of Indigenous Americans in the Sixteenth Century', in Saliha Belmessous (ed.), *Native Claims: Indigenous Law against Empire, 1500–1920*, Oxford University Press, New York, 2011, pp. 41–62.

6   Michael Pearson, *Indian Ocean*, Routledge, London and New York, 2003, p. 121. For some sample works on maritime pass systems, see Sebastian R. Prange, 'A Trade of No Dishonor: Piracy, Commerce, and Community in the Western Indian Ocean, Twelfth to Sixteenth Century', *American Historical Review*, vol. 116, no. 5, 2011, pp. 1269–93; Elizabeth Mancke, 'Early Modern Expansion and the Politicization of Oceanic Space', *Geographical Review*, vol. 89, no. 2, 1999, pp. 225–36.

7   On empires as systems of states, see Benton and Ford, Chapter 6.

8   Jane Burbank and Frederick Cooper, *Empires in World History: Power and the Politics of Difference*, Princeton University Press, Princeton, 2010.

9   The literature on premodern empires is vast. As an example, see Jonathan Karam Skaff, *Sui-Tang China and Its Turko-Mongol Neighbors: Culture, Power, and Connections, 580–800*, Oxford University Press, New York, 2012.

10 Helen Lacey, 'Protection and Immunity in Later Medieval England', in T.B. Lambert and David Rollason (eds), *Peace and Protection in the Middle Ages*, Centre for Medieval and Renaissance Studies-Pontifical Institute of Mediaeval Studies, Toronto, 2009, pp. 78–96.

11 Benton and Ford, Chapter 4.

12 Glanville; Orford.

13 Benton and Ford, p. 192.

14 For Ottoman uses of protection, see Gábor Kármán and Lovro Kunčević (eds), *The European Tributary States of the Ottoman Empire in the Sixteenth and Seventeenth Centuries*, Brill, Leiden, 2013.

15 The classic and much-cited work on the Chinese tributary system is John King Fairbank (ed.), *The Chinese World Order: Traditional China's Foreign Relations*. Harvard University Press, Cambridge, MA, 1968. More recently, a new generation of scholars has emphasised the limits of this traditional model by showing that, to quote Peter Perdue, 'tributary views were only one of a variety of Chinese world views, which appeared at certain times more prominently than others' ('The Tenacious Tributary System', *Journal of Contemporary China*, vol. 24, no. 96, 2015, p. 1007).

16 Lauren Benton and Adam Clulow, 'Empires and Protection: Making Interpolity Law in the Early Modern World', *Journal of Global History*, vol. 12, no. 1, 2017, pp. 74–92.

17 Benton and Ford, p. 115.

18 Anghie Antony, *Imperialism, Sovereignty and the Making of International Law*, Cambridge University Press, Cambridge, 2005.

19 Benton and Ford, Chapter 4.

PART I

Protecting Subjects, Projecting Power

Protection and the Channelling of Movement on the Margins of the Holy Roman Empire

LUCA SCHOLZ

Protection played a pivotal role in the channelling of goods and people in old-regime societies. In the fragmented political landscape of the Holy Roman Empire of the German Nation, escorts, guard patrols and letters of passage were often a precondition for unobstructed travel. At the same time the territorial rulers' protection of travellers and mobile populations could become a vehicle for gaining control over strategic thoroughfares and thereby provide considerable economic and political leverage. As this suggests, protection was an ambiguous notion, not only in early modern regimes of movement but also in the feudal collective imagination as a whole. It provided a fundamental justification for early modern state building while featuring in a range of key debates centred on the vexed relationship between protection, power and obedience.[1] Its prominence in early modern politics and thought has led some to the conclusion that 'security is *the* issue of modernity'.[2]

The co-existence of hundreds of fragmented, blurred and often overlapping polities that were integrated in a common imperial structure makes the Holy Roman Empire a valuable site for studying the role of protection in interpolity mobility in the premodern period. Made up of more than 300 quasi-sovereign political entities, the Old Reich challenges conventional conceptions of state formation.[3] The political entities at the heart of the so-called Westphalian system followed a 'manorial' rather than a 'territorial logic', and should be seen as 'aggregation of titles of ownership', rather than as 'states in the making'.[4] While the empire's political culture can be described in terms of 'organised hypocrisy',[5] aggressive pettiness and political deadlock, it provided religious toleration, the protection of the least powerful political units and a court system in which even peasants could appeal against their rulers.[6] Seen from afar, the empire's role was as pivotal as it was supine. As Brendan Simms has put it, the Old Reich lay 'at the heart of the European balance of power' and formed, together with its successor states, 'the crucible of the most important ideological changes in Europe: the Reformation, Marxism and Nazism were all incubated there'. Yet, as Simms notes, the Holy Roman Empire was politically weak and almost helpless in the face of the ambitions and conflicts of the major European powers.[7] Because of its peculiarity, the fragmented, polycentric complex of polities at the heart of Europe offers an opportunity for bridging the sometimes overemphasised gap that separates the historiography of Europe from that of its colonies and other parts of the early modern world. If early modern Europeans had wished to experience fully the idiosyncrasies of uneven, overlapping, fragmented territoriality that historians tend to associate with more remote parts of the world, a trip to Weimar or Frankfurt would have given them just that.

In many cases, the protection and governance of interpolity mobility in the Holy Roman Empire was framed as a matter of safe conduct. Consequently, in the first part of this chapter I will focus on this as a means of protection as well as an economic, political and symbolic instrument in the hands of the empire's territorial rulers. Here I provide a case study of a dispute around the dominion over a river in the empire's North during the late sixteenth and early seventeenth centuries in order to reconstruct a practical example of safe conduct. In the second part of this chapter I will survey the use of protection and security as strategic arguments for the justification of territorial expansion and a self-serving order of movement. In general I propose in this essay to broaden our understanding of protection's role in the ordering of movement by highlighting the importance of agency, contingency and ambiguity in everyday interactions between protector and protected.

DOUBLE-EDGED PROTECTION

Few institutions gave substance to hospitality and the protective duties of lordship as concretely as safe conduct. It was a routine institution throughout the medieval and early modern world.[8] However, in the context of the Holy Roman Empire's complex territoriality it acquired an extraordinary and lasting significance. It fulfilled important functions for the protection of travelling rulers and persons of rank, messengers, markets, and assemblies and their participants, especially during the Middle Ages. Safe conduct duties, which were levied on trade flows in addition to customs duties, sometimes merged with the latter to form a single transit duty.[9] Different forms of safe conduct letters for felons, debtors or foreigners, as well as safe conduct treaties between cities warranted their bearers' protection for limited periods of time.[10]

While safe conduct provided powerful means for securing 'the wayfaring man' and establishing public safety, certain forms of safe conduct lost their immediate protective function.[11] In the early modern period the institution gained considerable importance as a fiscal, political and symbolic instrument at the hand of territorial rulers.[12] The fiscal exploitation of safe conduct was particularly marked in the case of regalian safe conduct, which entitled the conductor to control, protect and tax movements of goods and people on public roads and rivers.[13] The letters of safe conduct that were issued to Jews as travel, residence or work permits could be a profitable source of income as well.[14] Different letters of safe conduct were granted to representatives of foreign potentates, especially those with whom the host was in enmity.[15] Letters were also issued when foreign officials performed acts that were seen as signs of sovereignty in the bestower's dominion, such as transporting prisoners. Physical acts of escorting were, moreover, an important means for symbolically asserting seigneurial prerogatives over roads and rivers and their boundaries.[16]

While regalian conduct was conceived as reciprocal in legal theory — the safe conduct authority being obliged to maintain the road and river infrastructure within its dominion and to vouch for the traveller's safety — this was not always translated into practice. Where travellers were physically escorted, safe conduct offered effective protection to travellers up to the nineteenth century,[17] but in many territories it was ministered by full- or part-time officials whose principal duty was to enforce the levy of conduct tolls and to patrol the roads in order to identify potential evaders.[18] Such regimes were more cost-effective than the physical escorting of travellers, and primarily served the fiscal and commercial interests of territorial rulers. Conversely, while the obligation of a ruler to pay compensation for damage and assaults suffered on his safe-conduct roads remained a cornerstone of the legal discussion of regalian safe conduct during the seventeenth century, it was not always satisfied in practice.[19] Thus, the history of safe conduct illustrates both the importance and the ambiguity of protection in early modern regimes of movement.

In times of crisis and conflict physical safe conduct remained the means of choice for protecting travellers. However, the same form of safe conduct could easily become a vehicle for territorial expansion and a means for advancing self-serving interests. The agents charged with protecting and policing passages on these thoroughfares played a pivotal role in brokering the mutuality of safe conduct. This can only be understood by observing interactions on the ground. The Weser, which was one of the most fiercely contested rivers in early modern Europe, provides a good example.[20] The last stretch of the waterway, called the Lower Weser, connected the city of Bremen with the North Sea (see Map 1). At the end of the sixteenth century Bremen numbered around 20,000 inhabitants and though it was de facto independent

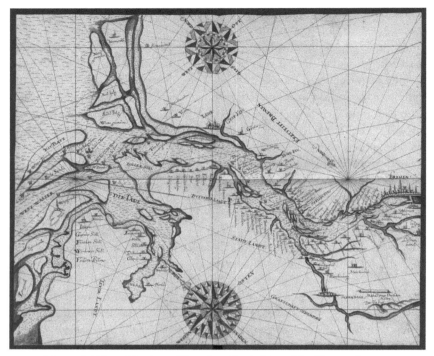

MAP 1: Manuscript Map of the Lower Weser from the Archives of the Elector of
Brandenburg, c. 1600–20
(Geheimes Staatsarchiv Preußischer Kulturbesitz, I. HA Geheimer Rat, Rep. 19 Strom-, Schifffahrts- und
Zollsachen, Nr. 71 a, Fasz. 2, © GStA PK)

and commanded its own extramural territory the city was formally subject
to the Prince-Bishops of Bremen on the right bank of the river.[21] To acquire
the status of a Free Imperial City had been one of the Bremen's most important political projects since the thirteenth century, but it only achieved this
after the Thirty Years' War. As the city's wealth and fiscal revenues largely
depended on maritime trade, another key ambition throughout the late
medieval and early modern periods was to secure safe passage on the Lower
Weser. In the Late Middle Ages the city had managed to acquire some strate-
gically important territories on the right side of the stream, but the possessions
were not sufficient to control the river.[22] Bremen's principal opponents in its
struggle for the Lower Weser were the neighbouring counts of Oldenburg.
During the sixteenth and seventeenth centuries the counts controlled most of
the left bank of the Lower Weser as well as some exclaves on the right side.[23]
Their aim was not so much to safeguard maritime trade but to levy transit
duties on the ships that navigated the river.[24]

Throughout the Middle Ages and the early modern period the Lower Weser had been troubled by pirates and freebooters.[25] With the beginning of the Dutch War of Independence in 1568, piracy on the North Sea increased significantly, as did the insecurity in the North-West of the empire. Both the Spanish and the Dutch required Bremen to supply ammunition, provisions and ships.[26] The Lower Weser and the river Jade presented lucrative hunting grounds for privateers. For example in 1592 a pirate looted a flotilla of twenty-two ships.[27] Comital subjects and officials colluded with the pirates.[28] Bremen stepped up its presence on the river during the 1570s. Its warships hunted the freebooters into the tributaries of the river Weser, where they fled on land. The counts of Oldenburg, however, denounced and opposed such pursuits as encroachments on their territory. The difficult terrain and the constant competition between the two polities thus favoured piracy in the region.[29] To counter the attacks of freebooters Bremen's convoys repeatedly escorted vessels to and from its ports during the sixteenth and seventeenth centuries.[30] In 1587 Bremen armed eight boats which accompanied ships from the sea to the city.[31] An ordinance from 1593 informed the travellers that the city's convoy ships would usher all vessels that requested this service.[32]

The ships that Bremen maintained on the Lower Weser were highly adaptable agents which the city hoped would help enforce a series of claims over the river. The protection of travellers was, it is evident, one of the soldiers' foremost duties. All instructions issued between 1620 and 1647 charged the captains with ensuring safe and unobstructed navigation.[33] This entailed monitoring and patrolling the entire Lower Weser (from Bremen unto the 'salty sea'), checking and inspecting suspicious vessels, escorting endangered ships, and persecuting freebooters and all those hampering navigation.[34] To ensure the enforcement of such measures the city gave its captains carte blanche. They were authorised to use whatever means 'the circumstances and exigency require[d]',[35] such as detaining delinquents and seizing or even sinking their vessels. Moreover, the warships were charged with ensuring the navigability of the river. This meant, for instance, removing the stakes to which local fishermen fixed their nets. Since the spikes could seriously encumber the river's navigability, the warships were instructed to remove all newly erected hazards. The city also enjoined its ships to prevent other parties from checking and inspecting ships using the river. This was aimed at officials of the Count of Oldenburg who had been attempting to enforce a toll of their own since 1624.[36]

Protecting trade and ensuring navigability, however, were not the warships' only purposes. They were also charged with preventing all actions 'to the prejudice, detriment and disadvantage'[37] of the city of Bremen and its subjects.

The open wording of this instruction illustrates the malleability of Bremen's territorial claims over the river. In practice, the instruction covered all potential encroachments on the city's titles of dominion. One of the most obvious of these was a vessel's refusal to strike its sails at the passage of the warships. This was not simply a technical question. By striking its sails, which forces it stop, a ship attested its subjection to the local rulers. Consequently, the city regarded the obligation as an important symbol of its superiority over the river.[38] The legal deductions commissioned by the city in defence of its prerogatives put a similar emphasis on the quarrel's symbolic dimension. In the 1630s, when Bremen increasingly presented the toll dispute as a question of territorial superiority, such badges of sovereignty gained in importance.[39] Indeed, the very capacity of a political agent to bar movements on a road or river could be regarded as a token of territorial superiority. In the disputes between the city of Regensburg and the Dukes of Bavaria regarding dominion over the river Danube, Regensburg, which could block the river with metal chains, argued that he 'who has the might to hinder the navigation on a public river can also ascribe the dominion over that river to himself'.[40]

In 1576 Bremen agreed to inspect armed vessels only but in practice its warships made civilian ships strike their sails as well. Many boatmen refused to comply with the requests of Bremen's warships even though the captains of the warships were authorised to shoot at them.[41] In May 1613 two boatmen gave revealing accounts of their encounters with Bremen's warships to a comital notary.[42] The two men had sailed on the river, each with one ship transporting construction material for the Count of Oldenburg. When the first vessel passed Bremen's warship, the boatman bared his head and wished the soldiers 'a good morning'. The latter, however, fired three shots at the sails without warning. When the boatman asked for an explanation the captain shouted that he should have struck his sails in the presence of Bremen's warship. The visitor replied that he knew Bremen's ship well, but that 'thank God, he was not aware of any war'. When the captain learned that the boatman was from Oldenburg, however, he let him leave. The second boatman found the official in a less affable mood. When he passed Bremen's warship the soldiers fired several times and forced him to sail towards them. He was then required to come aboard the man-of-war. The captain defiantly asked 'Is this the wilful knave who refused to halt?' at which the boatman replied that 'he was no knave' and that the river belonged to the Count of Oldenburg. When the captain asked him to pay a buoy toll the boatman retorted that, as a subject of the Count of Oldenburg, he was exempt. When the captain demanded an indemnity of half a *Reichstaler* for every shot fired at him the boatman laughed and asked whether he was serious. The captain, however, was in no mood for joking and asked: 'Do you hold the shot in such low regard[?] If you received it on your skin [. . .] you would perhaps speak differently.' Yet the captain's attitude changed entirely when the boatman showed him his pass, which was issued by the Count of Oldenburg. The captain excused himself, said that he had thought the boatman came from Frisia, and let him go with 'nice words'.

Like the 'beer money'[43] that Bremen's soldiers had requested on earlier occasions, asking boatmen to 'reimburse' the shots fired at their ships recalls the terminology with which early modern officials and travellers referred to bribes.[44] The exaction of 'beer money', 'voluntary presents' and 'reimbursements' was not uncommon. Some safe conduct ordinances even formally sanctioned officials' reception of 'voluntary presents' from travellers.[45] Moreover, these were not the only cases in which escorts posed a threat to the people they were supposed to protect. In 1480, for instance, the Doge of Venice claimed damages from the Duke of Jülich because an Italian traveller had been robbed by the very ducal escorts charged with protecting him.[46] In 1635 escorts of the Duke of Jülich took 25 new pistols from the gunsmiths of Aachen whom they were escorting, even though the gunsmiths possessed an imperial letter of safe conduct.[47] On another occasion the escorts ran away and abandoned the merchants whom they were escorting to the highwaymen.[48] While the significance of such cases should not be overstated they challenge the assumption — one might call it a 'myth of rationality'[49] — that feudal power relationships were, by and large, reciprocal and that protection always meant protection. As the example of the Lower Weser suggests, historians should be wary of taking premodern protection talk at face value.

Perhaps the most controversial of Bremen's activities was the taxation of shipping.[50] In 1585 the city began to levy a new toll in order to finance its fleet. Two of Bremen's warships, positioned at the mouth of the river, requested a receipt from every vessel proving that the conduct toll had been paid at Bremen.[51] The new impost was despised by many boatmen, as it forced every boat to proceed to the sea via Bremen in order to pay the tariff and receive a ticket.[52] Many crafts were thus forced to make a long detour if they wished to avoid any incident with the warships. This procedure very much resembled the *cartaz* system with which the Portuguese established monopolies along certain sea routes and collected revenues and prizes.[53]

In 1585 four boatmen complained about Bremen's practice to the Count of Oldenburg.[54] As they had entered the Lower Weser from the sea their vessels had been stopped and inspected by Bremen's soldiers. The captain then ordered them to travel to Bremen to pay the safe conduct toll, the buoy and beacon levy, and an excise duty. If they wanted to leave the river on their return they could only proceed if they presented a written confirmation from the hand of the toll keepers in Bremen. Otherwise, they would be violently chased up the river again.[55] This was not an empty threat. Another skipper testified that he had seen Bremen's soldiers violently pushing five ships towards Bremen to pay the duties.[56] A boatman from Emden, who complained about the request, was struck to the ground by Bremen's captain with a blow to the neck.

Unsurprisingly, opposition to Bremen's new toll rose quickly and several captains grumbled about the new duties to their authorities, who then protested to the Council of Bremen. The city of Emden, for instance, complained that it was without precedent and obstructed the commerce on the river, thus violating the empire's constitution.[57] The Council of Bremen reacted with incredulity and rejected the designation of the toll as a 'customs duty'. It was rather a temporary conduct levy to be enforced only as long as the navigability of the Lower Weser was endangered.[58] Instead of complaining, the merchants should thank Bremen for its protection. The Duke of Saxe-Lauenburg received an analogous reply in 1589 after he had forwarded the complaint of a subject whom Bremen's warships had forced to pay the impost.[59] Bremen replied that its 'safe conduct or protection toll'[60] benefited all merchants. If the city could no longer protect the river from piracy, Bremen threatened, there would be dire consequences.

SECURITY AND LEGITIMACY

The city's strong emphasis on protection in the debates around the legitimacy of its safe conduct duties was not coincidental. Bremen's use of defence against piracy as a political argument allowed it to take politics 'beyond the established rules of the game'[61] in a strategy of 'securitisation'.[62] Securitisation, Barry Buzan explains, describes a process in which an 'issue is presented as an existential threat, requiring emergency measures and justifying actions outside the normal bounds of political procedure'.[63] It amounts to an extreme form of politicisation at the end of a spectrum that ranges from non-politicised issues (not of public concern) through politicised issues (a matter of public policy) to securitised issues that are deemed to be beyond politics.

Protection thus became the figurehead of the eclectic body of arguments that Bremen used to justify its policies in the face of adversity.[64] As a matter of fact the city did contribute significantly to safeguarding navigation on the waterway both from piracy and obstructions of the channel, which added plausibility to its claim to be protecting the Lower Weser. In a commissioned legal disquisition of 1619 a jurist elaborately deduced Bremen's jurisdiction over the river from its service of protection.[65] Protection and jurisdiction were intrinsically connected, the argument went, because no polity could pacify a stream without having jurisdiction over it. Bremen's right to shield the merchants on the river was presented both as a consequence of and proof for its superiority and jurisdiction over the river.[66] The thesis echoed that used by Venice in its defence of its sovereignty over the Adriatic, namely that the Venetians had gradually acquired dominion over the sea by guarding it from pirates.[67] The logic also recalls the seventeenth-century debates around piracy in which ships were frequently understood as 'vectors of crown law thrusting into ocean space'.[68]

In order to succeed a securitising move needs to convince an audience that a threat is serious enough to endanger the very existence of the referent object and thereby justifies the breaking of rules.[69] The City Council of Bremen strongly emphasised the dangers that privateers and freebooters as well as the claims of the counts of Oldenburg posed to the navigability of the river. When justifying its conduct tolls to the Duke of Saxe-Lauenburg in 1589 the council painted a particularly bleak image. If the city were to remove its warships, traffic on the river would be exposed to 'barbaric confusion'.[70] With few exceptions all merchants would be robbed of their goods, ships and even their lives. All commerce would be interrupted. Ultimately, Bremen's retreat from the Weser would open the floodgates to 'the ruin of public peace'. In a letter to the Chapter of the Prince-Bishopric of Bremen the city argued that the benefits of its protection were acknowledged by the merchants themselves.[71] They were thankful and asked the city to continue its important service. No prince, city or subjects (except for Oldenburg) had complained about its protective measures.[72]

In Bremen's account pirates were not the only existential threat to navigability. As soon as Oldenburg's plan to introduce a toll on the Lower Weser had become likely to succeed, the city began presenting the new toll as a fundamental risk to commerce with devastating consequences for the whole empire. In a memorial to the envoy of the Landgrave of Hesse-Kassel from 1619 the council painted a dismal scenario.[73] Since large quantities of foodstuffs were transported to his territory via the Weser, the levy would cause a considerable rise in food prices. The inflation would hurt the already poor commoners.[74] Permanent price rises would 'exhaust and emaciate'[75] the landgrave's subjects and make them 'languish' to the bones. Moreover, the city predicted a reduction of the landgraviate's exports via the Weser and a considerable depletion of his own revenues derived from the river, which would lose its significance as a trade route.[76] Finally, Bremen suggested that Oldenburg's toll would set a dangerous precedent for other princes, who would seek to impose further tariffs on a river that counted already twenty-six toll stations.[77]

In a long plea to the Imperial Deputation, a 'miniature diet' assembled in Frankfurt in 1590, Oldenburg tried to expose Bremen's warnings as scaremongering; protection was merely a subterfuge for the advancement of Bremen's fiscal and political interests. With reference to the dramatic picture that Bremen drew of the Lower Weser as a thoroughfare on the brink of 'barbaric confusion', Oldenburg argued that the Dutch War of Independence had not affected navigation on the river and that there was 'no insecurity' because of the war, 'nor is there today'.[78] In view of the many instances of piracy on the Lower Weser this claim was problematic at best. Nevertheless, it supported the contention that Bremen's tolls did not contribute to navigability, but rather constituted an unlawful, permanent toll which benefited the city and endangered the economy of the entire region. While Bremen had emphasised that the conduct tolls constituted a temporary emergency measure and would only be levied as long as navigation on the river was too unsafe, Oldenburg claimed that the duties were not temporary but nothing less than 'eternal'. The new levy, Oldenburg continued, had nothing to do with the Dutch war, which had begun seventeen years before Bremen first introduced the new duties in 1585.[79] Although Bremen pretended that its activities averted dangers and insecurity from the river and redounded to the merchants' welfare, Oldenburg claimed, it could not prove that any prince, city or subject ever actually requested its protection.[80]

Instead, Oldenburg argued, Bremen's warships served the city's fiscal and commercial interests, causing heavy inflation and obstructing the passage of the Lower Weser. By obliging all ships to travel to the city, pay the duties and receive a pass if they wanted to leave for the sea, Bremen established 'a monopoly' on trade.[81] By directing boats into the city, Bremen enriched itself at the expense of its neighbours. What is more, Oldenburg denounced Bremen's navy, not pirates, as the actual source of insecurity on the stream. In the summer of 1587 the warships had attacked the town of Blexen with more than one hundred cannonades. The cannons damaged the dykes, the gardens and the churchyard of the town and struck one woman to the ground. Recounting many other instances of violent disputes with boatmen and repeated encroachments on its territory, Oldenburg thus accused Bremen's fleet of breaking the law of nations and public peace.[82]

CONCLUSION

The history of safe conduct sheds light on the complex role of protection in the ordering of interpolity mobility. In the fragmented landscape of the Holy Roman Empire safe conduct was an essential instrument for securing the movement of goods and people. Because of its peculiar territorial and political structure the Old Reich offers an important point of comparison for the study of mobility and border regimes in other parts of the early modern world. Bremen's safe conduct and dominion over the Weser demonstrates that safe conduct was double-edged: it was a protective service but it could readily be transformed into a vehicle for wider claims of dominion, acts of symbolic subjection and self-serving economic policies. Escorts and safe conduct officials were highly adaptable agents of state power, but they also pursued their own agendas with considerable room for manoeuvre. Bremen's safe conduct effectively defended boatmen from privateers but its unruly soldiers became a new source of insecurity for rivals and those whom the city had no interest to protect. And, as other chapters in the volume confirm, this was not an isolated case; rather it recurred across the early modern world, from the Indian Ocean to the Atlantic Triangle.

This chapter has shown that ostentatious claims of protection can point to dynamics of securitisation, a process in which an issue is presented as existentially threatened in order to justify emergency measures. It was not uncommon for authorities in the Old Reich to exaggerate threats to public safety in order to convince their subjects to perform security-related duties or to pay taxes.[83] By warning travellers and neighbouring polities of the catastrophic consequences of piracy on the Lower Weser, Bremen attempted to justify both exceptional security measures and its expanded grasp on the thoroughfare. Bremen's rivals, on the other hand, attempted to delegitimise the city's policies as scaremongering for the pursuit of its commercial, fiscal and political interests. Oldenburg tried not only to reject Bremen's self-fashioning as a disinterested protector of the disputed river but hoped to move the matter out of the sphere of security altogether.

The ambiguities and tensions inherent in the safe conduct regimes of the Holy Roman Empire illustrate that protection talk could amount to little more than 'normative projections'[84] and that premodern power relations were not necessarily upheld by the protected's trust in the validity of their protectors, but rather by 'massive motives of fear and hope'.[85] At the same time the history of safe conduct shows that the dynamics of protection cannot be accurately described with simple dichotomies that bluntly oppose violence and protection. Even though premodern protection could be highly exploitative, political rule was often 'acceptance-oriented', meaning that protectors attempted to obtain the co-operation and acceptance of the protected.[86] It is therefore important to appreciate the multiplicity of agents who negotiated the ordering of movement in practice and to highlight how protection and violence diverged or converged to varying degrees, depending on the persons, places and interests involved.

NOTES

1 See, for instance, Werner Conze, 'Sicherheit, Schutz', in Otto Brunner et al. (eds), *Geschichtliche Grundbegriffe*, vol. 5, Klett-Cotta, Stuttgart, 1984, pp. 831–62.

2 Andrea Schrimm-Heins, 'Gewißheit und Sicherheit. Geschichte und Bedeutungswandel der Begriffe "certitudo" und "securitas" (Teil 2)', *Archiv für Begriffsgeschichte*, vol. 35, 1992, p. 204, her emphasis. For recent research on the history of security, see Christoph Kampmann (ed.), *Sicherheit in der Frühen Neuzeit: Norm — Praxis — Repräsentation*, Böhlau, Köln, 2013.

3 See Joachim Whaley, *Germany and the Holy Roman Empire*, vol. 1, Oxford University Press, Oxford, 2012, pp. 2–7. See, moreover, Peter H. Wilson, *Heart of Europe: A History of the Holy Roman Empire*, The Belknap Press of Harvard University Press, Cambridge, MA, 2016.

4 Christophe Duhamelle, 'Drinnen und draußen. Raum und Identität der Exklave im Alten Reich nach dem Westfälischen Frieden', *Trivium*, vol. 14, 2013, pp. 5–6; Whaley, p. 40. See, moreover, Falk Bretschneider, 'Praxis der Grenze. Konflikte und Umgänge mit Territorialgrenzen im Alten Reich', *Jahrbuch für Regionalgeschichte*, vol. 29, 2011, pp. 36–44.

5 Barbara Stollberg-Rilinger, *The Emperor's Old Clothes: Constitutional History and the Symbolic Language of the Holy Roman Empire*, Berghahn Books, New York, 2015, p. 239.

6 See Whaley, p. 11.

7 Brendan Simms, *Europe: The Struggle for Supremacy, 1453 to the Present*, Basic Books, New York, 2013, pp. 4–5, 11.

8 See, for instance, Robert Ignatius Burns, 'The "Guidaticum" Safe-Conduct in Medieval Aragon-Catalonia: A Mini-Institution for Muslims, Christians and Jews', *Medieval Encounters*, vol. 1, no. 1, 1995, pp. 51–113.

9 Hans Kalisch, *Über das Verhältnis des Geleitsregals zum Zollregal*, Hermann, Berlin, 1901.

10 See, for instance, Georg Robert Wiederkehr, *Das freie Geleit und seine Erscheinungsformen in der Eidgenossenschaft des Spätmittelalters*, Juris, Zürich, 1976, pp. 28, 33–34.

11 For a recent assessment of the protective function of late medieval safe conduct, see Michael Rothmann, 'Innerer Friede und herrschaftliches Gewaltmonopol. Zur herrschaftlichen Funktion von Fehde und Geleit in Spätmittelalter und beginnender Früher Neuzeit unter besonderer Berücksichtigung von Frankfurt und dessen Umland', in Elsbeth Orth and Heribert Müller (eds), *'Ihrer Bürger Freiheit'. Frankfurt am Main im Mittelalter*, Kramer, Frankfurt am Main, 2004, pp. 89–124.

12 Kalisch, pp. 7–24.

13 On the evolution of regalian safe conduct, see, for instance, Ludolf Fiesel, 'Woher stammt das Zollgeleit?', *Vierteljahrschrift für Sozial- und Wirtschaftsgeschichte*, vol. 19, no. 4, 1926, pp. 385–412.

14 See, for instance, Karl Härter, 'Jüdische Migrationen im frühneuzeitlichen Alten Reich', in Stefan Ehrenpreis (ed.), *Kaiser und Reich in der jüdischen Lokalgeschichte*, Oldenbourg, München, 2011, pp. 67–92. See, moreover, Stephan Laux, *Gravamen und Geleit. Die Juden im Ständestaat der Frühen Neuzeit (15.–18. Jahrhundert)*, Hahnsche Buchhandlung, Hannover, 2010.

15 See Megan Kathryn Williams, 'Dangerous Diplomacy and Dependable Kin: Transformations in Central European Statecraft, 1526–1540' (PhD thesis, Columbia University, 2009).

16 See, for instance, André Krischer, 'Grenzen setzen: Macht, Raum und Ehre der Reichsstädte', in Christian Hochmut and Susanne Rau (eds), *Machträume der frühneuzeitlichen Stadt*, UVK, Konstanz, 2006, pp. 135–54; Otto Rieder, *Das pfalzneuburgische Geleite nach Regensburg und in das Kloster Prüfening*, Mayr, Stadtamhof, 1908.

17 See, for instance, Gebhard Weig, 'Das Ius conducendi der Bischöfe zu Würzburg. Eine Studie zur Rechtsstruktur, politischen Funktion und Organisation des Geleitsrechtes im Hochstift Würzburg während des 15. und 16. Jahrhunderts' (PhD thesis, University of Würzburg, 1970), pp. 180–94; Rainer Wilhelm, 'Die Handhabung des Zollgeleits in der Grafschaft und im Herzogtum Württemberg von den Anfängen bis zum Dreißigjährigen Krieg' (PhD thesis, University of Tübingen, 1957), pp. 77–78, 126–27.

18 For instance in Electoral Saxony, in the Ernestine Duchies of Thuringia, in the Prince-Bishopric of Würzburg, or in the Duchy of Württemberg.

19 See Martin Kintzinger, 'Cum salvo conductu. Geleit im westeuropäischen Spätmittelalter', in Rainer Christoph Schwinges and Klaus Wriedt (eds), *Gesandtschafts- und Botenwesen im spätmittelalterlichen Europa*, Thorbecke, Ostfildern, 2003, p. 322; Weig, pp. 197–98; Wilhelm, pp. 151–62.

20 I briefly discussed the conflict between the City of Bremen and the Counts of Oldenburg in my 'Frei und sicher? Geleitschutz und Bewegungsfreiheit im Alten Reich am Ende des 16. Jahrhunderts', in Tilman Haug et al. (eds), *Protegierte und Protektoren. Asymmetrische politische Beziehungen zwischen Partnerschaft und Dominanz*, Böhlau, Köln, 2016, pp. 335–39.

21 In the following I refer to the Imperial City of Bremen as 'Bremen' and to the Prince-bishopric of Bremen with its full designation. For this entire paragraph see Herbert Schwarzwälder, *Geschichte der Freien Hansestadt Bremen*, vol. 1, Röver, Bremen, 1975, pp. 289, 296–99, 344–50.

22 Ibid., p. 277; Michael Ehrhardt, 'Eine kleine Territorialgeschichte der Region Unterweser', in Hartmut Bickelmann (ed.), *Fluss, Land, Stadt: Beiträge zur Regionalgeschichte der Unterweser*, Landschaftsverband der ehemaligen Herzogtümer Bremen und Verden, Stade, 2011, pp. 162–70.

23 Ehrhardt, pp. 164–65.

24 Georg Sello, *Oldenburgs Seeschiffahrt in alter und neuer Zeit*, Duncker & Humblot, Leipzig, 1906, pp. 4–18.

25 Ibid., pp. 9–10.

26 See Friedrich Gläbe, *Die Unterweser. Chronik eines Stromes und seiner Landschaft*, Eilers und Schünemann, Bremen, 1963, p. 76.

27 Sello, p. 10.

28 See ibid., pp. 9–10; Gustav Rüthning, 'Seeraub im 16. Jahrhundert', *Jahrbuch für die Geschichte des Herzogtums Oldenburg*, vol. 15, 1905, pp. 154, 160.

29 Especially in the lands of Jever and Butjadingen. See Rüthning, pp. 154, 160; Schwarzwälder, pp. 268–69.

30 On the wider efforts of Nothern European polities to secure maritime trade against Muslim corsairs, see Magnus Ressel, *Zwischen Sklavenkassen und Türkenpässen. Nordeuropa und die Barbaresken in der Frühen Neuzeit*, De Gruyter, Berlin, 2012.

31 See Notice about the convoy ships from 1593, 2.R.10.aa.4, Staatsarchiv Bremen (henceforth StA Bremen).

32 See Ordinance of the Mayor and Council of the City of Bremen, 16 July 1593, 2.R.10.aa.13.a.1, StA Bremen.

33 See, for instance, Instruction for Captain Wilhelm Hoyer, 6 January 1620, fo. 2r, 2.R.10.aa.13.a.1, StA Bremen.

34 See, for instance, the instructions from 1620, 1628 and 1647 in 2.R.10.aa.13.a.1, StA Bremen.

35 Instruction for Captain Wilhelm Hoyer, 6 January 1620, fo. 3r, 2.R.10.aa.13.a.1, StA Bremen.

36 See, for instance, Instruction for Captain Meinart Meinerts, 13 June 1628, §§ 4–5, 2.R.10.aa.13.a.1, StA Bremen.

37 Instruction for Captain Wilhelm Hoyer, 6 January 1620, fo. 2v-3r, 2.R.10.aa.13.a.1, StA Bremen.

38 Deduction of Bremen's right to jurisdiction on the Weser, 1619, fo. 50, 53, 56, 77–79, 2-R.10.a.5, StA Bremen.

39 Ibid., fo. 53. For Oldenburg the question of territorial superiority became more important as Bremen was likely to obtain the status of a Free Imperial City (and thus become an Imperial state). Oldenburg had always claimed that only an Imperial state could exercise the jurisdiction over the river (ibid., fo. 67).

40 Rieder, pp. 211–12.

41 See Transcription of a proclamation requesting all ships not to pass the warships without striking the sails, 1613, 2-R.10.aa.13.a.1, StA Bremen.

42 Notarial instrument by Johannes Conters, 20 May 1613, 2-U.13.c.1.b.1, StA Bremen.

43 Count Johann VII of Oldenburg and Delmenhorst to Landgrave Wilhelm IV of Hesse-Kassel, 12 January 1591, fo. 180, 2–U.1.b.6, StA Bremen.

44 'Gifts' being another common term. See Stefan Gorissen, 'Korruption und merkantilistische Staatswirtschaft. Die preußische Zoll- und Akzisepolitik in Schlesien und in den westlichen Provinzen unter Friedrich II', in Niels Grüne and Simona Slanicka (eds), *Korruption: Historische Annäherungen an eine Grundfigur politischer Kommunikation*, Vandenhoeck & Ruprecht, Göttingen, 2010, pp. 327–28.

45 See Stefan Nöth, 'Gleußen und das sächsische Geleit: Zur Wiederaufrichtung der Geleitssäule "Heroldstein" dei Gleußen', in Nöth (ed.), *Coburg 1056 - 2006*.

Ein Streifzug durch 950 Jahre Geschichte von Stadt und Land, Wikomm, Stegaur-ach, 2006, pp. 91–92.

46 See Emil Pauls, 'Geleitsrechte des Herzogs von Jülich im Jülichschen und in Aachen', *Aus Aachens Vorzeit*, vol. 17, 1904, pp. 59, 103.

47 Ibid., pp. 66–67.

48 Ibid., pp. 113–14.

49 Stollberg-Rilinger, p. 8.

50 See Treaty between Count Anton I of Oldenburg and Delmenhorst and Mayor and Council of the City of Bremen, 16 July 1576, articles 5, 10, 20, 2.R.10.a.3, StA Bremen. See, moreover, Manfred Richter, *Die Anfänge des Elsflether Weserzolles. Beiträge zur Geschichte von Schifffahrt und Wirtschaft der Unterweser im 17. Jahrhundert*, Stalling, Oldenburg, 1967, pp. 5–6.

51 Rüthning, p. 156.

52 Christina Deggim, 'Aufgeblasen und abgebrannt. Seetonnen und Baken in Quellen der Bremer Handelskammer', in *Bremisches Jahrbuch*, vol. 79, 2000, pp. 78–80.

53 See Lauren Benton and Adam Clulow's chapter in this volume.

54 Copy of a notarial instrument with the testimonies of several subjects from Oldenburg and Havel, 16 August 1585, fo. 2r-2v, 2.R.10.aa.4, StA Bremen.

55 Ibid., fo. 2v.

56 Ibid., fo. 6v.

57 Council and Mayor of the City of Emden to Mayor and Council of the City of Bremen, 27 September 1585, 2.R.10.aa.4, StA Bremen.

58 Extract from letter of Council and Mayor of the City of Bremen to Council and Mayor of the City of Emden, October 1585, 2.R.10.aa.4, StA Bremen.

59 Mayor and Council of the City of Bremen to Franz II, Duke of Saxe-Lauenburg, 11 November 1589, 2.R.10.aa.4, StA Bremen.

60 Ibid., fo. 1r.

61 Barry Buzan et al., *Security: A New Framework for Analysis*, Lynne Rienner, Boulder, 1998, p. 23.

62 See ibid., pp. 23–24. For the application of the concept to historical research, see Eckart Conze, 'Securitization. Gegenwartsdiagnose oder historischer Analysean-satz?', *Geschichte und Gesellschaft*, vol. 38, no. 3, 2012, pp. 453–67.

63 Buzan et al., pp. 23–24.

64 Protection against pirates and privateers was, moreover, the pretext under which the alliance of the States General and several hanseatic cities defended their commer-cial interests against the Spanish and Denmark. See Schwarzwälder, p. 274.

65 See deduction of Bremen's right to jurisdiction on the Weser, 1619, 2-R.10.a.5, StA Bremen.

66 Ibid., fo. 33. In the Holy Roman Empire, other rulers, such as the Free Imperial City of Ulm, also attempted to deduce territorial superiority from the right of safe conduct. See Rolf Freitag, 'Das Geleit der Reichsstadt Ulm', *Ulm und Oberschwaben*, vol. 37, 1964, p. 100.

67 See, for instance, the arguments proposed by Venice's legal advisor, Paolo Sarpi, at the same time: Lilian del Castillo, *Law of the Sea, From Grotius to the International Tribunal for the Law of the Sea*, Brill, Leiden, 2015, pp. 52–53.

68 Lauren Benton, 'Legal Spaces of Empire: Piracy and the Origins of Ocean Regionalism', *Comparative Studies in Society and History*, vol. 47, no. 4, 2005, p. 704.

69 Buzan et al., p. 25.

70 Mayor and Council of the City of Bremen to Franz II, Duke of Saxe-Lauenburg, 11 November 1589, fo. 3v, 2.R.10.aa.4, StA Bremen.

71 Mayor and Council of the City of Bremen to Cathedral Chapter of the Prince-Bishopric of Bremen, 2 January 1586, fo. 6r, 2-U.1.b.5, StA Bremen.

72 Descriptions of piracy in such dramatic tones were fairly common in other parts of the early modern world as well, for instance during the British campaigns against pirates in the 1720s. While it was common to condemn pirates as enemies of all mankind in the rhetoric of universal jurisdiction, such calls were often accompanied by the more pragmatic treatment of pirates under the law of particular polities. See Lauren Benton, 'Toward a New Legal History of Piracy: Maritime Legalities and the Myth of Universal Jurisdiction', *International Journal of Maritime History*, vol. 23, no. 1, 2011, pp. 225–40.

73 Resolution for the Envoy of Landgrave Moritz of Hesse-Kassel, 29 October 1619, 2.U.13.c.1.a, StA Bremen.

74 Ibid., fo. 1v.

75 Ibid., fo. 2r.

76 Ibid., fo. 1r, 1v.

77 Ibid., fo. 1v, 2r.

78 Count Johann VII of Oldenburg and Delmenhorst to Deputy Princes and Estates in Frankfurt, 23 August 1590 (copy), fo. 16v, 2–U.1.b.6, StA Bremen. It is not clear whether the Count denies the insecurity on the river altogether or whether he only disputes it for the time before 1585 and then in 1590. In any case, there were instances of piracy on the Lower Weser both before 1585 and in 1590.

79 Ibid., fo. 2v.

80 Ibid., fo. 15v.

81 Ibid., fo. 3v.

82 See Ibid., fo. 4v.

83 See Karl Härter, 'Security and "Gute Policey" in Early Modern Europe: Concepts, Laws, and Instruments', *Historical Social Research*, vol. 35, no. 4, 2010, p. 49.

84 Gadi Algazi, *Herrengewalt und Gewalt der Herren im Späten Mittelalter: Herrschaft, Gegenseitigkeit und Sprachgebrauch*, Campus, Frankfurt am Main, 1996, p. 232.

85 Ibid., p. 228. The phrase is Max Weber's: *Wirtschaft und Gesellschaft. Grundriss der verstehenden Soziologie* (1922), Mohr, Tübingen, 1985, p. 822.

86 See, for the latter approach, Stefan Brakensiek, 'Akzeptanzorientierte Herrschaft. Überlegungen zur politischen Kultur der Frühen Neuzeit', in Helmut Neuhaus (ed.), *Die Frühe Neuzeit als Epoche*, Oldenbourg, München, 2009, pp. 395–406.

2

Containing Law within the Walls: The Protection of Customary Law in Santiago del Cercado, Peru

KAREN B. GRAUBART

In 1571 Peruvian Viceroy Francisco de Toledo inaugurated Santiago del Cercado on the outskirts of Lima. It was to be an Indian town surrounded by a high wall and breached by three doors. There, in the words of the Jesuits charged with overseeing the town's Catholic mission, 'the Indians who are dispersed around the city and the new immigrants might be brought together' and 'the Prelate [Archbishop Jerónimo de Loaysa] and those who govern this Republic will assure that they do not sin as much as they have on their own'.[1] The Cercado, as it was popularly known, became a significant indigenous neighbourhood in the vice-regal capital. Its initial residents were men carrying out the forced labour draft (*mita*) in the region, but they were quickly joined by permanent settlers who built homes and formed an Indian *cabildo* (municipal government) for its governance. Spaniards and Africans were excluded from residence there, as it was intended to separate Indians and thereby protect them.[2]

Historians have paid scant attention to the Cercado, mainly treating it as an unsuccessful episode in the history of colonial social control. Mario Cárdenas Ayaipoma once called it a 'vice-regal ghetto', arguing that such settlements were solely for the purpose of extracting tribute and labour, and the Cercado's walls were intended to keep its coerced residents from fleeing at night.[3] More sophisticated is Alexandre Coello de la Rosa's analysis of the Cercado as site of a conflict between royal officials, the Jesuit order, and the city's archbishop (representing secular priests) over control of indigenous spiritual care and thus political power.[4] In a different vein Lynn Lowry's work on indigenous Lima introduces the Cercado as the intended receptacle for a group of indigenous fishermen violently relocated from their river-side homes before expanding her treatment to consider it as part of the development of urban indigenous governance.[5] Within larger studies of the characteristics of the indigenous population of the Lima valley, Lowry, Emilio Harth-Terré,

Paul Charney, and I have used sparse notarial records to reconstruct the lives of some Cercado residents.[6]

Modern scholars largely accept the Viceroy's and the Jesuits' claims that the relocation was intended to control the Indian population, although they do so in the course of mounting a critique of the policy of segregation and with a belief that resistance was inevitable. The indigenous seventeenth-century critic Felipe Guamán Poma de Ayala offers a contrasting perspective in a letter to King Philip III, arguing that the physical separation of Indians, Blacks and Spaniards was 'one of the holiest things in the service of God and Your Majesty'.[7] He noted that in multiracial cities like Lima 'the Indians could not live in any manner due to the great peril caused by the Spaniards, their children and servants, their male and female Black slaves'.[8] Guamán Poma encouraged the monarch to promote a policy of separation and expulsion in order to protect indigenous communities and to return order to Andean society.

A longer historical memory finds more evidence for Guamán Poma's reading of walls such as those of the Cercado. In 1266 the Muslims of Murcia, through their spokesman Abengalib, complained to King Alfonso of Castile that they had received considerable injury from Christians entering Murcia, cheating and robbing them, and that they could not keep them out because of the lack of a wall.[9] Recently brought under Castilian control, the Muslim population requested an enclave free of Christian harassment. Alfonso agreed, and moved them from the main city to a neighbourhood, Arrejaca, with masonry walls and closed gates. There, they could have mosques and butcher shops, hear the call to prayer, and live together under Islamic law. The enclave physically contained and isolated this minority population, but it also stood as a symbol of their commitment to maintaining difference in the face of conquest.[10]

Iberian conquest societies required the participation of the conquered but the exact terms of this co-existence were complex. Muslims and Jews who resided in Iberian Christian kingdoms before their late fifteenth-century expulsions lived in an ambiguously pluralistic system that recognised their jurisdiction at the same time as this frequently impinged upon it.[11] They swore fealty to the monarch and paid their tribute directly into royal coffers as compensation for royal protection and as a sign of their humiliation. While New World Indians could not maintain their religious practices, they too lived within this legal pluralism. And, as a vanquished population, they could also be raided, expropriated and, under certain circumstances, enslaved. Murcia's Muslims understood their precariousness within the Christian kingdom, and they welcomed a wall that would keep Christians out and protect them from religious contagion.[12]

For Indians within the Spanish-dominated city of Lima, as for Muslims in thirteenth-century Murcia, walls served their own interests as well as those of their conquerors. They represented not only the material protection of their selves and property but also the legal protection of their status as subjugated peoples entitled to live under the governance of their own leaders and laws. The confluence in Lima of the wall and that protected status led to the unusual circumstance of delimiting a specific property regime for its indigenous residents, enforced by its own political agents. That property regime made the Cercado's residents materially distinct from other colonial subjects.

PROTECTION THROUGH SEPARATION POLICIES
IN THE IBERIAN AMERICAS

Along the lines of the medieval Iberian model for governing Muslim and Jewish communities, indigenous polities in the Spanish American colonies retained first-instance jurisdiction for many civil complaints. Customary law would be meted out by the prehispanic nobility (generally known as *caciques*) and by a new set of officials intended to challenge cacical authority within a republican form, the *pueblo de indios*. In the Americas, though, customary law would be stripped of what the church deemed its idolatrous content.[13] Native American vassals of the Spanish Crown — those populations that were pacified and thus legally considered to have accepted conversion — were to be considered fragile neophytes and deemed to need protection from many predators, especially their own conquerors. They would be granted the legal status of *miserables* or wretches, who deserved aid and support, particularly the paternalistic care of the Crown and church. As *miserables* they would receive individual benefits, such as free legal assistance, to make them less vulnerable. But as a group they were understood to require proximity to civilisation to guide their moral development: they were to be the recipients *par excellence* of what Michel Foucault called pastoral power, exercised over a flock of people for its salvation, wherein the pastor had to concern himself with every act of the individual as much as with the multiplicity.[14] In order to be saved, they would have to be collected, overseen and guided.[15]

Nearly from the beginning of Spanish colonisation in the Americas, the Crown called for the removal and reorganisation of indigenous populations as a way to protect them when they came into contact with Spanish settlers.[16] In 1516, after hearing concerns that Spanish *encomenderos* (recipients of royal grants of indigenous labour) were treating the natives of Hispaniola poorly, Charles V ordered the Hieronymite friars to move the native communities closer to the mines or pearl fields and away from the Spanish town, and to inform them that this was for their benefit.[17] Despite a general belief in freedom of movement, the Crown found it necessary to ban unmarried Spanish men, mestizos, mulatos, enslaved Africans and occasionally even *encomenderos* from entering or living in indigenous communities.[18] By the middle of the sixteenth century the policy of *reducción* (also known as *congregación*) was institutionalised, forcing members of indigenous settlements to live in concentrated *pueblos* often distant from their residences and fields.[19] Authorities believed that Indians had to be congregated in order to be evangelised, taught to live in *policía* or urban orderliness and good government, and be available to provide labour to Spanish masters.[20] Moreover, this often had to occur far from their original homes because it was thought that Christianised Indians could be tempted by old practices that were enshrined in the physical landscape.

Protection talk, as Lauren Benton and Adam Clulow note, was ubiquitous. But in the case of the Spanish colonisation of the indigenous Americas it was also multivalent.[21] Indigenous vassals of the Crown had to be protected from more predatory vassals and foreigners; new Christians had to be protected from those yet to be converted and from morally dangerous environments; and Spanish cities had to be protected from indigenous rebellion and disorder. Moreover, 'inside' and 'outside' registers were far from distinct. While pacified Indians were vassals of the Crown and thus within the political community, they were not always distinguishable from their unpacified brethren. Their proximity to African slaves — forever foreigners, outside the polity — rendered them both potential victim of and ally to an enemy.[22] And the incomplete civility of both Indians and Africans, who provided necessary labour for the creation of colonial *civitas*, brought disorder and unrest to Spanish settlements.

However, despite the repeated rhetoric of protection, and the clear desire to separate certain parts of communities, only infrequently in Latin America did Spaniards erect walls to enclose populations. There were a few exceptions to this rule. First, Spanish settlers built walls, *presidios* and garrisons to fortify settlements against attacks from hostile autochthonous populations or European competitors for conquest and treasure, usually on islands or at frontiers.[23] Second, the founders of convents and missions built walls to keep the secular world outside. A final, unique exception was the urban *reducción* of Santiago del Cercado. Its marked separation from the city as well as from rural indigenous settlements nearby made a strong protective statement: behind its walls and three gates, Indians lived on gridded streets around a central *plaza* and a church, in supervised *policía*. But the Cercado also marked a space of differential legal jurisdiction with respect to the rest of the city. Its walls protected not only its neophyte Christians but a particular form of Indianness, bound up with law and property.

SPACE, *POLICÍA* AND HUMAN DEVELOPMENT

Like many of the cities founded by Spaniards to govern their new possessions, Lima suffered from an internal threat in the form of chaotic settlements, mostly African and indigenous, outside the elite's *traza* (central footprint) or, worse, within its very streets. The city rapidly expanded beyond the plan laid out in 1535 and Spanish citizens began to complain about the disorder of the increasingly numerous African and indigenous populations, which they predominantly expressed in terms of their being masterless: they lived without direct Spanish oversight. Between 1550 and 1552 the *Real Audiencia* or royal high court of Lima approved a set of statutes aimed at restoring *policía* by creating Spanish oversight and accountability over the city's non-Spanish residents: temporary indigenous migrants were to live with their *caciques* on urban plots assigned to them; and indigenous and African residents working as domestic servants or independent agents were to settle with a permanent master and learn a trade. The *Audiencia* granted the *caciques* of the nearby Indian polities of Huarochirí and Magdalena political authority over the unadministered Indians, at least for the purposes of ensuring attendance at Mass and resolving minor civil issues.[24]

Yet none of these solutions did much to constrain the indigenous and African populations. The city continued to sprout *rancherías* or crowded camps full of poor people, and they were often housed in *callejones* or *corrales* (alleys) where packed rooms were grouped around common cooking spaces and chicken coops.[25] These settings produced intimate social mixture, polluted water and streets, and surrounded elite Spaniards with distasteful elements.

In 1568 Governor Lope García de Castro decided to confront the problem by constructing a *reducción* for the city's Indians. This was to be a contained town where they could be governed by their own authorities as well as by Jesuit priests and a royal official, and where tribute could be easily collected and labourers rounded up for public works. While Indian *pueblos* had been concentrated and relocated before, this experiment marked the beginning of a broader *reducción* policy across the Andes, and an unusual urban instantiation.

The form and content of the idealised Indian town served as a means to civilise the indigenous people by changing their spiritual and work practices. The architects of *reducción*, such as the jurist Juan de Matienzo, were explicit: 'Given the laziness of the Indians and their condition and that danger that follows from it, it is understood that to incline and compel them towards work is a good thing.'[26] He argued that providing each with land and wages would 'make them love to work, and thus *policía* will come to them'.[27] Matienzo also

recommended placing Indians in concentrated sites, near religious authorities, with streets running in an orthogonal grid around the buildings that
symbolised their new reality: a church, a meeting place for the Indian municipal government (*cabildo*), a jail and private residences.

The requirement that Indians would learn to love work and desire *policía*
meant that they had to be treated as neophytes not only spiritually but also
legally. They were collectively assigned to a limited version of the legal category
of *miserables* or wretches, a protected class like minor dependants,[28] it being
assumed that they had the infantile qualities of 'frailty, gullibility and lack of
constancy' and must be sheltered from the treachery of the ill-intentioned.[29]
This was done by assigning them a protector general as well as a bureaucratic
network of judges, solicitors, notaries and other officials.

Who were the ill-intentioned from whom Indians needed protection?
For the most part, officials understood Spaniards to be their greatest threat.
Spanish farmers and entrepreneurs rapidly acquired much of the Lima valley's
agricultural lands in the sixteenth century. Viceroys were specifically charged
to defend indigenous towns against the expanding Spanish city.[30] Authorities
also assumed malevolence on the part of the large and growing community of
enslaved and free Africans in the region. They issued a slew of laws intended
to manage Africans through curfews, requirements that they be accompanied
by Spaniards at all times, and constraints on their movement, particularly
with respect to Indian towns.[31] But in their extreme innocence and gullibility
Indians even had to be protected from their own *caciques* and nobles, of
whom one viceroy memorably noted: 'these will rob them and not even leave
them the wax in their ears'.[32]

In November 1568 royal officials determined to contain Lima's Indian
population within what became the walled neighbourhood of Santiago del
Cercado in order to protect them and train them in living in *policía*. For this
purpose Governor García de Castro ordered the expropriation of land parcels
at the city's edge from three Spaniards, compensating them with funds raised
from auctioning off the parcels originally distributed to house the city's *mita*
workers.[33] In 1571 the new viceroy, Francisco de Toledo, officially opened
Santiago del Cercado, placing its spiritual governance in the hands of the
Jesuits, recently arrived in the New World. The costs of building the walled
town, its church, *cabildo* house, a prison for unrepentant idolators and other
subsequent structures would have been significant. Some of these costs were
assigned to the *encomenderos* whose Indians were to be housed there, and met
out of tribute payments and directly through Indian *mita* labour.[34] Other
funds were raised from the indigenous communities of Lima, including a
tax on the corn beer they sold, as well as alms and bequests. The Crown
granted each of the two Jesuits in charge an annual income of 500 pesos.[35]

Moving the city's Indian population to the town proved difficult. The *mita* workers who were displaced from their urban plots were immediately relocated, each community being permitted to purchase lots (*solares*) based on the size of their regular contingents. Communities raided their treasuries to pay for these, perhaps selling off agricultural land back home.[36] Indigenous servants and apprentices living within Spanish households were exempted from moving as they were already considered to be under protection. Many indigenous men and women willingly took up residence in the Cercado in order to receive living space, gardens, and the promised religious and educational services. But the hundreds of independent artisans, labourers and vendors who still lived in the city sought to continue living where they were and so were the occasional target of threats of removal.

The most famous case of this concerned the shrimp fishing community (*camaroneros*) living on the north bank of the Rimac River in the parish of San Lázaro, which was the home as well to the quarantine barracks for disembarked African slaves, slaughterhouses, and a leper community. The *camaroneros* were an independent community that was used as a labour force by the city's *cabildo*. Now they became pawns in a battle between the Archbishop and the Jesuits, each considering themselves the spiritual overseers of all the city's Indians. The Jesuits had the support of Viceroy Cañete, and late one night in 1590 he had the *camaroneros* removed and their homes destroyed in the name of protecting their health and property from a flood plain.[37] The viceroy appropriated this land, donating two-thirds of it to the city to quell concerns.[38] Despite plaintive correspondence between the Jesuits, the Archbishop, the *Audiencia*, the Viceroy, the Pope and the King, the legal situation was not fully settled until 1598 when the King pronounced that his vassals all had the right to liberty and so those who wished to leave the Cercado would be allowed to do so.[39]

The Jesuits articulated the mission of the Cercado in the language of protection. The Indians, they claimed, would be safer within the confines of their walls, where they would be prevented from sinning excessively.[40] This language was repeated by Jesuits and their indigenous charges, as can be seen in litigation arising from an Indian woman's bequests in 1632. She issued a series of wills and codicils regarding a house she owned in San Lázaro parish, wavering between leaving the property to two Catholic confraternities, who took the dispute to court after her death. The Jesuit confraternity argued that its leaders were best able to carry out the wishes of the dead woman because they were subordinate to the Jesuits, unlike the leaders of Copacabana, who, because they were 'unattached' Indians, would dissipate her estate. An indigenous witness agreed that, outside the Jesuits' organisations, 'they were Indians who had no masters nor anyone to govern them'.[41] The Jesuits' opponents made the same claim, asserting that the Jesuits left their charges unprotected because the Indians' work outside the Cercado caused them to 'spend the whole day coming and going, lacking Christian education and falling into illness'.[42] The right living spaces were deemed to bring safety to particular bodies, through evangelisation, health, controlled interactions and law.

Despite its wall, the Cercado did not separate peoples. The vast majority of the city's Indians lived outside it. Even within, its gates had to remain open during the day to let workers go to their jobs and return home. Non-Indians could also enter the town in significant numbers. These included African slaves owned by well-off Indians (some of whom shared their residences), Spaniards and their servants and slaves who snuck in at night to steal fruit from the Indians' orchards, and churchgoers of all backgrounds.[43] Whatever protection its walls offered, it was not that of separation of bodies.

PROPERTY AND LAW

If social control for the purpose of evangelisation and labour mobility was the unrealised purpose of the Cercado's creators, its development as a neighbourhood gives us insight into other dimensions of the protective force of colonial law. Like any *reducción*, the Cercado had its own indigenous leadership and a *cabildo* on the model of a Spanish town. The Cercado's elected leaders (of whom little is still known) were men who tended to come from non-noble lineages and who rose to office through skilled trades, the Indian militia and service to the Catholic church. They were permanent residents who garnered moderate incomes and even wealth in the city, and worked their way up and through political office. They were charged with promoting the common good of the indigenous residents.

While the Indian leaders of the Cercado had jurisdiction over their residents' complaints, they were also part of a web of colonial legal recourses. The *corregidor* of the Indians was a royal official who was the de facto judge of the town (and, after 1603, the entire region's indigenous population), though his caseload suggests that his actual jurisdiction was fairly narrow.[44] The Indian *cabildo* also interacted with Lima's *cabildo*, but the Crown explicitly denied the latter power over the former as their interests so often conflicted. Cercado residents could also have access to the *Real Audiencia* (royal appeals court) and the Archbishop's court. Cercado residents cultivated relationships with all of these Spanish authorities as a means of righting wrongs.

Judging by the surviving archival record, these Spanish and Indian legal authorities sought to protect Cercado residents' property and certain definitions of property from predation. The *corregidor*, for example, was charged with ensuring that Spaniards did not purchase or steal property that indigenous communities needed for their survival. Spanish authorities in particular sought to manage the ways that indigenous actors came to engage with property in order to protect them from adopting certain forms of tenancy and ownership that might worsen their situation. Polo de Ondegardo, the *corregidor* of Cuzco in the mid-sixteenth century, argued strongly that these novices should embrace what was valuable from Spain but not give up all of their own practices. In protecting their *fueros* or customary law, they should avoid all 'evil and reprobate innovations'.[45] From this perspective, the purpose of the town's walls shifts.

Throughout the seventeenth century the indigenous leadership of the Cercado was called upon to manage internal property issues in particular ways. The initial organisation of the town's *solares*, as units purchased by and assigned to distant towns that sent temporary workers to Lima, was challenged within a generation. Indigenous residents permanently occupied and built structures on these *solares*, considering themselves owners of the houses, if not the land. A spate of wills written between 1605 and 1610 by Cercado residents illustrates this trend.[46] Four testators called themselves owners of houses in *solares* associated with the communities of Pisco and Huarochirí, though none of the testators hailed from these places. These houses were emerging from a new real estate market: Magdalena Yauri Chumbi observed that she had purchased her house and garden from another indigenous man, Juan Cabilca. Diego Sedeño offered more evidence for the process, noting that he had originally bought his house from Juan Paichucama, paying in cash. Since then he had added a bedroom and living room with draperies and unfinished roof, a locked door to the street and many fruit trees. These improvements marked the residence as his own even if he had no title to the *solar* on which it was constructed. Many contemporary testators who also lived in the Cercado did not claim ownership of homes, suggesting that it was a transfer of title, through inheritance or sale, which helped establish such a claim.

These changes, which only increased over time, were not taking place without the permission of the Cercado's authorities. Indigenous authorities drew up and witnessed these documents, lending oblique approval to the process. They also performed official acts, as when in 1687 Francisco de Contreras and Doña Juana Josefa de Contreras appealed to Hernando de Rivera, the town's *alcalde ordinario*, to have a *solar* and house they inherited from their late parents legally divided in two.[47] The indigenous officials gathered at the *solar* to measure out two equal sectors. The notary documented the acts for posterity and placed the papers in a locked box in the town for safety.

However, these changes happened informally and unevenly, which led to confusion. In 1686, the *alcalde ordinario* was called to adjudicate the ownership of a *solar*.[48] Ynes Lázaro claimed to have inherited it, in the site called *Olleros* (Potters), from her late father Captain Gerónimo Cansinos, but had no papers to prove her case. Her witnesses, some of whom titled themselves *vecinos* (citizens) of the Cercado, testified to Captain Cansinos' long occupation of the site, with a period of rental to a third party after his death, before his son removed the renter and moved his own family in. The indigenous *cabildo* found Ynes Lázaro and her husband to have legitimate possession of the *solar* by virtue of being Captain Cansinos' heirs. The renter's potential claim was pushed aside because of the legitimacy of the original claim and the secondary claim of inheritance.

The language of citizenship also altered over the seventeenth century. Community residents were often described by Spanish officials as *forasteros* (outsiders) when they were temporary residents on *mita* occupying the *solar* purchased by their community of origin. Those born in or with long-standing ties to the Cercado called themselves *naturales* (native-born). But owners of *solares* sometimes called themselves *vecinos*, the title used by propertied Spaniards with political rights within the city of Lima. As was often the case, Spanish authorities did not acknowledge the indigenous assertion of status, but it mattered to parties in establishing their social position, and, as in the 1686 case, was successful with an indigenous audience.[49]

Nevertheless, some recorded incidents indicate that property within the Cercado was handled differently from residential property in Lima, which, once titled to an individual by the Crown, could be bought and sold with few restrictions. In the Cercado it was treated more along the lines of property within rural *pueblos de indios*, where customary law as well as the common good could interfere with market relations.[50] For example, in 1691 the Cercado's *corregidor* received a petition from the town's solicitor requesting that Matheo Felipe, *vecino*, be assigned a vacant *solar* as a meritorious gesture.[51] Felipe had for many years been *mayoral* of the *solar* of Huaylas, that is, he either mustered the *mita* labour force from that community or acted as a local arbitrator or representative for the residents in the solar. He had for unstated reasons been dispossessed of his own home and forced outside the walls, where he and his family were living in a field. The solicitor requested that a vacant site in the *solar* of Quiquiz be reassigned to Felipe. The *corregidor* who investigated the matter learned that it was described as 'sin dueño' (without owner), suggesting that it had never been placed into private ownership, and so ordered that this be done. In the final ceremony Felipe held the indigenous *alcalde*'s hand and walked through the property 'calling possession possession

possession and threw rocks and did other acts in sign of possession' before they signed the documents that would establish his title to the site.

In summary, the surrounding of the Cercado with walls had the effect of making distinctions between different property regimes within greater Lima. Urban property, once distributed to settlers, could be resold with relatively little oversight whereas indigenous property, which was overwhelmingly rural, was heavily protected, at least in theory. The Cercado was, thus, a hybrid: it was collective property that sometimes became a kind of alienable individual commodity though not one that could be transferred to just anyone or under any conditions. In the name of protection the walls around the Cercado created a space in which indigenous people were urged to live as Spaniards and offered assistance that enhanced but also constrained their ability to do so.

THE CASE OF JUANA ÑUSTA

One case survives that clearly demonstrates how the Cercado protected and invented indigenous property law. In 1652 two elite indigenous men filed on behalf of the community of the Yauyos (a highland community west of the city) a complaint with the Viceroy to evict the widow Juana Ñusta (aka Juana de Avalos) from a *solar* in the Cercado.[52] The Yauyos had purchased their plot in the Cercado but had lost control of all or part of it, leaving them without a place to live while they tended to fields that they were renting in a nearby valley.

The Yauyos, through their lawyer, argued that the loss of their *solar* in the Cercado made it difficult for them to meet tribute and *mita* obligations, and moreover that their children 'lacked Christian doctrine and were being raised like barbarians' outside its walls.[53] They drew deftly upon the rhetoric of the *reducción*, which was intended to provide stability as they farmed and became Christians, and noted that the Crown was required to 'give protection (*amparo*) to these poor ones'. They also identified themselves as *forasteros* rather than residents, highlighting their transitory occupation of the site for the purposes of *mita* and tribute production rather than permanent residence. The rector of the Cercado, Father Luis de Teruel, gave testimony that 'the Yauyos have a site of two or three blocks, purchased with their community's funds, which, because it was unused, some have planted with gardens, but this is done with the knowledge of the caciques of said province, and thus whenever they have wished to take residence [*vecindarse*] in it, it must be restored to them as their own property'.[54]

The *corregidor*, Don Joseph de Carbajal Marroquín, under direction of the Viceroy, restored the property to the Yauyos in August 1653, in a ceremony with Father Teruel present. They established the boundaries and that the garden on it was 'called that of Domingo Francisco' and as they walked through it 'they closed and opened the doors, they broke branches and did other acts all in sign of the said possession which they took quietly and peacefully without contradiction and in this the said Corregidor gave them protection'.[55]

However, the following month the case returned to court. A lawyer representing Juana Ñusta, *vecina* and widow of Captain Domingo Francisco, and their children and heirs, asked the *corregidor* to assert her ownership of the *solar*. According to his account, Captain Domingo Francisco of the Indian militia, recently deceased, had spent 6000 pesos improving the site, which he left to his widow and children. The couple had occupied the site for more than fifty years continuously, and the story the Yauyos had presented just months before was merely a sinister, if convincing, fiction. Juana Ñusta, using a Quechua title of nobility rather than her family name of de Avalos, presented her late husband's will as evidence.[56]

The will is itself an illuminating document about the establishment of the Cercado. Along with other early wills, it demonstrates that service in the indigenous militia was a pathway to property ownership and economic success for some men.[57] Through purchases and inheritances, Francisco had managed to acquire a large portfolio of lands in the Late Valley (where the Yauyos also farmed), most of which he rented to Indian farmers on contracts. He received official title to the lands from the King during a land *composición* or official act of retitling and expropriation. In the will he took care to describe his *solar* in the Cercado, indicating that he already realised it was contentious:

> Item, I declare as my property a *huerta* [cultivated land] that I have in this *pueblo* of the Cercado, with its house … that I cultivated this *huerta* myself and it was purchased from different persons and because of the right that the Indians of San Cristobal [de los Yauyos] claimed to it, I have brought a lawsuit in this Real Audiencia and the judges found on my behalf, for myself and my heirs, and I made this *huerta* as it originally was an uncultivated field and it is entirely completed … which I have fenced in, and so I declare it as my property.

His will also detailed his estate of five African slaves, four horses with saddles, two *arcabuces* (muskets), a sword and dagger, a helmet and buckler, other pieces of a fine military uniform and luxurious clothing.

Francisco, in other words, was entirely civilised in the manner prescribed by those who created the *reducciones*. He was a Christian, requesting burial in the Cercado's church in the habit of San Francisco and leaving bequests to numerous confraternities. He had risen to a position of status within the colonial spaces offered to indigenous men, becoming captain of the city's Indian militia, and gaining the privilege of wearing a sword and dagger, riding a saddled horse and boasting a wardrobe of imported finery. He owned a number of African slaves, the most powerful symbol of colonial authority available to him. And, most to the point, he had bought the lands that indigenous communities were placing on the market and was provisioning the city by renting them back to landless Indians. He had had these lands officially titled by the Crown, removing them from indigenous patrimony, and he had sued to defend his property. He was the very model of a colonial Indian, exactly what Juan de Matienzo had hoped to produce by requiring Indians to learn Spanish ways and live in planned towns.

And yet the Viceroy and the *corregidor* of the Cercado ruled against him, returning the *solar* to the Yauyos as a collective. The *corregidor*'s decision, taken alongside the other cases over rights in land, reveals the Cercado's status as a space where Indians were both protected and arrested in their path to becoming colonial subjects. The depredations of indigenous territories in the valleys surrounding the city, where individuals and communities routinely sold and rented their lands to Spaniards, troubled the Crown. While royal officials sought to title individual (as opposed to community) lands and remove what they regarded as excess properties from shrinking communities through the process of *composición*, they acted aggressively to monopolise privatisation. While some of the community *solares* of the Cercado had almost immediately been transformed into private residences, the Crown reserved its preference for collective use of the land as part and parcel of the legal definition of its Indian subjects. The Viceroy's final word on the subject had been to tell the *corregidor* to 'demand that the alcaldes of the Cercado turn the solares over to [the Yauyos], wherein they can have a house and from there take care of their fields, where they find lands for rent, and charge the Jesuit to admit them and enroll them, like others, in the said town'.[58]

CONCLUSION

Walls served many purposes in the Iberian Empire. While defence against hostile onslaughts was the most dramatic reason to build such an expensive bulwark, in reality walls were most often erected to manage populations: they divided tax-paying citizens from customs-paying outsiders, created the illusion that they were preventing contagion (including of ideas and beliefs) and sexual activity across lines of difference as constituted by the authorities, and served to contain predatory behaviour of one community against another.

For those such as the Muslims of Murcia or Guamán Poma de Ayala, fearful that co-existence with their conquerors would be to their economic, social, and spiritual disadvantage, strong walls were an instrument of protection.

But urban walls were unusual in colonial Latin America. The exceptional cost associated with erecting them could not easily be justified. We mostly find massive walls at sea coasts against piracy or invasion (as would eventually enclose all of Lima in the late-seventeenth century, at great cost), and, on a smaller scale, around convents and monasteries, creating a barrier between *el siglo* (the material world) and the life of the religious. The Jesuits would take the model of the Cercado and bring it to frontier regions such as Paraguay, creating missions that incorporated willing Indian converts and made claims for Spanish territorial possession even in the absence of Spanish settlements. There, the walls are assertions of pastoral power and protection of neophytes, and an implicit threat of incipient Spanish claims.

The walls of Santiago del Cercado are unique because they denote something more. In a sense they are a direct throwback to the walls between Christians, Muslims, and Jews in medieval Iberia, because they were to protect not only a subjected people but a way of life that preserved its difference within a pluralistic project. These walls refer not only to bodies and souls, but to land and the law that was inscribed on the ground.

The Cercado was clearly intended to be a space wherein indigenous residents would be protected as neophytes, subject to a negotiated interpretation of customary law and embedded levels of indigenous and Spanish governance. The Jesuits were one of the instruments of this slow transformation with their spiritual oversight of the Cercado encompassing the role of managing property disposition through confraternities, confessional practices, administration of chaplaincies, and executing and witnessing wills. The numerous wills left by Indian men and women in Lima are literal testament to the efficacy of this project, and to the Catholic church's material benefit as it was the direct beneficiary of many wills. The Jesuits sought this status over the city's entire indigenous population, but were acutely aware that 'loose Indians' — those not living within the walls — often slipped beyond their control.

The impetus for building a wall around this *reducción* may have been concerns about the difficulty of keeping Indians separate from the city where they worked and interacted, or the desire for safety against predation that its advocates voiced. But the wall also protected what authorities understood as the customary law of the Indians from overly rapid disintegration. Indigenous law was unlike Islamic or Jewish law: it was not codified in a text nor interpreted and enforced in central locations outside the realm of conquest. In the Andes, it was local, diverse and subject to complex changes depending upon the level of entanglements with Spanish colonisers. However, the wall created a space wherein indigenous law, whatever it might be, had valence. It made it impossible for Spaniards to purchase Indian lands in ignorance, thereby diminishing the capacity of indigenous men and women to support themselves and pay tribute to the monarch. It clarified the line between republics and managed the transition of law between the two. It was intended to maintain difference even as it anticipated that change, protecting a group as neophytes, some of whom were already demonstrating their aptitude for mimicry, transculturation and success within the terms of their imperial masters. The Cercado's walls sheltered an imperial notion of Indianness, which justified the continuation of pastoral power even where neophytes were hard to discern from Old Christians.

NOTES

1 Antonio de Egaña (ed.), *Monumenta Peruana*, apud Monumenta Historica Societatis Iesu, Rome, 1954, vol. 1, p. 416.

2 A census of the Cercado taken in 1812 shows that Spaniards and Africans came to outnumber Indians in the late colonial period. Lynn Lowry attributes this to the 1767 expulsion of the Jesuits, ending the phase of protectionism ('Forging an Indian Nation: Urban Indians under Spanish Colonial Control, Lima, Peru, 1535–1765' [PhD thesis, University of California, Berkeley, 1991], p. 147).

3 Mario Cárdenas Ayaipoma, 'El Pueblo de Santiago: Un Ghetto en Lima Virreinal', *Bulletin del Institut Frances des Etudes Andines*, vol. 9, nos 3–4, 1980, pp. 19–48.

4 Alexandre Coello de la Rosa, *Espacios de Exclusión, Espacios de Poder: El Cercado de Lima Colonial (1568–1606)*, Instituto de Estudios Peruanos, Lima, 2006.

5 Lowry.

6 Emilio Harth-Terré, *Negros e Indios. Un Estamento Social Ignorado del Perú Colonial*, Librería-Editorial Juan Mejía Baca, Lima, 1973; Paul Charney, *Indian Society in the Valley of Lima, Peru, 1532–1824*, University Press of America, Lanham, MD, 2001; Charney, '"Much Too Worthy ...": Indians in Seventeenth-Century Lima', in Dana Velasco Murillo et al. (eds), *City Indians in Spain's American Empire: Urban Indigenous Society in Colonial Mesoamerica and Andean South America, 1530–1810*, Sussex Academic Press, Brighton, 2012, pp. 87–103; Karen Graubart, *With Our Labor and Sweat: Indigenous Women and the Formation of Colonial Society in Peru, 1550–1700*, Stanford University Press, Stanford, CA, 2007. Other studies that contribute to our knowledge of the Cercado include Woodrow Borah, 'Juzgado General de Indios del Perú o Juzgado Particular de Indios de El Cercado de Lima', *Revista Chilena de Historia del Derecho*, vol. 6, 1970, pp. 129–42, and Alcira Dueñas, 'The Lima Indian Letrados: Remaking the República de Indios in the Bourbon Andes', *The Americas*, vol. 72, no. 1, 2015, pp. 55–75.

7 Felipe Guamán Poma de Ayala, *El Primer Nueva Corónica y Buen Gobierno*, Siglo Veintiuno, México D.F., 1992, p. 414.

8 Ibid., p. 797.

9 Francisco Fernández y González, *Estado Social y Político de los Mudéjares de Castilla, Considerados en Sí Mismos y Respecto de la Civilización Española*, Real Academia de la Historia, Madrid, 1866, p. 359.

10 On the difficulties of this sort of integration, see the discussion of religious noise in O. Remie Constable, 'Regulating Religious Noise: The Council of Vienne, the Mosque Call and Muslim Pilgrimage in the Late Medieval Mediterranean World', *Medieval Encounters*, vol. 16, no. 1, 2010, pp. 64–95.

11 Lauren Benton, *Law and Colonial Cultures: Legal Regimes in World History, 1400–1900*, Cambridge University Press, Cambridge, 2002, Chapter 2. The expulsion or forced conversion of all Muslims and Jews in Castile took place between 1483 and 1501.

12 Maliki jurists often called upon Muslims to leave places conquered by Christians to avoid corruption. Khaled Abou El Fadl, 'Islamic Law and Muslim Minorities', *Islamic Law and Society*, vol. 1, no. 2, 1994, pp. 141–87.

13 See Francisco de Toledo, 'Ordenanzas para los Indios de Todos los Departamentos y Pueblos de este Reino', in *Relaciones de los Virreyes y Audiencias que han Gobernado el Perú: Memorial y Ordenanzas de d. Francisco de Toledo*, J.E. del Campo, Madrid, 1867, tomo I, p. 162; Karen Graubart, 'Learning From the Qadi: The Jurisdiction of Local Rule in the Early Colonial Andes', *Hispanic American Historical Review*, vol. 95, no. 2, 2015, pp. 195–228.

14 Michel Foucault, *Security, Territory, Population: Lectures at the Collège de France, 1977–78*, Palgrave Macmillan, New York, 2007, p. 129. On pastoral power in the Spanish colonies, see Daniel Nemser, 'Primitive Accumulation, Geometric Space, and the Construction of the "Indian"', *Journal of Latin American Cultural Studies*, vol. 24, no. 3, 2015, pp. 338–39.

15 On the moral development of indigenous converts, see Anthony Pagden, *The Fall of Natural Man: The American Indian and the Origins of Comparative Ethnology*, Cambridge University Press, Cambridge, 1982, Chapter 7, and Sabine MacCormack, *On the Wings of Time: Rome, the Incas, Spain and Peru*, Princeton University Press, Princeton, 2007, pp. 119–21.

16 As Luca Scholz (this volume) argues, controlling mobility could easily translate into seizing 'abandoned' territory formerly considered to be under another's dominium as well as into making claims on the new site. See also Nemser.

17 Academia de la Historia, España (ed.), *Colección de Documentos Inéditos Relativos al Descubrimiento* . . ., Sucesores de Rivadeneyra, Madrid, 1877, series 2, tomo 9, pp. 56–57.

18 For example, Richard Konetzke (ed.), *Colección de Documentos para la Historia de la Formación Social de Hispanoamérica*, Consejo Superior de Investigaciones Científicos, Madrid, 1953, tomo I, pp. 180, 213, 297, 400, 425.

19 On the policy of *reducción*, see Jeremy Mumford, *Vertical Empire: The General Resettlement of Indians in the Colonial Andes*, Duke University Press, Durham, NC, 2012. On the *reducción* as a model for creating *policía*, see Valerie Fraser,

The Architecture of Conquest: Building in the Viceroyalty of Peru, 1535–1635, Cambridge University Press, Cambridge, 2009, pp. 75–79.

20 On the multiple meanings of *policía* in the colonial Latin American context, see Richard Kagan, *Urban Images of the Hispanic World, 1493–1793*, Yale University Press, New Haven, 2000, p. 27.

21 Lauren Benton and Adam Clulow, 'Webs of Protection and Interpolity Zones in the Early Modern World' (this volume).

22 On the foreignness of 'sovereignless' blacks, see Sherwin Bryant, *Rivers of Gold, Lives of Bondage: Governing through Slavery in Colonial Quito*, University of North Carolina Press, Chapel Hill, 2014, p. 49.

23 Martha Pollak ascribes the ubiquity of the walled and gridded European city to militarisation and the appearance of military order (*Cities at War in Early Modern Europe*, Cambridge University Press, Cambridge, 2010).

24 Ordenanzas para la Ciudad de Lima (1550–51), Patronato 187 r. 14 image 2, 10, 11, Archivo General de Indias, Sevilla, Spain. Similar concerns were raised about Africans, who also lived '*sueltamente*' without masters and caused civil and criminal problems, images 13–14.

25 María Antonia Durán Montero, 'Lima en 1613: Aspectos Urbanos', *Anuario de Estudios Americanos*, vol. 49, 1992, p. 7.

26 Juan de Matienzo, *Gobierno del Perú* [1567], Compañía Sud-Americana de Billetes de Banco, Buenos Aires, 1910, p. 15.

27 Ibid., pp. 15–16. On the relationship between the civilising mission, governance and these economic behaviors, see Sabine MacCormack, '"The Heart has its Reasons": Predicaments of Missionary Christianity in Early Colonial Peru', *Hispanic American Historical Review*, vol. 65, no. 3, 1985, pp. 443–66.

28 On the legal status see Bianca Premo, *Children of the Father King: Youth, Authority, and Legal Minority in Colonial Lima*, University of North Carolina Press, Chapel Hill, 2005.

29 Cited ibid., p. 34.

30 Charney, *Indian Society*, Chapter 2.

31 'Ordenanzas para la Ciudad de Lima (1550–1552)'.

32 Viceroy Conde de Nieva to Consejo de Indias (1563), in Roberto Levillier (ed.), *Gobernantes del Peru: Cartas y Papeles, Siglo XVI*, vol. I, Sucesores de Rivadeneyra, Madrid, 1921–26, pp. 529–30.

33 Harkness Collection, documents 866–877, Library of Congress, Washington DC.

34 Lowry, p. 69.

35 Egaña, vol. I, pp. 343, 346, 416, 740, and vol. IV, pp. 478–49.

36 Derecho Indígena leg. 9 cuad. 130 (1653), f. 2v, Archivo General de la Nación (henceforth AGN), Lima, Peru.

37 Egaña, vol. IV, pp. 691, 728–30, and vol. V, pp. 92–96. On the *camaroneros*, see Lowry, pp. 39–48.

38 Lowry, p. 43.

39 Levillier, vol. XIV, pp. 85–86, 186–87; Lowry, 47–48; Egaña, vol. IV, pp. 678–91, vol. V, pp. 92–99. On early modern mobility, see Tamar Herzog, *Defining Nations: Immigrants and Citizens in Early Modern Spain and Spanish America*, Yale University Press, New Haven, 2003, Chapter 2.

40 Egaña, vol. I, p. 416.

41 Real Audiencia, Causas Civiles legajo 82 cuaderno 31 1631, ff. 112, 114v, AGN.

42 Egaña, vol. IV, p. 690.

43 Immunidad, leg. 1, exp. XXV (1603), Archivo Arzobispal de Lima, Peru.

44 Borah. The *corregidor* did not have direct oversight for litigation, as in Mexico, but mainly oversaw sales, rentals and apprenticeships involving indigenous residents of the region. On Mexico, see Brian Owensby, *Empire of Law and Indian Justice in Colonial Mexico*, Stanford University Press, Stanford, 2011.

45 Polo de Ondegardo, *Informaciones acerca de la Religión y Gobierno de los Incas* (1571), Sanmartí y Cia., Lima, 1916, vol. 3, pp. 47, 150.

46 'Testamento de Diego Lastara', 'Testamento de Magdalena Yauri Chumbi', 'Testamento de Catalina Carguay Chumbi', in Testamentos de Indios (hereafter TI) leg. 1A, AGN; 'Testamento de Diego Sedeño', TI legajo 1, AGN.

47 Corregimiento del Santiago del Cercado (hereafter CSC) leg. 1 doc. 4, 02.10.1687, Lima, AGN.

48 CSC leg. 1 doc. 3, 1686, Cercado, AGN.

49 For example, CSC leg. 1 doc. 3, Cercado 1686, AGN. Domingo Pascual calls himself *vecino* to add weight to his testimony about property ownership (f. 2). On the power of this language within indigenous communities, see Karen Graubart, 'The Creolization of the New World: Local Forms of Identity in Urban Colonial Peru, 1560–1640', *Hispanic American Historical Review*, vol. 89, no. 3, 2009, pp. 471–99.

50 David Vassberg, in his *Law and Society in Golden Age Castile*, Cambridge University Press, Cambridge, 1984, pp. 1–2, discusses the complexity of Spanish property relations, and the way that documentation obscures the importance of public ownership. That said, the Crown claimed dominium over any lands usurped from indigenous control, and, in cities like Lima, issued title through a governor or the *cabildo* to individuals intending to settle and populate the city. Those *solares* could be inherited or sold, and restrictions on sales were subject to enforcement.

51 CSC leg. 1 doc. 6 Cercado 1691, AGN.

52 'Autos que Siguieron los Indios Yauyos', Derecho Indígena, leg. 9, cuad. 130, 1653, AGN.

53 Ibid., f. 2v.

54 Ibid., f. 2v.

55 Ibid., f. 3v.

56 Ibid., f. 4.

57 See Charney, *Indian Society*, Chapter 3.

58 'Autos que Siguieron los Indios Yauyos', f. 2.

PART II

Conquest Reconsidered

3

Webs of Protection and Interpolity Zones in the Early Modern World

LAUREN BENTON AND ADAM CLULOW

References to protection were ubiquitous across the early modern world.[1] They were also notoriously imprecise, with many protection claims aimed at multiple audiences, both internal and external. This ambiguity guaranteed protection's pervasive appeal. Political agents or rulers might invoke protection in describing a pact between equals, in characterising a tributary relationship with a clear overlord and subordinates or in labelling quotidian domestic arrangements of stark inequality. Historical actors valued protection talk precisely because it applied so flexibly in so many different contexts. Put differently, protection was ubiquitous between the fifteenth and nineteenth centuries *because* it was so flexible.

This chapter traces the ways that intentionally capacious meanings of protection in early modern empires helped give rise to a distinctive, long phase of interpolity relations in world history. Early modern empires with fluid boundaries dominated regional and global regimes while also overlapping with other spheres of authority and control. Our analysis builds on the study of empires-as-networks and on insights from the literature on imperial borderlands, but the focus on protection also allows us to move beyond these approaches.[2] In the formations we are calling 'interpolity zones', claims about protection did not just influence or encompass empires; in a very real sense, such relationships *constituted* empires.[3] Protection also provided an effective mechanism for projecting imperial power selectively into areas where political and military control was tenuous. In borderland areas, mutually intelligible ideas about protection spanned very different political and social systems. The discourse of mutual protection framed alliances and gave them some stability, also embedding within them the possibility of conquest, a context in which only one power could claim the capacity to protect. As empires consolidated power, protection claims shifted away from languages of alliance to discourses of subjecthood, in the process casting shadows of sovereignty that anticipated imperial annexation.[4] The study of protection both reveals key forces that preserved interpolity zones over long periods and uncovers processes by which some imperial powers seized control and achieved global ascendance.

Our analysis commences with the seas. Sprawling maritime operations under the loose command of individual imperial powers utilised protection to establish their influence and channel their interests. Rather than ruling the seas, vessels and captains representing even the most powerful empires had to navigate overlapping networks of protection. We then apply some of these insights to territorial arrangements in which polities invoked protection to similar ends and effects. In analysing the way empires used protection to describe relationships of alliance we show how talk about protection could signal both the stability of political co-existence and the possibility that alliances prefigured conquest. The focus throughout is on the blurred lines between 'inside' and 'outside' registers of protection and the patterns of interpolity relations that were produced when networks of protection intersected and overlapped.[5]

EXTORTION AND REGULATION ON THE SEAS

The maritime licence has long been regarded as an indispensable tool of European expansion, with historians highlighting its use by the Portuguese in the Indian Ocean as well as by various successors and rivals.[6] The mechanics of the Portuguese *cartaz* system are well known. Capitalising on the military advantage provided by the light cannons their ships carried, the Portuguese sold *cartazes*, or shipping licences, to Indian Ocean shippers to force them to call at Portuguese-controlled ports. The system generated revenue and prizes for the Portuguese, who collected licence fees and also profited when they attacked vessels not carrying *cartazes*. There were Mediterranean precedents for such a system, and, in the seventeenth century, other European powers, including the Dutch and the English, developed similar pass systems in the Indian Ocean.[7] But scholars have challenged the view that such systems represented European innovation. The Indian Ocean was not a completely non-militarised space before European entry in 1500. The Mamluk Sultans of Egypt, for example, developed a maritime passport apparatus that looked remarkably similar to the Portuguese *cartaz*, and local rulers on the Malabar coast implemented their own systems of 'enforced tribute'.[8]

While valuable in undercutting assumptions about European exceptionalism, such analysis proceeds from a relatively narrow understanding of the *cartaz* system as a mafia-style protection racket in which a militarised sea power sold shelter from its own violence, extracting payments from merchants in exchange for ships' safe passage.[9] Even when an empire proffered protection as a means of extending and consolidating its influence, guarantees of safe passage worked as a flexible tool rather than the centrepiece of a singular strategy. And when other powers were in play, as they almost always were on the polyglot seas, many agents referred to protection, generating overlapping networks in the process. The result was not so much a regulatory order as a framework for desultory violence.[10] Looking more closely at the actual workings of the Portuguese *cartaz* system showcases the fluidity of such systems.

The promise of safe conduct by the Portuguese in the Indian Ocean took on many forms. Portuguese agents sold *cartazes* to Indian Ocean shippers, taxed *cartaz*-carrying vessels in Portuguese-controlled ports and regarded any ships without passes as fair game for capture.[11] The system generated some revenue but was mainly valuable in shoring up Portuguese monopolies for some commodities along particular trade routes and identifying a stream of legal prizes for continued raiding. Particularly during the first decades of Portuguese maritime presence in the Indian Ocean, we observe something more complex still: an array of intersecting strategies to apply safe conduct as an instrument to consolidate and sustain Portuguese power.

As they encountered Indian Ocean polities and traders, Portuguese agents adopted postures ranging from warfare to negotiation to withdrawal.[12] Portuguese arrangements of suzerainty with regard to coastal polities incorporated some of the same language and structures of maritime protection. Further, Portuguese officials resorted to similar proffers of protection when seeking to regulate the activities of often unruly and self-interested subjects. When viewed in the context of overlapping networks of Portuguese patronage and command sustained by raiding, profit and corruption, the *cartaz* system appears as one of a set of practices utilised to fashion the empire as a sprawling web of protection arrangements.[13]

The wide range of protection practices of the Portuguese is apparent in the commentary of Afonso de Albuquerque, who led campaigns at Goa and Melaka and established the network of ports that formed a key component of empire in the east. Protection arrangements underlay the Portuguese foothold in those ports. For example, Albuquerque's attack on Ormuz resulted in a truce that left it in the hands of the kingdom of Khaja Attar and 'ordained that the king should rule in the name of the king of Portugal' and provide tribute to the Portuguese.[14] The insecurity of the Portuguese position was more norm than exception. Even in Goa and Melaka, where his forces prevailed and the Portuguese installed themselves as rulers, Albuquerque worried about the tenuousness of Portuguese command. Imploring the Crown to send more arms and ships, he alerted the king that Moslem traders who had been forced to pay for Portuguese protection were 'wait[ing] for the moment when they can take the noose from their necks and set to work against you'. He warned of the absurdity of trying to keep even seemingly peaceful clients under control 'with fair words and offers of peace and protection'.[15] The dangers posed by the weak ties created through bonds of protection encompassed individual Portuguese subjects who ranged outside the narrow ambit of Portuguese jurisdiction.[16]

This volatility of protection arrangements in the ports extended to the way the Portuguese approached safe conduct on the seas. When merchants from the Coromandel coast appealed to Albuquerque for a safe conduct pass for ships sailing to Melaka and for a vessel ready to sail from Melaka with a cargo of textiles, Albuquerque reported the cases as examples of the profitability of exchanging safe conduct guarantees for 'the king's portion'.[17] Yet in the same letter Albuquerque bemoaned the loss of revenue resulting from the mere regulation of peaceful trade: 'Now that we have peace and friendship with everybody except the Sabaio and Calicut, there are no prizes or booty' from which to pay troops and maintain the fleet, he observed.[18] The benefits of providing protection had to be balanced against the opportunity costs of diminished raiding opportunities.

Already under Albuquerque, crown officials applied some similar tactics to the control of unruly Portuguese subjects in the east. It was after all by virtue of a licence from the king that the viceroy held the right to seize the property of non-compliant Portuguese and reassign captaincies of individual ships.[19] For example, the letter issued to Lopo Soares as Captain Major and Governor of India in 1515 invested him 'with the power of removing and displacing captains of the fortresses ... and captains of the *naos* or vessels ... and all other officials, even if they go from here by our order and warrant'. Opportunities for private profit drew individual Portuguese to act as independent agents and even to seek to establish themselves as semi-autonomous rulers: Diogo Veloso installed a king of Cambodia under his sway and constructed a fortress under his own command; Filipe de Brito e Nicote parlayed his service as a mercenary in Burma into a governorship there, established a *feitoria* and collected revenue in Lower Burma. Both appealed to Goa for recognition by the Portuguese Crown.[20] In such cases the difference between corruption and service to the king was a matter of interpretation.

Albuquerque labelled Portuguese captains as criminals for flouting his directives, and he confiscated and redistributed ships, providing protection to favoured subordinates by allowing them to sail in convoys with the fleet.[21] Taken together, the set of practices involving the sale or provision of protection, on land or on sea, in the Indian Ocean comprised a flexible framework for regulating both foreign and Portuguese shipping, and for structuring relations with local rulers and Portuguese subjects along a wide continuum of arrangements.[22]

Other pass systems, including those introduced by non-European powers, also evolved in unexpected ways by expanding to incorporate new groups or channelling violence toward foreign upstarts and potential rivals. This was the case with the famous vermilion-seal or *shuinjō* system, which was introduced in the early seventeenth century by the newly established Tokugawa regime in Japan. The *shuinjō* system was created as a domestic regulatory system with what seemed, at least at first, to be clearly defined boundaries. The Tokugawa military government or Bakufu issued passes or *shuinjō* authorising the holders to undertake individual voyages from Japan to stated destinations. The system was designed to monitor, control and restrict access to foreign trade. Only trusted merchants and lords received passes, thereby ensuring that the profits represented by long distance commerce did not spill out into unfriendly corners of Japan, especially to Kyushu-based rivals like the powerful Shimazu clan of Satsuma. Since the Tokugawa regime maintained no navy or indeed vessels of any kind, the system functioned at the harbour level rather than on the open seas. Only vessels carrying these passes were allowed to depart from Japanese ports, and the Tokugawa shogun wrote to rulers across East and Southeast Asia warning them that any vessel failing to carry one of these documents should not be permitted to trade.[23]

Although the system was created for domestic merchants, it began to bulge in unexpected directions once it became clear that the Tokugawa would intervene aggressively to guarantee the security of any vessel carrying one of these documents. In 1610, for example, the Portuguese watched in horror as one of their massive trading ships was sunk in Nagasaki harbour for a perceived infringement of a *shuinjō*.[24] In the aftermath of this episode foreign merchants, including later the Portuguese captains placed in charge of the crucial Macao-Nagasaki route, jostled to secure access to Tokugawa-issued shipping passes.[25] The result was the development of a lucrative marketplace where *shuinjō* were exchanged or sold by European and Chinese traders in order to secure the best combination of destination and timing.[26]

At the same time, foreign merchants with no capacity to claim these documents also clamoured for Tokugawa protection, and a string of aggrieved traders arrived in Edo to demand that the shogun intervene to secure their vessels.[27] The regime responded by tacking on additional provisions that significantly expanded the remit of its authority over the seas. In 1621 the Bakufu decreed that all merchants in Japanese coastal waters (very vaguely defined) were entitled to protection if they were attacked, regardless of whether or not they carried a *shuinjō*; in 1659 the Bakufu went one step further by stipulating that Chinese merchants on their way to Japan with goods intended for the Japanese marketplace could claim protection even if they were thousands of miles away from the archipelago.[28] The result was a significant expansion of the boundaries of what had started off as a domestic regulatory system and the insertion of Tokugawa protection as a key determinant in maritime conflicts in the East China Sea. In 1665, for example, the Dutch East India Company was forced to call off a maritime campaign directed against Zheng shipping based in Taiwan after Tokugawa officials made it clear that the shogun's protection extended to Chinese vessels transiting between Taiwan and Japan, even if the company was in open war with their home state.[29]

It was also the case that a single power could maintain very different, and sometimes fundamentally contradictory, protection systems. The Dutch East India Company (*Verenigde Oostindische Compagnie* or VOC) implemented a defined pass system, the *pascedullen* system, after the capture of Melaka, in 1641 in which all shipping was required to call at this port in order to purchase passes.[30] But prior to this the VOC operated overlapping protection systems, all functioning according to strikingly different principles. In places like the Banda archipelago, where the Company was determined to maintain monopoly control over key licences, it created a narrowly defined pass system in which any Bandanese craft 'found without a passport' might be 'taken by the Hollanders and declared as good prize with all their cargo'.[31] In Batavia, by contrast, VOC officials issued passes to Chinese merchants in order to provide security and develop the port as a regional hub. And in the Taiwan straits, the VOC simply took over pre-existing protection networks run by local pirates and targeting Fujianese fishermen who were required to provide a share of their catch in return for security.[32]

One of the reasons so many different pass systems co-existed was that they were not always engineered from the top down by imperial powers seeking to bring order to sea-lanes. Instead, such systems often emerged and derived strength from the actions of vulnerable merchants who petitioned relentlessly for passes and flags. Although the English East India Company had no formal pass system in Asian waters, English agents did supply documentation of protection. The head of the English factory in Japan, Richard Cocks, was kept busy issuing documents for diverse traders. On 27 February 1618 he handed over '2 lettrs of favour … w'th 3 flagges, two new and one ould' to Chinese merchants.[33] On 1 March he gave a flag and a letter for a Chinese merchant heading to Taiwan.[34] On 5 March he was back in action handing over 'an Eng. flag & a letter of favor' and a day later he gave a merchant called

Fingo Shiquan 'a letter of favour & an English flag', though he was not even sure where the vessel in question was sailing or what the name of the captain was, a lapse clearly evident in the two blank spaces in the diary where this information should have appeared.[35] In the space of just over a week Cocks had handed out five letters and six flags, each designed to assure particular merchants of English protection even in the absence of a wider officially sanctioned regime of English protection.[36] In these and other cases entrepreneurial merchants sought to bolster their connection with a European sponsor by carrying documents, displaying multiple flags and even taking on board European crewmembers.

If pass systems were essentially flexible, what legal identity or guarantees did carrying a pass actually confer? At times the answer seems to have been very little. A single vessel could carry multiple documents issued by both European and non-European powers. In 1622, for example, a Dutch East India Company ship eagerly looking for prizes to plunder sighted a strange junk in the waters near Taiwan. When questioned, the captain of the junk produced three documents, a letter from a Dutch merchant, a similar document issued by the head of the English East India Company factory in Japan and the 'Emperour's pass' or a Japanese *shuinjō*.[37] Such permutations were not limited to the first decades of European expansion but continued to characterise maritime encounters into the late-eighteenth century. In 1780, for example, an English ship encountered the *Istanbul*, which was owned by the wealthy Surat-based merchant Saleh Chalebi, on its way from Surat to Basra. Although he carried an English pass, the captain explained when questioned that he had no obligation to fly an English flag or claim English protection because he carried, in addition to this document, French and Dutch passes.[38] The proliferation of papers showing sponsorship in Indian Ocean shipping made the operation of pass systems at times very similar to maritime practice in the Atlantic, where sea-raiders routinely carried papers documenting authorisation by multiple, different sponsors as well as multiple flags, and calculated which documentation to produce in maritime encounters or prize courts.[39] Across the early modern world, mariners and merchants hoped to convert sometimes flimsy and even fraudulent paper claims into effective protection.

Some traders deployed ingenious systems to minimise costs. Gujarati merchants sometimes departed legally with a *cartaz*, or Portuguese safe conduct pass, then arranged for the same document to be sent back so that the next vessel could sail with it.[40] Sometimes the issuers of passes undercut the value of their own documents in order to secure advantage. In 1622, for example, Dutch warships attacked Indian vessels exiting Mocha harbour with passes issued by the VOC chief in that port, sparking a ferocious outcry from local merchants and rulers over what they termed 'false passes'.[41] In other cases, privateers and pirates deliberately forged passes to evade capture.[42]

Often a single document could be subject to very different interpretations. The multiple uses of protection by the Portuguese opened opportunities for conflicting interpretations of its legal significance by both Portuguese agents and those purchasing *cartazes*. Writing in 1727, one Portuguese viceroy, João Saldanha da Gama, argued that the purchase of *cartazes* transformed recipients into effective vassals of the Portuguese Crown, an outcome hardly consistent with a supposedly pervasive transactional logic.[43] Asian rulers with ships sailing under the protection of these documents often interpreted the arrangements very differently. For the Mughal emperors their receipt of free *cartazes*, together with the fact that some of the emperors' ships were permitted to sail without any licence as long as they paid customs duties at the port of Daman, enabled the regime to avoid any suggestion that carrying a *cartaz* required the acknowledgement of Portuguese suzerainty over the bearer.[44]

These examples show that pass systems operated with a recognised degree of ambiguity about the relation between the protecting sovereign and the ships and crews sailing with licences. Such ambiguities were consistent with a more systemic flexibility about the purpose of proffering protection. Issuing authorities guaranteed safe conduct on an ad hoc basis to ships belonging to formally recognised allies and opportunistically to others in efforts to establish monopolies on the trade of certain commodities or to control certain trading routes and ports. Passes were also produced haphazardly in response to merchant demands. At the same time very similar licensing arrangements aimed at regulating the commercial activities of diverse sets of subjects and subordinates.

The vagaries of pass systems made it difficult to pin down precise legal status and responsibility, even when parties had an incentive to do so. Records of litigation over captures provide a window on strategies to invoke protection in support of competing interests. Such conflicts posed questions about who was entitled to protection and about what precisely protection meant, in particular whether it conferred subjecthood on pass holders. Consider the case of the *Hamedy*, a Persian vessel seized by the Portuguese in 1725 after departing from the port of Bandar-Kung on the straits of Hormuz. The ship's owner, a wealthy Persian merchant called Aga Mehdy, had refused a *cartaz*, opting instead to sail under the protection of a French flag. The French bitterly protested against the capture and dispatched a representative, Louis de Saint Paul, to extricate the ship from Portuguese control and claim restitution. Saint Paul proceeded to marshal a string of arguments to prove that the *Hamedy* was bound to the French company, claiming among other things that carrying a

French commission conferred French nationality.[45] In much the same way an East India Company pass could convey subjecthood. Company passes stipulated that the holder could expect to receive the same protection as if 'actually in the said Right Honorable Company's Service'.[46]

A 1771 case involving the Portuguese and the English East India Company centred on the issue of subjecthood and provides a good illustration of the positioning of different powers over meanings of protection. In that year the Portuguese captured a vessel belonging to Dhanjishah Manjishah (Dunjee-shaw), a Parsee merchant who had served as an English broker in Surat.[47] The ship had sailed from Surat in November 1770 with a pass, but an English East India Company official had confiscated the document because of non-payment of convoy duties.[48] After Dhanjishah's vessel was captured, English and Portuguese officials clashed for months over differing interpretations of their rights. The English argued that the situation was entirely straightforward and that the vessel should be immediately restored to them with its full cargo. Anyone who held a pass, even if the pass was temporarily unavailable, was by definition a 'subject of the Hon'ble Company's as the Act of granting is a sufficient indication of it'.[49] The pass granted to Dhanjishah's vessel 'was of the usual Tenor and is such as serves a Protection to all our other Subjects'.[50] On the other side the Portuguese argued that when the ship was seized, it possessed no 'paper or Authentic pass that confirms her to belong to a person subject to the British government'.[51] When confronted with the pass itself Portuguese agents ridiculed the notion that it meant that Dhanjishah was an English subject. According to the governor of Goa, 'if the Hon'ble Company treat that Parseeman as a stranger why do they intend that I should repute and consider him as a Native of England'.[52] If Dhanjishah was not a subject, then the English had no right to issue him with a pass and by doing so English authorities had usurped 'the rights of the Crown of Portugal'.[53] The offence was not a minor one. For the English to issue such a document was 'the same as entering violently one of the Countries belonging to Goa and depriving its owner thereof'.[54]

The dispute called into question English rights to issue passes in the first place and the rights of holders of these documents to claim compensation based on their status as Company subjects. As a result, officials in Bombay determined that they must support their rights 'of granting Passes to all Persons' with all possible efforts.[55] When the Portuguese refused to back down, English officials determined to take action, and in late 1772 they convinced the Nawab of Surat to seize Portuguese property equal to the value of the captured ship and its cargo. In this way both the East India Company and the Governor of Goa sought to assert the authority not only to issue passes but also to determine their validity. Dunjeeshaw was unlucky, but he was not behaving illogically. His withholding of payment to the English recognised the imperfect nature of the protection the English agents were offering. Yet, when the ship was captured, he made the obvious choice of asserting English protection anyway.

This example and others like it caution against assuming that a particular imperial pass system was organising maritime relations in a particular place and time. Pass systems had ragged edges that shifted according to the strategies of rival powers, local authorities and merchants. The picture emerging from these profiles is one of overlapping protection networks of fluctuating strength and shifting dimensions. Imperial agents offered guarantees of safe conduct in different circumstances and arenas to subjects, allies and foreign traders without formal political affiliation. The fungible and flexible nature of promises of protection flowed both from mariners' manoeuvres and from the strategies of empires and their agents seeking to preserve the legitimacy of violent interventions in order to prop up their interests on seas and in ports. These webs of protection are best understood in many places as interpenetrating parts of a single interpolity legal regime, an image far removed from the standard account of sequential maritime imperial domination in the Indian Ocean. No one power conquered the seas. Every militarised maritime power structured its imperial enterprise around a family of relationships of protection. We now turn our attention to land, where similar networks of protection underpinned interpolity relations.

FROM PROTECTED ALLIES TO PROTECTED SUBJECTS

Protection talk frequently commenced with the possibility of an alliance in which two external powers promised to guarantee each other's security. In other cases imperial agents pledged to protect newly encountered groups without claiming political authority over them, and militarily weak groups found shelter under protective regimes without signalling their intention to cede sovereignty or abandon jurisdictional claims. In other words, accepting protection could mean no concomitant cession of sovereignty, but the same kind of protection talk could transition into a framework for claiming sovereignty and reclassifying allies as subjects. Protection talk framed, foreshadowed and in part constituted the process of conquest.

This process could happen with striking speed as putative allies suddenly found themselves reconstituted as subjects. The 1605 treaty concluded between the newly established Dutch East India Company and elders on the Banda islands, where much of the world's nutmeg was grown, stipulated that local authorities would take Dutch representatives under their 'care and protection' while the company promised to defend its newfound allies against outside aggression.[56] But four years later in 1609 the terms of the relationship shifted dramatically as VOC representatives demanded permission to build a fortress in order to protect the Bandanese properly against external foes such as the Portuguese and the Spanish. That the fort would turn them from allies into something far closer to VOC vassals was obvious, and the Bandanese responded by attacking and killing a Dutch admiral. The Company retaliated with overwhelming force, quickly bringing the Bandanese back to the negotiating table, where they were forced to sign a new treaty that dispensed with any notion of an alliance. By 1621 the Bandanese found themselves reconfigured as VOC subjects, compelled to sign a new treaty stipulating that they would recognise the Company and its officials as their sovereign without accepting any other 'princes or potentates'.[57]

In such cases protection served as a conduit for transforming relations. At the same time, as on the seas, the framework's appeal lay in its ability to support multiple interpretations simultaneously. An alliance between equals could, when viewed from a different perspective, represent a tributary relationship with clear overlord and subordinate. In many cases this kind of ambiguity was deliberately inserted from the beginning. When concluding what they regarded as vassalage agreements, the Portuguese in Goa made use of the term 'friend' to smooth the way and conceal a hierarchical relationship.[58] In the Kongo the relationship between Afonso I, the ruler of that kingdom (r. 1509–42), and the Portuguese Crown was infused with ambiguity. An incident in 1516 illustrates the way fragmented Portuguese authority in Kongo combined with formal recognition of the suzerainty of the Portuguese Crown to create a space for Afonso's autonomy. Portuguese agents were feuding over claims to local power, and the Portuguese factor Álvaro Lopes killed another Portuguese official. The accused murderer took sanctuary in the church, but Afonso extracted him and packed him off to Portugal for trial.[59] The episode tells us something about the limits of Portuguese royal authority in the Kongo, where the power to protect or discipline Portuguese subjects was weak and unreliable.[60] More tellingly the incident showcases Afonso's strategy of representing the royal houses as equals and characterising his relationship to Portugal as one of alliance. He referred to the Portuguese king as *irmão*, or brother, and called on him to act to contain the violence of his own Portuguese subjects. The Portuguese monarch responded with language emphasising his superiority to the Kongo king. Here the proxy for protection was tutelage. Royal letters to the Kongo outlined for Afonso how diplomacy should be conducted and addressed him as a subordinate.[61] Who was protecting whom? It depended on who was describing Portuguese-Kongo relations.

Similarly, in Spain's conquest in the New World, protection represented a useful framework, one that characterised pragmatic alliance-building as a process preparing the way for Spanish political dominance. For example, protection talk narrated the fluid and shifting power in relations between Spaniards and Tlaxcalans in sixteenth-century New Spain. It is commonplace to observe that Cortés would not have succeeded in taking Tenochtilán if not for the actions of the Tlaxcalans. Historians typically refer to the relationship as an alliance; Spaniards relied on the aid of Tlaxcalans in defeating the Aztecs, regarded as common enemies. Structures of composite political authority of both Spaniards and Tlaxcalans made sense of the idea of an alliance between groups of different political and military strength, allowing both sides to avoid talk of conquest in the context of their relationship.[62] But mutual understanding is not the point. Spaniards and Tlaxcalans differed sharply in their take on the nature of the alliance and how long it should last. If the alliance resulted from a pact – a security arrangement with mutual benefits – then it might dissolve (or evolve) once the object of war, the defeat of the Aztecs, was realised. But the relationship might also endure and evolve. Tlaxcalans angled to preserve the alliance while recognising that they were under the protection of the Spanish Crown; Spaniards argued that Tlaxcalans had assumed a subordinate place within the Spanish Empire, even as they retained elements of self-rule.

The ambiguities meant that no clear interpretation prevailed quickly. In 1529 the Spanish Crown granted Tlaxcalans an exemption from being assigned in *encomienda*, an act that affirmed their status as free vassals.[63] Tlaxcalan vassalage still provided space for autonomy. Tlaxcalan elites fought to retain recognition of their political community as a municipality, even travelling to Spain to make their case for their right to a direct relationship with the monarch rather than one mediated through Spanish overlords to whom they paid tribute and services. The arrangement established a form of self-government utilising Spanish institutions.[64] Here Tlaxcalans used the language of protection to manoeuvre for degrees of autonomy. The Crown, in turn, used the framework of protection in efforts to shelter Tlaxcalans from the worst abuses of Spanish colonists.[65] Here we see protection's range of meanings framing a political field of options that no one considered mutually exclusive: the preservation of limited indigenous authority, the subordination of indigenous political communities and the regulation of the power of imperial agents.

Such examples might suggest that protection functioned simply as a temporary cover for imperial aggression. But the interpolity dimensions of protection were sometimes relatively stable over long periods and vast spaces. Less powerful polities often helped to perpetuate competing networks of protection by shifting loyalties between overlords. In Cambodia, a weak state marooned between two more powerful polities, the lines were so blurred that local rulers were able to perform the apparently impossible balancing act of claiming political independence while also seeking shelter from two separate protectors: Siam as 'Father and the Vietnamese [emperor as] . . . Mother'.[66] The result was a string of contradictions concealed within a basic imprecision about the nature of protection, an arrangement that enabled Cambodia to function in the words of one contemporary as an 'independent country that is a slave of two'.[67] Part of the reason a state like Siam could tolerate such imprecision in its relations with less powerful neighbours was that it made use of a similar ambiguity in dealings with its putative overlord, Ming China, to which it offered tribute in return for protection. This ambiguity found perhaps its clearest expression in a single term, *jingong*, a Chinese word meaning tribute and the term used to describe the relationship between Siam and China. While Siamese rulers referred to *jingong* in documents dispatched to China, they avoided the Thai equivalent in Siamese royal letters and opted instead for the transliterated word *chim kong*, which lacked a precise meaning or clear associations with subordination. This sleight of hand allowed the Siamese kings to present themselves within Siam as brother monarchs of an independent country rather than as subservient vassals.[68]

Imperial centres also recognised the ambiguous status of semi-subordinate polities over which they claimed protection. The Tokugawa regime in early modern Japan cultivated a system in which the 'roles of inferiors . . . could simultaneously express both "autonomy" and "complete subservience"'.[69] The contradiction was so pronounced that some domains in the archipelago could appear as utterly subordinate political units in one moment and virtually independent countries in the next. While this incongruity has flummoxed generations of scholars, who have veered between radically different assessments of the power of the Tokugawa regime, the ability to tolerate these contradictions appears to stem from a crucial but largely neglected distinction between two key concepts: *uchi*, the (often) hidden inside, and *omote*, the outside façade presented to the world.[70] The Tokugawa regime's governing dynamic relied on keeping these two categories separate, allowing the domains considerable autonomy within their own spaces of operation as long they preserved the outward illusion of perfect subservience in their dealings with Edo. What this arrangement meant in practice was that domains made use of two separate languages, one for internal consumption within the domain and another for interactions with the central regime.

Protection talk reflected, and preserved for a long time, a similarly useful
ambiguity in relations between the English East India Company (EIC) and
Indian rulers. The Company had inserted itself into the sub-continent by
accepting the protection of the Mughal emperor. This relationship was soli-
dified by the latter's appointment of the EIC as Diwani of Bengal, Behar and
Orissa in 1765, an arrangement that established the Company's right to collect
taxes in those territories. Along with access to revenue came the obligation to
protect, and the Company was charged with maintaining 'a large Army for the
protection of the Provinces of Bengal'.[71] The Company also entered into an
exemplary pact with the Nawab of Awadh wherein the potentate agreed to pay
for the military services of the Company in exchange for a pledge to defend
Awadh. The treaty inaugurated a 'new pattern' in which Indian rulers found
themselves 'struggling to maintain their authority and to meet the imperious
demands of the East India Company for revenues to pay for their armies'.[72]
The British Empire in India was stitched together in a combination of mili-
tarism and diplomacy, as a series of treaties with Indian polities that combined
the cession of control over external affairs by Indian states with an obligation
for them to pay for the Company's military presence.[73]

The language of protection continued to permeate Anglo-Indian politics.
By 1803, with power relations shifting, the Company could assert that it was
placing the 'person, family and nominal authority' of the Mughal emperor
'under the protection of the British Government'.[74] What precisely this meant
was still unclear, and English officials described the relationship in different
terms depending on their audience.[75] The logic of protection framed even the
system's rupture. Following the Indian Rebellion of 1857 the Company placed
the emperor, Bahadur Shah II, on trial for treason as a 'subject of the British
government of India'.[76] His subjecthood was declared to have arisen when 'his
grandfather, Shah Alam, after having been kept in rigorous confinement by
the Mahrattas, on their defeat by the English in 1803, applied to the British
Government for protection'. After that moment, 'the titular kings of Delhi
became pensioned subjects of the British'.[77] This reading of the history
removed any trace of ambiguity about protection's meaning as subjugation
rather than alliance.

Although protection was an indispensable tool for European expansion, we
should be wary of assuming that protection arrangements functioned always as
vehicles for growing European power. If protective networks organised European imperial ambitions across the Americas, increasing European authority
within such webs was hardly certain or predictable. To be sure, Europeans
often boasted to metropolitan, settler and native audiences of their rights and

responsibilities as overlords. British and New York officials brought Mohawk 'kings' to London in 1710 as embodiments of the British suzerainty in New York more than a decade before signing the 1722 Treaty of Albany.[78] Across eastern North America Europeans encouraged American Indians to adopt the fictional kinship title of 'father' or the native category of 'greatest lord' in referring to Europeans. The political language of alliance persisted, meanwhile, with many recorded references by North American Indian groups to Europeans as brethren, a clear strategy to point to Europeans' and Indians' equality of status as allies and to support Indian claims for European gifts required to solidify pacts of mutual security.[79] In some circumstances such gifts operated as tribute and recognised the greater military power of Indians while casting Europeans as purchasers of protection.

Alliances were notoriously fragile. They broke down not only when colonists failed to deliver sufficient or proper gifts but also when networks of alliances functioned to spread violence, much like conduits carrying an electrical charge.[80] The volatility of relations of protection is illustrated by the Anishinaabewaki of the *pays d'en haut*, whose agents travelled to Montreal to participate in the signing of a peace pact in 1701 that would establish the French as arbiters of conflicts among Indian groups to the west. A short time later, Anishinaabewaki recognition of French protection disappeared as it became very clear that the French could not produce order even in French-controlled enclaves, much less in the vast middle reaches of the continent.[81]

Promises of protection could not by themselves convert unstable networks of fragile alliances into polities that we might recognise as full-fledged empires. Nor did slippery imperial rhetoric about receiving and providing protection always translate into increased influence. In Japan, for example, such notions proved nothing more than a dead-end. Beginning in the 1630s, Dutch officials, exactly as their English counterparts in India had done, began claiming that they were nothing more than loyal vassals intent only on serving the Tokugawa regime. Rather than providing a springboard for increased influence, this rhetoric came to trap the Dutch, who found themselves encased instead within a rigid requirement actually to deliver on that service by, among other things, dispatching a vessel to aid in the suppression of a domestic revolt at Shimabara in 1637–38.[82] In the Americas, protection featured prominently in the persistence of unevenly bounded spheres of influence. What we call 'empires' in thickly contested borderlands took the form of unstable webs of alliances, in some cases assuming more definite outlines in direct response to conflicts over jurisdiction and protection.[83] Protection claims cast shadows of sovereignty, but there was a great deal of movement in the shadows.

CONCLUSION

In this chapter we have pointed to the prevalence of protection in cross-polity interrelations in the early modern world. In different regions, protection established lasting, if elastic, frameworks within which relationships of political authority and jurisdiction combined and recombined. Rather than resolving into different types of protection systems — domestic licensing agreements or mafia-like protection rackets imposed on vulnerable outsiders on the seas, or relationships of alliance or conquest on land — empires activated a range of meanings of protection in responding to local circumstances and the political strategies of their interlocutors. Protection operated as a flexible framework for interpolity relations rather than simply a tool of imperial consolidation.

The key to protection's functions in structuring powerfully formative conflicts lay in the blurred divide between 'inside' and 'outside' protection. Parties to agreements about protection might describe them as voluntary arrangements and treaties between autonomous polities. At the same time, sophisticated actors on all sides knew that alliances did sometimes slide into configurations of unequal power. Both imperial agents and subordinate groups found reasons to associate protection with the recognition of subjecthood. A transition toward an 'inside' variant of protection in which it figured as a necessary good provided by a legitimate sovereign was not necessarily irreversible. Political communities absorbed into empires had reason to maintain the accoutrements of rule and their own claims to be providers of protection.

The resulting webs of protection structured both interpolity and intra-imperial relations in the early modern world. The institutional forms associated with protection arrangements changed, but the general framework remained stable over a long period. Empires took shape within these configurations as irregular and overlapping areas of influence, abutting and interweaving with spheres of power associated with rival empires and an array of less powerful polities. We look in vain for a doctrine of protection recognised across an early modern law of nations. Yet we do find a coherent and repeating set of practices and utterances about protection that spanned culturally and legally disparate parts of the world and that gave shape to overlapping spheres of imperial control.

Protection was not the only framing device in a repertoire of practices we label 'interpolity law'.[84] Protection talk joined a widely shared focus on protocol for marking authority, pervasive jockeying over jurisdiction and positioning with regard to possession to compose a recurring and recognised framework for organising relations across very different polities in the early modern world. This is not to say that there was anything approaching a universal law of nations.[85] Rather, the existence of parallel systems of political organisation meant that diverse political communities shared some basic characteristics that allowed legal actors to rely on analogies, rather than elusive cross-cultural understandings, as they engaged with other peoples and polities.[86]

The meanings of protection were multiple but finite. The blurring of 'inside' and 'outside' registers of protection was widespread and often purposeful, the result of observable strategies. Yet early modern imperial agents and others invested protection talk with specific alternative meanings in arguments over property, subjecthood and authority. The political configurations that emerged through the politics of protection held vast regions in thrall. In many ways the early modern world, on land and sea, was an age of protection.

NOTES

1 This chapter is adapted with permission from Lauren Benton and Adam Clulow, 'Empires and Protection: Making Interpolity Law in the Early Modern World', *Journal of Global History*, vol. 12, no. 1, 2017, pp. 74–92.

2 For these approaches see Alison Games, *The Web of Empire: English Cosmopolitans in an Age of Expansion, 1560–1660*, Oxford University Press, Oxford, 2009; Kerry Ward, *Networks of Empire: Forced Migration in the Dutch East India Company*, Cambridge University Press, Cambridge: 2008; Karen Barkey, *Bandits and Bureaucrats: The Ottoman Route to State Centralization*, Cornell University Press, Ithaca, NY, 1994. The literature on borderlands is vast, but see, for example, Chad Bryant (ed.), *Borderlands in World History, 1700–1914*, Palgrave Macmillan, Basingstoke, 2014.

3 On this point, and more generally on 'protection talk', see Lauren Benton and Lisa Ford, *Rage for Order: The British Empire and the Origins of International Law, 1800–1850*, Harvard University Press, Cambridge, MA, 2016, Chapter 4.

4 Lauren Benton, 'Shadows of Sovereignty: Legal Encounters and the Politics of Protection in the Atlantic World', in Alan Karras and Laura Mitchell (eds), *Encounters Old and New in World History: Essays Inspired by Jerry H. Bentley*, University of Hawai'i Press, 2017, pp. 136–50.

5 On 'inside' and 'outside' registers of protection, see the Introduction in this volume and also Benton and Ford, *Rage for Order*, 89, 102.

6 Elizabeth Mancke, 'Early Modern Expansion and the Politicization of Oceanic Space', *Geographical Review*, vol. 89, no. 2, 1999, pp. 225–36.

7 Markus Vink, 'Passes and Protection Rights: the Dutch East India Company as a Redistributive Enterprise in Melaka, 1641–1662', *Moyen Orient & Océan Indien*, vol. 7, 1990, pp. 73–101.

8 Luis F. F. R. Thomaz, 'Precedents and Parallels of the Portuguese Cartaz System', in Pius Malekandathil and Jamal Mohammed (eds), *The Portuguese, Indian Ocean,*

and European Bridgeheads, 1500–1800: Festschrift in Honour of Professor K.S. Mathew, Fundação Oriente and Institute for Research in Social Sciences and Humanities of MESHAR, Tellicherry, Kerala, 2001, pp. 67–85; Sebastian R. Prange, 'A Trade of No Dishonor: Piracy, Commerce, and Community in the Western Indian Ocean, Twelfth to Sixteenth Century', *American Historical Review*, vol. 116, no. 5, 2011, p. 1276. For a restatement of the older view that the legal regime emerging in the sixteenth century in the Indian Ocean represented a merging of Northern European and Mediterranean practices and their thrust into non-militarised space, see Philip Steinberg, *The Social Construction of the Ocean*, Cambridge University Press, Cambridge, 2001, pp. 86–89.

9 This characterisation runs from Lane to more recent accounts: Frederic Lane, *Profits from Power: Readings in Protection Rent and Violence-Controlling Enter-prises*, State University of New York Press, Albany, 1979; Michael Pearson, *Indian Ocean*, Routledge, London and New York, 2003, p. 121.

10 For a similar argument about the influence of British imperial law on the seas in the early nineteenth century, see Benton and Ford, Chapter 5.

11 Thomaz, p. 68.

12 A.J.R. Russell-Wood, *The Portuguese Empire, 1415–1808: A World on the Move*, Johns Hopkins University Press, Baltimore, MD, 1992, p. 43.

13 On the Portuguese Empire as a network or set of networks, see Erik Lars Myrup, *Power and Corruption in the Portuguese World*, Louisiana State University Press, Baton Rouge, 2015; and Victoria Garcia, 'From Plunder to Crusade: Networks of Nobility and Negotiations of Empire in the Estado da India 1505–1515', unpublished paper, Wesleyan University, 2012.

14 T.F. Earle and John Villiers (eds), *Albuquerque Caesar of the East, Selected Texts by Afonso de Albuquerque and his Son*, Aris & Phillips, Warminster, 1990, p. 57.

15 Ibid., p. 103.

16 Ibid., p. 111.

17 Ibid., pp. 117–19.

18 Ibid., p. 119; Albuquerque clearly regarded control of the ports and of adjacent waters as an interlocking system. Returning to the theme of the need for more men and arms sent from Lisbon, he explained in a letter to the king that Portuguese enforcement in and around specific nodes such as Goa had a ripple effect. Foreign traders and their sponsors bowed to Portuguese demands even in adjacent areas where enforcement was less sweeping (ibid., pp. 135–37).

19 'Letters Patent of Captain-Major and Governor of India Issued to Lopo Soares', Almeirim, 10 February 1515, *Documentos Sobre os Portugueses em Moçambique e na África Central, 1497–1840*, Vol. IV, Centro de Estudos Históricos Ultramarinos, 1965, Lisbon, pp. 211–13.

20 A.R. Disney, *A History of Portugal and the Portuguese Empire*, Vol. 2, Cambridge University Press, Cambridge, 2009, pp. 189–90.

21 For Albuquerque's treatment of Diogo Mendes, see Earle and Villiers, p. 143.

22 Garcia makes the point that historians have exaggerated the divide between a 'formal' and 'informal' Portuguese Empire; *fidalgos* operated across these spheres and manoeuvred through 'networks of nobility'.

23 Robert Innes, 'The Door Ajar: Japan's Foreign Trade in the Seventeenth Century' (PhD thesis, University of Michigan, 1980), p. 112.

24 Charles Boxer, *The Christian Century in Japan, 1549–1650*, University of California Press, Berkeley, 1951, pp. 430–31. The supposed infringement can be traced back to 1608. In that year a *shuinsen* belonging to Arima Haranobu, a prominent lord in Kyushu, arrived in Macao on its way back to Japan from a successful voyage to Cambodia. When the Japanese crew became involved in a violent riot, Portuguese authorities responded by executing at least one of the offenders. After Tokugawa officials learned of this incident – almost certainly via a doctored version of events that emphasised Portuguese culpability – they determined to take action for what was seen as an assault on Arima's trading licence. In an important new book that puts forward a different interpretation, Reinier Hesselink argues that the infringement was in fact nothing more than an excuse and that the Tokugawa Bakufu was trying to exert control over the wider Portuguese trade (*The Dream of Christian Nagasaki: World Trade and the Clash of Cultures, 1560–1640*, McFarland Publishers, Jefferson, NC, 2016).

25 W. Ph. Coolhaas (ed.), *Generale Missiven van Gouverneurs-Generaal en Raden aan Heren XVII der Verenigde Oostindische Compagnie*, 9 vols., Martinus Nijhoff, The Hague, 1960-, vol. 1, p. 149; Richard Cocks, *Diary Kept by the Head of the English Factory in Japan: Diary of Richard Cocks, 1615–1622*, edited University of Tokyo Historiographical Institute, 3 vols., University of Tokyo, Tokyo, 1978–80, vol. 3, p. 60.

26 In November 1617, for example, the head of the English factory in Japan sold a 'junk w'th the goshon [*shuinjō*], for 1200 *tais* [taels]' (Cocks, vol. 2, p. 204).

27 See Adam Clulow, *The Company and the Shogun: The Dutch Encounter with Tokugawa Japan*, Columbia University Press, New York, 2014, Chapters 4 and 5.

28 This happened even as the Tokugawa regime moved to end the *shuinjō* system in 1635 when it prevented most Japanese ships from leaving the archipelago (Michael Laver, *The Sakoku Edicts and the Politics of Tokugawa Hegemony*, Cambria Press, Amherst, NY, 2011).

29 Cynthia Viallé and Leonard Blussé (eds), *The Deshima Dagregisters, Vol. 13, 1660–1670*, Universiteit Leiden, Leiden, 2010, p. 162; John E. Wills Jr., *Pepper, Guns, and Parleys: The Dutch East India Company and China, 1622–1681*, Harvard University Press, Cambridge, MA, 1974, p. 62.

30 Vink.

31 J.E. Heeres and F.W. Stapel (eds), *Corpus Diplomaticum Neerlando-Indicum*, 6 vols., Martinus Nijhoff, The Hague: 1907–1955, vol. 1, pp. 123–24.

32 Weichung Cheng, *War, Trade and Piracy in the China Seas (1622–1683)*, Brill, Leiden, 2013, pp. 64–65; Tonio Andrade, 'The Company's Chinese Pirates:

How the Dutch East India Company Tried to Lead a Coalition of Pirates to War against China, 1621–1662', *Journal of World History*, vol. 15, no. 4, 2004, p. 428.

33 Cocks, vol. 2, p. 257. Cocks makes use of the Julian calendar. This date corresponds to 9 March in the Gregorian calendar.

34 Cocks, vol. 2, p. 258.

35 Ibid., p. 261.

36 Of course the English were hardly strangers to pass systems or the politics of maritime protection. On the English uses of protection in the early modern Mediterranean, see Tristan Stein, 'The Mediterranean and the English Empire of Trade, 1660–1748' (PhD thesis, Harvard University, 2011).

37 Anthony Farrington, *The English Factory in Japan, 1613–1623*, British Library, London, 1991, p. 1190.

38 Ghulam Nadri, *Eighteenth-Century Gujarat: The Dynamics of Its Political Economy, 1750–1800*, Brill, Leiden, 2009, p. 59.

39 Lauren Benton, *A Search for Sovereignty: Law and Geography in European Empires, 1400–1900*, Cambridge University Press, New York, 2010, Chapter 3.

40 Michael Pearson, *Merchants and Rulers in Gujarat: The Response to the Portuguese in the Sixteenth Century*, University of California Press, Berkeley, 1976, p. 99. Note that the practice of carrying multiple flags and commissions signed by several sovereigns extended into the Atlantic. See Benton, *Search for Sovereignty*, Chapter 3.

41 H.T. Colenbrander (ed.) *Jan Pietersz. Coen, Bescheiden omtrent zijn Bedrijf in Indie*, 7 vols., Martinus Nijhoff, The Hague, 1919–23, vol. 7.2, p. 938.

42 For one example, see William Foster (ed.), *The English Factories in India, 1634–36*, Clarendon Press, Oxford, 1911, pp. 239–40.

43 Da Gama explained that 'as a kind of vassalage they buy a cartaz' (João Melo, 'Lords of Conquest, Navigation and Commerce: Diplomacy and the Imperial Ideal During the Reign of John V, 1707–50' [PhD thesis, Swansea, 2012], p. 133).

44 Glen Ames, *Renascent Empire: Pedro II and the Quest for Stability in Portuguese Monsoon Asia ca.1640–1682*, Amsterdam University Press, Amsterdam, 1999, p. 151.

45 The subsequent fight over the nature of the connection created by *Hamedy's* licence extended to Europe, where the French ambassador at Lisbon protested against the seizure (Melo, pp. 146–48).

46 Philip Stern, *The Company-State: Corporate Sovereignty and the Early Modern Foundations of the British Empire in India*, Oxford University Press, Oxford, 2011, p. 44.

47 Adam Clulow is grateful to Ghulam Nadri for directing him to this case. Ghulam Nadri, 'Interdependence, Competition, and Contestation: The English and the Dutch East India Companies and Indian Merchants in the Seventeenth and Eighteenth Centuries', Unpublished paper, Global Company Conference, Heidelberg, 3–5 December 2015. The records for this dispute can be found in the British Library, Home Miscellaneous Series 108, ff. 83–125, 151–83.

48 Ibid., f. 85.

49 Ibid., f. 171.

50 Ibid., f. 165–66.

51 Ibid., f. 100.

52 Ibid., f. 181.

53 Ibid., f. 168.

54 Ibid., f. 179.

55 Ibid., f. 154.

56 Heeres and Stapel, vol. 1, pp. 37–38.

57 Ibid., p. 162.

58 Melo, p. 101.

59 See 'Carta d'el-Rei do Congo para Portugal Informando que Ali Tinha Chegado Álvaro Lopes (4 de Março de 1516)', Documento 9, António Luís Ferronha (ed.), *As Cartas do Rei do Congo D. Afonso*, Grupo de Trabalho do Ministério da Educação para as Comemorações dos Descobrimentos Portugueses, Lisbon, 1992, pp. 26–41.

60 John Thornton, 'Early Kongo-Portuguese Relations, 1483–1575: A New Interpretation', *History in Africa*, vol. 8, 1981, p. 195.

61 Ivana Elbl, 'Cross-Cultural Trade and Diplomacy: Portuguese Relations with West Africa, 1441–1521', *Journal of World History*, vol. 3, no. 2, 1992, p. 193.

62 R. Jovita Baber, 'The Construction of Empire: Politics, Law and Community in Tlaxcala, New Spain, 1521–1640' (PhD thesis, University of Chicago, 2005), p. 67.

63 Ibid., pp. 85, 95, 103, 105.

64 Ibid., p. 134.

65 Ibid., pp. 157–60.

66 Quoted in Thongchai Winichakul, *Siam Mapped: A History of the Geo-Body of a Nation*, University of Hawai'i Press, Honolulu, 1994, p. 85.

67 David Chandler, *A History of Cambodia*, Westview Press, Boulder, 1992, p. 119. Such relations recurred in different parts of Asia. The Tai state of Sipsongpanna occupied a similar position between Qing China and Burma. As C. Patterson Giersch notes, in 'this political world, it was acceptable to be the "son" of one or two distant suzerains' (*Asian Borderlands: The Transformation of Qing China's Yunnan Frontier*, Harvard University Press, Cambridge, MA, 2006, p. 87).

68 Erika Masuda, 'The Fall of Ayutthaya and Siam's Disrupted Order of Tribute to China (1767–1782)', *Taiwan Journal of Southeast Asian Studies*, vol. 4, no. 2, 2007, p. 117.

69 Luke Roberts, *Performing the Great Peace: Political Space and Open Secrets in Tokugawa Japan*, University of Hawai'i Press, Honolulu, 2012, p. 5.

70 Ibid., pp. 6–8.

71 William Bolts, *Considerations on Indian Affairs, Particularly Respecting the Present State of Bengal and its Dependencies*, London, 1772, p. 30.

72 Robert Travers, 'A British Empire by Treaty in Eighteenth-Century India', in Saliha Belmessous (ed.), *Empire By Treaty: Negotiating European Expansion, 1600–1900*, Oxford University Press, New York, 2015, p. 142.

73 On the British Empire and treaties in India, see H.V. Bowen, *The Business of Empire: The East India Company and Imperial Britain, 1765–1833*, Cambridge University Press, Cambridge, 2008, pp. 260–72; and especially Travers. On protection language in the consolidation of British authority on Ceylon, see Benton and Ford, Chapter 4.

74 Robert Martin (ed.), *The Despatches, Minutes, and Correspondence, of the Marquess Wellesley, K.G., During his Administration in India*, J. Murray, London, 1836–37, vol. 4, p. 156. This move was prompted by a desire to make sure that the emperor and hence Mughal legitimacy could not be seized by one of the Company's rivals.

75 Buckler's classic 1922 article observes that Wellesley presented the arrangement in two different ways depending upon his audience. When addressing Europeans, he described the relation in terms of a protectorate; when speaking to Mughal officials, he referred to a 'vassal's protection of his lord' ('The Political Theory of the Indian Mutiny', *Transactions of the Royal Historical Society*, fourth series, vol. 5, 1922, p. 91). Note, however, that Buckler argues that relations between the Company and the Mughal Empire were dominated by misunderstanding. More recently, historians observe that the layered qualities of Asian and European sovereignty created common ground; the EIC itself was, after all, a state operating with the authorisation of another state. See Stern; Travers; and Benton, *A Search for Sovereignty*, Chapter 5.

76 The quote comes from the charges laid against Bahadur Shah (Lucinda Bell, 'The 1858 Trial of the Mughal Emperor Bahadur Shah II Zafar for Crimes Against the State' (PhD thesis, Melbourne University, 2004), p. 259.

77 'Trial of Muhammed Bahadur Shah, Titular King of Delhi, and of Mogul Beg, and Hajee, all of Delhi, for rebellion against the British Government, and murder of Europeans during 1857', *Selections from the Records of the Government of the Punjab and Its Dependencies*, new series, no. VII, Punjab Printing Company, Lahore, 1870, p. 221.

78 Daniel Richter, *Facing East from Indian Country: A Native History of Early America*, Harvard University Press, Cambridge, MA, 2001, p. 166.

79 Ibid., p. 148.

80 Michael Witgen, *An Infinity of Nations: How the Native New World Shaped Early North America*, University of Pennsylvania Press, Philadelphia, 2012, p. 293.

81 Ibid., pp. 276–78.

82 Clulow, Chapter 3.

83 Pekka Hämäläinen, 'The Shapes of Power: Indians, Europeans, and North American Worlds from the Seventeenth to the Nineteenth Century', in Julianne Barr and Edward Countryman (eds), *The Contested Spaces of Early America*, University of Pennsylvania Press, Philadelphia, 2014, pp. 31–68; Brett Rushforth, *Bonds of Alliance: Indigenous and Atlantic Slaves in New France*, University of North Carolina Press, Chapel Hill, 2012; Lisa Ford, *Settler Sovereignty: Jurisdiction and Indigenous People in America and Australia, 1788–1836*, Harvard University Press, Cambridge, MA, 2010.

84 Lauren Benton and Adam Clulow, 'Legal Encounters and the Origins of Global Law', in Jerry H. Bentley et al. (eds), *Cambridge History of the World, Volume 6, Part 2*, Cambridge University Press, Cambridge, 2015, pp. 50–79.

85 C.H. Alexandrowicz, *An Introduction to the History of the Law of Nations in the East Indies*, Oxford University Press, Oxford, 1967; Jennifer Pitts, 'Empire and Legal Universalisms in the Eighteenth Century', *American Historical Review*, vol. 117, no. 1, 2012, pp. 92–121; C. H. Alexandrowicz, *The Law of Nations in Global History*, edited by David Armitage and Jennifer Pitts, Oxford University Press, Oxford, 2017.

86 Benton and Clulow, p. 82.

4

Plunder and Profit in the Name of Protection: Royal Iberian Armadas in the Early Atlantic

GABRIEL DE AVILEZ ROCHA

In the summer of 1523 Gonçalo Leite and Duarte Valadares found themselves in the service of the Portuguese Crown as captains of an 'armada of protection of the Strait [of Gibraltar]'. Instructed to work toward the king's 'service, protection and defense', Leite, Valadares and dozens of mariners and soldiers spent months plying the sea-lanes between Andalusia, southern Portugal and Atlantic Morocco.[1] At stake were the ambitions of the Spanish and Portuguese Crowns in the Maghreb, the Mediterranean and the broader Atlantic. For Iberian crown operatives the discourse of protection or protection talk routinely summoned patrol fleets that incited violence against perceived rivals in the region. In other words, in this case protection talk not only spurred defensive measures against designated foes but signalled a rationale for deploying violence to pursue material and political gain.

Many historians have tended to place the sixteenth-century Portuguese and Castilian Crowns and their operatives in isolation at the rivalrous vanguard of European expansion. As if encountering a separate Iberian Atlantic, they have cast the French, Dutch and English as latecomers, interlopers or parasites.[2] Meanwhile, the sixteenth-century Maghreb has been set apart entirely, despite the fact that it was also filled with expansionist polities.[3] One effective critique of this separate Atlantics model has come from political and legal historians of empire. Their work has shown how competition among emergent colonial powers forged a common political rubric for structuring coalescent institutions of empire in the early modern period.[4] Building on this perspective, we can discern a crucial and largely ignored element of Iberian imperial formation: that discourses justifying violence against others not only drew from dictates of Christian proselytisation but also from claims to protect and secure Ibero-African sea-lanes, the subjects travelling through them and the property they carried.

In this chapter I highlight some of the key ways that officials sought to deliver on claims of protection between the 1510s and the 1520s. The treasurers, tax collectors and factors of the Iberian Crown regularly armed, outfitted and hired mariners and soldiers to patrol Iberian and North African waters and wage violence against Mahgrebi mariners and coastal communities. As the first section of the chapter shows, protection talk in the 1510s was largely understood to support Portugal's territorial ambitions in the Maghreb. The second section traces how a crescendo of French privateer engagement in the northeastern Atlantic in the early 1520s, combined with a relative lull in the war theatre in North Africa, reoriented Iberian protection talk to the sea. Facing maritime attacks, Portuguese and Spanish monarchs continued to outfit armadas, feeding into a vicious cycle by which claims to protect gave increasing cover for plunder, trade and captivity. In the last section I argue that in the mid-1520s mariners and soldiers serving in Iberian royal patrol fleets weighed the state of protection talk, recognising and appraising the intensifying horizon of violence and commerce by land and sea and the royal pledges of protection that brought them into the fray. On that basis they were able to secure concessions from officials regarding shipboard modes of remuneration. Thus, maritime and military labourers bent protection talk, much as crown actors did, for their own material and political gain.

LEGITIMISING AGGRESSION IN THE NORTHEASTERN ATLANTIC

Usually built into the premise of a claim to protect is the implication that there is something to lose, and that this would be undesirable and so should be prevented. For about a century Iberian crown operatives had pursued different colonial enterprises to expand territorial holdings in the western and central Maghreb, eking out a string of military garrisons and trading posts on the Mediterranean and Atlantic coasts by the early 1500s. Recognising their vulnerability while pursuing expansionist policies, crown officials regularly organised 'armadas of protection' to patrol the Straits of Gibraltar and the Atlantic coast of Morocco. In North Africa the Crowns of Portugal and Castile had much to lose. Protection, for officials in the service of the Portuguese and Castilian monarchs, meant taking several measures to support Iberian garrisons in North Africa but also going on the offensive through alliances of convenience and sizeable military mobilisation.

Invoking protection directly and indirectly the military surrogates of the Iberian monarchs sought to expand the breadth of Portuguese and Spanish military occupations, some of which dated back to the fifteenth century, by exploiting deep divisions in Northern Morocco between the Wattasid Sultanate based in Fez and a broad array of autonomous polities in the Rif and south into Dukkala and the Sus, only some of which were nominally subject to Fez.[5] In the early 1510s members of the Portuguese and Castilian nobility sponsored a slew of military campaigns in North Africa, relying heavily on alliances of convenience with regional Islamic political leaders whom they called 'Moors of peace' (*Mouros de paz*).[6] Their efforts, which would have been impossible without the likes of ascendant Maghrebi power brokers such as Yahya-u-Ta'fuft, reinforced a decades-old string of Portuguese and Castilian military occupations in coastal fortresses from Tripoli, Algiers and Ceuta to the Atlantic ports of Tangier, Azemmour, Asilah, Safi and Agadir.[7] The expense to the royal exchequers of waging wars of conquest with heavy artillery and armies, which included the massive and unprovoked attack on Azammour in 1513 with a force of 18,000 soldiers and mariners, was enormous.[8] Combined with the cost of maintaining military personnel and provisions in such outposts, the drain on the Iberian crown treasuries and their aristocratic consorts was staggering.[9]

With much to lose, protection was of vital importance for many Iberian royal administrators in the early sixteenth century who recognised that the resources channelled by their respective Crowns toward expansion in North Africa would count for nothing if royal agents could not reliably provide material and personnel reinforcements across the Strait of Gibraltar. Periodic maritime raids by North African mariners called these functions into question. Licences, appointment letters and instructions to captains and crew for recurrent Crown-funded armadas in the 1510s commonly repeated the refrain that the outfitted vessels were intended to protect against Maghrebis at sea: fleets headed by the likes of Turkish privateers Aruj and Khizr (later known as the Barbarossa brothers), Kurtoglu Muslihiddin and others who operated with the support of the Hafsid Sultan of Tunis.[10] In those years North African mariners willing to resort to violence at sea found receptive trading partners in semi-autonomous towns on the Atlantic coast such as Tafetna and Tarkuku, and gradually succeeded in carving out their own enclaves of rule supported by Iberian Muslim refugees, most notably in Algiers but also in Bougie, Tetuan, Salé and Larache. Concerned with Maghrebi mariners as well as furthering Crown objectives across the region, Iberian monarchs regularly gave armadas of protection the task of carrying shipments of grain to military garrisons in coastal Morocco. The same fleets escorted merchant vessels contracted for the same purposes. And, crucially, they were empowered to seek out potential aggressors as targets of violence, captivity and extortion.

We can discern the centrality of violence in protection discourse in the organisation of a specific Portuguese armada in 1516 under the command of the nobleman Diogo Lopes de Sequeira. He would be neither the first nor the last to lead the royal Portuguese fleet known as the 'Armada of the Strait', which annually circulated in the waters and coasts of the western Mediterranean and the northeastern Atlantic for three- to six-month stints.[11] Similar to his predecessors and successors, Sequeira's formal royal appointment specified, in a clear articulation of the duties of protection, that the armada's task involved making the sea-lanes between Iberia and North Africa 'safer from the ships of the Moors'.[12] Sequeira's armada followed on the heels of a failed Portuguese attempt in early 1515 to take Marrakech, which ended in a Wattasid-led rout and a protracted siege of several months the following year against the Portuguese fortress in Asilah.[13] Providing relief to besieged troops at Asilah seems to have been a high priority for Sequeira's fleet of over thirty vessels, which left Andalusia in May and arrived off the coast of Asilah in early June. Clearly preoccupied with an ongoing confrontation with the King of Fez, Sequeira's royal interlocutors emphasised the precarious nature of regional maritime routes by calling for acts of pillage characterised as retribution. Iberians stationed in Asilah saw his arrival similarly, as a participant later recalled: 'not only to defend the town, but to venture out and fight Maghrebis on their lands'.[14]

Such perceptions were consistent with official mandates for Sequeira's armada. From his position as captain of the *Santa Maria do Cabo* Sequeira was informed of 'the principal thing' he was sent to accomplish with the king's fleet: 'to take all the ships of war and other types [of sea vessels] belonging to the Moors, confiscating those that can be taken and burning others so that there are none left'.[15] Singling out the town of 'Amanda Ranel' and surrounding settlements along the Oued Laou River southeast of Tetouan as a particular hotbed of corsair mobilisation, crown officials called for Sequeira to carry out a military expedition on land to enter and rob settlements in the region if he was able to muster local allies, and 'do all of the harm and damage' that he could.[16] Invoking the spectre of sea banditry led officials to articulate their intentions to wage campaigns of plunder that were essentially open-ended, extending far beyond the immediate concern of relieving the siege of Asilah. That they explicitly noted a necessity to forge alliances of convenience with North African factions whom they called 'Moors of peace' served to place religious imperatives of 'just war' in a minor key, amplifying protection as the key rationale behind Sequeira's incursions.

From the Andalusian port town of Málaga the Portuguese royal factor Nuno Ribeiro played a key role in mobilising Iberian armadas such as Sequeira's. Like his successors, Ribeiro was responsible for overseeing preparations for the armadas: recruiting mariners and military men, acquiring supplies and provisions, and ensuring that ships were well maintained.[17] In several documented

instances he and other Portuguese crown factors in Málaga passed on news of
North African fleets on war footing in the region and pressed the Crown to
meet such threats with squadrons of their own. In the months surrounding
Sequeira's armada Ribeiro noted in correspondence to Lisbon the presence
of over thirty-three Maghrebi vessels in the Strait of Gibraltar, urging royal
treasurers to release funds for a navy that 'with the help of our Lord will destroy
them all'.[18] In this way protection talk was dependent on the articulation of
an urgent threat.

   Yet the mobilisation that ensued soon hinged on other concerns and
objectives. Of the several uses to which armadas of protection were put, their
most consistent function entailed bringing provisions to Iberian outposts in
Morocco, often while escorting merchant vessels hired for the same task.
Arriving in Málaga in September 1516 Sequeira signed off on maintenance
work done on the *Santa Maria do Cabo* while also taking on victuals for the
crew; at the same time porters loaded the caravel with a bulk cargo of wheat
intended for the garrison in Asilah, recovering after the lifted Wattasid siege.
Sequeira also agreed to escort two other ships heading to Asilah with their own
shipments of grain.[19] Weeks later, the armada appears to have reached its
intended destination.[20] By November Sequeira and the crew of the *Santa
Maria do Cabo* were back on the Andalusian coast, this time in the town of
Puerto de Santa María, to collect provisions and salaries from the royal
factor.[21] The seemingly humdrum nature of their passages between Iberia
and the Maghreb confirm that the militant zeal in official instructions for
armadas of protection in Sequeira's time routinely gave way to the mundane
functions of the maritime transport trade.

   Nevertheless, by several accounts, Sequeira in key moments heeded his
more hawkish directives and attempted to organise a military campaign in the
Rif. He began by targeting a coastal town referred to by the Portuguese as
'Targa', a dozen leagues out of Ceuta in the direction of Tetuan.[22] Owing to a
difference of opinion between Sequeira and the military governor of Ceuta,
who had been asked to contribute troops to the endeavour, the campaign
never materialised. Sequeira reoriented his efforts southwest towards Ksar es
Seghir, in the vicinity of Dehar el Karroub.[23] Nothing of discernible consequence seems to have come of this venture either.[24] Yet the degree to which
Sequeira appears to have felt the need to mobilise *any* sort of incursion, even
after playing an important role in lifting the siege of Asilah and overseeing
relief efforts for the Portuguese garrison, is consistent with the incitement to
violence embedded in the protection talk of his instructions, and may be
discerned as an Iberian attempt among many others to implement royal
designs of military conquest across the region. Accordingly, despite the

lacklustre results of his territorial incursions, Sequeira's stint as captain of the armada did not jeopardise his future as a crown official.[25]

The Sequeira fleet's trajectory in 1516–17 underscores how framing the armada's responsibilities as heeding the defensive dimension of protection — pushing back against an endemic and multifaceted set of challenges faced by Iberian Crowns, merchant elites and their allies in the northeastern Atlantic — is ultimately misleading. The royal appointment may have gestured towards a wishful future marked by the absence of Muslim threats in the region, but Sequeira and the captains of Iberian armadas of his time were more immediately expected to transport provisions to existing garrisons, or act as reinforcements for existing traffic, in the run-up to attempting fully fledged territorial incursions.[26] Granting armada officials like Sequeira authority to wage war, crown officials hoped both to neutralise Maghrebi maritime and land-based initiatives targeting their subjects, and to go on the offensive. As Sequeira's instructions make explicit, directly unprovoked territorial raids were the 'principal thing' the armada was entrusted to undertake. When Norman corsairs and privateers decisively entered the fray in the early 1520s Iberian officials shifted their concerns of protection in the region to the Atlantic, making it far less likely that future Armadas of the Strait would pursue territorial incursions to the extent that Sequeira had attempted.

ENTER THE FRENCH

The outbreak of hostilities between adherents of Francis I and Charles V over patrimonial holdings in Italy and the Pyrenees spilled into the maritime sphere in the early 1520s.[27] At that time a broader assortment of Iberian, North African and Mediterranean maritime communities began to experience a concerted wave of Atlantic privateering ventures supported by French political and mercantile elites. Armed with letters of marque legitimising plunder as permissible under the customs of just war, Norman privateers followed the same routes of conflict and trade that North African mariners had long plied in the northeastern Atlantic while venturing further west toward the Azorean archipelago. Many recognised that Iberian infiltrations of the Atlantic and Indian Ocean worlds translated into captives and goods of more distant provenance increasingly fanning out across Iberian and Maghrebi sea-lanes. In the 1520s the momentous opening of sustained transatlantic and global sea routes did not eclipse the importance of the northeastern quadrant of the Atlantic but reinscribed it as a fraught space of potential loss and gain buffeted by North African and now French pressures. Iberian officials who had long used protection talk in mobilising armada fleets in the region against

Maghrebis found, with the arrival of the French, that their vulnerability increased. They responded by sending out further armadas of protection, but these were now turned increasingly towards perpetrating violence at sea. This shift in strategy would exacerbate regional tensions and compound the Iberian Crowns' difficulties in delivering on their promises of protection.

The earliest known French attack on Iberian shipping in the northeastern Atlantic during the Franco-Spanish conflict confirms the extent to which Norman privateers privileged traditional Ibero-African maritime routes. Well before a privateer from Dieppe, Jean Fleury, achieved fame for intercepting an early levy of loot dispatched by Hernán Cortés from the Aztec capital of Tenochtitlán, he attacked a Portuguese merchant vessel en route from Lisbon to the Moroccan port of Safi.[28] Other reports of French attacks on Iberian vessels during the same summer of 1521 trickled into Lisbon and Seville. Soon Castilian royal officials sounded alarms that the French were becoming an intractable obstacle for Atlantic trade, 'taking prizes from our vassals and *naturales*', and adopting the strategy of 'waiting for the ships that are expected every day from our Indies' in the sea-lanes between the Azores and the south-western coast of Portugal.[29] In a sober assessment of the state of affairs that anticipated decades' worth of turmoil, a Spanish crown adviser noted that French corsairs 'could do much damage' to the traffic leaving the Indies and the Atlantic and heading for Spain.[30] Clearly perturbed by these developments, Castilian crown officials dutifully mobilised their own armada captained by Rodrigo Bermejo, invoking the standard dictates of protection against maritime predations such as the need to 'patrol and secure the coast' of Andalusia against 'corsairs taking prizes from our vassals'.[31] The Portuguese Crown, too, outfitted an armada of four caravels headed by Simão da Cunha.[32] Yet outfitting more Iberian armadas of protection did little to diminish or neutralise the growing number of attacks on Iberian shipping.

In instances when they met their objectives of intercepting French fleets, armadas ran into problems of various kinds. In the summer of 1522, as Fleury extended his attacks against Iberian vessels in the northeastern Atlantic, another French privateer named Jean Fain, who was also supported by prominent Norman merchants, sacked the Castilian ship *La Madalena* on its return voyage from the Caribbean via the Azores.[33] In the immediate aftermath of this strike (which killed many passengers aboard *La Madalena*, brought others into captivity and resulted in the seizure of a sizeable cargo including sugar, leather, gold and pearls), the French were themselves attacked and captured by a royal Portuguese armada. Fain's crew soon faced trial in Lisbon, a sign that the armada of protection had accomplished its mission. But this moment of success soon dissolved into discord, as lengthy lawsuits unfolded in Seville and Lisbon over the property confiscated from *La Madalena*. Portuguese, Genoese and Andalusian merchants waged courtroom battles that reverberated across diplomatic relations between the Iberian Crowns.[34] The fallout from *La Madalena* shows that rare cases when royal armadas hit the mark did not necessarily result in clear victories for the Iberians.

French maritime predations in the early 1520s were not the only catalyst for the reorientation in the strategies of protection of Iberian Crowns.[35] With a devastating drought taking hold across the northwestern Maghreb between 1519 and 1521 Portuguese officials were forced into what one historian has called 'an economy of force posture' in the region.[36] A series of attacks at sea by North African mariners also significantly altered Iberian priorities. The successes of the Turkish privateer Khizr, who entered the service of the Ottoman Sultan and confronted Spanish troops directly in Algiers in 1519, were cited by the Portuguese when they deployed an Armada of the Strait in 1520.[37] In the same months as Fain sacked *La Madalena* and Iberians squabbled over the spoils a fleet of vessels under the command of an individual whom the Portuguese named 'Quartão', acting in alliance with Turkish corsairs, attacked the Andalusian towns of Palos, Moguer and Huelva, along with points on the Portuguese Algarve, including near Albufeira.[38] Privateers from Larache were also active in the same years, seizing Iberian vessels and taking crews captive in staggered simultaneity with French attacks.[39]

The long-standing nature of North African assaults on Iberian vessels and ports, compared to the more recent onslaught of French predations across the maritime sphere, helps to explain why in the same summer of 1522 Iberian mariners, merchants, fishermen and other maritime labourers voiced more concerns over North African corsairs to royal officials looking to hire them. In several entries in his account book in late April and early May 1522 the Portuguese factor in Andalusia noted that the mariners whom he attempted to enlist for a short trip to Tangier, such as Miguel Sanchez, a resident of Huelva, did not want to go there because of the possibility of being attacked by Maghrebi mariners.[40] Other Iberian ship captains, pilots and sailors in the same weeks invoked the 'great dangers of Moors'.[41] As we have seen, French privateers had not avoided the coast of North Africa in their ventures. Nevertheless the fact that mariners intending to provision Portuguese fortresses in Morocco did not mention them in voicing their concerns suggests that Iberian maritime communities with ties to the Maghreb still viewed the threat of French corsairs as minor when compared to attacks waged by North Africans. These perceptions, as we will see, would change rapidly in the following years.

As the likes of Jean Fleury and Jean Fain proliferated in the northeastern Atlantic an attendant increase in Iberian armadas of protection fed into a cycle of violence by which their presence added to the number of potential targets for French privateers. Fleury's travails, in this respect, provide another case in point. Although his attack on a Spanish fleet carrying loot from Tenochtitlán in 1523 is well known it is seldom appreciated that the vessels he took that had been hauling Cortés's shipment formed part of an armada of protection. As dusk descended on 28 May, ten leagues away from the Portuguese coast, the Spanish armada lost two of its three caravels to the Normans. Among the dead was a *conquistador* and ally of Cortés, Antonio de Quiñones. Carrying the lion's share of Mexica plunder, along with a large amount of artillery aboard the Spanish armada, some of the Normans brought back Spanish captives, including another *conquistador*, Alonso Dávila, to La Rochelle.[42] The rest continued to ply Atlantic waters in a way that suggested a deepening French engagement with the Maghreb, despite intensified Iberian efforts to prevent them from doing so.

A few days after coming into possession of the loot from Tenochtitlán Fleury's fleet forcibly took two more Spanish merchant ships outside Tenerife, both of which were carrying a great quantity of grains and wine from the Canaries.[43] Fleury then headed to the harbour of Asilah, where Sequeira's Armada of the Strait had given succour seven years prior. Now, Fleury intended to barter and trade some of the goods that he claimed to have seized as items of just war. He dispatched an unnamed Spanish captive to deliver a letter to the garrison's Portuguese officials requesting they contact a French merchant in town identified in Portuguese records as 'João de Cervano'. Fleury intended, through him, to find buyers for two ships from his fleet along with their cargo. Merchants in Asilah also came to learn that Fleury looked to sell a considerable quantity of sugar that they recognised as having American provenance. Fleury and other French privateers repeatedly conducted business in Asilah and other points of the North African littoral in ensuing years, finding willing buyers for the plunder they had in many cases acquired from Iberian vessels, including royal armadas.[44] Fleury's decision to trade in Morocco following his attack on Cortés' fleet reveals that early French involvement in the northeastern Atlantic thrived due to a greater array of maritime targets as well as pre-existing Euro-African connections in the coastal markets of the western Maghreb.

Compared to earlier years Iberians in 1523 more frequently recognised the embroiled nature of Maghrebi and Norman enterprises of war against them. Petitioners to Charles V in the Cortes of Valladolid in August noted that the coast of Andalusia was teeming with 'Moors and Turks and French and corsairs', asking that the Crown take the lead in 'cleaning up the seas so that people may go back to trading'.[45] Royal officials responded as they long had, noting that they were in the process of organising other armadas with orders to attack and confiscate. In this they heeded the advice of Alonso Dávila, the *conquistador* taken captive by Fleury's fleet and brought to La Rochelle, who had warned the Crown against retreating, and called instead for them to organise an armada 'to go after' and 'harm' the French.[46] Speaking of 'the protection and security of the coast' that year, merchants in Seville voiced the hope that royal-backed efforts would leave the sea 'clear of corsairs'.[47] Reports of continued attacks, such as the taking of a Portuguese vessel heading to London with sugar from Madeira, only lent further urgency to these appeals.[48]

Iberian pleas and claims of protection continued to call for violence, but times had changed from Sequeira's day. Outfitted armadas and other protection fleets continued to be tasked with supporting Iberian garrisons in North Africa, or escorting ships transiting in the region, but they were seldom required to make territorial raids in North Africa. The centre of gravity for Iberian concerns of protection had shifted to the maritime corridors of the northeastern Atlantic in the early 1520s. Confronted with a dynamic array of actors altering the order they sought in the maritime sphere, royal officials made more freewheeling promises to Iberians looking to reap profits from regional and long-distance trade. Merchants and mariners of elite and humble status alike could no longer but see the French as newly enmeshed with the long-standing spectrum of exchanges with Maghrebi mariners and traders, and attempted to meet a proliferating set of challenges head on.

OPENINGS IN PROTECTION TALK

By August 1523 grain shipments from Andalusia to North Africa almost entirely ground to a halt. In the ports of Málaga, Cádiz and Puerto de Santa María pilots, sailors and ship owners expressed trepidation when it came to conducting their habitual business with the Maghreb. Maritime workers had always interacted with royal agents over the conditions by which they would deliver on the Crown's pledges to escort vessels and protect regional sea-lanes. The manner by which they did so in late 1523 and the following year illustrates how a diverse array of actors beyond officialdom bent protection talk to further their own agenda of self-preservation. With French privateering and an Ibero-North African military struggle for the Maghreb converging in the northeastern Atlantic, sailors and soldiers in the service of the Iberian Crowns were well positioned to advance their interests. On 23 August 1523, loaded with a large cargo of wheat, the crew on Andrés Martínez's caravel refused to go to Tangier or any other place except Ceuta, the closest North African port to Málaga, 'for fear of the Moors and corsairs, of which there are many'. Sailors and pilots on at least six other ships in the surrounding weeks expressed similar apprehensions, sometimes citing other corsairs but always noting the threat of Maghrebi mariners.[49]

The chorus of concern came to fill the pages of the royal factor's account book. Behind the refrain was a widely shared assessment of the geopolitical situation in the northeastern Atlantic. Maritime workers weighed officials' long-standing, ongoing stratagems for advancing royal interests – especially clear in the protection talk that filled the air and the armadas that filled the waters – and calculated that pledges of royal protection could be translated into clear material gains for themselves. Their strategies underscore that protection talk may have fed off and reinforced adversarial relationships, as we have seen between Iberian royal agents and French or Maghrebi privateers, but that it also created openings for certain actors to position themselves obliquely in relation to ongoing conflicts and advance their own separate agenda.

Several key regional developments challenged the ability of both Iberian Crowns to organise armadas in late 1523 and 1524. First was the persistent tempo of French attacks from the coast of Portugal to the Canaries, made more dire by reports of a transatlantic expedition sponsored by the French Crown to the North American coast.[50] In another blow for the long-standing designs of the Iberian Crowns in the Maghreb Ahmad al-A'ruj and allies from the Sus conquered Marrakesh, taking an important inland city and establishing a de facto seat of Sa'adian power.[51] Rapidly changing circumstances in the Maghreb exacerbated the uncertainties of a Portuguese and Spanish presence which extended negligibly from the coasts. Dogged by intractable territorial and maritime challenges, the Iberian Crowns nevertheless boosted their long-standing strategies, putting forward more armadas of protection.

In October 1523, after weeks of greatly diminished traffic, Duarte Valadares and Gonçalo Leite began to escort vessels hauling grain to Asilah.[52] Tensions onboard appear to have run high. Laying anchor outside the harbour of Asilah, where Fleury had peddled New World sugar months before, Valadares' ship opened fire at a vessel that they identified as a 'small galleon of Moors'.[53] In mid-January 1524 Valadares and Leite's armada docked in Andalusia to replenish the crew's supply of victuals.[54] At that time the Portuguese factor stationed in Málaga offered back pay for the crew, doling out salaries for a prior month's work spanning November and December but reneging on the last three weeks because the month was not yet through, and it was tradition to pay wages for full months in arrears if the work was ongoing.[55] It would only be weeks later that the royal factor distributed funds once more to Leite and

Valadares, again in Málaga, for the two previous months ranging from December to February.[56] Discontent amid sailors and soldiers over lagging paydays, not a surprising occurrence, was rendered more acute as mariners, soldiers and officials shared a climate of heightened apprehension. Wage labourers for royal protection fleets could also see that by outfitting more armadas, Iberian administrators intensified mobilisation efforts to address their growing set of challenges in the Atlantic and North Africa.

A few weeks after receiving their wages in February the crew of Valadares' vessel waited aboard their ship, the *Santa Maria do Cabo*, anchored outside the harbour of Asilah.[57] While intending to support the Portuguese garrison under siege by a Wattasid army, the armada was approached and attacked by Fleury's fleet.[58] This time Fleury took a sizeable number of mariners and soldiers on the Portuguese armada ship captive. Leite returned to Málaga missing a large contingent of his crew. There, he put in a request to replace a small vessel that had been, he claimed, 'broken near Asilah and lost with the people' aboard.[59] Those 'lost' appear to have remained in captivity by the French for several months.[60] Much as Fleury had engaged in negotiations in Asilah, he once more used windfalls at sea as bargaining chips for trading along the North African coast. This time it was clear that armada crewmembers were, more than ever, on the front lines of these transformations.

Iberian officials responded by expanding the ranks of their protection armadas. In the same period that Fleury took dozens captive, the royal factor in Andalusia began to refer to a French ship, the *Santa Cruz*, which now formed part of the Portuguese Crown's Armada of the Strait.[61] The *Santa Cruz* was confiscated that summer from French merchant mariners on the African coast between Tangiers and Tarifa by Bastião Nunes, soon after receiving command of the *Santa Maria do Cabo* following the conclusion of Duarte Valadares' term.[62] As part of the king's protection fleet, the French-made, Portuguese-appropriated vessel followed the sea-lanes of the region between the Iberian coast, the Atlantic islands and North Africa under the command of Vasco Fernandes César, recently returned from a period of captivity in Dieppe.[63] For several months in the late summer and autumn of 1524 Portuguese royal funds provided for provisions and wages for the crew of the *Santa Cruz* in a now expanded Armada of the Strait, as reports confirmed the presence of at least fifteen French ships prowling the Portuguese coast.[64] Taking on the *Santa Cruz* was no small addition to existing expenses: the French man-of-war was significantly larger, holding roughly as many people aboard as the armada's two principal caravels combined.[65] Royal officials nevertheless lent their support for an expanded fleet, though the funds were not at the disposal of the factor in Málaga.

When the *Santa Cruz* put in at Málaga in September 1524 the sailors and soldiers made their discontent clear to the captain. 'I was unable to pay the full amount of the wages', reads the factor's account book, 'because [I] did not have money, as all that [I] had was spent on [the two main vessels], and so [I] sought borrowed funds so that the people [on the *Santa Cruz*] would work, since they wanted to leave the ship'.[66] Facing mass desertion, the factor's stop-gap loan bought him some time but did not solve the problem. On 6 September the French ship broke ranks with the Armada of the Strait to join another royal protection fleet. Its crewmembers promptly received the rest of the wages they had demanded from the treasurers of the Armada of the Strait.[67] Such a turn of events would likely not have occurred if agents for the Portuguese Crown had not felt significant pressure to fulfill increasingly hollow promises of protection. Aware of these realities, mariners and soldiers leveraged royal commitments to pursue Mahgrebi and French privateers in order to secure their wages, taking advantage of the reliance that crown actors had on their labour and the circumstances that rendered their participation more valuable.

This would not be the only occasion that year that mariners and soldiers forced the hands of Iberian elites who sought to make good their pledges of protection. In the autumn of 1524 many armada mariners and soldiers began to demand and receive their wages for the coming month as an advance, rather than in arrears. Prior to leaving the Tagus River aboard a Portuguese armada ship, a Genoese sailor identified as Tomasino requested the monthly salary of 700 *reais* immediately, like the others aboard whom he noted had received wages up front.[68] A caulker known as 'The Basque' brought aboard to tend to leaks also requested his monthly salary before setting foot on the ship. Otherwise, he claimed, he would not go.[69] In each instance the captain and the factor scrambled to meet the request, citing the difficulty they were encountering in hiring sailors for their ships.[70] Daring crown officials to renege on pledges of protection, maritime workers like Tomasino and 'The Basque' repurposed the articulation of threats and incitements of violence that had always formed the bedrock of royal Iberian protection talk in the region into guarantees that they would receive remuneration before embarking on the royal armada.

Repurposing protection talk sometimes extended beyond the issue of wages. When the daily rations of crewmembers on the *Santa Cruz*'s new fleet failed to include meat, César and the other captains heard loud and frequent objections. They took the complaints seriously enough to pay 6,000 *reais*, more than eight times the rate of a sailor's monthly salary, to buy six hogs in Tavira to feed the fleet.[71] It could surely be appreciated by some mariners that they would do well to face the risks of Atlantic sea-lanes with ample servings of meat. While sailors and soldiers arguably experienced more dangerous working conditions than previous years – further evidenced by a string of attacks by mariners from Larache against Iberian vessels in late 1524 and early 1525 – they negotiated from a stronger position when it was time to determine wages and certain aspects of their daily rations because of a prevailing sense that circumstances beyond the decks of their ships were spiralling further out of the control of Iberian officialdom.[72]

For those aboard armada vessels protection talk opened an avenue for gain that extended beyond the adversarial binary of the perpetrators and victims. Tomasino, the Basque and the numerous others who made up the crews of protection fleets were familiar with discourses of protection that brought them wages, and they realised that conditions were favourable for them to strike a better deal. The experiences of these armada crewmembers reveal that rationales of protection were malleable in ways that extended beyond the objectives of crown agents.

CONCLUSION

Iberian protection talk, while it apparently pertained to clashing interests at the crown level, actually underscored a conflictive arithmetic of appropriation and profiteering that drew a multitude of social actors into a contested but fundamentally shared political and economic arena. Norman and Moroccan mariners, among other non-Iberians, were more than parasites preying on Portuguese and Andalusian maritime trade. They were active participants and contributors to a toxic mix of violence and trade that accompanied unequal divisions of wealth and labour across the northeastern Atlantic. Even when Iberian Crowns delivered on their promises to intercept their adversaries, the results provoked further disruptions that ranged from disputes over prizes to how to maintain expanded armadas. In this context protection talk served a variety of ends that extended beyond defending the nebulous dictates of security on behalf of political elites.

If anything, pledges of protection made by royal Iberian officials entailed an appraisal of events that they could foresee but were essentially powerless to avoid. When they could, Iberian Crowns used protection talk as an incitement to forceful seizure and destruction that only served to deepen animosities against their traditional regional rivals. In the process of deepening conflict protection was more than the sum of the adversarial relations that its rhetoric implied. While royal Iberian claims of protection may have involved one-sided framing of protagonists and antagonists locked in conflict, it also provided openings for mariners and soldiers in the employ of the Crowns to pursue their own agendas that only partly overlapped with monarchical objectives. Oblique approaches to royal pledges of protection rechannelled initiatives of profit-oriented violence toward new ends.

Persistence in the patterns that first emerged in the 1520s suggests that protection talk helped to cement regional tendencies of conflict and exchange over a longer period. Two decades after Fleury raided and traded for years on end across the North African littoral, French mariners and merchants came to forge alliances with the Sa'di-sponsored campaigns that expelled the Portuguese from Agadir and other garrisons in the Maghreb.[73] Into the later sixteenth century and the seventeenth century the consolidation of the Sa'di dynasty and its heyday under al-Mansur, in conjunction with the establishment of 'corsair republics' in Rabat-Salé, Larache and Tetuan, which drew the support of Maghrebi, English and Dutch actors, all find clear precedents in the dynamics of the 1520s traced here. Paying attention to how Iberian crown operatives conceived of responsibilities to protect regional sea-lanes brings developments in North Africa, Iberia and the broader Atlantic into close alignment. In contending with the ongoing and overpowering presence of others, Iberian protection talk and its correspondent practices call into question the usefulness of the 'Iberian Atlantic' as a category of analysis, even for the supposedly precocious heyday of Portuguese and Spanish imperial expansion.

While the sources consulted here allow us little insight into the internal dynamics of crews on North African and French vessels, it is nevertheless reasonable to argue that the mariners of Larache or Dieppe pressed for shares of remuneration that they deemed acceptable, and were themselves roiled by internecine factionalism. Because Iberian political and mercantile elites recognised that they formed only one unstable faction within a dynamic multitude of collectives in the northeastern Atlantic, it is anachronistic to interpret their articulation of protection in terms of a normative sense of security defined by geopolitical rivalries in an 'Iberian Atlantic'. More pervasively, individuals of diverse backgrounds invoked shared discourses of protection to justify and attempt assaults, negotiations, exchanges and acquisitive forays of various orders. By this means ideals of protection contributed to the ways that individuals sought material gains while escalating violence across dynamic religious, ethnic and class divides in the early Atlantic.

NOTES

1 I translate the Portuguese *armada de guarda* and its Spanish equivalent as 'armada of protection'. Corpo Cronológico, p. 2, mç. 109, no. 30, Arquivo Nacional da Torre do Tombo (henceforth ANTT).

2 See, for example, Francisco Bethencourt and Diogo Ramada Curto (eds), *Portuguese Oceanic Expansion, 1400–1800*, Cambridge University Press, New York, 2007; John H. Elliott, *Empires of the Atlantic World: Britain and Spain in America, 1492–1830*, Yale University Press, New Haven, 2007; Saliha Belmessous, 'Greatness and Decadence in French America', *Renaissance Studies*, vol. 26, no. 4, 2012, pp. 559–79.

3 Recent calls for the necessity of including Moroccan perspectives on the formation of the Atlantic world include Amira K. Bennison, 'Liminal States: Morocco and the Iberian Frontier Between the Twelfth and Nineteenth Centuries', *Journal of North African Studies*, vol. 6, no. 1, 2001, pp. 11–28; and Lhoussain Simour, '(De)slaving History: Mostafa al-Azemmouri, the Sixteenth-Century Moroccan Captive in the Tale of Conquest', *European Review of History: Revue Européenne d'Histoire*, vol. 20, no. 3, 2013, pp. 345–65.

4 See, for example, Lauren Benton, *A Search for Sovereignty: Law and Geography in European Empires, 1400–1900*, Cambridge University Press, New York, 2010; and Ken MacMillan, *Sovereignty and Possession in the English New World: The Legal Foundations of Empire, 1576–1640*, Cambridge University Press, New York, 2006. For a defence of the 'national segmentation of the Atlantic basin', see Nicholas Canny and Philip Morgan, 'Introduction: The Making and Unmaking of the Atlantic World', in Canny and Morgan (eds), *The Oxford Handbook of Atlantic History*, Oxford University Press, New York, 2011, pp. 1–17.

5 For background on Ibero-Moroccan politics and warfare in the early modern period, see, for example, Andrew C. Hess, *The Forgotten Frontier: A History of the Sixteenth-Century Ibero-African Frontier*, University of Chicago Press, Chicago, 1978; Weston F. Cook, *The Hundred Years War for Morocco: Gunpowder and the Military Revolution in the Early Modern Muslim World*, Westview Press, Boulder, CO, 1994; and Alan Jamieson, *Lords of the Sea: A History of the Barbary Corsairs*, Reaktion Books, London, 2012, pp. 28–33.

6 Maria Leonor García da Cruz, 'As Controvérsias ao Tempo de D. João III sobre a Política Portuguesa no Norte da África', *Mare Liberum*, vol. 13, 1997, pp. 123–99; António Dias Farinha, *Os Portugueses em Marrocos*, Instituto Camões, Lisbon, 1999, pp. 30–54.

7 Matthew T. Racine, 'Service and Honor in Sixteenth-Century Portuguese North Africa: Yahya-u-Ta'fuft and Portuguese Noble Culture', *Sixteenth Century Journal*, vol. 32, no. 1, 2001, pp. 67–90.

8 Cook, pp. 147–49.

9 da Cruz, pp. 130–31; A.R. Disney, *A History of Portugal and the Portuguese Empire*, vol. 2, Cambridge University Press, New York, 2009, pp. 10–16; Farinha, p. 55; Natália Maria Antónia, 'Ceuta: "Muy Bom Sumydoiro de Gente de Uossa Terra e Darmas e de Dinheiro"', *Cadernos do Arquivo Municipal*, 2nd series, no. 4, 2015, pp. 125–52. North African conquests also took a toll on the Castilian crown treasury, which struggled to keep up with rising costs of war by applying funds from Caribbean receipts to maintain its garrison in Oran in 1518 (Indiferente 419, L. 7, ff. 744r–744v, 796r, 779r–779v, Archivo General de Indias [henceforth AGI]).

10 Jamieson, pp. 33–37.

11 Andreia Martins de Carvalho and Pedro Pinto characterise a series of armadas led by Duarte Pacheco Pereira between 1509–10 as one of the first concerted royal efforts to patrol the Portuguese coast for purposes of defence against maritime predations ('Da Caça de Mondragón à Guarda do Estreito de Gibraltar (1508–13)', *Anais de História de Além-Mar*, vol. 13, 2012, pp. 221–332).

12 David Lopes (ed.), *Anais de Arzila*, Academia das Ciências de Lisboa, Lisbon, 1915, vol. 1, p. 286.

13 Cook, pp. 154–55. Portuguese garrisons in northern Morocco in those years faced recurrent sieges by a loose coalition of polities under the Wattasid banner of Muhammad al-Burtugali, who was able to draw in allies from across the Wadi Lukkus valley and beyond.

14 Lopes, p. 198.

15 A. da Silva Rego (ed.), *As Gavetas da Torre do Tombo*, Arquivo Nacional da Torre do Tombo/Centro de Estudos Históricos Ultramarinos, Lisbon, 1960–77, vol. 5, pp. 520–30.

16 Ibid., p. 522. It is possible that the Portuguese were referring to Chechaouen, an independent principality founded by the sharifs of Jabal Alam in alliance with recent Muslim exiles from Iberia, responsible for organising many attacks against Portuguese and Spanish military garrisons in the Rif at that time (Hess, p. 49.)

17 Manuel Corte Real, *A Feitoria Portuguesa na Andaluzia: 1500–1532*, Instituto de Alta Cultura, Lisbon, 1967; Robert Ricard, 'Les Facteurs Portugais d'Andalousie (1509–1588)', in Paul Cénival (ed.), *Les Sources Inédites de l'Histoire du Maroc*, vol. 2, pt. 2, Paul Geuthner, Paris, 1946, pp. 564–73; Antonio Moreno Osorio, 'Apuntes sobre la Evolución de la Factoría Portuguesa en Málaga durante el Reinado de Carlos V (1516–1556)', *Isla de Arriarán*, vol. 29, 2007, pp. 65–79.

18 Núcleo Antigo 877, n. 4, ANTT. Merely dated 24 August, the letter is signed by Ribeiro and Pedro de Aguiar, the latter being identified as royal *escrivão* in Málaga. Aguiar first appears as *escrivão* in Ribeiro's account books in the late summer of 1516 (Núcleo Antigo 711, fol. 1r, ANTT), and Ribeiro served as factor until 1519, suggesting that this letter was written between 1516 and 1519 (Manuel Henrique Côrte-Real, 'Feitores e Escrivães na Andaluzia durante o Reinado de D. João III', *Do Tempo e da História*, vol. 1, 1965, p. 141).

19 Núcleo Antigo 711, ff. 35r, 75r, ANTT.

20 Chancelaria Manuel, Liv. 39, f. 117r, ANTT.

21 Núcleo Antigo 711, ff. 75v–76r, ANTT.

22 Targa appears in the 1513 Philesius edition of Ptolemy's *Geography*, neighbouring Tangier (Louis Massignon, *Le Maroc dans les Premières Années du XVIe Siècle: Tableau Géographique d'Après Léon l'Africain*, Adolphe Jourdan, Algiers, 1906, pp. 67–68).

23 The sixteenth-century chronicler Bernardo Rodrigues referred to 'Arraihana, a village of Farrobo'. Massignon finds other references in Portuguese records to a 'Sierra do Farrobo', surmising that these toponyms corresponded to al-Karroub (p. 241).

24 A cursory mention of the armada in an otherwise exhaustive elegy for Sequeira confirmed that the expedition did not meet its own standards of success but did not meet disaster either (Ronald B. Smith, *Diogo Lopes de Sequeira*, Silvas, Lisbon, 1975, pp. 58–59). Rodrigues dismissed the campaign by noting its participants 'did little more than nothing' (Lopes, p. 226).

25 Corpo Cronológico, pt. 2, mç. 73, n. 105, ANTT.

26 For consideration of analogous arrangements by the Crown of Castile in this period, see Fernand Braudel, 'Les Espagnols et l'Afrique du Nord de 1492 à 1577', *Revue Africaine*, vol. 29, nos 335–336, 1929, pp. 184–233 and 351–428; Rafael Carrasco, *La Empresa Imperial de Carlos V y la España de los Albores de la Modernidad*, Ediciones Cátedra, Madrid, 2015, pp. 32–35.

27 Robert Knecht, *Renaissance Warrior and Patron: The Reign of Francis I*, Cambridge University Press, New York, 1994, pp. 369–84.

28 Eugène Guénin, *Ango et ses Pilotes*, Imprimerie Nationale, Paris, 1901, pp. 30–31.

29 Indiferente 420, L. 8, f. 327v, AGI.

30 This proposal, which came in 1522, repeated the contours of the earlier report of 1521 (Indiferente 420, L. 9, f. 42r, AGI).

31 Contratación 5784, L. 1, f. 39r, 45v; Indiferente 420, L. 8, ff. 327v–328v, AGI.

32 Núcleo Antigo 709, f. 16r, ANTT; Corpo Cronológico, pt. 2, no. 98, doc. 58–59, 100, 125.

33 Justicia 697, R.4, p. 1, AGI. For a separate treatment of this case, see Gabriel de Avilez Rocha, 'The Azorean Connection', in Ida Altman and David Wheat (eds), *The Spanish Caribbean in the Long Sixteenth Century*, University of Nebraska Press, Lincoln, NE, forthcoming.

34 Some lawsuits were still going on as late as June 1527 (Indiferente 421, L. 12, f. 99v, AGI).

35 Treatments of piracy in the early Atlantic that involve both North African and French actors generally perceive them under separate headings. See Kris Lane, *Pillaging the Empire: Global Piracy on the High Seas, 1500–1750*, 2nd edn, Routledge, New York, 2016, pp. 8–18; and Luís Guerreiro, 'Pirataria, Corso, e Beligerância Estatal no Sudoeste Peninsular e Ilhas Adjacentes (1550–1600)', in Maria da Graça A. Mateus Ventura (ed.), *As Rotas Oceânicas (Sécs. XV-XVII)*, Edições Colibri, Lisbon, 1999, pp. 119–47.

36 Cook, p. 174.

37 Jamieson, pp. 37–39; Lopes, pp. 285–86; Núcleo Antigo 608, f. 35v, ANTT.

38 Lopes, p. 397.

39 Núcleo Antigo 721, ff. 43r, 47r–47v, ANTT.

40 Núcleo Antigo 709 f. 40r, ANTT.

41 Núcleo Antigo 709 f. 44r. ANTT.

42 Patronato 267, r. 1, no. 1 and no. 2, AGI; Paul Gaffarel, *Le Corsaire Jean Fleury*, Imprimerie E. Cagniard, Rouen, 1902, pp. 19–20.

43 Lopes, p. 400.

44 Ibid. Merchants in the Canaries noted that 'if the French did not have buyers for the things that they stole' they would find less reason to pillage.

45 Res. 214–11A, f. 11v, Biblioteca Nacional de Lisboa.

46 Patronato 267, N.1, R.1, AGI.

47 Patronato 269, N. 1, R. 1, doc. 2, AGI.

48 Corpo Cronológico, pt. 2, mç. 173, n. 36, ANTT.

49 Núcleo Antigo 710 ff. 26r–35v, ANTT.

50 Rego, vol. 5, pp. 330–31.

51 Hess, p. 52; Cook, pp. 174–78.

52 Núcleo Antigo 710, f. 36v, ANTT.

53 Corpo Cronológico, pt. 2, mç. 115, no. 71, ANTT.

54 Núcleo Antigo 720, ff. 89r–93r, 94r–95v, ANTT.

55 Núcleo Antigo 720 ff. 93v, 96r; Corpo Cronológico, pt. 2, mç. 113, no. 3, ANTT.

56 Núcleo Antigo 720, ff. 97r-101v, ANTT.

57 Manuel de Faria e Sousa, *Europa Portuguesa*, 2nd edn, vol. 3, Lisbon, 1680, p. 140; Cook, p. 176.

58 Guénin, p. 33.

59 Núcleo Antigo 720 ff. 102r–103v, ANTT; Corpo Cronológico, pt. 2, mç. 114, n. 68, ANTT.

60 Cénival, vol. 2, pt. 1, pp. 329–31.

61 Núcleo Antigo 720, f. 114v, ANTT.

62 Lopes, pp. 479–80; Corpo Cronológico, pt. 1, mç. 31, no. 44, ANTT.

63 Vasco Fernandes César first appears as an armada captain in 1520 (Núcleo Antigo 608 f. 35v, ANTT).

64 Corpo Cronológico, pt. 2, mç. 116, no. 23, ANTT.

65 Corpo Cronológico, pt. 2, mç. 118, no. 13 and mç. 119, no. 7, ANTT.

66 Núcleo Antigo 720 ff. 114v, 117r. ANTT.

67 Núcleo Antigo 617, ff. 15r–15v, ANTT.

68 Ibid., f. 11r.

69 Ibid., f. 8v.

70 Ibid., f. 11r.

71 Ibid., ff. 11v–12r.

72 Reports of separate attacks on Iberian vessels at this time attribute them to Maghrebi mariners taking captives to Larache (Núcleo Antigo 721, ff. 43r, 47r, 54v, 56r, ANTT).

73 Corpo Cronológico, pt. 1, mç. 73, no. 115 and mç. 71, no. 132, ANTT; J. Caillé, 'Ambassadeurs, Envoyés, Particuliers, et Représentants Officieux de la France au Maroc', *Hésperis*, vol. 38, 1954, p. 355–64.

PART III

Protection and Languages
of Political Authority

5

Protection as a Political Concept in English Political Thought, 1603–51

ANNABEL BRETT

'The end of Obedience', Thomas Hobbes declared in *Leviathan* of 1651, 'is Protection'.[1] Behind Hobbes' words lay a history of contestation over the political meaning and the political use of protection that stretched back beyond the immediate context of the English civil wars to the accession of James VI of Scotland and I of England in 1603, and beyond that, ultimately, to the wars of religion in late sixteenth-century France. On the one hand that process of appropriation and re-appropriation, for and against the Crown, inside and outside the state, demonstrates the potential of protection to push existing political vocabularies in new directions and thereby to reshape the available possibilities of political legitimation. On the other, it manifests the distinctive mix of rhetorical force and conceptual instability inherent in the term, as the crucial question of what actually constitutes protection remained unanswered. It was in fact Hobbes himself, in the Latin version of his political philosophy *De Cive* of 1642, who exposed the weakness of protection in a literal sense, and if protection is not *literally* protection, what is it? As much as in *Leviathan* Hobbes might have helped himself to its appealing fruits, his work joins other productions of the English civil wars in offering a much more critical reflection on protection as a political concept.

BACKGROUND

By the time of the civil wars the language of 'protect' and 'protector' had long been embedded in English legal and political culture. Both as a local privilege and as a personal relationship between lord and dependent, protection was a ubiquitous feature of medieval English legal thought and practice, sometimes in the technical sense of an immunity and sometimes in the sense of a preservation from attack or other molestation.[2] In the latter sense it was closely associated with 'peace', peace being thereby conceived as a personal

93

function of a lord just as was protection. Historians have analysed the process whereby the king's peace, from being a selective protection of royal servants, became universalised over the whole realm and all subjects under the common law, although latterly they have also emphasised that this did not mean that specific royal protections became redundant.[3] This universal peace of the king was invoked in Henry de Bracton's *De Legibus et Consuetudinibus Angliae*, written c. 1220–30: the king 'has also those things that are of peace, that the people entrusted to him may be quiet and restful in peace, and so that none should beat, wound or mistreat another, none take another's property by force and robbery, and none maim or kill a man'.[4] Bracton coupled peace with justice, both of which are inseparable from the Crown and belong to the Crown alone. However, justice, in which the king acts 'as the minister and the vicar of God' to 'give to each his own', is not the same as peace, which is a protective or defensive function, guarded by the sword which 'signifies the defence (*defensio*) of the realm and of the country'.[5] This association between protection and the Crown was underlined in the royal coronation oath, whereby the monarch-to-be promised to protect (*protegere*) the laws and customs of the land. It figured, too, in another element of the coronation ritual, the girding-on of the sword, during which a prayer was made that God bless and sanctify the sword as a protection (*proteccio*) and a defence (*defensio*) of 'churches, widows, orphans and all who serve God'.[6] Finally, 'protector' was also the title assumed by a regent during a king's minority, culminating with Edward Seymour, 1st Duke of Somerset, 'Lord Protector of the Realm' during the minority of Edward VI.[7]

Despite the prominence of this language in the common law of the later medieval and Tudor period, despite the continued use of the medieval coronation ceremony, and despite, or perhaps, partly, because of, the controversial figure of Protector Somerset, English political thought in the sixteenth century was not marked by an emphasis on this specifically *protective* sword. This is not to say that the sword was not prominent. It is well documented how Protestant political thought, especially, emphasised the sword of Romans 13, carried by the prince as the 'minister of God' who 'beareth not the sword in vain' as 'an avenger to execute wrath' upon the malefactor. The virtue of the subject in respect of 'the powers that be' was obedience, for those powers are 'ordained of God'.[8] But this sword was primarily a sword of justice rather than of protection. It is true that, especially in its external function, the sword was associated with the language of defence. However, in none of the English 'commonwealth' writers of the sixteenth century was protection, specifically, prominent as a political function or aim, or as part of the language of good government; nor was the failure to protect, specifically, the key mark of tyranny or of bad government. Protection was a language largely alien to the classical humanism of these authors. Their discourse centred instead on the 'common weal' of the body politic, that is, 'commonwealth' in the sense of a multitude united by law and justice.[9] It is certainly the case that, in addition to this horizontal dimension of mutual association and citizenship, their Protestant political theology also produced a marked emphasis on the vertical dimension of commonwealth: the relationship between rule and subjection. But that dimension was primarily articulated in terms of command and obedience, rather than protection and obedience.

In this as in so many other dimensions of European political culture, however, the wars of religion that ravaged France during the last quarter of the sixteenth century were to have a lasting impact. As in England, the idea that the king had a duty to protect his subjects and his realm was firmly embedded in medieval European law and political culture, articulated through the Roman private-law concept of *tutela* or guardianship. The king was *tutor regni*, guardian of the realm, and the realm or the people were conceived as having the legal status of a minor.[10] During the wars of religion, however, *tutela* was turned by Huguenot legal theorists against the Crown. The *Vindiciae, Contra Tyrannos* asserted that, while the king was indeed the principal *tutor*, he was not the only one; other officers of the kingdom had the legal status of co-*tutores*, empowered to act for the protection of the people should the king fail in his contractual duty.[11] Protection as guardianship or *tutela* (also *cura*, 'care' and *curator*, 'carer') thereby became implicated in the classic proposition of early modern resistance theory that the king was superior to individuals (*singuli*) but inferior to the people taken as a whole (*universi*) and to those who represent them in that capacity.

The Latin vocabulary of *tutela* (*tutor*, *tuitio*) employed by the *Vindiciae* was impeccably classical. Jean Bodin, in his *Les Six Livres de la République* of 1576, deployed the vernacular form of the post-classical *protectio* as a key part of his drive to redefine the commonwealth (*respublica*, *république*) in terms of a new concept of sovereign power.[12] His 1586 Latin version of the work shows, however, that the French word *protection* does not translate *tutela* but *clientela*, the Roman institution of patron and client, which Bodin might be read as polemically substituting for *tutela* in his absolutist reply to the theorists of resistance. The principal object of his self-consciously innovative chapter on *protection/clientela* in Book I of the *Six Livres* was not, in fact, the internal relationship between a sovereign and his people, but the external relationship between a protecting state and a protected ally. He was concerned to argue that protection in this sense was a relationship which respected the sovereignty of the protected, because the protector had no power over it and the protected owed only reverence and honour in return. Later writers would raise a dis-abused question mark over this international protection that was supposedly purely in the interests of the protected. In his striking *empresa*, *Protegen pero destruyen* ('They protect but they destroy'), the seventeenth-century Spanish political theorist Diego de Saavedra Fajardo depicted a pair of wings shelter-ing the land beneath but thereby casting a deep shadow over it where the sun cannot shine.[13] In Bodin, however, this external relationship of honour is contrasted with the internal relationship between sovereign and subject which *is* one of power; of a benefit to the individual that this brings ('security in goods, person and family'); and of a price paid for it in return ('faith, subjec-tion, obedience, assistance and aid'). In the internal domain Bodin used the feudal language of 'liegeman' to characterise this client-subject,[14] but what he had done was to rearticulate that relationship within a new theory of sover-eignty, the crucial attribute of which was power. The result was to efface the corporate body of the people and replace it with a series of individual subjects in a personal relationship to the sovereign.

PROTECTION AND KINGSHIP UNDER JAMES I AND CHARLES I

James I was the first English monarch to be crowned in a service that used English as the principal language, but it remained a close translation of the medieval Latin ritual, thus involving reference to both defence and protection as duties of the king.[15] James understood his kingship in terms of a royal absolutism based upon divine right, but the rhetoric of protection does not seem to have been central to his self-articulation as king. The word is not especially prominent in his own writings and speeches, although he does appeal to other terms implying some sort of protecting role, especially that of 'father'.[16] However, early on in his reign 'protection' received renewed emphasis within published legal and political discourse. The English civilian John Cowell's dictionary of English law, *The Interpreter*, published in 1607, was immediately a matter of political controversy because of the entry under 'King', which gave the king 'absolute rule' over the whole land and argued that he was above individual laws, if not the law itself. At the end of that entry, Cowell referred the reader to the passage of Bracton on the position of the king that we looked at above; as we shall see, it would be cited again in the royalist cause during the civil wars (though, as parliamentarians pointed out, there was much in Bracton that did not support the idea that the king was above the laws). Cowell included a lengthy entry on 'Protection' in which he invoked the king's prerogative. Protection, *protectio*, had according to him a general and a particular sense. The general sense was 'that benefit and safetie, that every subiect, or Denizen, or alien specially secured, hath by the Kings lawes'. The more specific sense of protection was 'an immunitie given by the king to a person against suites in law, or other vexations upon reasonable causes him thereunto moving, which I take to be a branch of his prerogative'. This included special protections for those on the king's service on the seas, abroad and on the marches, and, more controversially, a protection, called *moratoria*, for the king's debtor against any other suits until the debt to the king be paid.[17]

Of far greater impact on English political discourse than Cowell's entry under 'Protection', however, was Calvin's Case of 1608, reported by Sir Edward Coke. Argued by both Lord Ellesmere and Sir Francis Bacon, it concerned the issue of whether one born in Scotland after the accession of James I could take up an inheritance in England, given that English law stipulated that aliens could not inherit in England. At stake, then, was the definition of who was an alien. However, that question, in the handling of the court, involved the other side of the issue: who was a subject, and what was owed by subject to sovereign and vice versa. The first term of law that was examined was *Ligeantia*, a familiar concept in English common law which was here defined as 'a true and faithful obedience of the subject due to his Sovereign'.[18] The authority of the medieval lawyer Glanville was appealed to for the notion that ligeance is owed to the lord by every tenant 'that holdeth by homage'. But this feudal tie was transcended in the case of the sovereign: 'between the Sovereign and the subject there is without question a higher and greater connexion: for as the subject oweth to the King his true and faithful ligeance and obedience, so the Sovereign is to govern and protect his Subjects'. Bodin, too, had insisted that the protection of lords in respect of their vassals is 'much less' than that of the sovereign in respect of his subjects, which is 'the first, and the strongest protection that exists', and there may well be a direct influence given that Bodin's work was translated into English as *The Six Bookes of a Common-Weale* in 1606. In short, Coke's report asserted a 'mutual bond' of protection and obedience between sovereign and individual subject.[19]

This principle was then the basis for the much more controversial argument that, given 'the protection and government of the King is general over all his dominions and kingdoms, as well in time of peace by justice, as in time of warr by the sword ... seeing power and protection draweth ligeance, it followeth, that seeing the King's power, command and protection, extendeth out of England, that ligeance cannot be local, nor confined within the bounds thereof'.[20] Crucially, therefore, the association with power allowed protection, and thus sovereignty itself, to track not just the movement of the king's special agents, as previously, but the location of any subjects whom he might license outside the bounds of the realm as far as his effective power extended. Philip Stern's chapter in this volume highlights the significance of this concept of extensible protection for early modern commercial enterprises. More specifically, Keechang Kim and, especially, Christopher Tomlins have stressed the importance of the decision in Calvin's Case for English imperial and colonial activity in the early seventeenth century. Both authors concentrate on the link in the text between the naturalness of 'ligeance' and its exportability, yet neither comments on the language of power in the reciprocal relationship of protection.[21] However, the association between the extension of protection and the extension of power can be paralleled elsewhere in imperial discourse of around the same time, for example in Serafim de Freitas' *On the Just Empire of the Portuguese in Asia* (1625). Here, in the context of protection at sea, he argued that 'since the relevant area of the sea is not defined by natural law, in consequence we must say that in terms of control [*imperio*, 'empire'] and jurisdiction it can be widened, or restricted, according to the power of the lord'.[22] In a domestic context, however, the political potential of the argument from natural law was soon recognised. Johann Sommerville notes the judgement being cited in Parliament as early as 1610 for the principle that kings have a natural duty to protect their subjects.[23]

Following Charles I's accession to the throne there is some evidence that the language of protection had become widespread. In 1635 George Wither, the deliberately plain-styled, oppositional poet who would later write explicitly for the parliamentarian cause during the civil wars, published a much safer project in a very popular genre: a book of emblems with accompanying poems, which he dedicated to Charles.[24] The absence of specific political intent in this work allows the unpretentious verse to function as some index of popularly intelligible moral and political vocabulary. The sword figures frequently, sometimes on its own, sometimes held out by an arm or the figure of a king. The mottoes and poems accompanying these emblematic swords suggest an interesting fusion between the vengeful sword of Romans 13 and the protecting sword of the rearticulated, originally feudal relationship between lord and liegeman, now between sovereign and loyal subject. Emblem 3 of Book III, depicting a sword and mace, has a motto directly from Romans 13, *Non sine causa*. In the accompanying poem, the sword is there to punish malefactors; there is no mention of protection.[25] But Emblem 3 of Book I, with the motto *Lex regit et arma tuentur*, which Wither glosses as 'The Law is given to direct;/ The Sword, to punish and protect', extends the remit of the sword beyond the execution of justice.[26] Two further sword emblems are in a different register again, and hint at reason of state. Book III, Emblem 29, a king with law and sword, insists on the necessary conjunction of law and 'Armed pow'r' ('At home, in every Province of his Lands, / At all times, armed are his Trayned bands').[27] Emblem 30 in Book IV depicts another sword, in which the accompanying poem warns that 'Kingdomes, nor in Warre nor Peace, can stand, / Except the Sword have always some command', and 'Considering this, let none be so unwise / The Swords well-us'd protection to despise'.[28]

POLITICISING PROTECTION AT THE OUTBREAK OF THE ENGLISH CIVIL WARS

Wither's popular emblems are a good demonstration, at a relatively ordinary level of language, of the protean nature of protection: its ability to slip between different discursive registers. The multiple political possibilities of the language became fully apparent from the outset of the English civil wars. Charles I, or his advisers responsible for drafting the text, decided to play the protection card right at the start of his substantive answer to the XIX *Propositions*: 'The Demands being such, as we were unworthy of the trust reposed in Us by the Law, and of Our dessent, from so many great and famous Ancestors, if We could be brought to abandon that power which only can inable Us to perform what We are sworn to, in protecting Our people and the Laws'.[29] Here, Charles appealed to his coronation oath to portray himself as the protector of the laws and the personal protector of the people. But the key element of his answer was the relationship between power and protection: without de facto military might, the de jure function of protection cannot be exercised. As the judgement in Calvin's Case and Wither's demotic poetry had already suggested, therefore, protection was a concept on the interface between might ('*Armed* pow'r') and right.

   Henry Parker picked up on protection in his reply to Charles of 1642. '*But our King here, doth acknowledge it the great businesse of his coronation oath to protect us:* And I hope under this word *protect*, he intends not onely to shield us from all kind of evill, but to promote us also to all kind of Politicall happinesse according to his utmost devoyre, and I hope hee holds himselfe bound thereunto, not onely by his oath, but also by his very Office, and by the end of his soveraigne dignitie'.[30] Here, Parker drew the concept of protection into a 'commonwealth' understanding of government, with its Aristotelian teleology of *eudaimonia* or happiness within the body politic, and a corresponding conception of the duty or office of the king. Central to Parker's politicisation of protection was the distinction between the members of the commonwealth *ut singuli*, as individuals, and *ut universi*, taken as a whole.[31]

He developed the point in an extended critique of Charles' appeal to multiple relations of personal superiority (including father, husband and lord) to describe his position as king. A likeness of these personal relations may obtain, according to Parker, between individuals and the king, but it is quite otherwise with the people as a body, which cannot be to the king in a relation of creature, son, wife or servant.[32] Thus, 'protection' at a properly *political* level, and that means, for Parker, applied to the people *as a whole*, cannot be a kind of personal shielding but must involve the promotion of the 'Weale Publike'. It is noticeable that the distinction between protection and other forms of care or guardianship is lost in this expansive critique of the royal language of government.

Parker was happy enough to appeal to a sixteenth-century 'commonwealth' language of good government, with its accompanying Aristotelian distinction between political rule and the rule of a father or master. And yet he was also modern enough to invoke at the outset, as the aim of all politics, a term that by the mid-seventeenth century was ubiquitous in political discourse: *salus populi*, which could mean 'the people's welfare' but was generally translated 'the safety of the people'. As part of the phrase *salus populi suprema lex esto*, 'let the safety of the people be the supreme law', it was associated with the late humanist discourse of reason of state.[33]

Dudley Digges' response to Parker on behalf of, and authorised by, the king used precisely this language to politicise protection in a sense opposed to that of Parker. Thus, Digges argued that 'the ends which states ayme at ... are safety and plenty, To have riches, and not to be able to defend them, is to expose ourselves as prey; to be safe, and poore, is to be securely miserable'.[34] Here, the aim of the state as a whole is no different from that of the individuals within it, as Digges slid between the language of public safety and that of individual security. From this position he was able to attack Parker's new sense of 'protection' as providing for political happiness, while deliberately avoiding running together protection with other forms of care and guardianship: 'How should we conceave, that the Prince is obliged by oath to take care for his people in such a degree, as the most affectionate mother never yet took for her dearest children. . . Every particular subject hath a just title and may challenge an interest in whatsoever is meant by the word, Protection: Is the king therefore bound to promote every particular person to all kinds of politicall happinesse?'[35] For Digges, here, it is Parker's 'happiness' language that is personal rather than political; 'protection' is political only insofar as it is understood in a more narrow sense (although, as he pointed out, that sense is not entirely clear). But whatever that narrow sense is, it is a matter of both justice and interest for the subject, which are both clearly political terms, though the one belongs to the language of rights and the other to that of reason of state. Thus, a central part of Digges' strategy in rehabilitating a narrow sense of 'protection' was to prise it away from a paternalistic (or maternalistic) rhetoric of care for passive dependants and make it part of a language of active, lawful, subjection.

Digges developed this line of thought in his book of the following year, 1643, entitled *The Unlawfulnesse of Subjects Taking up Armes against their Soveraigne*. It was already indebted to the ideas of Hobbes, but, as we shall see, it has much more to say about protection specifically than either *The Elements of Law* (1640) or *De Cive* (1642).[36] The very Hobbesian opening asserts that 'in requitall for the submission of our private strength, we are secured by the united power of all, and the whole kingdome becomes our guard'.[37] Digges developed the position by pursuing Charles' argument from the coronation oath: the king, and only the king, being sworn to protect his subjects, he must have the power to do so.[38] It is indeed the law itself which arms the king with this power, and *populi salus*, the safety of the people, rests upon that law.[39] Citing in support the passage of Bracton that Cowell had already quoted, and also Bracton's definition of the sword, Digges further mobilised the kind of neo-feudal argument that had been articulated in Calvin's Case: the king is 'our Leige [sic] Lord' and 'all subjects are *homines ligii*, leige men.' 'Ligeancy is an obligation upon all Subjects to take part with their leige Lord against all men living . . . The Lord like wise is bound to governe, protect, and defend his leige people (so the English are often called in Acts of Parliament) according to the rights, customes, and Lawes of the Country'.[40]

As we have already seen, this vocabulary was at odds with classical conceptions of commonwealth and the people. It threatened to collapse the civil state into the state of personal protection enjoyed individually by all subjects in return for their allegiance. This was not, in fact, what Digges wanted; but his negotiation of the point was uneasy. On the one hand he insisted that 'the King is supreme head, not in respect of single persons, but the *universitas subjectorum* [the collective body of subjects]. For this is comprehended in a *body politique* compact of all sorts, and degrees of people. . . And it is evident, that hee is not the head of this or that man, but of all the members in conjunction, of the whole body, for else he would be the head of millions of bodies, and by consequence have as many distinct Kingdoms, as particular Subjects'. On the other hand it is false to say that the *universitas subjectorum* is greater than the king, because the 'same reason which makes him above one, makes him above two, and so above ten, & so ten thousands, & so ten millions of thousands; for their assembling together doth not dispense with their duty of alleagiance, many or few alters not the quality of the act'. Digges was here taking on an anonymous tract called *A Reply to the Answer*, which had argued that the *universitas* is a body qualitatively different from the individuals who make it up, so that, even if the *universitas* consisted only of two people, it would still be greater than the king; and that although individuals can owe allegiance, the body politic as a whole cannot.[41] Digges replied that 'the division of all persons in this Land is into King and Subjects, liege Lord and liege people, and therefore they must be placed in the latter ranke. It is a strange phansie to abstract the body politique from all the particulars whereof it is compacted', and he pressed his point against abstraction by referring to the very concrete 'hands of particular men' that were actually doing the fighting.[42] But his mockery of the metaphysics of corporation left it unclear what his own 'body politique' was, apart from a simple aggregate of individuals tied to the same person. He offered here no clear account of the *universitas* over which his King might be 'supreme', and which indeed was the basis of that supremacy.

THE INTERNATIONALISATION OF PROTECTION DURING THE 'ENGAGEMENT CONTROVERSY', 1649–1650

Two works from the time of the 'Engagement Controversy', both of them also indebted to Hobbes, likewise put protection centre-stage, but this time in an argument for the commonwealth rather than the king: Anthony Ascham's *Of the Confusions and Revolutions of Governments*, in the expanded edition of 1649, and Marchamont Nedham's *The Case of the Common-wealth* of 1650. Of the two, Ascham's is the more sustained and subtle argument, though Nedham put the nub of the protection–obedience relationship in his usual energetic manner: 'Protection implies a Return of obedience and Friendship from the persons protected, to those that protect them; otherwise they put themselves in the condition of Enemies, and by the Law of Nations, which indulges a liberty unto all that are in power to provide for their owne security, they may be handled as Publique Enemies, and Out-lawes.'[43] The marginal note (not particularly accurate) beside the 'Law of Nations' refers the reader to Hugo Grotius' *De Iure Belli ac Pacis*, and is an index of Nedham's debt to Ascham, much of whose work is a systematic application of Grotian thinking to the situation of civil war and conquest within England. That application depends upon the principle that civil war in a country in fact creates an international situation, one in which each side equally constitutes a nation, and in which, therefore, ambassadors may be sent to both sides.[44]

Like other works of this decisive moment following the execution of Charles I in 1649, Ascham's treatise confronts head-on the question of the relationship between de facto power and lawful subjection.[45] Ascham offered a direct parallel between international relations and the relation of individuals to de facto powers in their land. Contracts between states, he argued, are always made upon 'consideration of *the power which each Kingdome hath to afford benefit one to the other*'; it follows that, equally for subjects in a situation of 'internal' division, 'it is best and enough for us to consider, *Whether the invading party (just or unjust) have us or the meanes of our subsistence in their possession or no*'.[46] The line 'betwixt *Might* and *Right*' does not entirely disappear, but it is softened by the necessary role of the de facto power situation in determining the content of an oath of allegiance.[47] At base, however, the appeal to the fact of power, at least in the case of an individual, rested on the more fundamental principle that each man has a natural right to his own self-preservation and protection, asserted ringingly at the very start of the work: 'Of each mans Soveraigne Allegiance to himselfe'. Hence, 'if the said Armies fall into our quarters, and we be summoned to assist the unlawfull Party, we may then arm ourselves, not for him, but for our selves'; 'Nature commends me to my selfe for my owne protection, and preservation'.[48]

Here, then, once again, appears the active subject, for whom submission is an act of allegiance to himself, of *self*-protection. But, as for Digges, there is then the question what, if anything, is the civil state more than a series of essentially private protection deals. Ascham tackled the issue in Chapters XI and XII of Part II, which offer his own account of the origins of government. Chapter XI is largely Hobbesian in tenor, and contains an explicit acknowledgement of his work. Although we were at the beginning born in subjection to heads of family, as our natural magistrates, now following the confusion of families we are naturally under no subjection and live in mutual fear. As a result, we must seek our 'Security or Protection' through a renewed subjection, giving up much of our natural right as the price. Subjection is conditional upon power, but power without consent cannot stably ground subjection as a legal relationship. 'Wherfore Compact was judg'd a securer way than meer power for the coalition of society, and for the rule of Obedience and Subjection ... and that state is now the best which needs least force to maintain it'.[49] In the following chapter, clarifying the nature of the 'Compact', he followed the author of the *Vindiciae, Contra Tyrannos* by using the legal model of guardianship of a minor to analyse the relationship between a ruler and the people as a whole.[50] There being no father ('we must suppose him dead and buried') to perform the role naturally, the only possibility is that the minor, the people, must 'appoint this first and supreme Officer of State'.[51] Guardianship, then, was Ascham's answer to 'so many other Questions and scruples of the peoples rights': it makes the people the judge of the maladministration of their rulers,[52] and ensures that, just as 'a *Minor* cannot make a Contract to his owne prejudice', a people 'cannot by any Compact deteriorate their condition, and it is alwayes presum'd for their liberty, when dangers are threatened'.[53] Against Hobbes, and consistent with the intellectual origins of this argument in sixteenth-century French resistance theory, Ascham argued that the people must always retain a right of judging and punishing 'acts notoriously contrary to the light of nature and reason'.[54]

Besides the legal subjection of individuals for their protection, then, there was also a legal relationship between the people as a whole and its ruler(s). But that relationship was itself modelled on a relationship between individuals, and these two relationships seem to fuse in the final chapter, XVI, on 'Politicall justice', in which Ascham turned to the one exception he had made in Chapter XII on the minor's right to refuse a guardian, '*viz.* in a Controversie for his rights and estate, and then it is conceiv'd very equitable he should have some good done for him, even against his own peevish will'. In this final chapter, he argued that the simple fact of individuals' being able to enjoy the fruits of their labours, to 'communicate with one anothers Virtues', even to 'sleepe composed (without any Alarums) in their beds', is already protection for which allegiance is owed. It is thus no more than 'Politicall justice' that 'they who protect us and our Children in the Common-Wealth ... ought in equity to be rewarded'.[55] Here, the de facto nature of power, the fact that the 'good' is *already being done*, seems to reduce the distinction between a public 'people' and private individuals and their children sleeping in their beds, both enjoying protection. The line is blurred in an 'us' and a 'we' who must recognise the equity, the superior principle of justice operative in the existing state of affairs, and not demand the choice that stricter justice might seem to offer us.

A critic might object that Ascham had simply failed to address any of the hard (Diggesian and Hobbesian) questions about how a people is constituted as a people, distinct from private individuals. But the appeal to equity suggests that pressing hard (legal) questions is itself misplaced in certain situations. Moreover, a careful reading of Ascham's text suggests that there is more to 'Politicall justice' than a moral reframing in the face of de facto power, important though that is. Ascham's use of 'Politicall' here echoes the 'Politicall sence' he had earlier required as an interpretative condition of all public legal relationships.[56] As we saw, an international contract or oath between public persons – kings or princes – is said in Part I to be made on 'consideration of the power which each Kingdome hath to afford benefit one to the other'. However, the consequence Ascham drew is that therefore 'the contract is rather with the *places*, then with the persons'.[57] Why so? It appears that for

Ascham, the fact of power which is the enabling – indeed, in that sense, constitutive – condition of political society was fundamentally related to place or locality. This is confirmed in the contrast with natural society that he drew in Part II:

> What then after all can mortall men conclude to themselves, out of these *susque deque's* of the world, out of its confusions and revolutions, out of the uncertainty of the rights of particular persons, or bounds of Empires and places; out of those various circumstances, wherby we are now cimented, as pieces which accident, and not nature fastens in the same frame (unlesse it be in respect of the society of man-kind whose nature is not to be an *Ascriptus glebae particulari* like a Tree or a Rock, which alwayes keepe one place) what (I say) can we conclude, but that we of the People must be contented with those governours, into whose full possessions it is our destiny to fall?[58]

Here, place in the sense of locality provides a de facto horizontal dimension of political society, just as power provides the de facto vertical, and legitimates a fusion between the people and the people who live there ('we of the People'). Hobbes in *The Elements of Law* had refused any political significance to the fact of living in the same place: that was natural, not political.[59] But for Ascham, place is a central part of 'Politicall sence', and protection as a *political* concept is essentially a local as well as a personal relationship.[60]

OBEDIENCE AND PROTECTION IN THOMAS HOBBES

The powerful presence of Thomas Hobbes has been making itself felt throughout the previous two sections, and it is time finally to turn to his distinctive contribution to the debate. Hobbes' English masterpiece of 1651, *Leviathan*, appeared definitively to claim the concept of protection for the absolutist state, by lining up the personal relationship of protection and obedience with his denial of the existence of the collective people independent of the sovereign representative. Key to both was the conceptualisation of the sovereign in terms of 'a Common Power, to keep them in awe'.[61] Following a long tradition that we have already seen exemplified in Wither's work, Hobbes emblematised power with the sword, both in the famous frontispiece and in his declaration, in Chapter 21, that 'The end of Obedience is Protection; which, wheresoever a man seeth it, either in his own, or in anothers sword, Nature applyeth his obedience to it, and his endeavour to maintaine it'.[62]

Hobbes laid particular stress on 'the mutuall Relation between Protection and Obedience' in the 'Review, and Conclusion' to *Leviathan*, an emphasis which Noel Malcolm is surely right to connect with Ascham's and Nedham's tracts ('divers English books lately printed'). He is also right to argue that, despite these late references, the essence of Hobbes' position had been there since *The Elements of Law*.[63] But, although both *The Elements* and *De Cive* use the language of protection at times, connecting it with preservation, it is *security* that centrally preoccupies Hobbes in both. Ascham had used the two terms as if they were equivalent ('Security or Protection', above), but, although the two notions can be connected in a broad idea of a sheltered space of action, their connotations are not quite the same. Security, at least in Hobbes' handling, peculiarly involves the idea of *risk*, and it thus has a psychological dimension not shared by protection: an element of personal judgement (every man in the condition of nature is judge of 'the greatness of the danger'),[64] and also a personal affective attitude – of 'confidence', if we feel secure; of what Hobbes calls 'diffidence', if we do not.[65] Thus, every individual has, in the phrasing of *The Elements*, the natural right of protecting himself.[66] But what an individual actually goes about to do in the condition of nature is to increase his or her security by all means possible, by eliminating or at least controlling potential risks.

Famously, Hobbes argued that this pursuit is unending except by death, sooner rather than later. Reason (the law of nature) therefore demands that we give up our natural right through covenant, and create a sovereign which is nothing other than a power great enough to give us security. As Hobbes put it in *The Elements*:

> The end for which one man giveth up, and relinquisheth to another, or others, the right of protecting and defending himself by his own power, is the security which he expecteth thereby, of protection and defence from those to whom he does so relinquish it. And a man may then account himself in the estate of security, when he can foresee no violence to be done unto him, from which the doer may not be deterred by the power of that sovereign, to whom they have every one subjected themselves.[67]

In the parallel passage in *De Cive*, Hobbes refined the argument by appealing (implicitly) to the Roman law concept of 'just fear', *iustus metus*, defined as the 'fear that befalls a constant man' (not merely a timorous man who might be afraid of anything). Thus he defined 'to live securely' as 'so as not to have a just cause to fear from others, as long as he himself has not done injury to others. For to render men safe from mutual damage, so that they cannot be hurt or killed injuriously, is impossible; and therefore it does not fall under deliberation. But it can be looked for that there should be no just cause of fear'.[68] Protection, then, must and can be only to the extent (*unusquisque in tantum protegatur*) of providing security in the sense of the absence of reasonable fear. Even in *Leviathan* the sword of the famous frontispiece looms over the land, but this does not free its subjects from the caution of locking their doors at night, and neither do they expect it to.[69]

Hobbes was still capable, in *Leviathan*, of reproducing the royalist argument from protection much as Charles I had deployed it in his *Answer to the XIX Propositions*.[70] But his main argument was not centrally couched in the language of protection, and not of obedience, either. The laws of nature, listed in Chapter 15 of *Leviathan* as the moral virtues (that is, dispositions that conduce to peace), do not include obedience; from the body of the work, it is unclear where Hobbes would place it other than as a derivative of the justice of keeping the original covenant. Certainly, in the 'Review, and Conclusion', he added to the laws of nature one further: '*That every man is bound by Nature, as much as in him lieth, to protect in Warre, the Authority, by which he is himself protected in time of Peace*', and claimed that this law 'may bee drawn by consequence, from some of those that are there already mentioned'.[71] But it is not clear, nor did he trouble to argue, precisely how that deduction works. In short, the mutual relation between protection and obedience, of which Hobbes made so much in the 'Review, and Conclusion', was grafted on to a natural rights argument that could, in theory, do perfectly well without it. Indeed, it is noticeable that although both *The Elements* and *De Cive* occasionally gloss the original natural right as a right of self-protection, *Leviathan* does not use this formulation at all. Both Digges and Ascham had much better integrated their notion of natural right with the protection that is the ultimate aim of the civil state; but that is because theirs *were* centrally arguments about protection, whereas Hobbes' was not.

CONCLUSION: PROTECTION AS A POLITICAL CONCEPT

One conclusion to this chapter is quite simple. Protection was an extraordinarily malleable piece of legitimating language, available for manipulation in multiple causes and contexts. It fitted equally well into the moral discourse of natural law, the commercial language of colonial enterprise, and the pragmatic, power-orientated maxims of reason of state. Its beneficiaries could range from an orphaned child to shipping and plantations. It could operate both for and against the sovereign power: it delegitimated opposition – for who could complain of being protected? – but at the same time it handed a very powerful weapon to subjects in the form of the claim that they were *not* being protected. Its embeddedness in both common law and civil law was a further advantage, lending the happy lustre of legality to what it touched. It is not hard to conclude that this malleability was and remains the key to the exceptional usefulness of protection as a piece of legal and political rhetoric.

Beyond that, however, what the polemics of the civil wars show are the complexities involved in understanding protection as a political concept. The way in which the *Answer to the XIX Propositions* linked the liturgical language of the coronation ceremony with the king's control of garrisons and weaponry was embarrassingly inadequate.[72] On both sides in the civil wars, protection as a political concept was understood to involve the protected as well as the protectors. From this perspective, however, protection could be either maximal or minimal, inflated to cover the whole of political well-being or shrunk to a bare preservation; its object could be either the entire body politic or the individual at the point of the sword. The contest over the nature of protection was part of the political contest itself. At its most fruitful, the attempt to harness protection to either side produced a sustained and difficult reconsideration of the relationship between the individual and the body politic. Protection implied power, not in the abstract but in the physical sense of power to shield the body from harm, and relatedly to cause harm to bodies: a sense that the civil wars had made very real. Those writers of the wars who thought about this seriously were not content either with a simple restatement of Huguenot legal resistance theory or an equally simple appeal to de facto reason of state. None of them wanted to collapse the political state and political authority into private protection, but neither could the agency of the individual human being seeking the bodily safety and confidence of everyday life be adequately recognised or, indeed, respected, by an exclusive appeal to the body of the people. Protection, a concept on the interface between the personal and political, physical body and abstract body politic, de facto and de jure, pushed political thought in new and thought-provoking directions, even if the history of its rhetorical manipulation, especially in overseas dominions, can claim no such distinction.

NOTES

1 Thomas Hobbes, *Leviathan*, edited Richard Tuck, Cambridge University Press, Cambridge, 1996, p. 153.
2 Helen Lacey, 'Protection and Immunity in Later Medieval England', in T.B. Lambert and David Rollason (eds), *Peace and Protection in the Middle Ages*, Centre for Medieval and Renaissance Studies-Pontifical Institute of Mediaeval Studies, Toronto, 2009, p. 80, citing Sir Edward Coke from as late as the early seventeenth century: 'Protection is of two sorts, one, to give a man an immunitie or freedome from actions or suits, the second, for the safety of his person, servants and goods, lands and tenements whereof he is lawfully possessed from violence, unlawfull molestation or wrong.'

3 See Paul Hyams, *Rancor and Reconciliation in Medieval England*, Cornell University Press, Ithaca, 2003, Chapters 7 and 8; Lacey, pp. 82–83.

4 Henry de Bracton, *On the Laws and Customs of England*, translated Samuel E. Thorne with parallel Latin text by George Woodbine, Harvard University Press/Belknap Press, Cambridge, MA, 1968, Vol. II, p. 166, tit. *De Libertatibus et Quis Possit Concedere Libertates et Quae Sunt Regis*.

5 Ibid., p. 32, tit. *Quid Significat Gladius*.

6 *Liber Regalis*, in Leopold G. Wickham Legg (ed.), *English Coronation Records*, A. Constable & Co., London, 1901, pp. 88, 95. See also H.G. Richardson, 'The English Coronation Oath', *Speculum*, vol. 24, no. 1, 1949, pp. 44–75.

7 J.S. Roskell, 'The Office and Dignity of Protector of England, with Special Reference to its Origins', *English Historical Review*, vol. 68, no. 267, 1953, pp. 193–233; on Somerset, see Stephen Alford, *Kingship and Politics in the Reign of Edward VI*, Cambridge University Press, Cambridge, 2002, Chapter 3.

8 For a classic exposition, see Quentin Skinner, *The Foundations of Modern Political Thought*, Cambridge University Press, Cambridge, 1978, vol. 2, Chapter 1.

9 For a recent treatment of this kind of language, see Aysha Pollnitz, *Princely Education in Early Modern Britain*, Cambridge University Press, Cambridge, 2015.

10 Walter Ullmann, *Law and Politics in the Middle Ages: An Introduction to the Sources of Medieval Ideas*, Cornell University Press, Ithaca, 1975, pp. 58–59, 205–06.

11 George Garnett, 'Introduction', in *Vindiciae, Contra Tyrannos*, edited and translated by George Garnett, Cambridge University Press, Cambridge, 1994, pp. xxvi, xl-xli; Daniel Lee, *Popular Sovereignty in Early Modern Constitutional Thought*, Oxford University Press, Oxford, 2016, pp. 134–37, 152–55.

12 Jean Bodin, *Les Six Livres de la République*, edited Christine Frémont et al., Fayard, Paris, 1986, *Livre premier*, Chapter 7, 'De Ceux qui sont en Protection: Et la Difference entre les Alliez, Estrangers, et Subjects'. The very first sentence of the work lays down sovereign power, '*puissance souveraine*', as definitive for the existence of a commonwealth ('*republique*'). See Annabel Brett, 'Political Thought', in Hamish Scott (ed.), *The Oxford Handbook of Early Modern European History, 1350–1750: Volume II: Cultures and Power*, Oxford University Press, Oxford, 2015, pp. 32–33. Bodin's main chapter on sovereignty (Book I, Chapter 8) actually follows the chapter on *protection/clientela*, showing the structural position of the concept within his political theory more generally.

13 Diego de Saavedra Fajardo, *Idea de un Principe Politico Christiano. Representada en Cien Empresas*, Munich, 1640, pp. 627–31. The accompanying text foregrounds the inequality of power in changing protection to tyranny ('*Asi la proteccion suele convertirse en tirania. No guarda leyes la mayor Potencia*', p. 627) and exposes the protection of allies as a strategy of imperial domination, using primarily Roman examples. It also comments, however, on contemporary examples such as the presence of Swedish forces in Germany ('*Diga Alemania como se halla con la proteccion de Suecia*', p. 629).

14 Garnett, p. 17 note 20 notes that the relationship between the Roman *cliens* and the feudal vassal was a celebrated topic of debate among the legal humanists of sixteenth-century France.

15 J. Wickham Legg (ed.), *The Coronation Order of King James I*, F.E. Robinson & Co., London, 1902, p. 16 (promise to 'defend and uphold the laws'), p. 28 (sword as 'defence and protection').

16 See Johann P. Sommerville (ed.), *James VI and I: Political Writings*, Cambridge University Press, Cambridge, 1994.

17 John Cowell, *The Interpreter*, Cambridge 1607, sig. [Fff4]v, col. 1–2.

18 Steve Sheppard (ed.), *The Selected Writings and Speeches of Sir Edward Coke*, Liberty Fund, Indianapolis, 2003, vol. 1, p. 175.

19 The similarity of the 'mutual bond' to Hobbes' 'mutuall Relation' is striking, and is almost certainly in the background to it: Johann P. Sommerville, *Thomas Hobbes: Political Ideas in Historical Context*, MacMillan, Basingstoke, 1992, pp. 68–69; Noel Malcolm, 'Introduction', in Thomas Hobbes, *Leviathan*, edited Noel Malcolm, Clarendon Press, Oxford, 2012, vol. 1, p. 68.

20 Sheppard, pp. 187–88.

21 Keechang Kim, *Aliens in Medieval Law: The Origins of Modern Citizenship*, Cambridge University Press, Cambridge, 2009, pp. 176–99; Christopher Tomlins, *Freedom Bound: Law, Labor and Civic Identity in Colonizing English America, 1580–1865*, Cambridge University Press, Cambridge, 2010, pp. 82–92.

22 Serafim de Freitas, *De Iusto Imperio Lusitanorum Asiatico*, Valladolid, 1625, Cap X, note 40 (my translation).

23 Johann P. Sommerville, *Royalists and Patriots: Politics and Ideology in England 1603–1640*, 2nd edn, Routledge, London, 2014, p. 93.

24 For Wither, see David Norbrook, *Writing the English Republic: Poetry, Rhetoric and Politics, 1627–1660*, Cambridge University Press, Cambridge, 1999, who describes his 'prophetic voice' as 'subdued' in the 1630s (p. 87).

25 George Wither, *A Collection of Emblemes, Ancient and Moderne*, reprinted with Introduction by Rosemary Freeman and Bibliographical Notes by Charles S. Hensley, University of South Carolina Press, Columbia, SC, 1975, fo. 137.

26 Ibid., fo. 3. Compare the double function in another sword emblem, 37 in Book IV, with the tag: 'Protect mee, if I worthy bee; If I demerit, punish mee' (ibid., fo. 245).

27 Ibid., fo. 163.

28 Ibid., fo. 238.

29 *XIX Propositions, Made by both Houses of Parliament to the Kings most Excellent Majestie; With His Majesties Answer Thereunto*, in Joyce Lee Malcolm (ed.), *The Struggle for Sovereignty: Seventeenth-Century English Tracts*, Liberty Fund, Indianapolis, 1999, vol. 1, p. 158.

30 [Henry Parker], *Observations upon Some of His Majesties Late Answers and Expresses*, [London], 1642, p. 3.

31 As we have seen, this distinction, with the accompanying thesis 'the king is greater than individuals, but less than the whole' (quoted by Parker at p. 2), was key to the

'resistance theory' of the French wars of religion, here translated into the English context. See J.H.M. Salmon, *The French Religious Wars in English Political Thought*, Clarendon Press, Oxford, 1959.

32 Parker, pp. 18–19.

33 See, among many studies, Richard Tuck, *Philosophy and Government, 1572–1651*, Cambridge University Press, New York, 1993, Chapters 2 and 3; Noel Malcolm, *Reason of State, Propaganda and the Thirty Years' War: An Unknown Translation by Thomas Hobbes*, Clarendon Press, Oxford, 2007, Chapter 6.

34 [Dudley Digges], *An Answer to a Printed Book, Intituled, Observations upon Some of His Majesties Late Answers and Expresses*, Oxford, 1642, p. 3.

35 Ibid., p. 15.

36 For Hobbes' influence on Digges' thinking, see Tuck, pp. 273–74.

37 [Dudley Digges], *The Unlawfulnesse of Subjects Taking up Armes against their Soveraigne*, n.p., 1643, p. 6.

38 Ibid., p. 8.

39 Ibid., pp. 75–76.

40 Ibid., p. 82.

41 *A Reply to the Answer (Printed by His Majesties Command at Oxford) to a Printed Booke Intituled Observations upon Some of His Maiesties Late Answers and Expresses by J.M.*, London, 1642, pp. 17–18.

42 Digges, *The Unlawfulnesse*, pp. 148–50.

43 Marchamont Nedham, *The Case of the Common-Wealth of England, Stated*, London, n.d. [1650]), Chapter 3, p. 17.

44 Antony Ascham, *Of the Confusions and Revolutions of Governments*, London, 1649, Part I, Chapter VIII, p. 37. The principle is attributed to '*Grotius* in his Treatie *de legatis*' (i.e. *De iure belli ac pacis*, Lib. II, Cap XVIII, II. 3), but in fact it was first articulated by Alberico Gentili in his two treatises *De legationibus* (*On Embassies*, 1585) and *De Iure Belli* (*On the Law of War*, 1598).

45 Ascham is discussed at length, together with other writers of the 'Engagement Controversy', in John M. Wallace, *Destiny his Choice: The Loyalism of Andrew Marvell*, Cambridge University Press, Cambridge, 1968, Chapter 1. See also Deborah Baumgold, *Hobbes' Political Theory*, Cambridge University Press, Cambridge, 1988, Chapter 7. Noel Malcolm rightly singles out Ascham and Nedham as focused on protection in a way that other tracts of the 'Engagement Controversy' are not ('Introduction', pp. 66–71).

46 Ascham, pp. 37–38, and p. 34 (chapter title).

47 Ibid., Part II, Chapter IX, pp. 92–94.

48 Ibid., Part II, Chapter II, p. 48.

49 Ibid., Part II, Chapter II [recte XI], p. 108.

50 Ibid., Chapter XII, p. 111.

51 Ibid., p. 112. Ascham points out that in civil law, even if the minor cannot actively choose a guardian, 'yet he may at least refuse such a Curator as is offer'd him'.

52 Ibid., p. 114; he adds 'not an unpleasant observation', that although princes fail to allow in their own cases that the people has the right of judging them, they certainly allow it in the case of others. For example, 'the King of England by his receiving the late King of Portugalls Embassadors, avowd the change there made by the power and right of the people, just at that time, when his Scottish Subjects began the same Controversie with himselfe there'.

53 Ibid., p. 115.

54 Ibid., Chapter XIII, pp. 121, 123.

55 Ibid., Chapter XVI, pp. 147–48.

56 Ibid., Part I, Chapter VIII, p. 37.

57 Ibid., my emphasis.

58 Ibid., Part II, Chapter XII, p. 115.

59 This claim is made perhaps most starkly in *The Elements of Law*, in which he denies any political identity to 'the people of England', or 'the people of France', per se. If they are not united in a sovereign, the people of England is no more than the multitude of natural individuals who happen to inhabit that region (*The Elements of Law*, edited Ferninand Tönnies, 2nd edition, [Frank Cass, London, 1969], Part II, Chapter 2 n. 11, p. 124).

60 In this he was, in my view, being very true to his source Grotius, for whom space is critical to thinking about politics. See Annabel Brett, 'The Space of Politics and the Space of War in Hugo Grotius' *De Iure Belli ac Pacis*', *Global Intellectual History*, vol. 1, no. 1, 2016, pp. 1–23.

61 Hobbes, *Leviathan*, p. 120. Anne Orford highlights these aspects of Hobbes' argument in her critical genealogy of the modern doctrine of 'responsibility to protect', although she also analyses the qualifications that Hobbes introduces to the absolutist dynamic of protection/subjection through the conditionality of obedience and the subjectivity of judgement involved (*International Authority and the Responsibility to Protect*, Cambridge University Press, Cambridge, 2011, Chapter 3).

62 Hobbes, *Leviathan*, p. 153.

63 Malcolm, 'Introduction', p. 66. See also Quentin Skinner, 'Conquest and Consent: Thomas Hobbes and the Engagement Controversy', in his *Visions of Politics*, vol. 3, Cambridge University Press, Cambridge, 2002, pp. 287–307; Kinch Hoekstra, 'The De Facto Turn in Hobbes' Political Philosophy', in Tom Sorell and Luc Foisneau (eds), *Leviathan after 350 Years*, Clarendon Press, Oxford, 2004, pp. 33–73.

64 Hobbes, *The Elements*, Part I, Chapter 14 n. 8, p. 70 [recte 72].

65 Hobbes, *Leviathan*, p. 121, for 'confidence' in the civil state; ibid., p. 87 for 'diffidence' in the state of nature.

66 Hobbes, *The Elements*, Part I, Chapter 14 n. 13, p. 73; *jus protegendi nosmetipsos* in Thomas Hobbes, *De Cive*, edited Howard Warrender, Clarendon Press, Oxford, 1983, Cap. I, n. 14, p. 97.

67 Hobbes, *The Elements*, Part II, Chapter 1 n. 5, p. 110.

68 Hobbes, *De Cive*, Cap. VI n. 3, p. 138.

69 Cf. Hobbes, *Leviathan*, p. 89.

70 Hobbes, *Leviathan*, p. 127, considering what powers the sovereign may grant away 'and yet the Power to protect his Subjects be retained'. Compare Chapter 29, concerning things that weaken a commonwealth, highlighted by Malcolm ('Introduction', p. 31) as possibly relating to negotiations by Charles II at the time when Hobbes was composing *Leviathan*.

71 Hobbes, *Leviathan*, p. 484.

72 It is noticeable that another royalist reply to Parker's *Observations* passed rapidly over the issue of protection onto the safer ground of royal grace: John Bramhall, *The Serpent Salve, or, A Remedie for the Biting of an Aspe*, n.p., 1643, pp. 32–34.

6

Limited Liabilities: The Corporation and the Political Economy of Protection in the British Empire

PHILIP J. STERN

Much of the scholarly concern about the relationship between protection and empire has been focused on the ways in which discourses of protection served to produce subjects and expand both the territorial and extraterritorial claims of empire. This is appropriate. After all, it was the protection of the imperial state that helped produce the concept of Britain for settlers and itinerant imperial figures in the first place. As legal techniques from the extension of the protection of the common law to the protection of maritime shipping passes expanded the ambit of colonial state power, claims upon that protection constituted the legitimacy of its sovereignty. Yet, as the extension of protection included some, it excluded others, especially aboriginal inhabitants, from those very same rights and privileges of imperial subjects, extending the prerogatives of empire as a necessary paternalistic enterprise and producing new institutions and networks.[1] Thus, protection served simultaneously to make an inside and an outside, rendering some people subjects of imperial sovereignty by distinguishing its holders from those outside that protection and normalising them as subjects of that sovereignty, while rendering others as objects of that sovereignty by distinguishing them as those requiring special status and thus outside the status of subject or citizen. The protection of the state, especially the colonial state, in this sense could serve as both a means of assimilation and its alternative.

This concern as to how protection produced empire through inclusion or exclusion is an important one, but it conjures a binary relationship between protector and protected, ruler and ruled, coloniser and colonist. By contrast, this chapter, by placing protection within a political and economic language of pluralism, offers a preliminary examination of some of the ambiguities, tensions and multiplicities born of that dualism, namely the ways in which extra-European expansion and plantation produced, indeed, required, agents that played the role of *protected* and *protector* simultaneously. Protection, in this sense, was a key feature of a colonial sovereignty that was by its very nature layered, hybrid and plural.[2]

One of the most critical of institutions, though hardly the only, in this plural dynamic of empire-building across the early modern and modern periods was the overseas corporation. Corporations relied and capitalised on the protective and protectionist ambitions of the Anglo-British state-in-formation, all the while asserting and exerting their own rights to protect commerce, people, concrete places and abstract jurisdictional space. Thinking about the corporation's history as a protective and protected enterprise highlights the porous boundaries between public and private in the making of the British Empire. It also suggests breaking down other historiographical boundaries as well, between political theory and political economy as well as across the early modern and modern empire, or between mercantilist and free trade forms of empire. Protection, in this sense, can be seen as an enduring feature of imperial ideology, even as who was to protect and who was to be protected evolved over time. In the same spirit, empire, seen through this notion of protection, becomes less a binary between ruled and ruler than a concert, or quite frequently a cacophony, of various claims of sovereignty operating at the same time and in dependent relationship with one another.

THE SOVEREIGN AND THE MERCHANT

Protection of course is at the core of many if not all early modern conceptions of political authority. It was the price a ruler or rulers paid for obedience and obligation. For Hobbes it was the most fundamental nature of sovereignty, perhaps even its essence: 'For by Art is created that great LEVIATHAN called a COMMON-WEALTH, or STATE, (in latine CIVITAS) which is but an Artificiall Man; though of greater statute and strength than the Naturall, for whose protection and defence it was intended.'[3] For Bodin, likewise, the protection of sovereignty, and the liberty such protection provided, is what defined a citizen.[4] To Grotius not only was the commonwealth defined by 'self-protection through mutual aid', but placing oneself under another's protection was so powerful that it rendered the protected 'for the time being a part, as it were' of the protector, and committed to his welfare.[5] As Locke and many others suggested, it was the protection of the state that primarily allowed individuals to preserve and accumulate private property as well as to encourage their industrious labour.[6] For the most robust early modern theorists of resistance, in turn, it was precisely the failure to provide protection that dissolved the bonds of political obligation.[7]

Yet, as Annabel Brett observes in this volume, for many other early modern thinkers the problem of the relationship among obedience, protection and sovereignty was far more nuanced; for Hobbes, protection was not an absolute right of the sovereign but rather was delimited by the function of his responsibility to provide for a state of security that both removed the subject from a state of fear but also allowed for conditions in which arts, science and commerce could flourish. Moreover, such vivid descriptions of the sovereign as an effective protector tended to appear most emphatically on the pens of theorists in moments of crisis – such as civil war, revolution and displacement – when the consequences of the absence of such a stable protective state seemed most vivid. And, of course, there was no shortage of such moments across the seventeenth century. Early modern political thinkers did not necessarily equate the sovereign capacity or responsibility of protection with absolute title or property, a distinction which was particularly apparent in debates over sovereignty of the sea that emerged in the seventeenth century. Oceanic space revealed the limits of the relationship between *imperium* and *dominium*, resisting the ability to make ownership or even perhaps sovereign claims though at the same time representing one of the greatest crises of protection in the early modern world as European commercial and political impulses to expand into the extra-European maritime world demanded, as Philip Steinberg has put it, 'not only for protection against other states, but also against the sea itself'.[8] When claims to sovereignty over sea and land did emerge in the colonial world, they did not, as Lauren Benton has shown, 'cover space evenly but composed a fabric that was full of holes, stitched together out of pieces, a tangle of strings'.[9]

Imperial sovereignty was lumpy, as Benton describes it, not only in the way it was expressed in colonial space but also in the range of agents and institutions doing that expressing, from merchants to missionaries, from crown officials to corporate governors. Much political thought insisted it was the state's responsibility to protect the subject, and one of the key tenets of early modern political economy, was, in theory, the state's responsibility to protect the merchant and create conditions conducive to those profitable enterprises that benefited the sovereign.[10] Such a system has come to be known as mercantilism, which, perhaps not uncoincidentally, is a concept whose meaning is inseparable from modern nineteenth- and twentieth-century policy debates over free trade and neo-mercantilism, that is, *protectionism*.[11] If mercantilism was supposedly at the heart of early modern political economy it was also at the heart of its commercial empire. This has particularly seemed to be the case with the expansion of seventeenth- and eighteenth-century empire, where the proliferation of monopoly, coupled with instruments like the Navigation Acts and institutions like the ever-expanding Royal Navy, produced what Kenneth Morgan has called 'the protectionist mercantile system'.[12]

While it is doubtless true that merchants and colonial projectors sought protection from the monarchs and republics of early modern Europe, for incorporated companies and societies the most critical protection was not necessarily from the world beyond Europe but rather deeply within it, namely, protection from competitors, rivals and interlopers in the form of monopoly. Most chartered forms of incorporation prior to the mid-nineteenth century implied exclusive access or right, whether to a trade or some other form of activity within a particular, abstractly defined jurisdictional space. In early modern England monopolies had a peculiar place in legal discourse: almost universally reviled as illegal, they also represented the apotheosis of the Crown's legitimate protective prerogative. Especially when it came to overseas trade, monopoly was frequently the focus of critics of that prerogative, including and perhaps especially those who insisted they were fighting against the abuse of that power on behalf of the liberty represented by Parliament.[13] The moral and political judgment on monopoly was embodied in its definition in a number of early modern dictionaries simply as 'engrossing' or 'propounding'. The concept has not fared better in retrospect. For any number of economists since Adam Smith, monopoly was the heart of a mercantilism that encouraged any kind of non-productive economic behaviour that modern capitalism ideally did away with.[14]

Yet mercantilism was never simply a unidirectional system, running down a clear hierarchy from the state to the merchant. To the extent it did exist it was less a coherent programme than it was a set of interlocking ideas and practices that impacted discourses and practices of science, commerce and sovereignty alike.[15] Indeed, the defenders of early modern monopolies quite frequently did not defend monopoly per se but rather defended their particular exclusive privileges as exceptions to the rule. Such was the defence mounted by the Merchant Adventurers against their critics in the early seventeenth century, as too was it the substance of the East India Company's defence of its exclusive jurisdiction in the 1680s.[16] Defining monopolies as *unfairly* restricted commerce allowed for the possibility of an exclusive privilege, which was a justifiable restriction on commerce and freedom in the name of protection: protection of people, of goods, even of souls.[17] Exclusive rights implied not just monopoly of trade but of jurisdiction: in other words, a form of sovereignty. This was critical for 'Order and Government', as the early seventeenth-century economic writer Edward Misselden put it,[18] something all the more critical, as many advocates of overseas corporations insisted, in the extra-European, non-Christian world. 'The Standard rule is',

Charles Molloy argued in 1677, 'to know whether the Trade of the Place will bear a Campany [sic], or not'.[19]

Early modern incorporated companies were synonymous with some form of exclusive right or monopoly; 'no society of trading men', Charles Davenant put it towards the end of the seventeenth century, 'can bring about any great thing for the common good, who think themselves but in a precarious and momentary possession of their rights and privileges'.[20] Thus, if a chartered corporation sought the state's protection and was essentially defined by that protection, these rights were, like many early modern political rights, not only rights *to* something but rights *from* something: a charter not only dispensed trading privileges but restricted the Crown, along with its other subjects, from transgressing upon those rights. One could thus see this brand of mercantilist protection less as the state protecting the merchant in exchange for obedience than the merchant contracting for restraint on the part of the state and protection from the whims and vicissitudes of its various different and often uncoordinated agents. Or, to put it another way, sometimes protection came in the form of abdications, delegations, or fragmentations of sovereign power.

In turn much of the business of incorporated companies was to provide protection in the form of expenditures required to maintain armed ships, forts, factories, cities, garrisons and a juridical, diplomatic and governing infrastructure that could promote the common good and punish those who threatened it.[21] Quite often, such companies did the sort of protective work that government could or would not do.[22] Conversely, the protection of exclusive rights freed companies to exert forms of force and violence against those who violated that right, from interlopers, smugglers and pirates to other European and Asian companies and polities.[23]

In other words, a monopoly, or whatever one called it, over some corner of overseas commerce or plantation was a product of protection and produced a protective regime at the same time. This was not simply a spatial or jurisdictional distinction: that is, corporations protected at home became protectors abroad. In the metropole, corporations armed with the protections of corporate status and monopoly in turn exerted protection, jurisdiction and authority over employees and used legal and political systems to discipline transgressors, such as interlopers. Conversely, overseas corporations quite frequently called upon the Crown's protection, in the form, for example, of naval convoys or legal authority, to pursue rivals beyond England's jurisdiction. Moreover, many, from North America to the East Indies, required treaties, agreements, dispensations and offices from regional and local powers that provided some form of protection for exclusive commercial privileges, travel, military partnerships, factories, settlement and fortifications. Such protections were in turn mobilised against both locals and Europeans (again, most notably interlopers) keen on violating what its leadership perceived as its rights and responsibilities to governance.

This elision of political and economic forms of protection should hardly be surprising if one reflects on the conflicted ways in which the concept of monopoly has often been employed in economic thought – generally seen as a form of private advantage – and in political thought – where it is one hallmark of the very concept of public politics. Perhaps the most influential of these monopolies is found in Max Weber's well-known formulation of the state as the '*monopoly of legitimate physical violence* within a particular territory'.[24] The claim to monopolise legitimate violence is, in its converse, a claim to a monopoly on valid forms of protection. What are we to make, then, of early modern overseas corporations that sought monopolies on trade that in themselves implied at least an aspirational monopoly on legitimacy and violence over a particular jurisdiction?

When economic historians and theorists have tried to bridge this gap between our conception of monopoly as a form of private interest and monopoly as a form of public good, they have tended to do so in order to explain how the emergence of a public monopoly over violence more effectively and efficiently allowed private subjects better circumstances for commercial development. Perhaps most notably, Frederic Lane argued that protection itself essentially amounted to a form of economic rent in which the differential costs of controlling violence produced critical comparative advantages for the protected subject as well as the protecting state.[25] For Lane, protection was a commodity. Yet, in such a formulation, one finds the dissonant tones sounded by the recurrent distinction between public and private forms of protective enterprises: one, mercantilist monopoly, somehow regressive, premodern, and counterproductive for capitalist development; the other, the core of the political theory of the modern state and indeed, as Lane argued, a service sold by that state that produced the very conditions necessary for capital accumulation.

This is not the only way to envisage the relationship between economic and political forms of monopoly protection. One could see, for example, the converse process at work: that is, the protection that political authority frequently provides under monopoly conditions as nothing more than selling protection from itself, a process of state formation that, as Charles Tilly has argued in a Weberian vein, might very well be understood less as protection than as a form of protection racket.[26] Conversely, to Niels Steensgaard, protection is not so much a service, mobbed up or otherwise, but a form of entrepreneurship. That is, protection is not the end – the thing being sold, as Lane had imagined – but a means through which risk – in this case, violence – can be converted into a form of revenue. Seen from this perspective, the protector becomes a form of 'monopolist who, in his transactions, has great latitude to set costs and conditions, limited only by the threat (migration, revolution, invasion, and so forth) that subjects would ultimately seek their protection elsewhere'.[27]

Whether a criminal or capitalist enterprise (or both), early modern protection was hardly the preserve of a single form of sovereign agent; such a perspective echoes and exports overseas Brett's reading in this volume of Hobbes and other seventeenth-century theorists, which highlights the centrality of protection as a means of managing security and risk. In short, the modern state's claim to a monopoly on legitimate protection was neither inevitable nor even the most logical historical outcome.[28] Many such alternatives existed, from city-states to seigniorial lords, from the papacy to piracy. Making what is now a familiar point, Steensgaard soliloquised: 'Thieves or customs officers? How big must a band of robbers be in order to call itself an army? How extensive in time and space must the power of a robber chief be before he may be regarded a prince? In the trackless areas in between the organised states it was to the merchant immaterial whether he was a victim of a Sovereign Prince or of a private criminal, the price being determined by whoever happened to be in power.'[29] It is probably not worth belabouring that there was and always has been a fine and legally relative line between legitimate and illegitimate agents of protection, whether that is between the state and organised crime, or, as Augustine famously put it, between a pirate and an emperor.[30]

The point here is not that protection was simply diffused across institutions, including chartered companies, but that the fusion of the public and private functions of protection of those institutions was central to colonial expansion. As Steensgaard argued, it was precisely the ability of the English and Dutch East India Companies to internalise the transaction costs of protection that not only allowed them to outpace their European rivals, especially the Portuguese, but fundamentally to transform the nature, and thus, as Miles Ogborn has observed, the spatial and economic geography of the maritime Indian Ocean trade.[31] The organisational principle of corporations internalising the function of protection had ideological backing from Grotius, among others, whose justification of Dutch East India Company violence against the Portuguese in early seventeenth-century Southeast Asia was founded upon a principle of the right to make alliances with infidels for mutual protection.[32] The Grotian notion of the ocean was that such agreements were not vested in states alone, but that, especially outside the bounds of Christendom, the right to self-preservation implied that any private individual, or the bodies into which they formed themselves, like companies or states, possessed rights of war and reprisal: 'even though people grouped as a whole and people as private individuals do not differ in the natural order, a distinction has arisen from a man-made fiction and from the consent of citizens. The law of nations, however, does not recognise such distinctions; it places public bodies and private companies in the same category'.[33] As such, a company had as much a right of just war in protection of an ally as a monarch or republic, 'since whatever is right for single individuals is likewise right for a number of individuals acting as a group'.[34] This was a conception of sovereignty as divisible and embedded within a pluralistic and overlapping political system, parcelled out among monarchs, republics and corporations alike.[35]

The fact that chartered corporations required protection to provide protection was not simply historical irony; it was the very source of their power. The capacity of the corporation – city, company or colony – to turn its monopoly into a protective enterprise provided support for their continued existence. In other words, the protection of the English state may have been a necessary condition for the emergence of the overseas monopoly corporation, but that corporation's capacity to make claims on the protection of trade and subjects formed a continuing foundation for its protection from the state's continual efforts to rein in those corporate privileges. Conversely, the failures of corporations, apparent or real, to protect, and a claim on the royal protection instead, were quite frequently the justification for rebellions and resistance to corporate rule. It was, for example, the Virginia Company's ostensible failure to protect its subjects and the English monarch's responsibility 'to protect, maintain, and support the same' that was used by the Crown to justify the abrogation of its charter and its dissolution in 1624. Likewise, early patents to corporations like Virginia as well as individual adventurers such as Humphrey Gilbert and Walter Raleigh expressly defined the scope of chartered responsibility as a feature of royal protection; thus, for example, failure to make restitution for wrongs committed against other Europeans would render the patentee 'out of our allegiance and protection, and free for all Princes and others to pursue with hostility'.[36] Yet, as much as charters provided such protection in theory, the actual protection of subjects in the colonial context often fell not to the Crown alone but to various agents, planters, proprietors, governors and corporators, who might or might not have been direct delegates of that sovereignty. Even after the removal of the Virginia Company from power, John Bargrave's outsized plan for reforming the colony under royal authority conceptualised protective authority as falling under a kind of authority that mixed a prefeudal lordship of Alfredian hundreds with the corporate shares of the Somers Isles: 'The first degree [of settler] is the patriot or patrician, they are such as are first named patentees in the particular plantations of colonies, cities, and corporations, thease shall bee such as haveing good estates in England they shall carrie or drawe over with them to the number of 300 men as their parteners and adherences of whom they must be protectors and for whose good abeareing they must bee pledges.'[37]

FROM PROTECTION TO PROTECTORATE

In both practice and theory the obligation for protection was never easily confined to the binary of ruler and ruled, but rather nested protective enterprises within others. One offering protection might very well have required protection as well, a situation that created a spatially diffuse and complex geography for imperial power, particularly as Europeans negotiated the pluralistic conditions of establishing forms of juridical authority in the extra-European world. The tension and ambiguity of this relationship was there at the very beginning. From the *quo warranto* assaults on the Virginia Company to Edmund Burke's critiques of the East India Company a century and a half later, there was a lively argument over whether companies of merchants could or should legitimately exercise the functions of state. As Burke noted in his speech on Fox's India Bill, while the East India Company had certain rights as a chartered corporation, 'no charter of dominion shall stand as a bar in my way to their [i.e., South Asians'] charter of safety and protection'. Conversely, it was not simply the Company's abdication of protection that justified upsetting its established constitution; it was the active harm its protection did: 'The Tartar invasion was mischievous; but it is our [i.e., the Company's] protection that destroys India. It was their enmity, but it is our friendship ... Every rupee of profit made by an Englishman is lost for ever to India'.[38] As a feature of sovereignty, protection was thus a political yardstick against which the legitimacy of those claims to govern could be measured.

If protecting and being protected went hand in hand it should be no surprise that into the nineteenth century debates over the state's protective functions, in the form of the rise of policies and ideologies of free trade, coincided with the ever-intensifying assault on the independent, protective capacities and rights of the colonial corporation, under the banner of reform. The repeated inquiries and interventions into the East India Company's government in India were in this sense inseparable from wider legislative efforts to reform corporations of all stripes, from municipalities to joint-stock companies. Yet, nonetheless, various forms of chartered corporate privilege endured. Joint-stock companies expanded into new economic sectors, while through the 1830s and 1840s critiques of chartered incorporation were met with new experiments, such as the 'quasi-corporation', which would possess patents from the Crown but not official parliamentary incorporation.[39] Companies, including the East India Company, also continued to play a critical role in British politics.[40] Indeed, despite its reputation as an era of free-trade liberalism and, even more so, as free-trade imperialism, the first half of the nineteenth century also conjured a vibrant opposition ideology that maintained the importance of active government involvement in economic life, and in *protection* in particular. David Macpherson, for example, echoed earlier defences of the Company from both the seventeenth and eighteenth centuries when he suggested that the East India Company's commercial sovereignty rendered it analogous to the British commonwealth; such a position also suggested that to upend the Company's monopoly and its territorial power would not only undermine the commercial and revenue value of India but amount to a violation of its charter and property rights and a violent toppling of the very constitution of British India.[41]

Thus, while the East India Company's monopoly and independence was progressively eroded through the first half of the nineteenth century, it did not cease to remain for some an example of an ideal form of colonial governance. When, in the 1820s, James MacQueen proposed a chartered West African company that was self-consciously modelled on the East India Company, he made the very same argument as his predecessors in that company did, namely, that what he called for was not in fact a monopoly but an 'exclusive privilege'.[42] Some years later, the political theorist and East India Company employee John Stuart Mill similarly suggested that bodies like the East India Company served important purposes for a liberal polity attempting to govern distant dependencies. 'It has been the destiny of the government of the East India Company', he opined, 'to suggest the true theory of the government of a semi-barbarous dependency by a civilised country, and after having done this, to perish'.[43]

The endurance of the colonial chartered corporation, supposedly a relic of a bygone mercantilist age, into the mid- and late-nineteenth century is remarkable not least because the very legal mechanism of chartering corporations had supposedly been done away with by a series of acts of parliament, beginning in 1834, in favour of a non-political administrative and registry process. As will be known to anyone with even a passing familiarity of nineteenth-century colonial enterprise in Africa and Asia, chartered incorporated colonial companies did not wither into obsolescence; rather, they resurged with a renewed intensity, no less ambivalent in their conception of protection than their early modern predecessors. However, to this modern context was added a new institutional and juridical category that made that relationship ever more explicit: the protectorate. As Barnaby Crowcroft explains in his chapter in this volume, protectorates were an obscure device converted by nineteenth-century colonialism into a ubiquitous if variable constitutional form. By their very nature protectorates were forms of hybridised sovereignty, theoretically rendering the external protection the responsibility of Europeans but reserving nominal sovereignty internal to the protectorate for the non-European government, though in practice of course such distinctions broke down quite quickly and in a variety of different ways.[44]

This was made even more complex by the fact that a number of protectorates, indeed some of the most notorious, in western and southern Africa, North Borneo and elsewhere, arrived in the form of or under the auspices of chartered colonial companies. As Lord Granville, the Secretary of State for Foreign Affairs, insisted in the parliamentary debate over the charter for the North Borneo Company in 1882: 'As to military protection expected or hoped for by the Company, they have distinctly stated that the Charter would entail no responsibility upon Her Majesty's Government for the protection of the country beyond that which is inseparable from the nationality of those engaged in developing its resources.' Where the Crown claimed dominion, such as Hudson's Bay or New Zealand, there was an implication of military protection, but in places like North Borneo there was, Grenville asserted, 'no dominion ... from which such an obligation can flow'.[45] Under the later North Borneo protectorate agreement the colony was explicitly if ambiguously defined as an independent state, governed by the Company but under Britain's protection.[46] The British South Africa Company similarly led the charge to maintain, and absorb the charges of, the Bechuanaland Protectorate, including the construction of a railway, the maintenance of the security of the frontier (with the South African Republic), and even potentially the missions on Lake Nyasa. As imperial historian Ronald Robinson recognised over a half a century ago, the use of chartered companies to undertake imperial expansion in Africa not only saved the British government the expense but managed to distance the state from the enterprise, assuaging both imperialist and anti-imperialist sentiments in British politics. Yet it also mobilised institutional forces that in many ways exceeded the power of the state. In Robinson's words, 'the expansionist power of private enterprise dwarfed that of an imperialist ministry'.[47]

In the end there was no single idea of what status a protectorate had within the constitution of the late nineteenth-century empire. Protectorates were not colonies: they were monitored and supervised by the Foreign Office, not the

Colonial Office. Yet, they were not clearly *not* colonies, and the process by which they should be acquired and how they should function, especially in times of war, was never worked out clearly. British representatives at the Berlin West Africa Conference of 1884–85 suggested that protectorates implied lesser responsibility for European states than colonies in that they permitted the persistence of forms of indigenous law and sovereignty. In this context the introduction of the neologism of a colonial protectorate, borrowed from French and German examples, and with boundaries defined by international negotiation rather than extant colonial jurisdictions, only made matters all that more confusing.[48]

So, as in centuries prior, protection – the form of protectorates, colonial companies, or both – permitted inclusion within an imperial regime but also a form of exclusion from its fundamental constitution. Companies needed protection to provide protection, and their provision of protection protected them from other claimants and rivals, including the encroachment of the British state itself. Once again, monopoly reared its head as a key category of concern. As the explorer Joseph Thomson, an occasional employee of both the Niger and South African Companies, put it in 1899: 'Much has been said and written against the iniquity of granting charters to private individuals or companies, as being little more nor less than monopolies. The arguments of such critics may hold good in Britain, but in Africa it is not so . . . More than all, a chartered company is enabled to maintain an effective control over the traffic and stop what is deleterious to the natives and harmful to the country, and therefore to the company itself.'[49] That Thomson's arguments reflected the wider ideology of chartered company rule in the late-nineteenth century was not surprising; that such ideology reflected clearly the arguments of the later-seventeenth century is more remarkable.

Thomson's erstwhile employer, George Goldie, was one of the most articulate late-nineteenth-century ideologues of corporate colonial rule, not only in favour of his own African ventures but also other similar efforts, from Cecil Rhodes' British South Africa Company to the North Borneo Company. For all these ventures Goldie argued that companies protected not only imperial subjects but empire itself, and were especially valuable in places too barbaric or uncivilised to be incorporated into British governance.[50] It was a position that did not match easily with either liberal or conservative ideas of protection or, more to the point, it seemed to possess elements of both. As he suggested in 1888, it was a 'radical vice in the system of government' that failed to persuade African natives that a government that protected their commercial and political stability was in their own best interests: 'They yield a ready obedience to those who, like a commercial and industrial company, bring them material prosperity as an equivalent for the surrender of their previous tribal independence.'[51]

In this sense a body like the Royal Niger Company was not only key to profit and efficiency; it was more likely to earn the tacit or explicit consent from the governed by protecting them and encouraging their prosperity. As Sir James Fergusson, the Undersecretary of State for Foreign Affairs, noted in defending the bill for chartering the Niger Company, the Company had engaged in 237 treaties, many granting exclusive rights and privileges to the Company and its predecessors, often in exchange for some form of protection.[52] Defending the Niger Company's interest in extending their jurisdiction to the Oil Rivers district, Goldie similarly argued, 'the council of the company have – incredible as it may seem to *les esprits forts* – a strong and disinterested ambition, as they had when they founded the company, to see these regions, with which they are so closely connected, grow under their auspices from barbarism to civilisation, from anarchy to order, from slavery to freedom, and from universal poverty to a source of wealth both to the natives of the country and to the overcrowded working classes of Great Britain'.[53] Yet critics of this position also circled back themselves to the very same arguments as their predecessors centuries earlier as well. As the *Times* suggested in January 1887, the Company had met 'very serious resistance on the part of the natives ... who decline to recognise the sovereign rights of persons, who[m] they view only as monopolist traders'.[54] As it had been had centuries earlier, the question of whether the protection of private rights was concomitant with, or in contradiction to, public responsibility to protect was central to how one understood the nature of colonial power. This issue arose not only in the divergent understandings of economic and political roles of large colonial companies, but also in relation to myriad forms of smaller, private associations and civil organisations that similarly produced protection critical to the colonial enterprise, whether in enterprises such as the Aborigines' Protection Society, formed in 1837, or conservation groups, such as the Society for the Preservation of the Wild Fauna of the Empire, founded in 1903.[55]

Protection was thus a central feature of the colonial enterprise from the origins of the British Empire in the sixteenth and seventeenth centuries until the era of decolonisation. Yet its history highlights the inherently complex and pluralistic nature of imperial sovereignty itself. From one perspective the very concept of protection lies at the core, from Hobbes to Carl Schmitt, of a political theory of absolute sovereignty. However, when it is examined in practice and from a more global and spatial perspective, protection also underwrites a far more layered, hybrid and fragmented concept of sovereign power, one in which various agents, such as corporations, could enjoy forms of protection that in turn engendered the right and responsibility to protect. Much like categories of ruler and ruled, there was no clear and stable binary between protector and protected. Rather, these were slippery categories that could be occupied simultaneously; protection often involved, as Moses Ochonu points out in this volume, ambiguous and elastic relations among a range of actors and gradations of power. Moreover, who should do the protecting, and be protected, was never a settled matter of imperial ideology. Indeed, the category of protection was a key terrain on which ideas about the nature and constitution of empire was contested. While hardly the only story worth telling about the history of colonial protection, the relationship between colonial corporations and the concept of protection, and the crucial continuum from discourses of commercial monopoly to colonial state formation, suggests at least a picture of the development of empire through institutional forms that resists easy chronological divisions between early modern and modern empires and complicates some of the more enduring distinctions that determine our accounts of the history of empire: inside and outside, public and private, protector and protected.

NOTES

1 Alan Lester and Fae Dussart, 'Trajectories of Protection: Protectorates of Aborigines in Early 19th Century Australia and Aotearoa New Zealand', *New Zealand Geographer*, vol. 64, no. 3, 2008, pp. 205–20; Shaunnagh Dorsett, 'Travelling Laws: Burton and the Draft Act for the Protection and Amelioration of the Aborigines 1838 (NSW)', in Shaunnagh Dorsett and John McLaren (eds), *Legal Histories of the British Empire: Laws, Engagements, and Legacies*, Routledge, Abingdon and New York, 2014, pp. 171–86; Tony Ballantyne, *Entanglements of Empire: Missionaries, Māori, and the Question of the Body*, Duke University Press, Durham, 2014.

2 Lauren Benton and Richard Ross (eds), *Legal Pluralism and Empires, 1500–1850*, New York University Press, New York, 2014.

3 Thomas Hobbes, *Leviathan*, edited Richard Tuck, Cambridge University Press, Cambridge, 1991, p. 9; John Dunn, 'Political Obligation', in his *The History of Political Theory and Other Essays*, Cambridge University Press, Cambridge, 1996, p. 69.

4 Daniel Lee, *Popular Sovereignty in Early Modern Constitutional Thought*, Oxford University Press, Oxford, 2016, p. 173.

5 Hugo Grotius, *Commentary on the Law of Prize and Booty*, edited and introduced by Martina Julia van Ittersum, Liberty Fund, Indianapolis, 2006, pp. 36, 172–73.

6 David Armitage, *Foundations of Modern International Thought*, Cambridge University Press, Cambridge, 2013, pp. 82, 127; Andrew Fitzmaurice, *Sovereignty, Property and Empire 1500–2000*, Cambridge University Press, Cambridge, 2014.

7 Richard J. Ross and Philip J. Stern, 'Reconstructing Early Modern Notions of Legal Pluralism,' in Benton and Ross, pp. 109–42.

8 Philip E. Steinberg, *The Social Construction of the Ocean*, Cambridge University Press, Cambridge, 2001, p. 99.

9 Lauren Benton, *A Search for Sovereignty: Law and Geography in European Empires, 1400–1900*, Cambridge University Press, Cambridge, 2010, p. 2.

10 Lars Herlitz, 'Conceptions of History and Society in Mercantilism, 1650–1730', in Lars Magnusson (ed.), *Mercantilist Economics*, Springer Science+Business Media, New York, 1993, p. 110.

11 Lars Magnusson, *The Political Economy of Mercantilism*, Routledge, New York, 2015, p. 16.

12 Kenneth Morgan, 'Mercantilism and the British Empire, 1688–1815', in Donald Winch and P.K. O'Brien (eds), *The Political Economy of British Historical Experience, 1688–1914*, Oxford University Press, Oxford, 2002, p. 170.

13 David Harris Sacks, 'The Countervailing of Benefits: Monopoly, Liberty, and Benevolence in Elizabethan England', in Dale Hoak (ed.), *Tudor Political Culture*, Cambridge University Press, Cambridge, 1995, pp. 272–91.

14 See, for example, Robert Ekelund and Robert Tollison, *Mercantilism as a Rent-Seeking Society: Economic Regulation in Historical Perspective*, Texas A&M, College Station, TX, 1982, and *Politicized Economies: Monarchy, Monopoly, and Mercantilism*, Texas A&M, College Station, TX, 1997. For a response, see Salim Rashid, 'Mercantilism: A Rent-Seeking Society?', in Magnusson, *Mercantilist Economics*, pp. 125–42. Of course, for later Marxists, following Lenin, it is precisely out of the intensification of capitalist competition – as increasingly competition produces winners and losers, production becomes concentrated in fewer and fewer hands – that monopoly arises as imperialism itself (V.I. Lenin, *Imperialism: The Highest Stage of Capitalism* [1917] in Lenin, *Selected Works*, Publishers, Moscow, 1963, available at Marxists Internet Archive, www.marxists.org/archive/lenin/works/1916/imp-hsc/).

15 Some of these themes of the problems with rigid definitions of mercantilist thought and practice are explored more fully in Philip Stern and Carl Wennerlind (eds), *Mercantilism Reimagined: Political Economy in Early Modern Britain and its Empire*, Oxford University Press, New York, 2014.

16 Stephen D. White, *Sir Edward Coke and the Grievances of the Commonwealth*, Manchester University Press, Manchester, 1979, p. 118; Philip J. Stern, *The Company-State: Corporate Sovereignty and the Early Modern Foundations of the British Empire in India*, Oxford University Press, New York, 2011, p. 48.

17 For a fuller discussion of this theme and the discussion below, see Philip J. Stern, 'Companies: Monopoly, Sovereignty, and the East Indies', in Stern and Wennerlind, pp. 177–95, and Philip J. Stern, 'The Ideology of the Imperial Corporation: "Informal" Empire Revisited', *Political Power and Social Theory*, vol. 29, 2015, pp. 15–43.

18 Edward Misselden, *Free Trade, Or, the Meanes to Make Trade Flourish*, London, 1622, p. 84.

19 Charles Molloy, *De Jure Maritime et Navali, or, A Treatise of Affaires Maritime and of Commerce in Three Books*, London, 1677, p. 434.

20 Charles Davenant, *Discourses on the Publick Revenues, and on the Trade of England. Which More Immediately Treat of the Foreign Traffick of this Kingdom*, vol. 2, London, 1698, pp. 422–23.

21 W.R. Scott, *The Constitution and Finance of English, Scottish and Irish Joint-Stock Companies to 1720*, Cambridge University Press, Cambridge, 1912, vol. 1, pp. 452–53, vol. 2, p. 9.

22 Michael Braddick, 'The English Government, War, Trade, and Settlement, 1625–1688', in Nicholas Canny (ed.), *The Oxford History of the British Empire, Vol. 1: The Origins of Empire*, Oxford University Press, Oxford, 1998, p. 293.

23 I have discussed these issues more fully, especially with regard to the East India Company, in my *The Company-State*, especially Chapter 2.

24 Max Weber, 'Politics as a Vocation' in Weber, *The Vocation Lectures*, edited David Owen and Tracy B. Strong, Hackett, Indianapolis, 2004, p. 33, his emphasis.

25 Frederic Lane, *Profits from Power: Readings in Protection Rent and Violence-Controlling Enterprises*, State University of New York Press, Albany, 1979, pp. 24–25.

26 Charles Tilly, 'War Making and State Making as Organised Crime', in Peter Evans et al. (eds), *Bringing the State Back In*, Cambridge University Press, Cambridge, 1985, pp. 169–91.

27 Niels Steensgaard, *The Asian Trade Revolution of the Seventeenth Century: The East India Companies and the Decline of the Caravan Trade*, University of Chicago Press, Chicago, 1973, p. 18; Vadim Volkov, *Violent Entrepreneurs: The Use of Force in the Making of Russian Capitalism*, Cornell, Ithaca, 2002.

28 Hendrik Spruyt, *The Sovereign State and its Competitors: An Analysis of Systems Change*, Princeton University Press, Princeton, 1994, p. 85.

29 Steensgaard, p. 61.

30 Rev. Marcus Dods (ed.), *The Works of Aurelius Augustine, Bishop of Hippo: Vol. 1, City of God*, T & T Clark, Edinburgh, 1878, p. 140; Anne Perotin-Dumon, 'The Pirate and the Emperor: Power and the Law on the Seas, 1450–1850', in James D. Tracy (ed.), *The Political Economy of Merchant Empires: State Power and World Trade, 1350–1850*, Cambridge University Press, Cambridge, 1991, pp. 196–227.

31 Steensgaard, pp. 114, 412; Miles Ogborn, *Indian Ink: Script and Print in the Making of the English East India Company*, University of Chicago Press, Chicago, 2007, p. 47. See also Douglas North, 'Institutions, Transaction Costs, and the Rise of Merchant Empires', in Tracy, pp. 22–40.

32 Richard Tuck, *The Rights of War and Peace: Political Thought and the International Order From Grotius to Kant*, Cambridge University Press, Cambridge, 2001, p. 94.

33 Grotius, pp. 158–59.

34 Grotius, p. 302; Tuck, p. 85.

35 Eric Wilson, 'The VOC, Corporate Sovereignty and the Republican Sub-Text of De Iure Praedae', in Hans W. Blom (ed.), *Property, Piracy and Punishment: Hugo Grotius on War and Booty in De Iure Praedae – Concepts and Contexts*, Brill, Leiden, 2009, pp. 310–40; Peter Borschberg, *Hugo Grotius, The Portuguese and Free*

Trade in the East Indies, National University of Singapore, Singapore, 2011, pp. 103, 153–62; Renée Jeffery, *Hugo Grotius in International Thought*, Palgrave, Basingstoke, 2006, p. 6.

36 Charles I, *A Proclamation for Settling the Plantation of Virginia*, London, 1625; Ken Macmillan, '"Bound by Our Regal Office": Empire, Sovereignty, and the American Colonies in the Seventeenth Century', in Stephen Foster (ed.), *British North America in the Seventeenth and Eighteenth Centuries*, Oxford University Press, Oxford, 2013, pp. 86–87, 96–97; Elizabeth Mancke, 'Chartered Enterprises and the Evolution of the British Atlantic World', in Elizabeth Mancke and Carole Shammas (eds), *The Creation of the British Atlantic World*, Johns Hopkins University Press, Baltimore, 2005, p. 253.

37 [John Bargrave], 'A forme of Polisie to plante and governe many families in Virginea, soe as it shall naturally depend one the soveraignetye of England', (1623?), reprinted in *American Historical Review*, vol. 19, no. 3, 1914, p. 565; Peter Thompson, 'Aristotle and King Alfred in America', in Peter Onuf and Nicholas Cole (eds), *Thomas Jefferson, the Classical World, and Early America*, University of Virginia, Charlottesville, 2011, pp. 202–03.

38 *The Works of Edmund Burke, Vol. II*, London, 1892, pp. 179, 194.

39 Mark Freeman et al., *Shareholder Democracies? Corporate Governance in Britain and Ireland before 1850*, University of Chicago Press, Chicago, 2012, p. 32.

40 Tim Alborn, *Conceiving Companies: Joint Stock Politics in Victorian England*, Routledge, London and New York, 1998.

41 Anna Gambles, *Protection and Politics: Conservative Economic Discourse, 1815–1852*, The Boydell Press, Woodbridge, Suffolk, 1999, pp. 158–65.

42 James M'Queen, *A Geographical and Commercial View of Northern Central Africa: Containing a Particular Account of the Course and Termination of the Great River Niger in the Atlantic Ocean*, Blackwood, Edinburgh, 1821, pp. 267–68, 269–70; Stern, 'Ideology', pp. 29–30.

43 John Stuart Mill, *Considerations on Representative Government* (1861), in J.M. Robson (ed.), *The Collected Works of John Stuart Mill, Vol. XIX: Essays on Politics and Society*, University of Toronto, Toronto, 1977, pp. 573, 577; Duncan Bell, 'John Stuart Mill on Colonies', *Political Theory*, vol. 38, no. 1, 2010, p. 43; Stern, 'Ideology', p. 31.

44 Antony Anghie, *Imperialism, Sovereignty and the Making of International Law*, Cambridge University Press, Cambridge, 2004, p. 87; more generally, see C.H. Alexandrowicz, *The European-African Confrontation: A Study in Treaty Making*, Sijthoff, Leiden, 1973.

45 *British Parliamentary Debates*, House of Commons, 13 March 1882, series 3, vol. 267, column 716.

46 'North Borneo: Agreement Between Her Majesty's Government and the British North Borneo Company, 12 May 1888', Frederick Madden with David Fieldhouse (eds), *Select Documents on the Constitutional History of the British Empire and Commonwealth, Vol. V: The Dependent Empire and Ireland, 1840–1900*, Greenwood Press, Westport CT, 1991, p. 555.

47 R.E. Robinson, 'Imperial Problems in British Politics, 1880–1895', in E.A. Benians et al. (eds), *The Cambridge History of the British Empire, Vol.* 3, Cambridge University Press, Cambridge, 1959, p. 174.

48 William Roger Louis, *Ends of British Imperialism: The Scramble for Empire, Suez, and Decolonisation*, IB Tauris, London, 2006, p. 114; Fitzmaurice, p. 284.

49 Joseph Thomson, 'Downing Street versus Chartered Companies', *Fortnightly Review*, vol. 52, 1889, p. 182.

50 George Taubman Goldie, 'Britain in Africa', in D.J.M. Muffett (ed.), *Empire Builder Extraordinary: Sir George Goldie: His Philosophy of Government and Empire*, Shearwater Press, Douglas Isle of Man, 1978, p. 287.

51 George Taubman Goldie, 'The Niger Territories', *The Times*, 21 December 1888, p. 14.

52 *British Parliamentary Debates*, House of Commons, 21 March 1887, series 3, vol. 312, column 831, 7 April 1887, series 3, vol. 313, columns 676–77.

53 George Taubman Goldie, 'The Royal Niger Company', *The Times*, 4 January 1889, p. 4.

54 'Disturbances on the Niger', *The Times*, 1 January 1887, p. 10; Stern, 'Ideology', p. 38 note 2.

55 John MacKenzie, *The Empire of Nature: Hunting, Conservation and British Imperialism*, Manchester University Press, Manchester, 1988, p. 201; James Heartfield, *The Aborigines' Protection Society: Humanitarian Imperialism in Australia, New Zealand, Fiji, Canada, South Africa, and the Congo, 1836–1909*, C. Hurst & Co, London, 2011.

7

From Nurturing to Protection in
Nineteenth-Century Japan

DAVID L. HOWELL

Japan became an empire in the nineteenth century. Exactly *when* in the century this imperial transformation occurred is a matter of debate with political as well as academic overtones. Discussions about Japan tend to link sovereignty and empire because threats to Japanese national sovereignty lay behind the impulse to build an empire in the first place. The empire grew as Japan forced sovereign states to cede to it territories like Taiwan and Karafuto (southern Sakhalin) and absorbed the previously sovereign Korea and nominally sovereign Ryukyu kingdom (now Okinawa Prefecture). This chapter focuses on an outlier region – Hokkaido, the northernmost of Japan's main islands – and its indigenous Ainu people. Never sovereign and never under the suzerainty of any state other than Japan, Hokkaido does not fit easily into typical modes of discourse about empire in the Japanese context.

In addition to its discursive links to sovereignty, empire was part of the project of making Japan modern along western lines. It took control of its first colony per se – that is, the first one described as such at the time both within Japan and internationally – only in 1895, with the acquisition of Taiwan from Qing China after the Sino-Japanese War. However, one could reasonably date the birth of the Japanese empire to 1879, when the state completed the process of annexing and absorbing Ryukyu, or 1869, when the nascent Meiji regime asserted full sovereignty over Hokkaido. One could suggest still other dates, some even a bit before the Meiji Restoration of 1868, but in any event discussions of Japan's emergence as an imperial power are almost always framed in terms of its engagement with, and longing for, western-style modernity.

I begin with this question of dating Japan's emergence as an empire because setting a date inevitably doubles as a comment on the place of Okinawa and Hokkaido in the Japanese polity. Relying on the conventional starting point of 1895 implies that Okinawa and Hokkaido have always been Japanese territory, whereas a choice between the other two dates represents a decision to privilege, or not, Ryukyu's lost status as a nominally independent state. Put another way, the choice of 1879 implicitly excludes Hokkaido and its indigenous Ainu inhabitants from a chronology of empire and leaves undetermined, at least at the level of scholarly discourse, the Ainu's status as Japanese or colonial subjects. (In strictly formal, legal terms, the Meiji state classified the Ainu as Japanese for most purposes, though officials in Hokkaido often went out of their way to differentiate Ainu from other subjects; in daily life, ordinary Japanese and Ainu distinguished themselves from one other.)

A few scholars and activists have begun to push back against the tendency to link empire and a longing for western-style modernity in their discussions of Hokkaido and the Ainu. They see Ezo, as the Japanese called Hokkaido before 1869, as a colony of the Tokugawa shogunate and the relationship between Wajin (majority Japanese) and Ainu as one of imperial domination. These writers do not, of course, treat the early modern Japanese empire as equivalent to its self-consciously modern Meiji counterpart, but they do see essential continuity from the shogunate's (and its proxies') domination of the Ainu in the early modern period to the Meiji state's domination of them after 1869.[1]

Looking at the discourses of protection employed by the early modern and modern states provides insight into the changing position of the Ainu while sidestepping the politics that inevitably colour any discussion of the place of indigenous people in modern nation-states. Rather than treat the empire's nature as a settled fact from which all further arguments radiate, let us look for the character of the Japanese empire in the Ainu's relationship with the Japanese state across the divide of 1868 (and 1879 and 1895).

Perhaps this issue is particularly pressing in the Japanese case, where all discussions seem to proceed either from strong a priori assumptions about the identity of the Japanese nation with the Japanese archipelago or, conversely, equally strong a priori assumptions about the essential outsideness of islands like Hokkaido and Okinawa. Scholars literally inscribe such assumptions in research through their choices of ethnonyms and toponyms. My use of 'Wajin' and 'Hokkaido' sends a message from the opening paragraphs of this essay quite different from the one I might have sent by calling majority Japanese by the Ainu term *shamo* or simply Japanese and the island *Ainu moshir* or Ezo.[2] To be sure, ethnonyms and related terms of reference are a point of contestation in many contexts – 'Indians' or 'Native Americans' or 'First Nations'? upper-case 'Indigenous' or lower-case 'indigenous'? – but in the Japanese case it is not unusual to see thoughtful scholars nearly paralysed by the double meaning of 'Japanese' as ethnonym and nationality, for it seems to them that distinguishing between 'Ainu' and 'Japanese' suggests that Ainu in contemporary Japan are not fully 'Japanese' citizens.[3] Reading their work, one might not realise that many other modern nation-states bear the names of their predominant ethnic groups.

Matsumae, the autonomous *daimyo* domain that served as the custodian of relations between Japan and the Ainu during the Tokugawa period (1603–1868), nominally legitimised its domination over the Ainu in terms of its caring for (*kaihō*) them.[4] However, the first systematic attempts to nurture the Ainu as an explicit policy goal began only after Russia emerged as a threat around the end of the eighteenth century and the Tokugawa shogunate assumed direct control over most of Hokkaido. After the Meiji Restoration, the modern state replaced the language of nurturing with a discourse of protection (*hogo*). In the pages that follow, I examine Japanese policies that claimed to nurture and protect the Ainu in the context of the state's attempts to situate itself in a world of nation-states and empires. I will look as well at the Ainu's accommodation of, and resistance to, Japanese policies of nurturing and protection.

Let us begin with the keywords themselves. *Buiku*, which I have rendered here as 'nurturing', is not a word in the everyday vocabularies of Japanese people today. The authoritative Japanese dictionary, *Nihon kokugo daijiten*, defines it as attentive and loving care and cultivation, as that of a parent for a child, with a secondary sense of coddling or spoiling. In the Tokugawa period, officials occasionally used the term to name welfare institutions, in which case it suggested a meaning closer to 'succour', that is, to provide presumably temporary assistance to the weak and vulnerable.[5] Incidentally, the term (pronounced *fuyu* in Chinese) appears often in Qing dynasty (1644–1911) records, but not in connection with policy toward non-Han peoples.[6] *Hogo*, in contrast, is a common word in modern Japanese and 'protection' is a reasonably straightforward translation.

I do not want to put too much weight on policymakers' word choices, especially when the reality of their policies rendered the words euphemisms at best and bitter ironies at worst. Still, it is worth pausing at least briefly to consider them, for they reflect, at the very least, the state's ambitions toward the Ainu. As noted above, *buiku* and *hogo* both refer to the strong taking care of the weak or defenceless, but *buiku* shares with the English 'nurturing' a suggestion of looking toward the future. (The character for *bu* 撫 means to 'pet' or 'stroke', as a cat or a beard, while *iku* 育 means to 'raise' or 'cultivate'.) The term *buiku* thus suggests a future self-sufficiency for the dependent once the requisite period of loving attention is done. *Hogo* is a more static idea: the object of protection need not be animate, much less in the process of growing or developing. Protection could be a temporary or permanent state; the term itself suggests nothing either way.

THE AINU IN EARLY MODERN JAPAN

Unlike the indigenous peoples absorbed into states founded by settler colonists in North America, Australia, New Zealand and elsewhere, the Ainu never lived in a precontact state before encountering the Wajin, or majority Japanese. The Ainu and Wajin share Neolithic ancestors and have been in contact with one another throughout recorded history. Indeed, Ainu culture, at least as defined by archaeologists, emerged out of preceding Neolithic cultures around the thirteenth century as a result of regular ties of trade and exchange with Wajin.[7] Key dates in the Ainu's relations with the Japanese state include Koshamain's Rebellion of 1457, which secured Wajin pre-eminence in southern Hokkaido; 1590, when the Kakizaki (later Matsumae) house submitted to the authority of the Japanese hegemon Toyotomi Hideyoshi and thereby made southernmost Hokkaido securely a part of the emergent early modern polity; and, above all, 1669, when an alliance of regional Ainu chieftains under Shakushain rose unsuccessfully against Matsumae's blocking of their direct access to trading partners in Honshu.

The failure of Shakushain's Rebellion led immediately to the loss of the Ainu's vestigial political and economic autonomy. Their opportunities to trade for Japanese commodities such as rice, cloth, sake, tobacco, lacquerware and ironware were limited to coastal trading stations established under the authority of leading Matsumae retainers. These stations evolved by the early eighteenth century into fisheries contracted to merchants, who used a mixture of Ainu and seasonal Wajin labour to harvest herring, salmon, kelp and other marine products for export to Honshu markets. Generally speaking, the degree of the Ainu's dependency appears to have correlated with proximity to areas of Wajin economic activity: that is, Ainu living near the rich herring fisheries of the Japan Sea coast of western Hokkaido or kelp and salmon fisheries on the Pacific Coast of southeastern Hokkaido relied more on fishery labour than those in remote areas in the far east and north. Nevertheless, by the end of the eighteenth century, few if any Ainu anywhere in Hokkaido remained aloof from the world of the contract fisheries. Even those who did not work at fisheries depended on the commodities that flowed through them.[8]

It is important to note that, even after Shakushain's Rebellion, the Matsumae domain did not rule directly over most of Hokkaido or its Ainu inhabitants.

The domain's home territory in the Oshima peninsula in southernmost Hokkaido was politically and institutionally fully part of Japan, albeit with a few quirks owing to its location. For our purposes, the principal quirk was that the domain legitimised its existence to the shogunate by asserting its status as the sole custodian of trade and other relations between the Ainu and Japan. Shakushain's Rebellion had challenged the domain's monopoly over contact from the Ainu side. To maintain it on the other side, Matsumae followed a policy of separation and dissimilation. It prohibited Wajin fishers from moving permanently beyond the domain's borders in southern Hokkaido and policed the ethnic boundary between Wajin and Ainu by insisting that Ainu not learn Japanese or adopt Japanese clothing, hairstyles or names. No doubt the ethnic boundary was often breached in real life, particularly in the realm of language, but the domain steadfastly maintained the façade of absolute separation.[9]

Dependence on Japanese commodities and the labour required to acquire them had profound and deleterious effects on Ainu culture and society. Diseases like smallpox and measles, endemic in Honshu, decimated the population during epidemics that struck every generation or so. ann-elise lewallen has demonstrated that for women, the constant threat of sexual assault or outright appropriation by Wajin men imperilled families and destabilised Ainu society more generally.[10] Notwithstanding the vulnerability engendered by dependence, however, the Ainu did not experience deculturation during the Tokugawa period. On the contrary, there is plenty of evidence of creative and vital adaptation to the reality of subordination to Wajin and the Japanese state that stood behind them.[11]

As fishery labourers, Ainu workers faced harsh treatment, though this image has been tempered recently by evidence that male workers enjoyed a surprising degree of agency and even authority at some herring fisheries in Hokkaido.[12] Whatever the actual conditions, which no doubt varied, little documentary evidence survives of collective flight or resistance among workers at the well-established fisheries along the Japan Sea coast of Hokkaido.

The only moment of resistance significant enough to draw the shogunate's attention occurred in 1789 at two sites that had only recently been integrated into the contract-fishery system. The incident occurred at fisheries in Menashi, on the Shiretoko Peninsula of Hokkaido, and Kunashiri Island, which lies opposite Menashi across the Nemuro Strait in the southern Kuril Islands. Managers working for Hidaya Kyūbei, an influential merchant who had just taken over the fisheries, began badly by ignoring ritual protocols governing trade, which no doubt cost them the goodwill of the local Ainu community. They then squeezed the Ainu by raising the price of rice and other trade goods while turning a blind eye to the egregious abuse of fishery workers.

The conflict's immediate trigger was the death of an Ainu leader after consuming some rice or sake, which other Ainu attributed to poisoning. According to the standard interpretation of the uprising, this death stoked fears of a mass poisoning and led 130 Ainu workers to attack Wajin at the two fisheries, killing seventy-one of them. Domain officials, with the assistance of influential Ainu chieftains in northeastern Hokkaido, negotiated the rebels' surrender. The domain eventually executed thirty-seven Ainu and, to forestall further resistance, stripped Hidaya of his contracting rights and took measures to alleviate material hardship at fisheries in the area. The Tokugawa shogunate itself stepped in to conduct what it called 'relief' (*osukui*) trade at fisheries in the far northeast of Hokkaido.[13]

Iwasaki Naoko cautions against seeing Kunashiri and Menashi as representative of the abusive working conditions at contract fisheries. Indeed, she expresses scepticism about abuse per se as a cause of the conflict because, at that time, Ainu in far northeastern Hokkaido, in contrast to those further south, were not yet deeply integrated into the Japanese fishing economy and therefore not dependent for their subsistence on labour; presumably, they could have abandoned the fisheries and returned to self-sufficient hunting and gathering if working conditions were truly intolerable. Iwasaki argues that the conflict was, most likely, the result of failed negotiations for compensation (*tsugunai*) after the leader's death rather than the lashing out of people driven to material or physical desperation.[14] Iwasaki's carefully researched critique of the dominant narrative is compelling, especially because she endows her Ainu subjects with a degree of agency missing from other accounts. Yet both the Matsumae domain and the shogunate reacted as if the standard account were correct, that is, that mismanagement and mistreatment caused the uprising rather than deeper issues of Ainu agency and autonomy.

Perhaps the uprising at Kunashiri and Menashi drew the shogunate's attention not so much as a result of its unprecedented violence but rather because of the fisheries' proximity to areas of Russian activity. Russian overtures for trade and diplomacy began in the 1780s and continued regularly, despite adamant Japanese refusals, until the rise of Napoleon drew Russian attention away from the east. The shogunate, hearing reports of Russian beneficence toward the Ainu in Sakhalin and the Kuril Islands, worried that the persistent maltreatment of indigenous workers at contract fisheries would eventually turn the Ainu into an Orthodox Christian fifth column ready to assist in a Russian takeover of the entirety of the Ezochi, that is, all territories inhabited by Ainu, including the Kurils, southern Sakhalin and all but southernmost Hokkaido.

The combination of fear of Russian aggression and a lack of confidence in the Matsumae domain's ability to serve as custodian of relations between

Japan and the Ainu led to a shogunal takeover of Hokkaido, beginning with
eastern Hokkaido in 1799 and expanding to the entire island in 1807 after
a series of Russian attacks on fisheries in northern Hokkaido and Sakhalin.
(Two lieutenants of Nikolai Rezanov, apparently acting on their own, carried
out the attacks in retribution for what they perceived as the injustice of the
shogunate's refusal of Rezanov's requests for diplomacy and trade.) Ruling
through magistrates posted in southern Hokkaido, the shogunate administered
the island until 1821, when the Russian threat seemed to have receded enough
to restore Matsumae to its former position.

Habuto Masayoshi, the magistrate sent to oversee shogunal policy in
Hokkaido until 1807, wrote that 'nurturing' the Ainu was a necessary response
to the Russians' 'devious method' of subjugation, already successful in 'many
lands', in which they eschewed attacks and battles in favour of displays of
'fleeting benevolence' and 'false charity'. The Ainu, resentful of their long
suffering at the hands of the Matsumae domain and its merchant proxies, were
susceptible to these tricks. And since Hokkaido's vast size made it impossible
to defend through military means alone, Habuto argued that the 'the state's
benevolence' simply had to be extended to the Ainu 'by generously nurturing
them'. 'We have no alternative', he insisted, 'but to teach them to join their
hearts as one and resist the foreigners' overtures'. The way to go about nurturing
the Ainu was for the government to take over the trade and thereby ensure that
past misdeeds, such as giving the Ainu spoiled goods or short-changing them in
exchange, were not repeated. The government should also provide Ainu fishers
with nets and other gear and offer them fair returns for their catches.[15]

Shogunal officials described nurturing as the use of trade to win over the
Ainu. In Nagasaki, Habuto pointed out, the shogunate allowed Chinese and
Dutch merchants to trade but had no interest in caring for them. By contrast,
nurturing the Ainu was the entire point of trade in Hokkaido. There was no
need for the exchange to be profitable.[16] An order from the finance magistrate,
which oversaw the shogunate's economic policies, reinforced this point. It
called for the suspension of the usual rules of supply and demand, and asserted
that the losses the shogunate might suffer in trade would actually be cause to
rejoice. The Ainu should be encouraged to harvest as many fish or other trade
goods as possible. The robust rewards they earned would not just discourage
them from falling into indolent habits but would spur them to work hard and
happily, 'thus ensuring the greater prosperity of the Ezochi [Hokkaido] and
fulfilling the fundamental goal of the [shogun's] august nurturing (*gobuiku*)
policy'.[17] Along the same lines, a subsequent order to the Hakodate magistrate
charged officials in Hokkaido with nurturing the Ainu as a way to prevent the
decline of industry in the island.[18]

Habuto and his colleagues in the shogunate's administration of Hokkaido were undoubtedly sincere in their desire to nurture the Ainu through trade and thereby secure Japanese claims to Hokkaido. In practice, however, the policy was short-lived and limited to just a few fisheries in the northeast that the shogunate administered directly. Before long, nurturing the Ainu devolved into the provision of outright grants of goods (*kudasaremono*) to mark import-ant events such as officials' inspection tours, holidays, or ceremonies. In many respects, this represented a return to the ritual relationship that already existed between Ainu leaders and Matsumae domain officials (and the domain's proxies, the contract-fishery operators), with the important exception that the premise of reciprocity had been stripped away in favour of the one-way provision of welfare.

As Kikuchi Isao has argued, this arrangement in practice did nothing to encourage the Ainu's development as self-sufficient actors. Quite the contrary, the shogunate's intervention merely furthered the Ainu's dependence, occur-ring as it did after the erosion of Ainu society's integrity under the influence of the contract-fishing economy.[19] Soon after the shogunate took over the entir-ety of Hokkaido, Habuto was gone, forced out of office on charges of mis-handling the response to the Russian attacks. His successors abandoned all pretence of nurturing the Ainu by endowing them with economic agency. Instead, an order noted that the attackers' decision to spare Ainu and their property demonstrated yet again Russian designs on the native people's hearts and minds. Hence, it continued, it was imperative to nurture Ainu in western Hokkaido 'by granting to them sake, tobacco and other goods and thereby encourage them to submit sincerely' to Japanese control.[20]

The shogunate's attention returned to Hokkaido after the beginning of diplomatic relations with the western powers. In 1855, the southern Hokkaido town of Hakodate opened to foreign shipping as one of Japan's first two treaty ports. The need to secure Hakodate, combined with renewed apprehension over Russian designs on Hokkaido, led the shogunate to resume direct admin-istration over almost the entire island the same year.

Japanese notions of territorial sovereignty differed quite radically from those we accept as commonsensical in the post-Westphalian order of nation-states. Rather than clearly defined national boundaries, early modern Japan had 'ragged edges', as Kären Wigen has put it.[21] The ambivalent status of Hok-kaido, subject to Japan but not fully part of it, reveals this quite clearly. During the last decade and a half of Tokugawa rule, the shogunate began an accom-modation to western rules of sovereignty that its successor regime, the Meiji state, would later complete. Officials in the late Tokugawa period understood western geopolitics surprisingly well and proved quite adept at negotiating with imperialism when the need arose in the middle of the nineteenth century.[22] Somehow, for instance, even in the midst of dealing with numerous 'troubles at home and problems from abroad' (*naiyū gaikan*), the shogunate in 1862 secured an internationally accepted claim to the Ogasawara (Bonin) Islands, despite the fact that none of the archipelago's few dozen inhabitants were Japanese (the men were mostly American whalers and the women Hawaiians or other Polynesians).[23]

In Hokkaido, officials took steps to secure sovereignty in ways that Russians and other westerners would understand, while at the same time fixing the island's place in the polity in terms that made domestic sense as well. Anxiety about sovereignty had informed Japanese policy at the beginning of the nineteenth century, of course. Habuto described nurturing in part as a response to the Russians' success at 'taking possession of some twenty islands' in the Kurils by winning over the Ainu there.[24] The shogunal officials who took charge of eastern Hokkaido in 1799 erected a stele on Etorofu Island in the southern Kurils that claimed it as Japanese territory, a claim that Russia honoured. The shogunate even effectively shared the administration of Sakhalin with Russia – neither country could make a persuasive claim to the island – from 1854 until the Sakhalin-Kuril Exchange of 1875.[25]

The concern about specific encounters between Ainu and Russian traders or naval officers that had animated the nurturing policy during the first shogunal takeover of Hokkaido gave way to more general anxiety over Japanese national sovereignty in the face of the full force of western imperialism. Events like the Opium War and the Indian Mutiny demonstrated that Japanese control of the island could not depend on the goodwill of its Ainu inhabitants.

During the second period of direct shogunal rule, the focus of Japanese policy toward the Ainu shifted from nurturing to assimilation (*kizoku* – literally a 'return' to quotidian 'customs', a term usually used to refer to Buddhist monks and priests who had returned to lay life). A memorandum affirming the continuation of material aid stated that Ainu would henceforth be free to speak Japanese if they wished and that Ainu children should be encouraged to learn the language.[26] In the months that followed, the shogunate reversed the Matsumae domain's other explicit policies of dissimilation in favour of a new set of measures that pushed Ainu men, and the community leaders among them in particular, to assume new identities as Japanese commoners.[27] They did this by providing material incentives in the form of grants of rice, sake and other commodities to those who took on the outward characteristics of Japanese peasant villagers: Japanese-style names, dutifully logged into a village population registry; clean-shaven faces; hair worn in a topknot with the pate shaven; and kimono folded to the right. When positive incentives did not work, officials apparently pressured Ainu to comply, but they seem to have avoided outright physical coercion. In 1856, shogunal authorities stopped calling the Ainu 'Ezo' ('barbarians') and instead referred to them officially as *dojin*, or 'natives', a term that eventually took on the same pejorative overtones of the English word, but at the time simply meant the native people of any locale.[28]

The assimilation policy, with its focus on outward 'customs' (*fūzoku*), did not really aim at changing anyone's ethnic identity, at least not in the way that concept is generally understood in the contemporary world. Rather, the point was symbolically to incorporate Hokkaido into Japan by endowing its Ainu inhabitants with the makers of civilisation. Made into commoners in the Tokugawa social-status order, the Ainu would no longer be alien 'barbarians' (Ezo) but the direct beneficiaries of the shogun's benevolent rule (*jinsei*). A concrete expression of the idea of benevolent rule was the vaccination of Ainu against smallpox at many of the same fisheries that had seen efforts at assimilation.[29] Whether Ainu themselves understood either assimilation efforts or vaccinations as benevolence – all evidence suggests they did not – is almost beside the point. They were the object of these policies, but not their real audience, which lay in Japan and, to some extent, Russia.

Before moving on to a discussion of Meiji protection policies, let us briefly take stock of the early modern Japanese state's engagement with the Ainu, particularly as it pertains to a consideration of the imperial character of the Tokugawa state. The Matsumae domain, acting as custodian of Japanese-Ainu relations, formally pursued policies of dissimilation while encouraging, through trade, ritual and labour, Ainu dependence on Japanese commodities. Hokkaido (other than the Wajin homeland in the far south) was considered to be outside the boundaries of the Japanese state, yet tied to it through Matsumae's relations with the Ainu. This was a form of indirect imperial control along lines not unfamiliar elsewhere in East Asia, particularly if one sees it, as Matsumae did, as an essentially tributary relationship. The Ainu themselves expressed their ties to Japan as those of free agents pursuing trade, even though they surely understood that material dependence, backed by violence or the threat of it, undermined their freedom of action in actual practice. Although their options were limited, as individuals they deployed various 'weapons of the weak', including flight; in at least one case, in Sakhalin in 1862, this took the form of an appeal to Russian protection. The Russians indeed protected the man, Tokonbe, saying that since the Ainu had no 'king' they were free to work for the Japanese or Russians as they pleased, just as they were free to accept nurturing from either side as they chose.[30]

The notion that Hokkaido lay beyond Japan's borders obtained even during the first period of direct shogunal administration in Hokkaido. Direct administration meant government operation of some fisheries and official oversight over the others, but except for a small number of nominally assimilated Ainu in Etorofu – the border island in the southern Kurils – the authorities never assumed direct rule over Ainu communities.[31] Nurturing policies rested on the fiction that the Ainu were free agents who, with the proper support and encouragement, could be persuaded to cast their lot with Japan rather than Russia. Advantageous trade arrangements and even the outright granting of goods as gifts served imperial purposes, both deepening Ainu dependence on Japan and helping to secure Japanese claims to Hokkaido in the face of Russian encroachment, but they did not alter pre-existing institutional structures of Ainu control.

The assimilation efforts of the second period of direct rule touched only a minority of Ainu, and even they were affected only fleetingly. Yet they are significant in their assertion of a mechanism by which Ainu could lose their erstwhile 'barbarian' status and become full-fledged Japanese commoners, and their homeland, presumably, an integral part of Japan. (The shogunate never formally absorbed Hokkaido into its core territories, but it did take an important first step by allowing year-round Wajin residence, beginning in 1855.) These policies certainly represent an imperial expansion of the Japanese state into the Ainu homeland. However, their central ambition to erase formally the distinction between Ainu and other Japanese subjects through the manipulation of mostly somatic markers of male identity sets the early modern empire as decisively apart from its modern counterpart.

THE AINU IN MEIJI JAPAN

With the collapse of the Tokugawa shogunate in 1868, the succeeding Meiji regime immediately assumed control over Hokkaido. The announcement to the Ainu of the 'restoration of monarchical rule' (*ōsei fukko*) began with an explanation of the emperor's divine ancestry and superiority over the samurai who had hitherto administered Hokkaido. It followed an expression of regret for the failures of past policies to nurture them with a list of modest quantities of rice, tobacco and sake to be granted to every Ainu woman, man and child.[32]

Although the Meiji state is known for its aggressive engagement with western-style modernity, in fact it came into power with a promise to restore Japan to the institutions of the ancient past, including imperial rule. Two of its earliest policies in Hokkaido – renaming the island from Ezo to Hokkaidō (literally, 'northern sea circuit') and dividing it and the Kurils (but not

Sakhalin) into eleven provinces – had the symbolic effect not only of incorporating Hokkaido fully into Japan but to suggest it had *always* been part of Japan because circuits and provinces dated to the seventh century. The gesture was purely symbolic, too, since neither had functioned as administrative units for centuries and would not do so, even nominally, in the Meiji era.

Thus, in a formal, institutional sense, the nascent Meiji regime declared as clearly as it could that Hokkaido was not an external colony of Japan but an integral part of it. This holds even though the state's actual administration of the island highlighted its differences from the rest of the archipelago. The Development Agency (Kaitakushi), which governed Hokkaido from 1869 to 1882, was charged with building infrastructure, developing industry and encouraging agricultural immigration to the island in the hope of exploiting the productive potential of its interior. Insofar as Meiji Hokkaido became a settler colony, the tendency of some writers to see its development as the beginning of Japan's modern empire is neither surprising nor unreasonable.[33]

In the early years of Meiji, the state devoted little attention to Ainu affairs per se.[34] Indeed, it is safe to say that the government had no systematic Ainu policy at all. Most Ainu continued their lives as seasonal fishery labourers, eligible for the first few years of Meiji to receive goods under pre-existing nurturing policies, but otherwise generally ignored. Between 1871 and 1876, the Development Agency prohibited a number of Ainu customs, including the tattooing of women's faces and hands, the burning of houses after the death of a family member and various traditional hunting methods. Many Anglophone scholars – particularly those more concerned with exposing the Meiji state's many sins than engaging with Ainu history per se – make much of these prohibitions, incorrectly assuming that the Development Agency tried systematically to enforce them.[35] These were all core practices, so if the prohibitions had been enforced the violence to Ainu culture would have been incalculable. Even as statements of state aspirations they are significant. However, it is also important to note that the prohibitions coincided with, and indeed ought to be seen as a continuation of, government-sponsored campaigns throughout the archipelago against 'backward' and 'barbarous' customs, including ubiquitous popular religious practices like dancing during the annual summer *bon* festival to honour the spirits of dead ancestors.[36]

In the late 1870s and early 1880s the Meiji state finally turned its attention to the Ainu. The overriding goal of its policy was to make the Ainu into ordinary Japanese subjects. In an early memorandum along these lines, a Development Agency official argued in 1875 that the only way to 'enlighten' (*kyōka*) the Ainu and get them to abandon of their own volition their 'evil customs' (*heishū*) was to treat them the same as Wajin, albeit with some provisions to shield them from employers' mistreatment.[37] Assimilation – now *dōka* ('to make the same', a neologism coined in 1872) rather than *kizoku* – was certainly the ideal, but so far as I can tell it was never stated explicitly as such. In practice, officials worked to render the Ainu as nearly invisible as a distinct population as possible. Ainu were not supposed to be distinguished from other subjects in household registrations or other official documents, but when it was necessary to single Ainu out the state mandated the use of the neologism *kyūdojin*, or 'former aborigine'.[38]

Nomenclature aside, the keystone of Ainu policy was the encouragement of agriculture, which officials assumed to be essential to the Ainu's prospects for stable livelihoods. This assumption reflected their deep suspicion of hunting and fishing as occupations, whether practised independently or for wages at commercial fisheries. Imagining Japan as a nation of farmers, they sought to have the Ainu blend into that nation as farmers themselves. Thus, the early 1880s saw a number of schemes to assign Ainu in various localities with land and tools to make a go at agriculture. They all failed, most almost as soon as they were launched. The most ambitious among them was Nemuro Prefecture's plan to assign every one of the 825 Ainu households in its jurisdiction a plot of land. The plan was doomed from the start. Even aside from the Ainu's lack of experience or interest in farming, the prefecture assigned each household ridiculously small plots of just 1.2 to 2.5 acres each, on which they were to grow potatoes, *daikon* radishes and other hardy crops suited to the region's short summers and long, bitterly cold winters. The novice cultivators were to receive training and material assistance (such as grants of seed and loans of tools) during their first season, but by the second year they were to be completely self-sufficient. Of course no one succeeded.[39]

Despite their lack of success, policies like Nemuro's became the model for the Meiji state's most thorough effort to protect the Ainu. The Hokkaido Former Aborigine Protection Act (*Hokkaidō kyūdojin hogohō*) was enacted by the Japanese Diet in 1899 and remained in force in amended form until 1997. Under the law, Ainu households were eligible to receive grants of up to about 12.25 acres of agricultural land, subject to various restrictions. The law was an ill-conceived and ill-fated effort to turn the Ainu into small farmers and thereby protect them from their inclinations to follow unsettled or unstable livelihoods. By becoming farmers, the Ainu could over time blend into Japanese society and in that way make Hokkaido fully part of Japan once and for all. In practice, very few Ainu established themselves as independent farmers under the protection law. Many, perhaps most, recipients of land grants eventually lost their small holdings to Wajin, despite elaborate provisions to prevent that from happening.[40]

In addition to its centrepiece goal of turning the Ainu into farmers, the protection law included provisions to support Ainu education and hygiene; these measures assaulted the integrity of Ainu culture in the name of humanitarianism. As Ogawa Masahito notes, the law's immediate intellectual roots lay in a discourse on the 'Ainu problem' in the 1890s, in which doctors, officials and journalists lamented what they saw as the Ainu's unsettled livelihoods, poor health and inability to make their way in a Hokkaido that was changing rapidly in response to a dramatic influx of immigrants from the Japanese mainland.[41]

Hokkaido Ainu could generally avoid the state's efforts to protect them with inadequate grants of marginal farmland by remaining in the fishing economy or seeking other work as wage labourers. Much more tragic was the fate of two groups of Ainu, one a party from Sakhalin relocated to central Hokkaido after the Sakhalin-Kuril Exchange in 1875, the other a group from the far northern end of the Kuril Island chain, who were moved in 1884 to Shikotan, one of the southernmost Kurils.[42] The Sakhalin Ainu had experience with the Japanese commercial fishing economy, and over time many disappeared into the fisheries of Hokkaido. The officials who moved them to Hokkaido, however, tried to get them to take up farming in the vicinity of Sapporo. As was the case elsewhere, that scheme failed utterly, but not before cholera and smallpox epidemics had cut the Ainu population by about half. The ninety-odd Kuril Ainu were sea-mammal hunters, not farmers or even fishers, but when they were forcibly moved to Shikotan in 1884 they had no choice but to rely on fishing and small-scale agriculture because the sea-otters and pinnipeds on which they had previously relied did not live in local waters. Even fishing was difficult, and in the end the Kuril Ainu were virtually wards of the state, dependent on grants of food to survive.

The keyword of Japanese policy toward the Ainu in the Meiji era was protection. The word appears most prominently in the title of the Hokkaido Former Aborigine Protection Act of 1899 and the proposals that preceded it. Its other major use came in the mid-1890s, when the government set aside tracts of 'protected lands' (*hogochi*), nominally (in practice only imperfectly) reserved for Ainu squeezed out of their homelands by mass immigration from the mainland. Despite the ubiquity of 'protection' in the titles of these measures, the term appears only incidentally, if at all, in their texts.[43] That is, policymakers took for granted the protective function of agriculture, education and hygiene.

In the Hokkaido prefectural archives, the oldest references to 'protection' refer not to Ainu subjects but to groups of disfranchised samurai who immigrated as agricultural settlers despite lacking experience in farming.[44] The only documents regarding the Ainu that routinely invoke 'protection' relate, in fact, to the first stages of the scheme that would eventually result in the relocation of the northern Kuril Ainu to Shikotan. The official who drafted most of the documents, Orita Heinai, emphasised the need to 'protect' the islanders so that they would not 'regret' their decision to relocate, and argued that 'only by absorbing the beneficent influence (*kunka o itadaki*) of this country' would the Ainu come to 'accept Japan's protection'.[45]

Note that even when the Japanese state pushed Ainu to relocate to farm-land, there was never any thought given to establishing Ainu 'reservations' along the lines of those created in the United States. This was not for a want of knowledge. The Development Agency hired a number of prominent Ameri-can educators and officials, including even a former Secretary of Agriculture, Horace Capron, to advise the government on developing Hokkaido's agricul-tural and mineral resources. However, the idea of segregating the Ainu into reservations would not have made sense to Japanese officials, for it would have committed the state to a policy that acknowledged essential and permanent difference between the Ainu and other Japanese subjects. It might even have required a recognition of the Ainu as a sovereign people, if only nominally. In that event, 'protection' would have suggested a desire to shield the Ainu from the effects of a rapidly modernising economy, when in fact the state sought only to protect them from their own culture.

NOTES

1 The most thoughtful proponent of this position is ann-elise lewallen. See her *The Fabric of Indigeneity: Contemporary Ainu Identity and Gender in Colonial Japan*, School for Advanced Research Press, Santa Fe, NM, 2016.

2 By using 'Wajin' and 'Hokkaido', I follow the predominant academic practice in Japan, which includes Hokkaido and the Ainu within 'Japan', though not without some consciousness of the violence this does to an autonomous 'Ainu history'. Most Anglophone scholars prefer 'Ezo' to refer to the island before 1869, even though (among other problems) it does not, strictly speaking, refer solely to the island of Hokkaido. *Shamo* has a vaguely derogatory nuance, not unlike the term *haole*, used to refer to Caucasians in Hawai'i; like 'Ezo', '*Ainu moshir*', 'the land of humans', does not refer only to Hokkaido, but rather includes places like southern Sakhalin and the Kuril Islands, which once had Ainu populations.

3 Sasaki Toshikazu, 'Ainushi wa seiritsu suru darō ka', in Hokkaidō-Tōhoku Shi Kenkyūkai (ed.), *Kita kara no Nihonshi*, Sanseidō, Tokyo, 1988; Ogawa Masato, *Kindai Ainu kyōiku seidoshi kenkyū*, Hokkaidō Daigaku Tosho Kankōkai, Sapporo, 1997, pp. 4–5 note 1.

4 Takakura Shinichirō, 'The Ainu of Northern Japan: A Study in Conquest and Acculturation', translated and annotated by John A. Harrison, *Transactions of the American Philosophical Society*, new series, vol. 50, no. 4, 1960, pp. 27–28. This work is a partial translation of Takakura Shin'ichirō, *Ainu seisakushi*, Nihon Hyōronsha, Tokyo, 1943. The term *kaihō* is very close in meaning to *buiku* (discussed below) and was used throughout the Tokugawa period.

5 The Chōshū domain's 'assistance bureau' (*buikukata*), established in 1762, served as a general fund for extraordinary expenditures, including the provision of emergency grain during famines, but it also lent funds for economic development schemes, including agricultural land development. In 1836, the Nakatsu domain in Kyushu set up an 'assistance exchange' (*buiku kaisho*) to assist samurai retainers and townspeople in distress. See *Kokushi daijiten*, svv. 'Buikukata' and 'Buiku kaisho'.

6 Mark Elliott, personal communication, 29 September 2016.

7 Archaeologists trace Ainu culture to an amalgam of Satsumon culture, which thrived in northernmost Honshu and Hokkaido from the eighth until the thirteenth centuries, with elements of Okhotsk culture, which flourished in Sakhalin, the Kuril Islands and northern Hokkaido from the third to thirteenth centuries. Aside from the incorporation of Okhotsk elements into it, the key marker of the transition is that the bearers of Satsumon culture entirely abandoned pottery-making, presumably because they enjoyed ready access to ironware and pottery received in trade with Wajin. In English, see Mark J. Hudson, *Ruins of Identity: Ethnogenesis in the Japanese Islands*, University of Hawai'i Press, Honolulu, 1999. In Japanese, perhaps the strongest statement of the Ainu's long history of interaction with Wajin is Segawa Takurō, *Ainugaku nyūmon*, Kōdansha, Tokyo, 2015.

8 On the fishing economy, see David L. Howell, *Capitalism from Within: Economy, Society, and the State in a Japanese Fishery*, University of California Press, Berkeley, 1995. On the Ainu's economic dependence on Wajin more generally, see David L. Howell, *Geographies of Identity in Nineteenth-Century Japan*, University of California Press, Berkeley, 2005, pp. 110–30. Brett L. Walker, *The Conquest of Ainu Lands: Ecology and Culture in Japanese Expansion, 1500–1800*, University of California Press, Berkeley, 2001, examines both Ainu agency in trade and their subjugation to Wajin dominance, mostly outside of the context of the fishing economy.

9 See David L. Howell, 'Ainu Ethnicity and the Boundaries of the Early Modern Japanese State', *Past and Present*, no. 142, 1994, pp. 69–93.

10 See ann-elise lewallen, '"Intimate Frontiers": Disciplining Ethnicity and Ainu Women's Sexual Subjectivity in Imperial Ezo', in Christopher P. Hanscom and Dennis Washburn (eds), *The Affect of Difference: Representations of Race in East Asian Empire*, University of Hawai'i Press, Honolulu, 2016, pp. 19–37; Brett L. Walker, 'The Early Modern Japanese State and Ainu Vaccinations: Redefining the Body Politic 1799–1868', *Past and Present*, no. 163, 1999, pp. 121–60.

11 For examples of Ainu cultural vitality, see Howell, 'Ainu Ethnicity'; Utagawa Hiroshi, *Iomante no kōkogaku*, Tokyo Daigaku Shuppankai, Tokyo, 1989; Sasaki Toshikazu, 'Iomante-kō: Shamo ni yoru Ainu bunka rikai no kōsatsu', *Rekishigaku kenkyū*, no. 613, 1990, pp. 111–20. On deculturation, see James F. Eder, *On the Road to Tribal Extinction: Depopulation, Deculturation, and Adaptive Well-Being among the Batak of the Philippines*, University of California Press, Berkeley, 1987.

12 Tajima Yoshiya, *Kinsei Hokkaidō gyogyō to kaisanbutsu ryūtsū*, Seibundō, Osaka, 2014, pp. 336–60.

13 The most detailed account of the Kunashiri-Menashi Rebellion in English is Takakura, pp. 44–47.

14 Iwasaki Naoko, *Nihon kinsei no Ainu shakai*, Azekura Shobō, Tokyo, 1998, pp. 169–201. Kikuchi Isao, *Ainu minzoku to Nihonjin: Higashi Ajia no naka no Ezochi*, Asahi Shinbunsha, Tokyo, 1994, p. 126, notes as well that far northeastern Hokkaido was brought under Matsumae's control only after Shakushain's Rebellion and was thus relatively autonomous at the time of the contract fisheries' creation.

15 Habuto Masayoshi, 'Kyūmei kōki' (1807), in Kokusho Kankōkai (ed.), *Zokuzoku gunsho ruijū*, 16 vols., Kokusho Kankōkai, Tokyo, 1912; repr. *Zoku gunsho ruijū* Kanseikai, Tokyo, 1978, vol. 4, p. 504.

16 Ibid., p. 562.

17 Ibid., p. 571.

18 Ibid., p. 587.

19 Kikuchi Isao, *Hoppōshi no naka no kinsei Nihon*, Azekura Shobō, Tokyo, 1991, p. 111.

20 Habuto, p. 639.

21 Kären Wigen, *A Malleable Map: Geographies of Restoration in Central Japan, 1600–1912*, University of California Press, Berkeley, 2010, p. 122.

22 Michael Auslin, *Negotiating with Imperialism: The Unequal Treaties and the Culture of Japanese Diplomacy*, Harvard University Press, Cambridge, MA, 2004.

23 David Chapman, *The Bonin Islanders 1830 to the Present: Narrating Japanese Nationality*, Lexington Books, Lanham, MD, 2016.

24 Habuto, p. 504.

25 See John J. Stephan, *Sakhalin: A History*, Clarendon Press, Oxford, 1971.

26 'Tōzai shimajima jikishihai ni tsuki dojin buikukata, wago shiyō sono hoka mōshiwatashi no ken', 1856/6, item 11 in 'Kitaezochi goyōdome', *bosho* 10, Archives of Hokkaido (hereafter AH), Sapporo.

27 Howell, *Geographies of Identity*, pp. 142–48.

28 Kikuchi Isao, *Bakuhan taisei to Ezochi*, Yūzankaku, Tokyo, 1984, pp. 158–60.

29 Walker, 'The Early Modern Japanese State'.

30 James C. Scott, *Weapons of the Weak: Everyday Forms of Peasant Resistance*, Yale University Press, New Haven, CT, 1985; Kikuchi, *Hoppōshi no naka*, pp. 294–95.

The Tokonbe case occurred during the period of the Russo-Japanese condominium in Sakhalin and the Matsumae domain had no authority over him or the Japanese fishery at which he worked, but production at the fishery occurred under conditions very similar to those that had prevailed at contract fisheries established in Hokkaido and southern Sakhalin under Matsumae's auspices.

31 On Etorofu, see Kikuchi Isao, *Etorofu-tō*, Yoshikawa Kōbunkan, Tokyo, 1999.

32 The Archives of Hokkaido includes several versions of the announcement, among them 'Ōsei fukko ni yoru tennō shihai tō fukoku no ken', ca. 1868/8, item 1 in 'Kisoku kakidome', A4/330, AH.

33 The classic English-language study of Hokkaido history, John A. Harrison, *Japan's Northern Frontier: A Preliminary Study in Colonization and Expansion, With Special Reference to the Relations of Japan and Russia*, University of Florida Press, Gainesville, 1953, takes this approach, as its sub-title suggests. For more recent scholarship, see Michele M. Mason, *Dominant Narratives of Colonial Hokkaido and Imperial Japan: Envisioning the Periphery and the Modern Nation-State*, Palgrave Macmillan, New York, 2012, and the essays collected in Michele M. Mason and Helen J.S. Lee (eds), *Reading Colonial Japan: Text, Context, and Critique*, Stanford University Press, Stanford, CA, 2012, which treat Hokkaido and Okinawa, along with continental imperial acquisitions, as 'colonial Japan'.

34 The following account of Ainu policies in the Meiji period is drawn from Howell, *Geographies of Identity*, pp. 172–85.

35 Komori Yōichi, 'Rule in the Name of "Protection": The Vocabulary of Colonialism', translated by Michele M. Mason, in Mason and Lee, p. 66; Katsuya Hirano, 'Thanatopolitics in the Making of Japan's Hokkaido: Settler Colonialism and Primitive Accumulation', *Critical Historical Studies*, vol. 2, no. 2, 2015, p. 211.

36 See Oku Takenori, *Bunmei kaika to minshū: Nihon kindai seishinshi danshō*, Shinhyōron, Tokyo, 1993, pp. 23–25, for examples.

37 'Hokkaidō dojin kyōka, buiku no ken', 18 May 1875, item 37 in 'Kaitakushi kōbunroku (Honchō), bosho 5815, AH.

38 Kaitakushi notice (*tasshi*) no. 20, 4 November 1878, in Kōno Motomichi (ed.), *Tai-Ainu seisaku hōki ruishū*, Hokkaidō Shuppan Kikaku Sentā, Sapporo, 1976, p. 49.

39 The key documents related to Nemuro Prefecture's scheme have been reprinted in Ogawa Masahito and Yamada Shin'ichi (eds), *Ainu kindai no kiroku*, Sōfūkan, Tokyo, 1998, pp. 433–37.

40 For a discussion of the law and its aftermath, see David L. Howell, 'Making "Useful Citizens" of Ainu Subjects in Early Twentieth-Century Japan', *Journal of Asian Studies* vol. 63, no. 1, 2004, pp. 5–29.

41 Ogawa, pp. 99–108. Major examples of this literature include Dohi Katsumi, *Ainu mondai*, n.p., 1895, and Sekiba Fujihiko, *Ainu ijidan*, Sekiba Fujihiko, Sapporo, 1896.

42 For a fuller account, see Howell, *Geographies of Identity*, pp. 186–93.

43 Kōno, pp. 113–26, reprints the texts of various proposed and amended versions of the protection law and, p. 226, the text of an 1894 prefectural law establishing 'protected lands' in the Chitose area.

44 See, for example, Kitagaki to Hiromoto, 15 July 1873, item 6 in 'Meiji rokunen burui shōroku', A4/425, AH, regarding samurai from the Inada domain on Awaji Island.

45 'Shumushu-tō dojin Uruppu-tō e tenseki no ken', 30 October 1878, item 82 in 'Chōkan ukagairoku', *bosho* 2567, AH.

PART IV

Protection and Colonial Governance

8

Protection Claims: The British, Maori and the Islands of New Zealand, 1800–40

BAIN ATTWOOD

In the decades prior to the British government's annexation of New Zealand in 1840 protection was the keyword in discussion about the islands, as claims for or of protection were made by a range of players, including missionaries, traders, settlers, colonisation companies, government officials and Maori themselves. For those familiar with protection's long history this will come as no surprise. Yet few historians of New Zealand have noticed both the ubiquity of protection talk and the fact that it comprised multiple, sometimes contradictory, strands. Instead they have argued that a single discourse of protection, which they have called humanitarian, was at work and that its influence was confined to the mid- to late 1830s.[1] This chapter suggests instead that over a longer period of time several players made good use of various notions of protection and that protection consequently performed several vital tasks.

Grappling with the history of protection talk in regard to the islands of New Zealand is important for several reasons. In the most general sense it reveals the various possibilities that were contained within protection talk and thus the different permutations that protection can take; it also shows that the uses to which British government put the notion were in keeping with the broad changes that took place in the early to mid-nineteenth century, whereby protection shifted from being a term compatible with interpolity relationships of alliance to one that connoted imperial lordship over subjects. More particularly, it demonstrates that the influence of the so-called humanitarian discourse of protection pales in comparison with that of a very different strand of protection talk which the British government had long deployed in order to deal with jurisdictional politics. Finally, it enables us to recover the fact that protection talk was central to the famous Treaty of Waitangi of 1840, which has often been regarded, and especially in recent decades, as the means by and upon which the nation was founded, and so to understand better its role and place in the making of this agreement.

The story I tell has this basic trajectory. In 1817 the British government disavowed its claim to sovereignty in the islands of New Zealand but at the same time upheld a claim of possession by projecting an image of itself as the protector of Maori. In seeking to lend authority to this ambiguous stance British agents began to treat Maori as though they were sovereign; this generated over the following two decades a relationship with Maori whereby they were constituted as something like an ally. At the same time the imperial government repelled demands from various quarters that it provide protection to both Maori and British subjects in the islands by continuing to maintain that it had to respect that fact the islands were not within the dominion of the British Crown. In the late-1830s the government fended off demands that it annex the islands by asserting that the islands actually fell under the sovereignty of Maori. Finally, in deciding to assume sovereignty the government adopted a form of protection talk which was a hybrid of the notions of protection that it had long found useful and the 'humanitarian' notions of protection that had recently advanced by evangelical philanthropists and colonisation companies; this resulted in a sudden but by no means complete shift from a notion of protection that had cast Maori as more or less sovereign and treated them as an ally of the British Crown to a notion of protection that portrayed Maori as a people who should cede that sovereignty so that they could become the subjects of the Crown and enjoy the rights and privileges of British subjects.

PROTECTION AND ALLIES

In the wake of the British government forming penal settlements in New South Wales and on Norfolk Island in 1788 a growing number of Europeans were attracted by seals, whales, flax, timber, food and water in the islands of New Zealand some 2000 kilometres away. As this economic penetration grew and contact with Maori increased, churchmen, traders and colonial administrators began to call on the British government to intervene. They mostly couched their requests in the language of protection. In one sense this is hardly surprising. While a British agent, James Cook, had claimed sovereignty in some of the islands of New Zealand on behalf of the British Crown in 1769–70, the British government had never made good that claim by authorising the occupation of any part of the islands and so the territory was deemed to be both inside and outside the imperial legal order. Rather than being exceptional, this brought New Zealand into line with other imperial situations where protection talk was often deployed.[2]

The first calls for protection were made in 1808 by the principal Anglican chaplain of the colony of New South Wales, Samuel Marsden, as he began to plan a mission among Maori in northern New Zealand. Marsden knew that any mission in the southeast Pacific had to secure the goodwill and support of the colonial government (New South Wales), the imperial government and the native people themselves. He set about trying to establish what amounted to a chain or even a circle of protection. To begin he sought to convince the Church Missionary Society in London that a mission founded under the patronage of the established (Anglican) Church would be regarded by the government of New South Wales as a part of it and so any governor of that colony would recognise that it was his duty to afford it protection. (It is apparent that Marsden simply accepted the ancient convention that the British Crown had a duty of protection to its subjects even when they were living in a territory beyond the boundaries of its empire.) Next, Marsden told the Church Missionary Society's committee that it should seek to persuade the British government to sanction the sending out of the missionaries and to recommend them to the Governor of New South Wales. This would commit both the British government and New South Wales governor to support the mission. Marsden further proposed that the missionaries should proceed from New South Wales under the patronage of the Governor and with his recommendation, thereby further committing the Governor to the mission as well as helping to secure the support of Maori. In turn, Marsden insisted that on their arrival in the Bay of Islands in northern New Zealand the missionaries were to place themselves as well as their property 'under the protection of the Chief'. (At this time he believed there was such a form of authority, and he was drawing on the lessons missionaries had learned in Tonga and Tahiti where they had secured the goodwill of powerful native dynasties to protect their defenceless missions.) Further, the missionaries should seek to convince Maori of their superiority in terms of what they could offer, which included protection. Finally, Marsden would support the plans of Sydney merchants to plant a settlement not far from the Bay of Islands on the assumption that this could be a further source of protection. It seems clear that Marsden was only able to conceive of his mission by envisioning these protective arrangements. It is also apparent, as was often the case with protection talk, that it was quite unclear what was to be protected, who was to protect whom, and to what end. Despite this ambiguity, or probably because of it, Marsden was able to secure the promises of protection that he needed from the various parties and thus realise his plan to form the mission. This finally occurred in 1814.[3]

In the meantime Marsden became increasingly aware that the masters and crews of vessels in the South Pacific were mistreating native peoples.

Consequently, he began to regard Maori as not only a source of protection but a recipient as well. He started to campaign systematically for the protection of islanders against the maltreatment by lawless British subjects, forming a philanthropic society largely for this purpose. As we will see, the question of how to acquire some means of control over lawless Britons in the islands of New Zealand in order to protect Maori as well as British subjects and trade and commerce was to prompt a series of claims for protection as well as claims to protect over the next twenty-five years.[4]

In December 1813 and again in November 1814 the Governor of New South Wales, Lachlan Macquarie, responding to representations from Marsden, issued proclamations that were designed to stop masters committing offences against the natives of New Zealand or any other islands in the South Pacific. Protection was fundamental to these proclamations in two ways. First, Macquarie assumed that British subjects had a duty of obedience to the British Crown because the Crown had an obligation to provide protection to British subjects wherever they went. Second, and more importantly, in order to bolster his claim to some British jurisdiction in these islands he declared that the native peoples were under the protection of the British Crown. In both cases Macquarie's claims or promises to protect were a way of imagining and thereby conjuring up a form of British authority that did not otherwise exist. This amounts to what Lisa Ford has called, in her chapter in this volume, protection-as-jurisdiction. Such claims had long been made in circumstances in which a polity actually enjoyed no dominion in the territory concerned but wanted to create some form of criminal jurisdiction. It might also be argued that Macquarie's intervention was consistent with a notion that the British Empire had a duty to protect groups of vulnerable subjects that had been gaining adherents since the late-eighteenth century, but it is clear that he made no humanitarian case for acting on behalf of the native peoples.[5]

It was one thing for an imperial agent to make a claim to protect, quite another to ensure that the claim had some substance. During the next twenty years this was an object that a succession of governors of New South Wales would pursue in regard to the islands of New Zealand. In Macquarie's case he sought the power he required in two sources. He called on the imperial headquarters to introduce legislation that would bestow on his government extraterritorial power to subject masters and crews of vessels to a series of regulations. But he also invested authority in three Maori rangatira (chiefs), Ruatara, Hongi Hika and Korokoro, in whose protection Marsden had placed the mission, in order to ensure the compliance of British subjects with those regulations. To be able to make this arrangement Macquarie had to treat Maori as though they were a sovereign polity, albeit one that he knew was divided between hapu (tribes). Taking that step was by no means axiomatic. Only some natives were deemed by European powers to be capable of crude government and thus able to exercise some of the functions of a state. That Macquarie chose to regard Maori rangatira as more or less sovereign was a function of the need for some sources of power to bolster his claim to authority. But it also owed something to the fact that Marsden had been representing Maori rangatira (who had long been visiting Sydney) in this manner, and this was a product of the relationship that he had forged with rangatira in seeking to win their agreement to protect his mission. As a result of Macquarie's claim to protect, Maori rangatira were not only treated as though they were sovereign but were constituted as an ally of the British Crown. As we will see, this status for Maori, and the relationship between the Crown and Maori that it generated, was to deepen in the course of the next twenty-five years, and though more a product of improvisation than design they were to have profound implications for the terms on which the British government would later annex the islands by dint of the Treaty of Waitangi.[6]

PROMISING PROTECTION

In the wake of Marsden's proposal for a mission, New South Wales' traders and merchants and British entrepreneurs sought permission to establish small settlements in northern New Zealand. In doing so they called on the British government to provide them with protection. They no doubt assumed that they had a right to claim this on the grounds of the age-old understanding that the bond between the British Crown and its subjects was not severed where the latter moved beyond its jurisdiction. But in time these supplicants typically made several arguments in their claims for protection: Britain's commercial interests would be advanced; the Maori chiefs had expressed an interest in obtaining a protecting government; and the islands had to be placed under British protection in order to ensure that the French did not establish themselves and thereby obtain an ascendancy that could threaten Britain's vital interests in the area. For their part successive governors of New South Wales endorsed these requests because they were keen to expand the reach of the colony, advance British trade and shore up Britain's strategic interests in the South Pacific vis-à-vis other imperial powers. But they did so on the condition that traders, merchants and entrepreneurs obtained the permission of the native chiefs.[7]

By contrast the imperial government proved reluctant to countenance such claims for protection. Yet at the same time it made its own claim to protect. The circumstances were these: Marsden had tried to have several ship captains prosecuted in New South Wales courts for their maltreatment of Maori, but he had failed (because the magistrates had declared that they had no jurisdiction to try British subjects for wrongs committed in the islands of New Zealand) and so had called on the Church Missionary Society and the London Missionary Society to put pressure on the imperial government to enact further measures. In response, Westminster introduced a bill in 1817 seeking the power to bring to trial masters and crews of ships who had committed manslaughter and murder in Honduras and the islands of New Zealand and Tahiti once those men had returned to British soil.[8]

The Murders Abroad Act, as it came to be called, has long been regarded by New Zealand historians as an act by which the British Crown put an end to any claims that it enjoyed jurisdiction in the islands of New Zealand.[9] However, while the British parliament certainly disavowed any sovereignty in the places and islands mentioned in the legislation by declaring that they did not lie within His Majesty's dominions, it simultaneously implied that it had some claim to possession in those places and islands by asserting that they were under the protection of the British Crown. This lent weight to the British government's attempt to forge extraterritorial jurisdiction just as it ensured that it would not incur any of the costly administrative responsibilities that could arise if it claimed sovereignty. In other words, a promise to protect was both a practical and cheap means of creating some kind of imperial order. There are in fact many diverse examples of imperial powers finding such protection talk invaluable in attaining such a goal.[10] This helps to explain why claims to afford protection were such a recurring part of the imperial repertoire.[11]

It is also evident that claims to protect not only had this kind of inside register but also an outside register (to adopt the terms suggested by Lauren Benton and Adam Clulow in their chapter in this volume). By making a promise to protect that alluded vaguely to a claim of possession the British government could shore up its interests vis-à-vis those of its European imperial rivals, especially the French.[12] Agents of the British government resorted to this kind of manoeuvre in regard to the islands of New Zealand on more than one occasion. At the same time, to revert to the inside register once more, by asserting that the islands did not lie with the dominion with the British Crown the imperial government acquired a ready means of repelling demands by British subjects that colonies be planted in the islands of New Zealand.[13]

Yet it soon became apparent that the 1817 Murders Abroad Act was of little use in checking the increasingly lawless conduct of escaped convicts, castaways, sealers, whalers and adventurers in the islands of New Zealand. It only covered violence that ended in death, did nothing to address other causes of conflict and proved to be virtually unenforceable. Consequently, over the next twenty years, Marsden, the Church Missionary Society missionaries in the Bay of Islands, Sydney-based traders and successive governors of New South Wales repeatedly called on the imperial government to make effective its promise to protect by providing the legislative or the military means that were required to give it some teeth.[14]

These calls became especially pronounced in April 1831 when news reached Sydney that a British merchant vessel called the *Elizabeth* and its captain had been involved in an expedition in which a leading Ngati Toa rangatira, Te Rauparaha, and his supporters had launched an attack on the settlement of another Maori tribe (the Ngai Tahu), slaughtering approximately a hundred people, and torturing and executing several more whom they had taken prisoner. Marsden, who had been troubled for some time that lawless Europeans could provoke Maori to attack British subjects as well as foment internecine Maori warfare, seized upon this incident to call on the Governor of New South Wales, Sir Ralph Darling, to afford every protection to Maori against the acts of violence that British subjects committed upon them. Yet who in fact needed protection remained ambiguous. Marsden asserted that the affair had created considerable anxiety among Maori and claimed that they looked to the British government for redress and protection according to a promise that King George IV had apparently made to two leading Nga Puhi rangatira, Waikato and Hongi Hika, when they had an audience with him in London in 1820. But he also warned that Maori would take power into their own hands and redress these wrongs themselves unless they could be persuaded that the British government would provide them with protection.[15]

Later the same year Maori rangatira in the Bay of Islands also deployed the language of protection in representations they made to the British government. Becoming apprehensive about French designs on their territory, thirteen signed a petition that asked King William IV to 'become [their] friend and the guardian of the[ir] islands'. Maori probably had their own notions of protection but it is difficult to recover these from the historical sources. However, it seems clear that they assumed that an appeal in these terms would consolidate the relationship between themselves and the British Crown that they believed Waikato and Hongi Hika had forged in 1820. There can also be little doubt, though, that a Church Missionary Society missionary, William Yate, and his colleagues in northern New Zealand had encouraged, perhaps even coached the rangatira to couch their petition in the language of protection and direct it to the British government rather than some other European government.[16]

In response to the pleas for greater protection made by both Marsden and Maori rangatira following the *Elizabeth* affair, Darling decided to send a

Resident to New Zealand as a means of assuring Maori chiefs that the British government would afford protection to them. The appointment of a Resident was a long-established British practice in regard to princely courts in Mughal and Maratha India. Such appointments were deeply ambiguous in nature: on the one hand they supposed that the British Crown had disavowed any claim to sovereignty and recognised the local polity as sovereign, on the other they constituted a means of assuming some control over British subjects as well as bolstering the integrity of a local polity so that it could be manipulated by the Resident.[17]

In response the Colonial Office seemed to be pointing to a new kind of protection talk. In January 1832 Goderich told Sir Richard Bourke, Darling's successor as the Governor of New South Wales: 'The unfortunate natives of New Zealand, unless some decisive measures of prevention be adopted, will, I fear, be shortly added to the number of those barbarous tribes, who, in different parts of the globe, have fallen a sacrifice to their intercourse with civilised men, who bear and disgrace the name of Christians'. The historian Tony Ballantyne has argued that this reveals that a 'humanitarian discourse of protection' had convinced the imperial government that the Maori were in need of protection and that some greater form of British intervention was necessary to provide it. However, the Colonial Office and more especially the Admiralty had been refusing for some time to accede to demands for more effective protection. More to the point, they continued to do so. In 1823 the imperial government had merely introduced legislation that included a section that extended the terms of the Murders Abroad Act by empowering courts in New South Wales to try offences that were committed by British subjects and British ship crews on the high seas or in places in the Indian and Pacific oceans including New Zealand that were not subject to the British Crown or the authority of any other state, while in 1828 it just replaced this legislation with a similar act that had the same purpose. And, now, Goderich acceded to Darling's decision to appoint a British Resident but refused to provide that officer with the means he needed to carry out his duties effectively and thereby protect Maori, despite the fact that Bourke pointed out that it would be useless to proceed with this appointment unless the British government provided the requisite legal authority and the military means to enforce it. This suggests that Goderich probably employed the rhetoric noted by Ballantyne because the government was flatly refusing to meet Bourke's demand that it provide more effective protection and consequently he felt it necessary to appease Bourke.[18]

It has become standard for scholars such as Ballantyne and Paul McHugh to argue that the imperial government was actually constrained from intervening in New Zealand's affairs by a series of legal rulings that clearly defined

New Zealand's status in the eyes of the British Crown by disavowing British sovereignty and pronouncing Maori to be the islands' owners and sovereigns.[19] Two examples from the available evidence suffice to call this into question.

First, as we have already seen, in the Murders Abroad Act of 1817 the Crown disavowed British sovereignty in the islands but implied it had some claim to possession, and so the status of the territory was actually vague. The second concerns advice the Colonial Office's legal counsel, James Stephen, gave in 1830 after a British entrepreneur, Robert Torrens, asked to be vested with some authority over British subjects who comprised an establishment he had made in northern New Zealand, having previously requested military protection from the British government for this endeavour. Stephen began by drawing attention to what he seems to have regarded as the key legal point, namely that the islands of New Zealand were not a part of His Majesty's dominions (as per the 1817 Murders Abroad Act). Consequently, the king could not invest his subjects with any authority in the islands. Next, in a passage more than one scholar has treated as the crux of this advice but is really something of a digression, Stephen speculated that Torrens might not only want to be able to keep his own men in order but take military action against the natives, whom Stephen called *'the owners and sovereigns of the soil'*. Stephen had close connections to the movement for the abolition of slavery and was inclined to rhetorical flourishes such as this one, but there is little if any evidence that he attached any precise legal significance to them. Moreover, returning to the matter at hand, he emphasised that, independent of any legal objections that might be raised to the government assuming the authority in the islands that Torrens had sought, foreign states might regard this as an indirect extension of British power in the region. Finally, Stephen proceeded to argue that the real question at stake was actually whether the government was willing to sanction a military occupation of New Zealand since this would 'inevitably and shortly lead to the assumption of a permanent dominion'. The answer was a resounding *no*. On this as well as many other occasions the British government held that it could not afford to provide the resources that would be required in founding another colony. In short, it seems clear that the considerations that constrained the imperial government from intervening in the affairs of New Zealand were essentially economic and political in nature, not legal.[20]

Legal rules of the kind McHugh, Ballantyne and others have emphasised undoubtedly played some role in the position that the British government took but they did not determine its position. Rather, they were simply part of a repertoire that the government deployed to support whatever stance it was inclined to adopt at any particular time. As we have seen, asserting that the islands of New Zealand were not within the dominion of the British Crown and implying that Maori were sovereign served a number of useful purposes.

Moreover, if the imperial government had really wanted to intervene in New Zealand's affairs to offer Maori greater protection it could have done so, for example by acquiring sovereignty through negotiating a treaty with Maori for its cession, which is precisely what it decided to do in 1839–40. For the time being, however, it saw no reason to alter its ambiguous stance on the matter of the sovereignty of the islands of New Zealand or abandon the strand of protection talk that sustained it.[21]

Maori not only continued to have the same status and relationship with the British Crown as they had previously; these were enhanced as a result of what happened after the imperial government appointed James Busby as Resident to the islands. In the first instance Governor of New South Wales Bourke, who was acutely aware that the imperial government had failed to furnish Busby with the power and authority he needed in order to perform his duties, realised that he had little choice but to recommend that Busby try to constitute the Maori rangatira as a unified sovereign authority.[22]

Busby arrived in the Bay of Islands in May 1833 bearing a letter in the name of the King (which responded to the 1831 petition from thirteen Maori rangatira begging the King to become their tribes' guardian) that once more figured the rangatira as allies by saying that the British government expected them to give Busby assistance and support to enable him to provide greater protection. Furthermore, several months after his arrival, Busby took steps to forge a sense of national sovereignty among Maori by creating a national flag and securing the imperial government's recognition of it. A further eighteen months later he used a rumour that a Frenchman, Baron Charles de Phillipe de Thierry, was threatening to establish an independent state at Hokianga in northern New Zealand to call rangatira there together and urge them to sign a Declaration of Independence of New Zealand that he had drafted. In this, they declared an independent state under the designation of the United Tribes of New Zealand and pronounced that all the sovereign power and authority in the territories of the United Tribes resided in this state and that they would not permit any other to exist unless it was by persons appointed by them and acting under the authority of laws enacted by the state; but the rangatira also agreed to forward the Declaration to the King and ask him to act as the parent of what they called their infant state and protect it from any challenges to its independence.[23]

Clearly, the Declaration expressed the same ambiguity in regard to the matter of sovereignty that had been articulated previously by British claims to protect. In this case, however, Busby made it clear to the Colonial Office that he actually regarded it as a means by which the British Crown could make the country a dependency in all but name. Moreover, three months later, he abandoned any pretence that Maori could or should be regarded as sovereign by arguing that Maori would be glad to yield government of their country to the British Crown and become British subjects, though he also suggested that the government would need to give an undertaking to protect their rights, including their rights in land, in order to assume sovereignty. However, for the time being, the imperial government saw no reason to change its position.[24]

FROM ALLIES TO SUBJECTS

In the mid- to late-1830s evangelical philanthropists led by the Quaker Thomas Fowell Buxton started to pay considerable attention to the islands of New Zealand. In the process, they began to make use of what historians have called the humanitarian language of protection. For many scholars such language was instrumental in convincing the British government to change its stance and intervene in the islands' affairs. However, it seems clear that it did not have the transformative effect often ascribed to it. Indeed, when placed alongside other kinds of protection talk, and especially protection-as-jurisdiction, it loses much of the power that has been bestowed upon it.

In July 1835 Buxton persuaded the House of Commons to appoint a select committee that gathered information not only about the cruel treatment of the aboriginal inhabitants in Britain's colonies of settlement but also the deleterious impact that British subjects were having on native peoples in islands in the South Pacific, including New Zealand. In its final report to parliament, tabled in June 1837, the committee asserted that the British people had a special duty towards native peoples: 'The disparity of the parties, the strength of the one, and the capacity of the other, to enforce the observance of their rights constitutes a new and irresistible appeal to our compassionate protection.' Clearly, these philanthropists deemed natives such as Maori to be fundamentally weak and thus to be regarded as subjects rather than sovereign and a party to be treated as allies, though at the same time it did assert that they should enjoy the rights of British subjects. Yet the specific recommendations the select committee made merely repeated the calls for more effective protection that had been made for some time.[25]

This may not be said for the gentlemen who soon formed a body called the New Zealand Association for the very purpose of promoting the systematic colonisation of the country. In order to win the government's support the Association's principal figures spoke the same language of protection the evangelical philanthropists were wielding but they argued that colonisation was already occurring in New Zealand and threatening Maori with extermination, and that what was required was systematic colonisation and the assertion of British authority in order to extend British protection over all of the islands. The missionary societies were aghast. Church Missionary Society secretary Dandeson Coates believed that the Association was fundamentally entrepreneurial in nature and so was being disingenuous in adopting the philanthropic language of protection. He was especially critical of the fact that the Association was calling on the British government to sanction the colonisation of parts of a country over which he said it had no claim, and argued that the colonisation being proposed would inflict great wrongs on Maori and interrupt or even destroy the work of the missionary societies. Coates maintained that the government was best to preserve the fundamentals of its protective arrangements in New Zealand but make them more effective.[26]

In mid-December 1837 the Secretary of State for the Colonies, Lord Glenelg, raised many of the same objections that the missionary societies had made to the New Zealand Association's scheme. But his opposition to the Association's plans counted for little. The Association's founders were politically well connected; more to the point, the government was dependent on the support of its chairman for its survival. Consequently, Prime Minister Lord Melbourne leaned on Glenelg, and by the end of December he had relented and offered the Association a charter to colonise New Zealand, albeit with certain conditions.[27]

Not surprisingly, Glenelg and his colleagues at the Colonial Office required some rationale to explain this volte-face. They found it in a long report they had just received from Busby in which he mobilised the metropolitan philanthropic language of protection to paint a picture of Maori in a state of crisis and argue that this situation demanded the imperial government intervene to create a protecting state. This is often depicted as a key moment in which the government made a crucial change in its stance about the state and status of New Zealand, which was merely confirmed in 1839 by its decision to annex the islands. Yet this seems unlikely. First, the missionary societies took the matter to the House of Commons where the majority was of the opinion that any colonisation of New Zealand had to be placed under the protective oversight of the Crown, and consequently a bill the Association had introduced to win sanction for its colonisation scheme (after it had refused to accept the charter it had been offered) was defeated, which prompted the collapse of the Association and its scheme.[28]

Second, Glenelg was almost certainly relieved by this turn of events. He had in fact anticipated the defeat of the Association's bill and had asked Stephen, now the permanent undersecretary of the Colonial Office, to consider what course the government might take to meet the apparent need for greater protection in New Zealand. Stephen outlined a proposal made in a report Bourke had commissioned on the state of New Zealand by a visiting naval officer, William Hobson, that merely recommended the government provide greater protection to both Maori and British subjects by creating trading stations at several places (including the Bay of Islands) and bringing them within British jurisdiction as dependencies of New South Wales, and that British officers in these places be credited as political agents to the chiefs who had been responsible for the Declaration of Independence. In short, it appears that the Colonial Office still believed that the fundamental position it had taken on the islands for some time – providing a sufficient amount of protection to sustain the Crown's claim of possession but little more than that – could and should be maintained.[29]

However, in November 1838 Coates received a letter from one of the Church Missionary Society's senior missionaries in which he argued that none of the measures that Coates had championed to protect Maori would suffice any longer because of the increasingly lawless state of the country, the growing volume of land sales and the inability of Maori to form a national government. Coates and the Church Missionary Society were so deeply troubled by the contents of this letter that they were now prepared to concede that the acquisition of sovereignty by the British government was the best means of protecting Maori. Coates showed Glenelg the letter and urged him to adopt this measure. But for the time being Glenelg merely seemed to be of a mind to adopt Hobson's proposal for a limited form of intervention and to negotiate a cession of sovereignty in just some parts of the islands. And even this proposal stalled when Glenelg resigned as Secretary of State for the Colonies in February 1839 and his successor decided that the decision to intervene should be postponed.[30]

Several weeks later, however, a body calling itself the New Zealand Company, which had recently been formed by the principal figures of the New Zealand Association, forced the Colonial Office's hand when it despatched a party to New Zealand to purchase large swathes of land. The government realised that in order to prevent a potential mess in regard to both land and native affairs it had to assert its authority and take steps to acquire sovereignty in the islands. At much the same time the Colonial Office appears to have accepted the advice of its appointee as Consul, William Hobson, that the measures he had previously recommended for the islands would not suffice and that the British government needed to assume sovereignty over the entire country.[31]

To take this momentous step the Colonial Office assumed that it had to disarm several players, not least the missionary societies. But its principal figures also had to persuade themselves of the merit and virtue of this move since they were reversing their position on the matter of sovereignty in the islands. They found what was needed in the 'humanitarian' strand of protection talk. For example, Undersecretary of State for the Colonies Henry Labouchere told the House of Commons that the government had decided to take steps that would probably lead to the founding of a colony in New Zealand on the grounds that it was 'the duty of the government to protect' a people who were 'quite unable properly to protect their own interests'. Most of the work of legitimising the Colonial Office's decision, however, was to be performed by the preamble to the instructions that it drew up for Hobson in his role as the colony's first governor.[32]

Here the protection talk the Colonial Office adopted amounted to a hybrid of protection-as-jurisdiction that it had long found useful and the 'humanitarian' notion of protection the evangelical philanthropists had been articulating. It began the preamble by arguing that the government was reluctant to intervene in the island's affairs given the impact that any colonisation would have on Maori and by claiming that it had previously deferred to the opinion expressed by the evangelical philanthropists in the select committee report on aborigines that this step would be fraught with calamity for Maori. Next, it claimed that the right of sovereignty and title to the land of Maori in the islands of New Zealand were indisputable and that this had been solemnly recognised by the British government. This done, the Colonial Office proceeded to contend that it had become all too apparent that the government had to acquire sovereignty because Maori would be exterminated if the extensive colonisation that was now under way were not constrained. This was to argue that the government's apparent acknowledgement of New Zealand as a sovereign state was binding on the faith of the British Crown but that since Maori were now enfeebled and the authority of the rangatira was so very precarious and little more than nominal it was now in the best interests for Maori to cede that sovereignty and thereby enjoy the benefits of British protection. However, at the same time, the Colonial Office acknowledged that the position the imperial government had taken on the status of the islands and its people as it pursued protection-as-jurisdiction obliged it to negotiate with Maori for the cession of that sovereignty. And, with an eye to another aspect of protection talk it had deployed in order to ward off claims to New Zealand by other foreign governments, the Colonial Office asserted that the British government disclaimed any pretension to seize the islands of New Zealand or govern them as a part of the dominions of Britain unless it could first obtain the consent of Maori chiefs to ceding their sovereignty. Finally, in the first part of the actual instructions to Hobson, the Colonial Office advised

Hobson how he might acquire that consent by negotiating a treaty, aware that the Maori rangatira would be suspicious about the reasons why the British government was now seeking to assume sovereignty and annex their territory.[33]

The Colonial Office's rhetoric in these instructions (which became public knowledge) seems to have disarmed the Church Missionary Society and the Wesleyan Missionary Society, not least because their secretaries Dandeson Coates and John Beecham were led to believe that the government was no longer contemplating the granting of a charter to a body such as the New Zealand Association and that its primary object was not the advancement of colonisation or commerce but the protection of the interests and rights of Maori. Consequently, Coates and Beecham instructed their missionaries in New Zealand to give Hobson their full support. In fact these missionaries needed no persuading. By contrast with the position Marsden had long maintained, they had come to believe that the only way to save Maori lay in the British government assuming sovereignty and taking them entirely under its protection. Yet they were also of the view that the government had to promise to uphold at least some Maori independence as well as maintain their territorial rights. And, as the focus of matters moved to New Zealand, the roles of Maori and the British Crown and the relationships between them that had been brought into being by protection-as-jurisdiction would assert themselves in the making of the treaty by which the British government would claim to have annexed New Zealand.[34]

Protection figured prominently in the English language draft of the treaty that was prepared in the Bay of Islands shortly before it was presented to the Maori chiefs who gathered at Waitangi on 5 February 1840.[35] In the preamble the Queen (as the current embodiment of the Crown) emphasised that she was anxious to protect the rights and property of Maori in the course of explaining why the British government had deemed it necessary to appoint Hobson to treat with them for a cession of sovereignty. Furthermore, in the first clause of the second of the treaty's three articles the Crown effectively promised to protect Maori in the possession of their lands, though its inclusion did not spring from the Colonial Office's instructions to Hobson but was instead the result of the intervention of the former British Resident, James Busby, in the drafting of the treaty, which was prompted by his and the missionaries' understanding of what the government's promise of protection had to entail if the Maori rangatira were to agree to cede sovereignty. Finally, in the treaty's third article the Queen undertook to extend to Maori her 'royal protection and [impart] to them all the rights and privileges of British subjects'. In presenting the treaty at Waitangi it appears that Hobson followed his instructions by telling the rangatira gathered that the British Crown could only acquire the authority it needed to be able to protect them if they were willing to cede sovereignty to the Queen. Presumably on the advice of Busby and the missionaries, Hobson also reminded the chiefs that they had often asked the British monarch to extend them protection and made clear that this was what the Queen was now offering.[36]

The ground for the treaty-making had been prepared over many years by the generation of a relationship between Maori and the British Crown as a function of protection-as-jurisdiction. In the 1810s Marsden and Macquarie had forged a relationship that had envisaged Maori as allies, and during the 1820s and 1830s the Church Missionary Society missionaries had encouraged Maori rangatira to request and look to the protection of the British monarch. This undoubtedly helped to deepen among some of the rangatira a sense of a formal relationship between themselves and the British Crown, but more especially it familiarised them with the language of protection. In more recent years Maori rangatira in northern New Zealand realised that they were failing to curb the British intrusion and began to lose confidence that they could deal with the problems of governance this was causing. They acknowledged that they needed new answers to these new problems and came to believe that a political arrangement with the British government might serve their purposes. But, not surprisingly, in 1839–40 they still assumed and expected that they would continue to be able to enjoy an alliance with the British Crown that would not only provide them with protection but a considerable degree of autonomy. They appear to have signed the treaty in accordance with this assumption and expectation. In other words, this way of regarding the terms of the treaty was very much in keeping with the way in which a notion of protection had long been presented to them and which they had embraced.[37]

What is more, despite the sudden shift in the way that protection was being conceived by British agents and the fact that this led to the transfer of sovereignty, the implications of this change were far from certain at this stage. Critical matters were yet to be even considered. For example, how was Maori possession of land or native title to be defined; would Maori custom be replaced by British law wholly or only in part; and were Maori forms of government to be recognised in the new legal order? The years that followed would see enormous struggle between various parties over these questions.

CONCLUSION

A close study of the discussions about the islands of New Zealand in the opening decades of the nineteenth century reveals that references to protection were ubiquitous. This can be explained in large part by the fact that talk of protection – as demonstrated again and again in this volume – is capable of performing a considerable range of tasks in a variety of contexts. In this case several players made good use of a notion of protection. They included missionaries, philanthropists, traders and agents of colonisation companies, all of whom used protection talk in the sense of claims for protection as a way of seeking or securing support from the British government for various schemes to plant a settlement in the islands of New Zealand. In doing so they relied on an age-old convention that they had a right as British subjects to seek such protection from the Crown even when they were living in a territory beyond the boundaries of its empire. But, as we have noted, in seeking to plant new colonies one of the most important claimants of protection did not regard the British Crown as the only source of protection. Most significantly, Marsden and his backers conceived of Maori performing this role as they tried to forge a chain or a circle of protection for their endeavour.

But the language of protection would not have assumed such importance if it was confined to missionaries and traders. As elsewhere, government officials also found protection talk very useful in reference to the islands of New Zealand. Making a promise to protect constituted a means of imagining a form of authority that would not have otherwise existed. Such claims had long been made in circumstances in which a polity actually enjoyed no dominion in the territory concerned since it enabled an imperial power to create a form of criminal jurisdiction and thereby forge some sense of order. But, as we have seen, claims to protect or what can be called protection-as-jurisdiction could serve other purposes as well. By making a claim to be a protector an imperial power could shore up their interests vis-à-vis those of their imperial rivals. By the same token, a promise to protect could be a means of projecting a claim to possession rather than staking a claim to sovereignty, which could ensure that an imperial power did not incur the costly burden of administering a colony that was often the consequence of claiming sovereignty. In other words, it could help a government deflect demands that it intervene more in a region. What was fundamental here, as with other kinds of protection talk, was a considerable degree of ambiguity or vagueness, even to the extent that it could be unclear which party was the protector and which the protected.

Protection talk in the case of the islands of New Zealand was also typical in the sense that it could give rise to relationships between parties that ranged between those of allies to those of overlords and subjects, and something in between. As we have seen, the promises to protect that were made by the British Crown led its agents to treat Maori as though they were sovereign and to generate a status of ally for them. Recovering the history of protection talk in its various guises in the islands of New Zealand enables us to understand why the British Crown came to treat Maori as more or less sovereign. Whereas several historians have argued that this was primarily the result of certain legal conventions or rulings, I have shown that this was largely the outcome of the protection talk that the government chose to adopt, largely for political reasons.

The changes in the uses to which the imperial government put notions of protection in New Zealand reflected the broad shift that took place in many contexts that saw many native peoples become the subjects rather than the allies of an imperial power. But, as we have observed, in the New Zealand case this only took place in a halting fashion. Most importantly, while the reasons for the imperial government deciding to annex New Zealand undoubtedly owed much to a so-called humanitarian discourse of protection that had cast Maori as weak and as subjects, the terms upon which it did this were a function of the status of Maori as sovereign that had been generated by two or more decades of a very different strand of protection talk. By recovering this relatively long variegated history of protection talk we are able not only to recognise the centrality of protection to the terms of the Treaty of Waitangi but to grasp better the meanings it had for the British agents and the Maori rangatira that were party to making it.

NOTES

I am indebted to my fellow editors and Shaunnagh Dorsett, Mark Hickford, Miranda Johnson and Andrew Sharp for their incisive comments on a draft of this chapter.

1 See, most recently, Tony Ballantyne, *Entanglements of the Body: Missionaries, Maori, and the Question of the Body*, Duke University Press, Durham, 2014, especially pp. 218, 248–49. Cf. Peter Adams, *Fatal Necessity: British Intervention in New Zealand 1830–1847*, Auckland University Press, Auckland, 1977.

2 Lauren Benton and Lisa Ford, *Rage for Order: The British Empire and the Origins of International Law, 1800–1850*, Harvard University Press, Cambridge, MA, 2016, pp. 115–16.

3 Samuel Marsden to Josiah Pratt, 24 March 1808, 7 April 1808 and 3 May 1810, Church Missionary Society, London: Records Relating to the New Zealand Mission, Hocken Library, MS-0498. In this paragraph I have drawn heavily on the insights of Andrew Sharp, *The World, the Flesh and the Devil: The Life and Opinions of Samuel Marsden in England and the Antipodes, 1765–1838*, Auckland University Press, Auckland, 2016, pp. 220–21, 361–64, 736.

4 Marsden to Pratt, 3 May 1810, 25 October 1810 and 19 November 1811, Church Missionary Society, London: Records Relating to the New Zealand Mission, Hocken Library, MS-0498; Minutes of the Founding Meeting of the New South Wales Society for Affording Protection to the Natives of the South Sea Islands and

Promoting their Civilisation, 20 December 1813, MS-0439/116, Hocken Library; John Rawson Elder (ed.), *The Letters and Journals of Samuel Marsden 1765–1838*, Otago University Council, Dunedin, 1932, pp. 64–68, 78–79, 97; Sharp, pp. 368, 374–75.

5 Marsden to Governor Lachlan Macquarie, 1 November 1813, Records Relating to the New Zealand Mission, General Inward Letters, March 1808 - November 1812, MS-0498, Hocken Library; Governor Lachlan Macquarie, Proclamation, 1 December 1813, Robert McNab (ed.), *Historical Records of New Zealand*, vol. 1 (henceforth *HRNZ*), pp. 316–18; Marsden to Pratt, 15 March 1814, Copy of Correspondence of Rev. Samuel Marsden 1813–1814, PC-0118, Hocken Library; Macquarie to Earl Bathurst, 17 January 1814, *Historical Records of Australia* (henceforth *HRA*), series 1, vol. VIII, p. 96; Macquarie, Proclamation, 9 November 1814, *HRNZ*, pp. 328–29; Sharp, p. 377; cf. Andrew Porter, 'Trusteeship, Anti-Slavery, and Humanitarianism', in Andrew Porter (ed.), *The Oxford History of the British Empire: Volume III: The Nineteenth Century*, Oxford University Press, Oxford, 1999, pp. 200–01.

6 Macquarie to Bathurst, 17 January 1814, *HRA*, series 1, vol. VIII, pp. 96, 98; Judith Binney, *The Legacy of Guilt: A Life of Thomas Kendall*, Oxford University Press, Auckland, 1968, p. 25.

7 Simeon Lord et al. to Macquarie, 3 October 1814, *HRNZ*, pp. 324–27; Macquarie to Bathurst, 24 June 1815, *HRA*, series 1, vol. VIII, p. 561; Extract of Bathurst to Macquarie, 9 April 1816, *HRNZ*, p. 407; Baron Charles de Thierry to Bathurst, 23 December 1823, *HRNZ*, p. 615; Marsden to Pratt, 4 June 1824, *HRNZ*, p. 628; Samuel Enderby et al. to Bathurst, 24 April 1826, CO 201/221, National Archives of the United Kingdom (henceforth NA); Robert Torrens to Lord Goderich, c. 25 January 1831, CO 201/224, NA.

8 Marsden to Pratt, 15 June 1815, 25 October 1815, 26 October 1815 and 6 November 1815, Collected Papers of and Relating to Rev. Samuel Marsden, MS-0055, Hocken Library; Marsden to Pratt, 16 March 1816, Collected Papers of and Relating to Rev. Samuel Marsden, MS-0056, Hocken Library; Memorial of the Church Missionary Society to Earl Bathurst, undated [July 1817] and appendices, McNab (ed.), *Historical Records*, pp. 417–27; 57 Geo III (1817) c. 53; Sharp, pp. 315–16, 379. This bill resembled legislation that had been enacted in the 1780s in respect of British interests in India.

9 See, for example, E.J. Tapp, *Early New Zealand: A Dependency of New South Wales, 1788–1841*, Melbourne University Press, Melbourne, 1958, pp. 40–42.

10 Geo III (1817) c. 53.

11 For other examples, see, for instance, Elizabeth Kolsky, *Colonial Justice in British India*, Cambridge University Press, New York, 2010, especially Chapters 1 and 2; Mary Dewhurst Lewis, *Divided Rule: Sovereignty and Empire in French Tunisia, 1881–1938*, University of California Press, Berkeley, 2014, especially pp. 63–64.

12 For a discussion of the various uses to which claims of possession could be put, see Lauren Benton, 'Possessing Empire: Iberian Claims and Interpolity Law', in Saliha Belmessous (ed.), *Native Claims: Indigenous Law against Empire, 1500–1920*, Oxford University Press, New York, 2012, pp. 19–40.

13 R. Wilmot Horton to de Thierry, 10 December 1823, *HRNZ*, p. 615; Extract from the Minutes of the New South Wales Executive Council, 31 October 1831, New Zealand Estrays collected by Sir William Dixson, 29 December 1830–1845, DLNAR 3, Mitchell Library; Governor Patrick Lindesay to Goderich, 4 November 1831, *HRA*, series 1, vol. XVI, p. 442; Lauren Benton, *A Search for Sovereignty: Law and Geography in European Empires, 1400–1900*, Cambridge University Press, New York, 2010, pp. 197–98; Benton and Ford, p. 86.

14 John Bigge, Questions to Church Missionary Society missionaries and their answers, 8 November 1819, *HRNZ*, p. 445; Bigge to Bathurst, 27 February 1823, *HRNZ*, pp. 587, 594–96; *Sydney Gazette*, 30 September 1824; Marsden to Governor Ralph Darling, 2 August 1830, CO 209/1, NA; Darling to Sir George Murray, 12 August 1830, *HRA*, series 1, vol. XV, pp. 702–03.

15 Marsden to Darling, 18 April 1831, *British Parliamentary Papers* (henceforth *BPP*) 1836, Report from the Select Committee on Aborigines (British Settlements), Paper no. 538, p. 484; Marsden to Dandeson Coates, 18 April 1831, *HRNZ*, p. 716; Marsden to Rev. E. Bickersteth, 25 April 1831, *HRNZ*, p. 718; Sharp, p. 721.

16 Warerahi et al., Petition to King William IV, undated, and William Yate to Colonial Secretary of New South Wales, 16 November 1831, *BPP*, 1840, Correspondence with the Secretary of State Relative to New Zealand, Paper no. 238, p. 7; Judith Binney, *Stories Without End: Essays 1975–2010*, Bridget Williams Books, Wellington, New Zealand, 2010, p. 355.

17 Darling to Goderich, 13 April 1831, *HRA*, series 1, vol. XVI, pp. 237–41; Paul McHugh, '"A Pretty Gov[ernment]": The "Confederation of United Tribes" and Britain's Quest for Imperial Order in the New Zealand Islands during the 1830s', in Lauren Benton and Richard J. Ross (eds), *Legal Pluralism and Empires, 1500–1850*, New York University Press, New York, 2013, p. 241.

18 4 Geo IV (1823) c. 96; 9 Geo IV (1828) c. 83; R.W. Hay to John Barrow, 14 June 1826, CO 201/221, NA; Barrow to Hay, 15 June 1826, CO 201/175, NA; George Elliot to Lord Howick, 7 January 1831, CO 209/1, NA; Hay, Minute, 29 January 1831, CO 201/224, NA; Sir Richard Bourke to Goderich, 23 December 1831, *HRA*, series 1, vol. XVI, pp. 482–83; Goderich to Bourke, 31 January 1832, *HRA*, series 1, vol. XVI, pp. 510–13; Lord Fitzroy Somerset to Hay, 6 February 1832, CO 201/228, NA; Hay, Minute, 10 February 1832, CO 201/228, NA; Barrow to Hay, 24 March 1832, CO 201/228, NA; Memo, New Zealand, undated, [24 March 1832], CO 201/228, NA; Goderich to Bourke, [2]8 March 1832, *HRA*, series 1, vol. XVI, pp. 561–63; Ballantyne, pp. 230–31.

19 McHugh, pp. 237–40; Ballantyne, pp. 230–31. See also Shaunnagh Dorsett, 'Metropolitan Theorising: Legal Frameworks, Protectorates and Models for Maori Governance 1837–1838', *Law&History*, vol. 3, 2016, p. 8.

20 James Stephen, Memorandum, 25 May 1830, CO 201/215, NA.

21 Barrow to Hay, 24 March 1832.

22 Goderich to the Chiefs of New Zealand, 14 June 1832, *BPP*, 1840, Correspondence with the Secretary of State Relative to New Zealand, Paper no. 238, pp. 7–8; Bourke to James Busby, 13 April 1833, *BPP*, 1840, Correspondence with the Secretary of State Relative to New Zealand, Paper no. 238, p. 6.

23 Busby to Hay, 3 April 1834, New Zealand Estrays collected by Sir William Dixson, 27 March 1833 - 20 April 1848, DLNAR 1, Mitchell Library; The Declaration of Independence, 28 October 1835, CO 209/2, NA.

24 Busby to Alexander McLeay, 31 October 1835 and 26 January 1836, Busby, Despatches from the British Resident 1833–70, qMS-0344, Alexander Turnbull Library.

25 *BPP*, 1837, Report from the Select Committee on Aborigines (British Settlements), Paper no. 425, pp. 3, 14–22, 85–86.

26 Resolutions of the Committee of the Church Missionary Society, 6 June 1837, in Dandeson Coates, *The Present State of the New Zealand Question Considered, In a Letter to J.P. Plumptre, Esq.*, MP, Richard Watts, London, 1838, pp. 3–4; [Edward Gibbon Wakefield and John Ward], *The British Colonisation of New Zealand*, John W. Parker, London, 1837, pp. 40–41, 54–58; Coates, *The Principles, Objects and Plan of the New Zealand Association Examined, in a Letter to the Right Hon. Lord Glenelg*, Hatchards, London, 1837, passim.

27 Lord Melbourne to Lord Howick, 14 December 1837 and 16 December 1837, Papers of Henry George, 3rd Earl Grey, B115/1/85 and B115/1/107, University of Durham University Library Special Collections; Lord Glenelg, Memorandum, 15 December 1837, CO 209/2, NA; Glenelg to Durham, 29 December 1837, *BPP*, 1838, Report of the Select Committee on New Zealand, Paper no. 582, p. 148.

28 Busby to Bourke, 16 June 1837 and Sir George Grey et al., Minutes and Notes, 18 December 1837, on this despatch, CO 209/2, NA; *British Parliamentary Debates*, House of Commons, 1 June 1838 and 20 June 1838, columns 542–53 and 871–83; Adams, pp. 14, 101–02.

29 William Hobson to Bourke, 8 August 1837, CO 209/2, NA; Stephen, Memo, 4 May 1838, CO 209/3, NA.

30 George Clarke to Coates, 1 March 1838, Letters from Henry Williams to the Church Missionary Society 1822–1851, vol. 2, 1831–40, MS 91–75, Auckland War Memorial Museum Library; Coates to Glenelg, 30 November 1838, Church Missionary Society Home Letterbooks (Outwards) 1838–1842, Church Missionary Society Archives, C.H./L3, Australian Joint Copying Project, Reel M238.

31 Hobson to Glenelg, 21 January 1839, CO 209/4, NA; William Hutt to Henry Labouchere, 29 April 1839, *BPP*, 1840, Correspondence with the Secretary of State Relative to New Zealand, Paper no. 238, pp. 22–27.

32 Stephen to Labouchere, 15 March 1839, CO 209/4, NA; *British Parliamentary Debates*, House of Commons, 25 June 1839, column 829.

33 Lord Normanby to Hobson, 14 August 1839, *BPP*, 1840, Correspondence with the Secretary of State Relative to New Zealand, Paper no. 238, pp. 37–38.

34 Coates to Church Missionary Society missionaries in New Zealand, 17 July 1839, quoted in Coates to Lord Stanley, 14 August 1844, *BPP*, 1844, Return to an Address of the Honourable the House of Commons, Paper no. 641, pp. 2–3; John Beecham to the Chairman of the New Zealand District, 2 September 1839, cited J.M.R. Owens, 'Missionaries and the Treaty of Waitangi', *Wesleyan Historical Society (New Zealand) Journal*, no. 49, 1986, p. 12; Sharp, pp. 720, 738.

35 There is no extant copy of the final English language text of the Treaty. For how it probably read, see Ned Fletcher's reconstruction in his 'A Praiseworthy Device for Amusing and Pacifying Savages? What the Framers Meant by the English Text of the Treaty of Waitangi' (PhD thesis, University of Auckland, 2014), pp. 34–35.

36 William Colenso, Memoranda of the Arrival of Lieutenant Governor Hobson in New Zealand 1840, MS 1611, Folder 1, Alexander Turnbull Library; Busby, 'The Occupation of New Zealand 1833–43', p. 90, James Busby Letters and Papers, MS 46, Box 6, Folder 1, Auckland War Memorial Museum Library; Busby to G.W. Hope, 17 January 1845, *BPP*, 1845, Copies of Letters from Mr Shortland and Mr Busby to Lord Stanley and Mr G.W. Hope, Paper no. 108, p. 15; Williams, 'Early Recollections', in Hugh Carleton, *The Life of Henry Williams, Archdeacon of Waimate, Vol. 2*, Wilsons & Horton, Auckland, 1877, p. 12; William Colenso, *The Authentic and Genuine History of the Signing of the Treaty of Waitangi*, Government Printer, Wellington, 1890, pp. 16–17.

37 Claudia Orange, *The Treaty of Waitangi*, Allen & Unwin/Port Nicholson Press, Wellington, 1987, p. 58; Michael Belgrave, *Historical Frictions: Maori Claims and Reinvented Histories*, Auckland University Press, Auckland, 2005, pp. 57, 59–60, 62; Lyndsay Head, 'Land, Authority and the Forgetting of Being in Early Colonial Maori History' (PhD thesis, University of Canterbury, 2006), pp. 8, 49, 53–54, 66–68, 144, 166–67, 202, 208–10, 212.

9

Protecting the Peace on the Edges of Empire: Commissioners of Crown Lands in New South Wales

LISA FORD

In the 1820s and 1830s Australian Aborigines fought a life and death battle on the frontiers of the colony of New South Wales. A new and insatiable demand for Australian wool induced settler entrepreneurs to march millions of sheep and cattle along the sparse waterways of the otherwise arid interior. For Australia's indigenous people this invasion was disastrous. It threatened more than dispossession from ancestral hunting grounds: food and water, the very stuff of life, was at issue. Consequently, Aborigines attacked livestock and speared shepherds. In turn, settlers shot, poisoned and brutalised Aborigines. News of these unequal conflicts trickled into Sydney and, eventually, into London. There, it joined accounts of similar events from Canada and southern Africa. It slowly dawned on imperial reformers that slavery was not the only, nor perhaps even the worst injustice wrought by Empire. The result, in 1837, was a parliamentary select committee report on the welfare of Aboriginal peoples residing on the fringes of British settlements. Aboriginal peoples, the report declared, needed Empire's protection.

The project of Aboriginal protection has a rich historiography. The best of it is deeply entwined with the study of webs of Empire. Those historians have taught us that the impulse to protect Aborigines grew directly out of the evangelical networks that had led the campaign to reform slavery. At the movement's epicentre lay a cluster of families living near Clapham Common. The 1837 Select Committee report on aborigines was a family effort, authored by Thomas Fowell Buxton's cousin, Anna Gurney.[1] Its signal achievement (or its biggest failure) in New South Wales was the establishment of the Aboriginal Protectorate in the Port Philip District. A tiny group of missionaries was deployed there between 1839 and 1849 to proselytise Aborigines, both dissuade and shield them from the worst frontier violence and, at some point, encourage them to settle on reserves.[2]

Viewed from Sydney, the Port Phillip Protectorate was an exceptional and exceptionable conceit: the efforts of four green missionaries in the southern wilds had little to do with the protection of Aborigines elsewhere in New South Wales, or indeed in the other fledgling colonies in the island continent. This chapter focuses on a very different and arguably much more important sphere of activity: the plans hatched in the late 1830s and only partly rolled out by Governor George Gipps on all of the other pastoral frontiers of the enormous colony. These plans had a very different focus. They explicitly linked the protection of Aborigines to the establishment of an effective magistracy and police force beyond the boundaries of settlement. Throughout the colony, Commissioners of Crown Lands and border police were charged with protecting Aboriginal people by bringing them within the pale of the law.

As Roger Milliss showed clearly some time ago, these efforts, like the Port Phillip Protectorate, were soon overwhelmed by violence and cynicism.[3] Nevertheless, I argue here that Gipps' plans for protection deserve further attention. This is so because they covered much more ground than the Protectorate, operating on every frontier of New South Wales and closely resembling models of protection adopted in South Australia and Western Australia soon after.[4] Most importantly, Gipps' project of protection had clearer roots in other imperial initiatives to protect vulnerable people than did the Protectorate. If the protectors shared the zealotry of the anti-slavery campaign, then Gipps' version of protection shared the ideology and methods of official efforts to ameliorate slavery in the 1820s. This change of view matters because it suggests that squatter interests alone cannot explain the scheme of Aboriginal protection implemented by Gipps in the western and northern borderlands of New South Wales after 1838. Gipps' scheme forms part of, and casts light on, a broader imperial story.

In this chapter I argue that both anti-slavery and Gipps' plans for Aboriginal protection were jurisdictional projects, imagined and instantiated as efforts to bring slaves and indigenous people within the Queen's peace and, therefore, within the reach of the Queen's courts. Gipps shared with anti-slavery a deep faith that incorporating new and old subjects under British jurisdiction would provide a cheap means of civilising marginal subjects and of making Empire more just without making it less autocratic. Viewed in this context, his efforts to police the pastoral frontier are enormously instructive because they help us to understand the ideational limits of the project of protection-as-jurisdiction by laying bare the Faustian bargain underpinning humanitarian legal reform. In Gipps' New South Wales equality before the law became the most compelling argument for *and* against Aboriginal protection.[5]

THE MAKINGS OF FRONTIER CONFLICT

A peculiar problem of governance confronted settler polities from the 1820s when industrialisation in Britain fed explosive colonial growth.[6] An overwhelming number of European migrants went to the United States after 1800, but enough people went to Australia to support the establishment of four new colonies between 1825 and 1852. More importantly, population growth, investment and changing industrial technologies fed the uncontrollable expansion of pastoralism. Sheep numbers grew exponentially when imperial wool tariffs were reduced in 1823, and again in 1828 when a parliamentary select committee in London declared that Australian wool was a viable alternative to German wool. In 1823 alone, wool exports from Australia jumped from 175,400 pounds to 400,000 pounds.[7] By 1831 Australia and Van Diemen's Land produced two and a half million pounds of wool, and by 1844 that figure had grown to thirteen and a half million pounds.[8]

In arid Australia this army of sheep required an enormous amount of land. At first pastoralists usurped grazing runs without the imprimatur of government and almost always without the consent of Aboriginal people. Their trespasses earned them the title of 'squatters'. Although squatters occupied land without crown consent it was neither feasible nor economical for the New South Wales government to halt their egress: the Empire was parsimonious and infrastructures of governance were pathetically small in the colony. The Crown settled for trying to preserve some fragile title to land. In 1826 and 1829, Governor Ralph Darling declared that the borders of the nineteen settled counties marked the boundaries of location beyond which no land would be surveyed or sold, and in 1833 his successor, Sir Richard Bourke, enacted legislation providing that 'the unauthorised occupation' of land would not be 'considered as giving any legal title thereto' through adverse possession or any other device of common law.[9] Successive acts of the local Legislative Council tried to turn illegal occupiers into paying licensees, holding the conditional right to depasture cattle temporarily on Crown Land but given none of the other benefits of tenure.

Collecting licence fees from far flung pastoralists was hard enough. Distance and difference made ordering relationships between Aborigines and settlers on pastoral frontiers harder still. Violence had marred Aboriginal-settler relations from the outset of colonisation but from the mid-1820s rapid pastoral expansion meant that violence was both more intense and largely removed from view. From 1836 skirmishes became so frequent that their recitation took on a quotidian character in the Governor's correspondence.

The depth of the problem became painfully apparent in three much discussed massacres, two of them presided over and covered up by government officials. The Surveyor-General of the colony, Thomas Mitchell, killed an unknown number of Aborigines near the Darling River in 1835. Nothing was done. Three years later the new Governor, Sir George Gipps, was still asking awkward questions about this incident.[10] In January 1838 Major James Nunn killed an unspecified number of Aborigines on the Gwydir River. Nunn's misdeeds were particularly troubling as his expedition marked the first foray into the squatting districts by a mounted police force. Nunn was supposed to model restraint on the pastoral frontier. In typical form the colony's Legislative Council insisted that an inquiry into the massacre should be completed by the local magistracy. Local sympathy and laws that precluded Aboriginal evidence meant that the inquiry could find precious little evidence of police wrongdoing.[11] Finally, in June 1838, a group of shepherds killed as many as thirty men, women and children at Myall Creek on the Liverpool Plains, only to be acquitted (at least initially) by a sympathetic jury.[12]

EMPIRE AND PROTECTION

Events like these were extremely disturbing for British reformers who had been engaged in multilayered projects of imperial protection for several decades. Massacres were disturbing because they highlighted a new sphere of colonial evil. This moral failure of the colonists foreshadowed a broader, imperial failure to govern and police settler peripheries. Imperial protection, in this context, had a legal as well as a moral valence.

As Lauren Benton and I have argued, the idea of protecting vulnerable people became a touchstone in British thinking about interpolity and intrapolity legal orders by the early nineteenth century. Protection was a flexible notion underpinning an array of jurisdictional claims over the poor and oppressed at home and subjects and foreigners abroad. Protection justified the rewriting of the Ionian constitution over the objections of local elites. Protection even wove into plans to incorporate new places into Empire. For example, protection of Kandyan people from tyrannical local law became an excuse for invasion in 1816.[13]

The most important of these projects, for my purposes, was the amelioration of slavery in Empire that spanned 1780 to 1833. This, too, was a jurisdictional project. The logic of imperial intervention in colonial slavery went thus. A master's proprietary claim to his or her slave removed both the master's and the slave's malefactions from the purview of the state. That derogation from the King's power to keep the peace corrupted government because colonial legislatures existed to serve slave masters in both the oppression of slaves and the protection of slaveholders against creditors.[14]

To achieve moral improvement in general, and slave protection in particular, required a shift in the constitutional balance from the periphery to the centre. Under this scheme imperial protection would be delivered through supervised acts of jurisdiction. Core proposals for slave protection opened the master-slave relationship to policing. The process was intimate and intensive, as the briefest look at the Trinidad Slave Code of 1822 demonstrates. That order in council required slave masters of Trinidad to respect slave marriages, allow slaves to honour the Sabbath, and record the most quotidian (in the context of plantation work regimes) of slave punishments. Their compliance would be scrupulously policed and recorded by the Protector of Slaves, who was also charged with mediating master-slave disputes and representing slaves before island courts. Even slave protection legislation passed by self-governing colonies – on which Aboriginal protection in New South Wales was clearly based – opened the master-slave relationship to state policing. From the late-eighteenth century island legislatures invested magistrates with new jurisdiction to govern masters and slaves chiefly in order to ward off abolitionist-inspired metropolitan intervention in slavery.[15] For example, the Nevis Protection Act named all the justices of the peace on the island 'collectively and individually ... to be protectors of slaves', an arrangement that James Stephen Jnr, legal counsel for the Colonial Office, thought cynical.[16] However, Mindie Lazarus-Black has demonstrated that even these half-hearted efforts to expand the jurisdiction of island magistracies opened new and real opportunities for slaves.[17]

Slavery ended in 1833, but the concern of anti-slavery campaigners with Empire did not. In 1835 Thomas Fowell Buxton convinced the British parliament to appoint a select committee to inquire into the treatment of indigenous people in the Empire's settler colonies. The result was the aforementioned Select Committee Report on aborigines (British Settlements) of 1837, whose recommendations were embraced by Lord Glenelg, Secretary for State for the Colonies.

Jurisdiction as a basis for protection formed a key strand in the 1837 Report. The Committee, in its own words, had been appointed 'to secure to [native inhabitants] the due observance of justice and the protection of their rights; to promote the spread of civilisation among them, and to lead them to the peaceful and voluntary reception of the Christian religion'.[18] Echoing arguments made about Caribbean legislatures by the great anti-slavery crusader James Stephen Snr in 1802, the Committee resolved that the Crown should take charge of the protection of aborigines because local legislatures could not be trusted to rule in their interests.[19] The chief duties of the protectors would be to ensure that Aborigines had enough land to hunt on and to manage their interface with British culture and British law. The Committee thought it in equal measures absurd *and* essential to punish Aborigines under British law, even if Aborigines had no idea what it comprised. It proposed that Aboriginal protectors should craft a 'temporary and provisional code' to bring Aborigines within 'the pale of the law'.[20] The office of protector was thus imagined through the prism of the magistracy, the courts, and criminal law.

In January 1838, in a very brief dispatch, Glenelg announced the establishment of the protectorate on an incredibly modest scale. George Augustus Robinson, who had overseen the deportation of indigenous survivors of the Black War in Van Dieman's Land to Flinders Island, was to move to Port Phillip to serve as Chief Protector. There he would supervise four assistant protectors deployed from Britain and handpicked for their missionary zeal. Each of these assistant protectors was to 'attach himself as closely and constantly as possible to the Aboriginal Tribes' and wander with them 'until they can be induced to assume more settled habits of life'. He would 'protect them . . . from any encroachments on their property, and from acts of Cruelty, of oppression and injustice', educate them, oversee their '*moral* and *religious* improvement' and learn their language. To this end, Glenelg instructed, 'it will be desirable to invest each protector with a commission as magistrate'.[21]

Five men scattered around one of the many enormous pastoral frontiers of New South Wales could never be expected to exhaust efforts to bring the benefits of the Queen's peace to Aborigines. So trifling was Glenelg's gesture that Gipps took months to reply. He tabled the letter at a meeting of the Executive Council in early July even as the Legislative Council gathered to discuss the Nunn affair and the Myall Creek massacre. And he only responded to Glenelg in November, pointing out rather brusquely that he had had more pressing matters to deal with.[22] In fact, from early in that year Gipps had been working on a different and much larger programme for protection in the colony.[23]

JURISDICTION ON THE EDGES OF EMPIRE

The 1837 Report was only one avenue through which jurisdiction wove into Aboriginal-settler relations in New South Wales. Jurisdiction had long since emerged as an inconsistent strand of local thinking about Aboriginal protection, imported to the colony by lawyers with humanitarian connections. From the beginning of settlement, government responses to settler-indigenous violence inhabited an ambiguous space between war, protection and policing.[24] However, the arrival of the first Attorney General and the first properly staffed

Supreme Court in 1824 prompted a marked swing away from the language of war and towards the language of jurisdiction. Attorney General Saxe Bannister oversaw the first declaration of martial law in the colony in 1824. He convinced the Governor, Sir Thomas Brisbane, that any government sponsored violence against Aborigines in the vicinity of Bathurst required a suspension of civilian law. As he told Brisbane's successor, Sir Ralph Darling, in 1826, the 'indiscriminate slaughter of offenders, except in the heat of immediate pursuit or other similar circumstances, requires preliminary solemn acts; and that to order soldiers to punish any outrage in this way, is against the law'.[25] This was an unprecedented jurisdictional claim. Bannister's conviction did not mark a decisive shift, however. In 1825, Secretary of State for the Colonies Lord Bathurst had instructed Darling to treat Aboriginal depredations 'as if they proceeded from subjects of any accredited State'.[26] And, despite Bannister's protestations, Darling refused to legitimise violence against Aborigines in the Hunter region in 1826 with a declaration of martial law.[27]

The creation of the mounted police in 1825 marked a more ambiguous but also more enduring shift from war to jurisdiction. This specialist force was staffed with armed and mounted men, many seconded from military service. As such it indulged in few of the pretences that had made police acceptable to a wary British public. Yet the very name of the force gestured to new jurisdictional aspirations towards Aborigines. In theory at least, police did not make war; their task was to keep the peace on the King's land among the King's subjects. The reality was quite different, as the 1827 trial and acquittal of Nathaniel Lowe for summarily executing an Aboriginal man in the Hunter Valley demonstrated.[28]

At the same time, the Supreme Court of New South Wales started to consider seriously the status of Aboriginal people vis-à-vis the Crown. This, too, was a halting process. The first indigenous person was tried in a settler court in 1816 but he was a cultural intermediary, proficient in English and raised in a settler family. The next was tried in 1822 for murdering a settler, and after this indigenous defendants began to appear once or twice a year for interracial violence. Many were acquitted on the grounds that they did not understand the proceedings. The jurisdictional qualms of the court were articulated most explicitly when Aborigines were arrested for killing their countrymen in settler towns. In 1828, the Supreme Court refused to try Ballard or Barret for killing another Aborigine in Sydney because Aboriginal peoples had not been conquered by the British Empire and so were governed by their own laws for crimes *inter se*. Aboriginal Australians only fell within settler jurisdiction when they committed crimes or needed legal remedies against settlers.[29]

The Supreme Court began to assert its jurisdiction over Aborigines much more consistently as violence increased in the 1830s. In 1835, twenty-one Aboriginal men were arrested and tried for a range of offences related to frontier violence. In the following year, in the case of R. v. Murrell, the court reversed its opinion in Ballard and declared that violence between Aborigines fell within British jurisdiction. The author of this decision, Justice William Burton, reasoned that Aborigines were governed by settler law because British sovereignty was a territorial measure of authority that could not share space with Aboriginal law. He also argued that Aboriginal law was not sophisticated enough to warrant recognition. Therefore, every Aboriginal person fell under the King's peace and protection. Law was the mechanism of both civilisation and protection. Here Burton drew directly on his own work on slave amelior-ation. He had been involved in legal reforms at the Cape Colony aimed at opening slavery and indentured servitude to government scrutiny. He was also in correspondence with controversial New South Wales missionary Lancelot Threlkeld about how best to serve Aboriginal people. In a letter to Burton, filed with notes on the Murrell case, Threlkeld had argued: 'it would be mercy perhaps to them were they placed under the *protection* as well as the *power* of the British laws, & much more safe for the country resident & his family.'[30]

For Burton, bringing Aborigines within the King's peace and protection did not promise equal protection under the law but rather special protection. Aborigines would enjoy an attenuated legal subjecthood: 'These are ... citi-zens of an inferior order, & are united & subject to the society without participating in all its advantages.'[31] The logic of rendering Aborigines as something less than subjects was more than dismissive chauvinism. As partial legal subjects, Aborigines (like slaves) could be treated differently by law, especially vulnerable to legal abuse, but also especially distinguished by legal protections and controls. Arguably Burton's complicated formula has formed the de facto basis of Aboriginal status ever since. As Heather Douglas and Mark Finnane have shown, from 1836 indigenous people were overpoliced yet never fully integrated into Australian criminal law.[32]

Burton's plans for Aboriginal protection drew even more explicitly from slave amelioration. In 1838 he drafted a bill for Aboriginal protection that, he said, adapted the Imperial Slave Code of 1830 (which was derived, in turn from the Trinidad Ordinance of 1822). The bill outlined a system of protec-tion for Aborigines that was based on intensive governance within the settled counties. Police magistrates would be given special powers to encourage Aborigines to live in designated places and discourage them from begging or hunting for subsistence. They would be authorised to oversee Aboriginal labour for government and disperse Aboriginal gatherings before they could end in affray. Mirroring concerns expressed in the Cape Colony about combining commissions of the peace with slave protection, police magistrates in New South Wales would be aided by dedicated district protectors whose task was to document the births and deaths of Aboriginal people, facilitate and vet their contracts for labour with settlers, and supervise their moral comportment. Burton noted that this sort of management could be effected through vagrancy law, but he hesitated in recommending it. Vagrancy law had proved a powerful tool in the oppression of emancipated slaves in the Caribbean since 1833, to the growing disquiet of both activists and the Colonial Office.[33] Instead, Burton suggested that labour should be at least semi-voluntary: a service given in return for subsistence.[34] The bill never passed, yet Amanda Nettelbeck has noted that very similar instructions were given to the first protectors in the colonies of South Australia and Western Australia at the end of the 1830s.[35] Thus, Burton anticipated the template of protection of Aborigines elsewhere in the continent.

In the end, a much simpler orthodoxy defined official thinking about the legal status of Aborigines after 1836. Secretary of State Glenelg told Governor Bourke in 1837 that 'all the natives inhabiting these territories must be considered as subjects of the Queen and as within Her Majesty's allegiance. To regard them as aliens with whom a war can exist, and against whom H.M.'s troops may exercise belligerent right, is to deny that protection to which they derive the highest possible claim from the sovereignty which has been assumed over the whole of their ancient possessions'.[36] Protection in this casting was more generic, that is, the protection owed Aborigines was the same protection owed any subject by their sovereign.

PROTECTION AND JURISDICTION

It was this simple orthodoxy that underpinned Gipps' plan for protection in 1838. At its core rested a new kind of magistracy reinforced by paramilitary police.[37] In April, just two months after his arrival, Gipps resolved to declare Commissioners of Crown Lands to be protectors of Aborigines and magistrates.[38] The office of Commissioner of Crown Lands had been created by Bourke's 1833 Crown Lands Act. Commissioners were authorised to 'do and perform any lawful acts matters and things for preventing intrusion encroachment and trespass' on Crown lands outside the boundaries of location. This was not a broad mandate because there were precious few 'acts matters and things' that a Commissioner who was not a magistrate could lawfully do. Only magistrates could police crimes or levy fines. Gipps' proposal, therefore, was a radical one. Combining the powers of the Commissioner

and Justice of the Peace and issuing special instructions that he wield his
powers in the defence of Aborigines signalled a new, and for squatters, a
daunting prospect. It threatened to bind up powers to grant and withdraw
licences with Aboriginal protection.

Gipps presented a proclamation to this end to the Legislative Council in
early April.[39] After reports of several murders in Gwydir (in retaliation for
Major Nunn's massacre) and of an attack by 300 Aborigines on thirteen men
driving cattle in Port Phillip reached Sydney late in April, the Council
requested that Gipps defer publication of the proclamation until public
anxiety about Aboriginal resistance had died down.[40] Meanwhile, the proclamation went back into draft, and a series of related controversies about
continuing violence, the use of the Land Fund for Aboriginal Protection,
and the creation of the Port Phillip Protectorate wracked the government.[41]
Ongoing discussions between Gipps and Assistant Colonial Secretary Thomas
Harington about the precise wording of the proclamation reveal ambivalence
about Aboriginal legal status.[42] One version suggested that Aborigines could
be 'governed by their own ancient usages, wherever these do not interfere
with the rights or safety of their more civilised fellow subjects' and that the
Commissioners might make and enforce treaties with indigenous people.[43]
A minute suggests that Justice Burton had quickly objected to the former.
Harington objected to the latter, pointing out the impossibility and the
unpopularity of treating with the Queen's subjects. Gipps, evidently attached
to the idea, suggested replacing 'treaty' with 'agreement'.[44]

These exchanges also reveal some deep ambiguities in the nexus between
jurisdiction and protection. Harington stressed the need to articulate that
protection was due to 'whites as well as blacks', as this was a grounding
principle of equality before the law. He warned: 'If Europeans, especially at
the outstations, are to be prevented from having recourse to *native law*, i.e. to
summary punishment inflicted by the person or party injured, is not the govt
morally bound first to provide adequate protection, consistent with the principles of English law?' He suggested that the final draft of the proclamation
should be submitted to the Attorney General or the judges to iron out the
thorny relationship of protection with sovereignty and the constitutional rights
of Englishmen. Several iterations later, the Governor was still worrying about
words. In his minute on another Harington commentary on the proclamation,
Gipps wondered if it was 'dangerous to enumerate their rights, lest we be
called on to acknowledge their right [to] the possession of the soil'.[45] As the
Legislative Council quibbled about whether to call the Aborigines' claim
on government a right to 'countenance' or 'protection', Gipps took issue
altogether with the clumsiness of the phrases 'protector of natives' and

'protector of Aborigines'.[46] These discussions were cut short by the Colonial Office's decision to create a protectorate for Port Phillip. When Gipps and the Council revisited the issue they avoided the problem by not naming Commissioners 'protectors' at all. Milliss argues that this decision reflected squatter lobbying and the subsequent compromise of Gipps' humanitarian principles.[47] His argument is compelling but I also think that Gipps' pragmatism cut through the rhetoric of humanitarianism to the main game: protection through jurisdiction and policing. Thereafter, investing the Commissioners with the powers of magistrates became Gipps' key tool of protection on pastoral frontiers throughout the colony.

The Governor had prerogative power to invest whomever he chose with the powers of magistrates, including Commissioners. The main task, therefore, was to pass legislation defining the powers of Commissioner-magistrates beyond the settled counties. The Crown Lands Unauthorised Occupation Act of 1838 (No. 23a) gave magistrates the power to revoke the licences of squatters summarily 'convicted on the oath of any one or more credible witness or witnesses of any offence which in the opinion of such Justice or Justices shall render such person unfit to continue to hold such lease or license'.[48] Judges John Walpole Willis and James Dowling remonstrated against this power. They argued that giving magistrates power to revoke a licence might also be 'unconstitutional inasmuch as it vests any Justice or Justices with the power of declaring any lease or license null and void'.[49] Dowling quickly backed down in the face of the Governor's disapproval, but Willis continued to press the case into 1839, urging the Governor to base the powers of Commissioners not on the authority of the legislature but on the less formal powers of emergency vested in the Queen.[50]

Surprisingly, the concerns of the Legislative Council and of parties testifying before a committee formed to discuss the 1839 Crown Lands Bill were much more temperate. Most merely objected to a single Commissioner's power to seize cattle and revoke licences without the aid and assistance of another magistrate. Some even asked that the Commissioners' powers be expanded to settle master-servant disputes beyond the boundaries.[51] To ward off constitutional critique Gipps altered the Crown Lands Unauthorised Occupation Act in 1839 to make the Commissioners' powers marginally more specific.[52] The 1839 Act also went much further than its predecessor by creating a new paramilitary police force. 'For the protection of the rights of the Crown and for the mutual protection and security of all persons lawfully occupying, resorting to, or being upon the Crown Lands of this colony', it placed a border police force under the orders of the Commissioner. This move was much more popular with the squatters. As the Committee's report made clear, 'all parties agree that a Border Police will prove of the greatest assistance in keeping peace and good order'.[53]

In his explanations to the Colonial Office, Gipps noted that the Act made 'no mention ... of the protection of the Aborigines' even though it was crafted with the goal 'of putting a stop to the atrocities which have been committed both on them and by them'. The Act did not need to mention Aborigines because, 'as it respects the Aborigines', the law 'required neither improvement nor alteration'. Aborigines were already the Queen's subjects and thus fell within her protection. Therefore, Gipps sought only 'the means ... of putting the law in execution'. These means, he hoped, would be supplied by the border police force established under the Act.[54] This force was an instrument of Aboriginal protection, Gipps explained, because it would keep the peace beyond the boundaries of location. To this end, standing orders issued to officers gave remarkably vague instructions that they should behave 'in a kind and humane manner to the natives, and [endeavour] to gain their confidence and esteem, as well as to civilise and improve them'.[55]

When, in May 1839, Gipps finally issued his thirteen-month-old proclamation, he made the link between his Commissioners, policing and Aboriginal protection much clearer. He warned pastoralists that 'extensive powers ... are now vested in the Commissioners of Lands acting beyond the boundaries of location', and that 'Commissioners are now magistrates of the territory'. Henceforth there would be no talk of 'aliens', 'war' or 'belligerent rights'. Such talk was 'no less consistent with the spirit of that law than it is at variance with the dictates of justice and humanity'. Commissioners were 'to cultivate at all times amicable intercourse' with Aborigines; to ensure they obtained 'redress for any wrong'; and to prevent 'interference on the part of white men with their women'. Coroners would investigate Aboriginal deaths, as they would white ones. But Aborigines would also be punished for their wrongs. They should be informed of 'the penalties' for 'aggression on the persons or properties of the colonists'. Nor would there be talk of special protection for Aborigines. Commissioners were not protectors of Aborigines; they were, instead, protectors of the peace dispensing 'equal and indiscriminate justice'.[56]

For all this talk there was no equal justice to be had by indigenous people before settler courts. Wrongdoing seldom made it into court. Many Commissioners of Crown Lands were pastoralists themselves and actively collaborated with their neighbours to cover up their atrocities.[57] In practice, their investment in protection extended little further than overseeing the distribution of blankets and submitting perfunctory annual reports about the population and fate of indigenous people in their districts.[58] Meanwhile, the disallowance of the New South Wales Aboriginal Evidence Act by the British government and the refusal of settler juries to convict their own rendered courts unable to deliver justice to Aborigines in those rare instances when settlers came to trial.

Practicalities aside, the promise of formal equality before the law opened ideological fissures in protection that had even wider ramifications. The most important of these emerged in discussions about what the state owed to squatters. In 1839, in what seemed to be an unrelated case, Justice Willis declared that Robert and Helenus Scott could sue George Dight for trespass for depasturing his sheep on their cattle run on the Liverpool Plains. He declared that 'the right of occupancy exists so long as the party occupies the land, and as it was proved that the defendant took his sheep into the best part of the plaintiffs' run, there was undoubtedly a trespass'.[59] *Scott v. Dight* seemed innocuous enough until Willis revisited the question of licensee rights in a murder case in Port Phillip in 1841. In *R. v. Bolden*, he pronounced that 'if a person receives a licence from the government to occupy a run, and whether white or black comes on that run to commit a depredation on the party's property, he is fully authorised to use any lawful means in his power to protect it . . . They have a right to turn either [a] black or a white off'.[60] That right extended to lethal force. In the stroke of a pen a licence to depasture stock became a licence to kill Aborigines.

Gipps responded to *Bolden* by suggesting that licences be altered to expressly declare licensees were 'in no way authorised to expel Aborigines from the Lands they occupy', and therefore could not 'stop Aborigines from hunting, fishing or encamping' on any part of their run that was not 'inclosed [sic] or cultivated'.[61] The acting Attorney General, Roger Therry, was less concerned. He articulated the power of Willis' logic very clearly: 'it has been held over and over again in the Supreme Court that the holder of a license for depasturing on Crown lands may maintain a trespass in respect of an injury done to his run.' This right could be used against Aborigines as well as settlers. Indeed, Therry could not 'see how any proviso could be made in their favour in the depasturing license without involving admission of a principle which the law has as yet decidedly negatived – vizt. a distinction between black and white'.[62] Keeping the frontier peace, in this view, could amount to nothing more than policing Aborigines. So, protection-as-jurisdiction collapsed into the rule of law.[63]

CONCLUSIONS

Efforts to protect Aborigines in New South Wales grew out of imperial discourses of protection that were decades old. As historians of protection have long pointed out, the Select Committee into the plight of aborigines in British settler colonies in 1837 was led by evangelist, anti-slavery crusaders. The men sent to Port Phillip to run the Protectorate were also evangelists, clients of the same movement. Burton's 1839 draft legislation explicitly borrowed from the Imperial Slave Code of 1830. And, most importantly, Gipps' magistrate-protector followed the cut-rate model of protection embraced extensively in self-governing slave colonies at the turn of the nineteenth century. Aboriginal protection in New South Wales thus fits into a broad imperial story because of its investment in protection-as-jurisdiction. It shared with anti-slavery a deep faith that incorporating new and old subjects within the reach of the Queen's courts under centrally reformed colonial law and procedure would provide a cheap means of civilising marginal subjects and making Empire more just without making it less autocratic.

The clear similarities between imperial and colonial strategies of protection in the pre-1833 slave colonies and in post-1835 Australia do not mean that slave protection and protection of Aborigines were the same. The jurisdiction sought by anti-slavery crusaders was intimate, detailed and encompassing. Only Burton's bill approached that level of engagement, promising as it did to concentrate Aboriginal populations and to half-encourage and half-coerce them into orderly living arrangements and state-sponsored work. In contrast, the problem of governance beyond the boundaries of settlement in New South Wales was one of distance, not of the legal and physical intimacy of masters and slaves. State efforts there were directed towards claiming a monopoly on violence and thus bringing the pastoral frontier within the Queen's peace. Gipps' goal was to project the presence of the state to frontiers through a mobile paramilitary police force under the leadership of an itinerant magistrate who held the authority if not the power to withhold licences and impose penalties. This was a very different sort of policing but it shared the goal of using criminal law to protect and police vulnerable subjects.

The task Gipps set his Commissioners and the border police was clearly impossible: a tiny government constrained by penury could not contain interracial violence on such a vast geographical scale. Few Commissioners even tried to do so. We need to do more work on the mechanics of that failure in order to better understand how the Commissioners worked and what they did. A very preliminary glance at the Armidale Commissioner's records in the 1840s suggests that they policed convict workers, settled occasional disputes between licensees, and did very little else besides.[64]

However, I have argued here that the failure of this system was not merely practical. Focusing on discussions about protecting Aborigines through jurisdiction in New South Wales after 1836 helps us to understand the *ideational* limits of the imperial project of protection on a grander scale. In 1838 Gipps thought law was perfect: if Aborigines fell within the Queen's peace they were already proper objects of the Queen's protection. However, the same logic meant that the only way to justify Aboriginal protection through law on New South Wales frontiers was to police and protect all of the Queen's subjects equally. Thus, Aboriginal subjecthood flattened the project of protection into a project of ordering subjects in space. The liberal promise of treating people equally in law destroyed the ideological bases for special protection, opening fissures in what had been an immensely powerful logic among imperial reformers. In the end the only way to instantiate special protection through law was to reanimate Burton's logic of 1836: to make Aborigines perpetual wards of the state.

NOTES

This research was conducted with the support of the Australian Research Council, DE1020100593.

1 Zoe Laidlaw, '"Aunt Anna's Report": The Buxton Women and the Aborigines Select Committee, 1835–1837', *Journal of Imperial and Commonwealth History*, vol. 32, no. 2, 2004, pp. 1–28; Elizabeth Elbourne, 'Imperial Politics in a Family Way: Gender, Biography and the 1835–36 Select Committee on Aborigines', in Bain Attwood and Tom Griffiths (eds), *Frontier, Race, Nation: Henry Reynolds and Australian History*, Australian Scholarly Publishing, Melbourne, 2009, pp. 111–35.

2 M.F. Christie, *Aborigines in Colonial Victoria, 1835–1886*, Sydney University Press, Sydney, 1979, pp. 81–106; A.G.L. Shaw, *A History of the Port Phillip District: Victoria before Separation*, Miegunyah Press, Melbourne, 1996, pp. 111–43; Richard Broome, *Aboriginal Victorians: A History Since 1800*, Allen & Unwin, Sydney, 2005, pp. 135–53. For a more recent account, see Jessie Mitchell, *In Good Faith? Governing Indigenous Australians through God, Charity and Empire, 1825–1855*, Aboriginal History, Canberra, 2011, pp. 173–97. In regard to squatting, the best book remains Stephen H. Roberts, *The Squatting Age in Australia 1835–1847* (1935), Melbourne University Press, Melbourne, 1964.

3 Roger Milliss, *Waterloo Creek: The Australia Day Massacre of 1838, George Gipps and the British Conquest of New South Wales*, McPhee Gribble, Melbourne, 1992.

4 Amanda Nettelbeck, '"A Halo of Protection": Colonial Protectors and the Policy of Aboriginal Protection as Punishment', *Australian Historical Studies*, vol. 43, no. 3, 2011, pp. 396–411; Amanda Nettelbeck, Russell Smandych, Louis A. Knafla and Robert Foster, *Fragile Settlements: Aboriginal Peoples, Law and Resistance in South-West Australia and Prairie Canada*, University of British Columbia Press, Vancouver, 2016.

5 S.G. Foster, 'Aboriginal Rights and Official Morality', *Push from the Bush*, no. 11, 1981, pp. 68–97.

6 James Belich, *Replenishing the Earth: The Settler Revolution and the Rise of the Anglo-World, 1783–1939*, Oxford University Press, Oxford, 2009, pp. 126–33.

7 Roberts, p. 42. In general, see Lisa Ford and David Roberts, 'Expansion, 1820–1850', in Alison Bashford and Stuart Macintyre (eds), *The Cambridge History of Australia, Volume 1*, Cambridge University Press, Melbourne, 2013, pp. 121–48.

8 Roberts, pp. 42–43.

9 *Crown Lands Encroachment Act*, 1833, 4 Will. 4, no. 11a, X, New South Wales, www.austlii.edu.au/au/legis/nsw/num_act/clea1833n11268/ (accessed 7 September 2016).

10 Colonial Secretary to Attorney General, 8 March 1838, 4/3745, State Records of New South Wales (henceforth SRNSW).

11 Executive Council Minute, no. 20, 7 June 1839, and Executive Council Minute, no. 22, 9 July 1839, 4/1520, SRNSW.

12 For exhaustive treatment of the Nunn and Myall Creek cases, see Milliss, pp. 166–203, 274–311; Brian W. Harrison, 'The Myall Creek Massacre and Its Significance in the Controversy over the Aborigines during Australia's Early Squatting Period' (BA Hons thesis, University of New England, 1966); R.H.W. Reece, *Aborigines and Colonists: Aborigines and Colonial Society in New South Wales in the 1830s and 1840s*, University of Sydney Press, Sydney, 1974, pp. 34–48, 146–74; 'Special Issue', *Push from the Bush*, no. 20, 1985.

13 Lauren Benton and Lisa Ford, *Rage for Order: The British Empire and the Origins of International Law, 1800–1850*, Harvard University Press, Cambridge, MA, 2016, pp. 85–116.

14 James Stephen, *The Crisis of the Sugar Colonies, or, An Enquiry into the Objects and Probable Effects of the French Expedition to the West Indies*, Hatchard, London, 1802, pp. 133–34.

15 Lauren Benton and Lisa Ford, 'Magistrates in Empire: Convicts, Slaves, and the Remaking of the Plural Order in the British Empire', in Lauren Benton and Richard J. Ross (eds), *Legal Pluralism and Empires, 1500–1850*, New York University Press, New York, 2013, pp. 173–98.

16 James Stephen to Governor Charles Maxwell, 27 January 1829, CO 323/46, ff. 80–81, National Archives of the United Kingdom. Stephen did note that the Nevis Act had the redeeming feature of providing 'the most ample and liberal concession which has hitherto been made in any part of the West-Indies' for recognising the testimony of slaves (f. 82).

17 Mindie Lazarus-Black, 'Slaves, Masters, and Magistrates: Law and the Politics of Resistance in the British Caribbean, 1736–1834', in Mindie Lazarus-Black and Susan F. Hirsh (eds), *Contested States, Law, Hegemony and Resistance*, Routledge, New York, 1994, pp. 252–81; Mindie Lazarus-Black, 'John Grant's Jamaica: Notes towards a Reassessment of Courts in the Slave Era', *Journal of Caribbean History*, vol. 27, no. 2, 1993, pp. 144–59.

18 *British Parliamentary Papers*, 1836, Paper no. 538, Report from the Select Committee on Aborigines, British Settlements, p. iii.

19 Stephen, pp. 133–34.

20 *British Parliamentary Papers*, 1837, Paper no. 425, Report from the Select Committee on Aborigines, pp. 83–84.

21 Lord Glenelg to Sir George Gipps, 30 January 1838, *Historical Records of Australia* (henceforth *HRA*), series 1, vol. 19, pp. 254–55, original emphasis.

22 Gipps to Glenelg, 10 November 1838, *HRA*, series 1, vol. 19, p. 668; Executive Council Minute, no. 33, 7 July 1838, 4/1520, SRNSW.

23 Executive Council Minute, no. 22, 10 August 1838, *New South Wales Votes and Proceedings*, 1838, p. 59.

24 See Lisa Ford, *Settler Sovereignty: Jurisdiction and Indigenous People in America and Australia, 1788–1836*, Harvard University Press, Cambridge, MA, 2010.

25 Saxe Bannister to Governor Ralph Darling, 9 September 1826, taken from Saxe Bannister, *Statements and Documents Relating to Proceedings in New South Wales in 1824, 1825 and 1826*, W. Bridekirk, Cape Town, 1827, p. 99; Reece, p. 112.

26 Earl Bathurst to Sir Ralph Darling, 14 July 1825, *HRA*, series 1, vol. 12, p. 21. See also Reece, p. 113.

27 Ford, pp. 173–74.

28 Ibid., pp. 125–27.

29 *R. v. Ballard or Barrett*, Decisions of the Superior Courts of New South Wales, 1788–1899, www.law.mq.edu.au/research/colonial_case_law/nsw/site/scnsw_home/ (accessed 19 October 2016); Bruce Kercher, 'Native Title in the Shadows: The Origins of the Myth of Terra Nullius in Early New South Wales Courts', in Ralph C. Croizier et al. (eds), *Colonialism and the Modern World: Selected Studies*, M.E. Sharpe, New York, 2002, pp. 100–19.

30 Lancelot Threlkeld to Justice William Burton, Memorandum, 2 March 1836, his emphasis, taken from Arguments and Notes for Judgment in the Case of Jack Congo Murrell, February 1836, Original Documents on Aborigines, 1797–1840, 5/1161, no. 48, pp. 234–36, SRNSW, www.law.mq.edu.au/research/colonial_case_law/ nsw/other_features/correspondence/documents/ (accessed 19 October 2016).

31 Emerrich de Vattel, quoted by William Burton, 'Arguments and Notes for Judgment in the Case of Jack Congo Murrell', February 1836, *Original Documents on Aborigines*, no. 48, pp. 234–36.

32 Heather Douglas and Mark Finnane, *Indigenous Crime and Settler Law: White Sovereignty after Empire*, Palgrave Macmillan, Basingstoke, 2012.

33 Mary Turner, 'The British Caribbean, 1823–1838: The Transition from Slave to Free Legal Status', in Douglas Hay and Paul Craven (eds), *Masters, Servants, and Magistrates in Britain and the Empire, 1562–1955*, University of North Carolina Press, Chapel Hill, 2004, pp. 303–22.

34 William Burton, Untitled draft legislation, in Burton to Gipps, 12 June 1838, Copies of Minutes and Memoranda Received, 4/1013, SRNSW. For one of the few pieces of scholarship to deal with the draft in detail, see Shaunnagh Dorsett, 'Travelling Laws', in Shaunnagh Dorsett and John McLaren (eds), *Legal Histories of the British Empire: Laws, Engagements and Legacies*, Routledge, London, 2014, pp. 171–83.

35 Amanda Nettelbeck, 'Creating the Aboriginal "Vagrant"', University of New South Wales History Seminar, Morven Brown, University of New South Wales, 6 September 2016.

36 Glenelg to Sir Richard Bourke, 26 July 1837, *HRA*, series 1, vol. 19, p. 48. For a careful exposition of official orthodoxy, see Foster, pp. 68–98.

37 Gipps to Glenelg, 6 April 1839, *HRA*, series 1, vol. 20, pp. 90–92.

38 Gipps to Glenelg, 27 April 1838, *HRA*, series 1, vol. 19, pp. 397–98.

39 Executive Council Minute, no. 24, 6 April 1838, 4/1520, SRNSW. See also Milliss, pp. 232–33.

40 Gipps to Glenelg, 27 April 1838, *HRA*, series 1, vol. 19, pp. 397–400; Executive Council Minute, no. 25, 22 May 1838, 4/1520, SRNSW.

41 Milliss, pp. 399–503.

42 Foster, passim; Milliss, pp. 238–45.

43 See the minute referring to the 'objections of Judge Burton' on undated document 'Aborigines' in Thomas Harington's hand (Copies of Minutes and Memoranda Received, 4/1013, SRNSW). Gipps was clearly conflicted about Aboriginal subjecthood. In a minute on Harington to Gipps, 25 April 1838, he noted that 'Different doctrine has been held elsewhere, but which is right I will not say' (Copies of Minutes and Memoranda Received, 4/1013, SRNSW).

44 Minutes on Harington to Gipps, 25 April 1838, Copies of Minutes and Memoranda Received, 4/1013, SRNSW.

45 Undated annotated draft, Copies of Minutes and Memoranda Received, 4/1013, SRNSW.

46 Ibid.

47 Milliss, pp. 612–23.

48 *Crown Lands Unauthorized Occupation Act*, 1838, 2 Vic., no. 23a, XIX, s. 5, New South Wales, www.austlii.edu.au/au/legis/nsw/num_act/cluoa1838n23418/ (accessed 7 September 2016). See every witness before the Committee on Crown Lands Bill, New South Wales Legislative Council, *Votes and Proceedings*, 1839.

49 Remonstrance from the judges of the Supreme Court, 11 October 1838, taken from Papers relating to the Regulation of Squatting, part 1, 1839–44, 5/4774.2, SRNSW, original emphasis.

50 John Walpole Willis to Gipps, 19 March 1839, reproduced in Chief Justice Letterbook, 4/6652, SRNSW.

51 Report from the Committee on the Crown Lands Bill, New South Wales Legislative Council, *Votes and Proceedings*, 1839, pp. 19–20, 30.

52 *Crown Lands Unauthorized Occupation Act*, 1839 2 Vic., c. 27, www.austlii.edu.au/au/legis/nsw/num_act/cluoa1839n1418/ (accessed 7 September 2016).

53 Report from the Committee on the Crown Lands Bill, New South Wales Legislative Council, *Votes and Proceedings*, 1839, p. 1.

54 Gipps to Glenelg, 6 April 1839, *HRA*, series 1, vol. 20, pp. 90–92.

55 Standing Orders, Border Police, in Gipps to Glenelg, 22 July 1839, *HRA*, series 1, vol. 20, p. 258.

56 Colonial Secretary, Public Notice, 22 May 1839, Papers relating to the Regulation of Squatting, part 1, 1839–44, 5/4774.2, SRNSW. This was not a simple assertion of jurisdiction: instructions to Commissioners also pointed out that they should appeal to chiefs to assist in policing.

57 Hilary Golder, *Evidence and Accountability: Revisiting and Reading the Public Record*, History Council of New South Wales, Sydney, 2006.

58 Many of these are reproduced in the *HRA* in Gipps' era. See, for example, the enclosures in Gipps to Lord Stanley, 3 April 1843, *HRA*, series 1, vol. 22, pp. 648–54.

59 *Scott v. Dight*, (1839) 16 NSW Supreme Court.

60 *R. v. Bolden, Port Phillip Patriot*, 6 December 1841.

61 Gipps, 10 February 1842, Papers relating to the Regulation of Squatting, part 1, 1839–44, 5/4774.2, SRNSW.

62 Acting Attorney General to Colonial Secretary, 28 February 1842, 5/4774.2, SRNSW.

63 Note that these caveats were included in some pastoral licences: Henry Reynolds and Jamie Dalziel, 'Aborigines and Pastoral Leases: Imperial and Colonial Policy 1826–1855', *University of New South Wales Law Journal*, vol. 19, no. 2, 1996, pp. 315–77.

64 In general, see Border Police Court Armidale, Letterbook, 1/5488, part 2, SRNSW.

10

British Protection, Extraterritoriality and Protectorates in West Africa, 1807–80

INGE VAN HULLE

Protection, as more than one chapter in this volume makes clear, had a long history in Africa where it was woven into diverse interactions between Europeans and local polities. In the seventeenth and eighteenth centuries, protection was used to forge political and military alliances. This chapter is concerned with a shift in the uses of protection that took place in the nineteenth century. During the early and middle decades of the nineteenth century treaties or alliances of protection were concluded in West Africa by British imperial agents with indigenous people that entailed increasingly expansive transfers of sovereign rights to the protecting state. Originally relationships of protection were primarily of a military nature, but during the period under discussion protection and extraterritoriality became inherently linked with each other for the first time as Britain was given rights to adjudicate disputes between British and African subjects and even disputes that exclusively involved African subjects. The growth of extraterritorial jurisdiction circumvented traditional adjudication of disputes by African rulers and extended British influence informally without the need to acquire territorial sovereignty. This amalgam of extraterritorial rights in areas that stood under British protection was later referred to by the British government as a new form of imperial governmental control called the protectorate or, in order to distinguish it from its European counterpart, the colonial protectorate but, as I show here, its practices were embedded in an earlier period. However, extraterritoriality was not part of a policy, centrally directed by the imperial government, but something that grew organically, primarily at the instigation of imperial agents on the spot.

In this chapter I consider the use of protection in legal relations between Britain and African communities in the Gold Coast, Sierra Leone and the Niger Delta and examine in particular the British arguments for the extension of protection and extraterritoriality over native societies. I demonstrate how the acquisition of a limited set of sovereign rights became a valuable tool for Britain to exercise tailor-made control over economic and judicial resources.

THE HAPHAZARD NATURE OF EXTENDING PROTECTION AND EXTRATERRITORIALITY

During the early decades of the nineteenth century British imperial agents, having established a commercial presence on the West coast of Africa in the course of the seventeenth and eighteenth centuries, created relationships of protection, often through treaty, with indigenous communities in the Gambia, Sierra Leone, the Gold Coast and the Niger delta. This extension of protection, and the accompanying gradual creation of new modes of governance, was not part of a coherent strategy devised by the British government. In fact, until the 1880s, enthusiasm for colonies in West Africa generally remained small and the British government made available only limited funds as it generally deemed these settlements to be unprofitable and expensive. Indeed, there was considerable debate as to whether they should be kept at all. This ambivalence was reflected in imperial law. The acquisition of complete territorial sovereignty was held to be undesirable as it would bring with it significant costs both in administrative and governmental responsibilities in areas that were still wholly unfamiliar to the British government. What was needed instead was a legal instrument tailored to accommodate the government's specific objectives in West Africa, which consisted mainly of the facilitation and development of legitimate trade as efficiently and inexpensively as possible.

The early relationships of protection grew organically and were often the result of independent action undertaken by imperial agents on the ground. Since it took months for correspondence from London to arrive on either coast of Africa, orders, approvals or decisions by the imperial government invariably lagged behind events while official geographical knowledge of the area was limited.[1] In these circumstances, when decisions needed to be taken quickly, imperial agents were left to their own devices and were even expected by the central government to act on their own initiative. This was also true in respect to the conclusion of treaties of protection and the extension of extraterritoriality. Initiatives often came from colonial governors, consuls and naval officers who acted independently or pressured the British government into adopting legislation. This was certainly the case in the Gold Coast where the Company of Merchants Trading to Africa (known as the African Company), which administered the British trading forts on the West coast, took the first steps towards combining protection with a project of extending British laws over indigenous communities.

During the 1810s and 1820s the Company became embroiled in a local conflict between the Fante states, which surrounded the British forts, and the Ashanti.[2] The political situation on the Gold Coast was further complicated by the fact that the African Company paid a yearly allowance to Ashanti according to a seventeenth-century agreement. The allowance was laid down in so-called notes constituting ground rent for the forts.[3] Originally the sum had been paid to the Fante as the immediate neighbours to the forts, but in 1807 the Ashanti had claimed that the notes had reverted to them on the basis of their conquest of Fante territory.[4] Meanwhile, the relationship between the African Company and the Fante could be best described as that of an implicit defensive alliance as the Company provided the Fante military aid through the erection of a defensive wall.[5] Yet, even after 1807, trouble between the Fante and Ashanti continued.[6]

As tensions between Ashanti and the Fante continued to rise the African Company began to view a commercial treaty with Ashanti as a way to defuse a charged political situation. Consequently in 1817 the Company sent a mission to negotiate a commercial treaty with the King of Ashanti, Osei Tutu.[7] Both in the instructions given to the negotiators and during the treaty negotiations with Osei Tutu the Fante were consistently referred to as falling under the protection of the Company.[8] The term protection was also inserted several times in the final version of the treaty. Colin Newbury has pointed out that the granting of military protection in return for access to resources and surpluses of production was not unknown in West Africa.[9] However, this kind of protection usually formed part of client-patron relationships and were a means for powerful chiefs to maintain their authority. Therefore, the British claim of protection actually challenged the presumption on the part of the King of Ashanti that he exercised overlordship over the Fante.

The treaty stipulated that there would be perpetual peace between both Ashanti and the British forts as well as between Ashanti and all the nations that resided under the protection of the Company's forts and settlements.[10] Furthermore, it instituted a system of dispute settlement. In case of aggression on the part of the natives under British protection the Ashanti king was to complain to the Governor-in-Chief to obtain redress. Yet this provision seems to have gone further than merely placing the Company in the position of a mediator in cases of a conflict between Ashanti and the Fante, since it made the Company the guarantor for any misbehaviour on the part of the Fante and obliged it to provide redress. Hence it could be said that the clause amounted to a partial claim of sovereignty, foreshadowing the increase in extraterritorial powers that the British would acquire over the surrounding Fante states during the course of the nineteenth century.

The treaty of 1817 quickly ran into trouble when new disagreements arose between the Company and Ashanti.[11] Indeed, by 1820 Ashanti and the British merchants were on the brink of war.[12] Consequently, the Colonial Office decided that the matter could not be left in the hands of the African Company, resolving instead to dispatch a mission to the Gold Coast to negotiate a new treaty. The negotiations for this treaty reveal that the Ashanti King considered his sovereignty over the people residing under the British forts to be undisputed,[13] and that he had equated the British claim to protection over the Fante to an unjust claim to sovereignty. Despite these objections the new treaty stated that while the British acknowledged Ashanti's claim to Fante territory this was only on the condition that the King agreed that the natives in the vicinity of Cape Coast Castle resided under British protection and were subject to British laws.[14] While previously protection had merely entailed military protection and dispute settlement by the Company, now it entailed the Fante being subjected to British laws. However, due to internal rivalry on the Gold Coast, the treaty of 1820 quickly suffered the same fate as its unfortunate predecessor and was not ratified by the imperial government.

Moreover, a borderland, which comprised a geographical zone immediately adjacent to Britain's West African possessions, where many British traders, missionaries and liberated African slaves tried their luck on the territories of African rulers, and where on more than one occasion they became embroiled in disputes with the local people, undermined the British government's attempt to limit its presence in Africa as it made clear that the interaction of British subjects with Africans outside of the official settlements could not be left entirely unsupervised.[15]

These confrontations between British and African subjects outside of the boundaries of Britain's settlements caused two main problems. First, they exposed British subjects to what the British government deemed to be barbarous indigenous law. From the 1840s onwards, as Britain was slowly expanding its influence on the West coast, ideas of torture, human sacrifice and slavery as punishment fuelled claims that indigenous African legal systems were backward and that extraterritorial rights were needed in order to protect the lives and property of British citizens.[16]

Second, even small-scale disputes between British and African subjects that were provoked by reckless British adventurers could endanger the resources the British government had invested in the suppression of the slave trade and the development of commercial relationships with neighbouring African rulers. In other words, these problems revealed that while British influence was vast and expanding beyond its official territories, the imperial government had no real authority there.[17]

It was held that the best way to gain such authority while preserving the informal character of Britain's presence was through the adoption of a limited set of sovereign responsibilities in African territories and the division of jurisdictional tasks between British colonial administrators and African rulers. From 1843 it is possible to discern a veritable boom in legislation providing for the exercise of extraterritorial jurisdiction and the creation of consular posts.[18] The primary purpose of the establishment of this extraterritorial authority was the creation of an atmosphere of law and order.

This heralded the gradual extension of Britain's extraterritorial jurisdiction whereby African rulers ceded authority to Britain, and by the end of the nineteenth century the hinterland adjacent to the British settlements on the Gold Coast, Sierra Leone, Lagos and in the area of the Niger delta had all been transformed into British protectorates.

'BARBAROUS' CUSTOMS IN THE GOLD COAST AND SIERRA LEONE

Avoiding or even effacing indigenous native legal customs that were considered to be uncivilised became one of the driving forces for the extension of extraterritoriality and protection in many regions of West Africa where Britain exercised informal and formal control. The starting-point for the adoption of new legislation that allowed for such extension was Governor George Maclean's illegal use of British law on the Gold Coast during the 1830s.

During this period Maclean adjudicated civil and criminal cases between British subjects and African people that were brought before him even though he had not acquired any sort of official cession of jurisdiction from the Fante rulers. The substantive law that was applied was primarily African indigenous law, which was moderated whenever it conflicted with the rules of English law.[19] In 1842 a British parliamentary select committee evaluated Maclean's administration of the Gold Coast.[20] It confirmed that in principle British jurisdiction was confined to the forts and could not be exercised over African subjects unless through agreement, but it nonetheless applauded his illegal exercise of jurisdiction. It did so on the grounds that it was deemed to have a civilising effect on African customs. The committee recommended that Maclean's policy of suppressing barbarous customs should be continued, stating that the agreement to be concluded for the regularisation of jurisdiction should at least include the suppression of 'barbarous customs'.[21] This meant that extraterritoriality on the Gold Coast became officially linked with the project of civilising indigenous people.

In order to acquire the consent of the Gold Coast African rulers an agreement was devised in 1844, the so-called bond, consisting of three articles to be signed by the African rulers living in the vicinity of the British forts.[22] In the first article the African states adjacent to the British forts on the Gold Coast recognised the power and jurisdiction exercised by Britain on their behalf.[23] In other words, the bonds provided an official legal basis for an already existing situation and confirmed a practice that had already been established for some years.[24] However, new elements were also inserted. The bond condemned human sacrifice and other so-called barbarous customs as 'abominations'. It also recognised them as contrary to law, which meant that they were elevated to the level of crimes. Moreover, it conferred broad jurisdiction to Britain in criminal cases.[25] These were to be adjudicated by British judicial officers in concert with the native chiefs, who together would mould 'the customs of the country to the general principles of British law'.[26] While criminal jurisdiction was thus shared and not entirely ceded to the British, the overarching goal was still to move towards the application of British law to African subjects. Despite this rather explicit statement with regard to the 'moulding' and 'civilising' function of Britain's extraterritorial jurisdiction, legal reform on the Gold Coast during the 1840s and 1850s reserved an important role for African custom, at least in theory.[27]

Before long the exercise of adjudicatory jurisdiction over the territories adjacent to the British forts no longer seemed sufficient for the administration of the Gold Coast. The British authorities believed that, apart from judicial extraterritoriality, legislative extraterritoriality was needed in order to stimulate trade, either through raising customs tariffs or through direct taxation of the protected territories for which actual legislative authority was needed.[28] The former proved problematic as it required some co-ordination with the Dutch authorities that also held possessions on the Gold Coast. The latter was therefore more attractive and was consequently adopted.[29]

Yet how was the tax to be imposed outside of the British forts where Britain did not exercise full territorial sovereignty? The relationship between Britain and the adjacent territories was a legal twilight zone and the government was unsure of how to make the imposition of direct taxation binding on the native chiefs over whom they recognised they exercised no territorial jurisdiction and who they knew were not British subjects.[30] In order to introduce direct taxation in 1852 the British government opted to convene the neighbouring African rulers at Cape Coast Castle and create a Legislative Assembly consisting of the chiefs, the governor and his council.[31] The African rulers of the protected territories would thereby give by agreement to Britain the power to legislate within their territory. The British governor was to act as its president and would have the power to convene the Assembly. Once the enactments had been approved, they became binding on all the individuals under British protection.

Subsequent to its creation the Assembly adopted direct taxation in the form of a poll tax consisting of an annual stipend per head.[32] The poll tax ordinance was styled as a kind of quid pro quo whereby in return for the blessings of British protection African rulers would contribute financially.[33] While the creation of the Legislative Assembly and the poll tax seem like important concessions on the part of the African rulers to British authority, it has recently been pointed out by the historian Rebecca Shumway that the collection of revenue was a recognised part of indigenous systems of government.[34]

A similar story unfolded in Sierra Leone, where the principal reason for extending jurisdiction was the British concern with respect to the adjudication and execution of criminal law outside of British territory. Crimes against or perpetrated by British subjects outside of the confines of British dominions had gone unpunished or were dealt with by African indigenous law. The extension of British extraterritorial jurisdiction was meant to preserve peaceful relations between the British settlements and its neighbours. Noble as these intentions were, they also stemmed from a sense of British superiority towards African indigenous law and a belief that justice would only prevail with the application of English criminal law. In reality, therefore, there was as much a civilising mission in Sierra Leone as there was on the Gold Coast.

In 1841 an Act was passed by the Colonial Council of Freetown that provided Sierra Leonean courts with powers of extraterritorial jurisdiction. It extended the laws in force in Sierra Leone for the punishment of crimes and other offences committed in territories 'adjacent to or connected by treaty' with the Colony of Sierra Leone within the geographical zone of twentieth degree north latitude and twentieth degree south latitude.[35] The Act seemed to adhere to the idea that consent of the African rulers was necessary for an extension of extraterritorial jurisdiction, but it was actually more ambiguous than that. The phrase 'connected by treaty' suggested that for those territories at least the consent of African rulers had been obtained. However, this was not the case for those territories described as being simply 'adjacent to' Sierra Leone. The Act did not extend jurisdiction to African subjects but confined itself to British subjects and placed liberated Africans on the same footing as British subjects. The Act further provided that any such crimes or offences committed within the aforementioned territories would be cognisable in the courts of Sierra Leone.

The reasons for this extension of extraterritorial jurisdiction were clearly stated in the Act itself. British subjects were frequently found to commit violence against indigenous people and property beyond the borders of Sierra Leone with impunity 'owing to there being no established judicatures therein, for the punishment of such offences'.[36] In other words, the existing system of

African custom did not live up to British expectations of an 'established judicature'. However, the Act was short-lived since it was deemed that only the British parliament could enact laws binding upon British subjects.[37]

Cases whereby British subjects committed crimes outside of the boundaries of Sierra Leone or even meddled in native wars nevertheless continued to occur.[38] In 1849 the Colonial Office, in order to protect British subjects from barbarous punishment by African rulers, decided that the easiest and most cost-efficient way of promoting civilisation in West Africa was through an extension of British jurisdiction without what were held to be the manifold disadvantages of acquiring territorial sovereignty.[39] These considerations in many ways foreshadowed the dawning of the same legal policy that had gradually been pursued at the Gold Coast of extending protection in the form of extraterritorial jurisdiction. It is no surprise that the neighbouring territories surrounding Sierra Leone in 1893 became formally incorporated into the Sierra Leone Protectorate, which legally formed a separate entity next to the Crown Colony of Sierra Leone.[40]

In Sierra Leone the message was clearly received. In the next few years treaties were concluded in rapid succession with neighbouring African rulers who had not already ceded their powers of criminal jurisdiction to Britain with respect to British subjects who committed crimes on their territories.[41] The treaties completely withdrew the power to take cognisance of offences committed by or against British subjects from the authority of native rulers and recognised the predominance of English criminal law.[42] The Order in Council that was finally adopted in 1853 to regulate extraterritorial jurisdiction recognised that courts in Sierra Leone were competent to hear criminal cases concerning British subjects in those adjacent territories where jurisdiction had already been recognised or would be recognised in future on the basis of treaties.[43]

EXTRATERRITORIALITY AND COMMERCIAL CONTROL IN THE BIGHTS OF BENIN AND BIAFRA

During the 1840s a new type of jurisdiction was developed by British consuls in the areas surrounding the river Niger in which Britain did not have any settlements and where consequently there were no neighbouring or adjacent areas that needed to be protected. Here, the rationale behind extending extraterritorial jurisdiction was to gain control over Anglo-African commercial relations. In the Bights of Benin and Biafra there had been an increase of the trade in palm oil to the extent that the area was referred to as that of the 'oil rivers',[44] and the heightened volume of trade brought with it an increase in disputes between African and European traders. Traditionally, the rules and regulations of trade between African and European merchants in this area had rested to a great extent on interparty trust and on age-old informal and unwritten agreements on how trade was to be conducted.

One of the ways in which the British consuls attempted to resolve quarrels was through the establishment of informal courts known as courts of equity, which were to decide on all manner of commercial disputes. This approach was not exclusive to the Niger River, as similar institutions had been set up in Lagos before its acquisition by Britain in 1861.[45] The lack of specification concerning the procedural and substantive details of dispute settlement in the Anglo-African treaties of the delta region was in the case of the equity courts resolved through the creation of so-called bye-laws.[46] Many of them were used as the norms on the basis of which equity courts resolved disputes. They were negotiated and sanctioned by the British consul or vice-consul, but technically they could not be placed under the heading of interstate treaties as they constituted agreements between a group of merchants and African rulers.[47] In this way a type of anomalous extraterritorial jurisdiction emerged as the bye-laws and courts of equity presented a means for British consuls to extend their influence beyond the substantive limits of their jurisdictional powers in the delta region, often without the sanction of the British government.

The bye-laws were only partly based on existing African commercial customs and often entailed entirely new provisions aimed at giving greater powers to the British merchant community.[48] More importantly, British involvement was formalised in the bye-laws, as the British consul was made responsible for appeals against decisions by the courts of equity.[49] These commercial arrangements were not conducive to equitable trade relationships. Consuls themselves repeatedly intervened on the side of the British merchants and aided them in establishing commercial monopolies.[50] In doing so they often appropriated for themselves informal magisterial powers.[51]

The imperial government's initial response to the bye-laws of the courts of equity was one of hesitation. To all appearances the agreements did not constitute treaties and so did not even require its approval. Nevertheless, the Foreign Office generally refused to sanction outrageously discriminatory bye-laws and attempted to restrain the practice of consuls in their lending of support to the supercargoes.[52]

Despite these unfavourable tidings, courts of equity continued to be set up by consuls, which compelled the Foreign Office to come up with a solution for regularising jurisdiction in the Niger delta region and stem the abuse of the courts of equity. However, in the Niger area it was entirely unclear on what basis jurisdiction had been exercised. This had supposedly happened through 'uniform "usage and sufferance"' and so it was held that it would be impolite to ask a 'formal grant of such jurisdiction' from an African chief.[53] In other words, similar to discussions in the Gold Coast and Sierra Leone during this period, the government appeared reluctant to awaken the suspicions of the African chiefs as to the possible illegality of the jurisdiction that British consuls had hitherto exercised.

In 1872 an Order in Council was prepared which finally regulated consular jurisdiction in the territory of the Niger delta by allowing the establishment of consular courts. Perhaps more important than the consular courts was the fact that the order gave the courts powers to settle minor trading disputes subject to the sanction of the consul. Only British traders would preside over the court.[54] While the order mainly confirmed a practice whereby consuls had extended their authority over the courts of equity, its symbolic value was great. Now, through the order the equity courts had been officially appropriated by Britain. The legal difficulty of consent of native rulers was neatly circumvented: the courts were competent to hear disputes among British subjects and between British subjects and natives, albeit solely on the basis of the agreement of both parties.[55] By doing so, the time-consuming process of treaty-making was avoided while at the same time the British government secured the consent of each person appearing before the court.

Administrative institutionalisation and the creation of a legal framework by Britain was one thing, acceptance by African communities of the new judicial arrangements was quite another matter. The requirement of consent created problems of its own, as consent could be withdrawn when circumstances changed. Martin Lynn and Gwilym Jones have both pointed out that the African rulers did not uniformly accept the equity courts since by this time they were rightly considered to be British institutions.[56] The continuing problem of local rejection of British adjudicatory and institutional authority and the uncertainty as to its legal basis were left in abeyance until 1884 when foreign competition pushed Britain into a race for treaties of protection, which inaugurated the formal creation of the Niger Protectorate.

PROTECTION AND EXTRATERRITORIALITY AS AN IMPERIAL TOOL

The piecemeal manner in which Britain gradually extended its jurisdiction in the areas adjacent to its forts is illustrative of the flexibility of the concept of protection as opposed to the outright acquisition of territorial sovereignty. It foreshadowed a tactic that was used in the late nineteenth century whereby the protectorate was deployed by European powers to acquire full territorial

sovereignty. At this stage, however, the British administration was not interested in acquiring full territorial sovereignty on the Gold Coast beyond the
precincts of the forts. In cases of full territorial acquisition British legislation
would automatically apply to the acquired territory, including the Slavery
Emancipation Act. As West African societies relied to a large extent on slavery
it was believed that the implementation of the Act would destroy the peace of
the region and cause an uprising.[57]

The concern over slavery played an important role in the decision of the
British government to limit its responsibilities to the mere exercise of extraterritorial rights on the Gold coast. The continued existence of domestic slavery
on the Gold Coast was a public embarrassment but nevertheless no direct
prohibition of slavery was believed to be feasible. The most plausible alternative was to use Britain's claims to jurisdiction to moderate the native customs
with respect to slavery through the application of British justice. These considerations together with the continued desire to levy customs in the Gold Coast
in order to acquire more revenue prompted the government to extend once
more British jurisdiction in the adjacent territories.[58]

The continued extension of extraterritorial rights and protection in West
Africa was therefore an imperial tool to limit British responsibilities to what
was both realistically feasible in African societies and preferable in terms of
British imperial objectives concerning commerce and informal influence.
The rudimentary form of governance occasioned by extraterritoriality was
from the 1860s regularly referred to by the British government as a 'protectorate' with respect to the Gold Coast and the immediate vicinity of Lagos. For
the areas adjacent to Sierra Leone this was the case from the 1870s onwards.[59]
Prior to that time, the adjacent areas had been described as the 'protected
territories' or occasionally as 'quasi-protectorates'.[60] The use of the term
'protectorate' therefore coincides with the increased use of extraterritorial
jurisdiction. This evolution suggests that the protectorate did not emerge as
a separate international legal concept in practice until a rudimentary exercise
of governance on the part of Britain over neighbouring African communities
could be identified.

However, the haphazard way in which extraterritorial jurisdiction was
extended laid bare one of the fundamental problems connected with jurisdiction in West Africa: the uncertainty of territorial boundaries. Geographical
limitations in treaties of cession often referred to vaguely described natural
boundaries, leaving room for speculation as to the exact limits of British
territory when British subjects settled on the borders or in the vicinity of
these natural boundaries. Consequently, it was in some cases entirely unclear

which territories belonged to Britain and at which geographical point British territorial jurisdiction ended. This caused problems when new legislation that would again increase Britain's extraterritorial powers had to be adopted. If the boundaries of territorial jurisdiction could not be clearly drawn, then at least an equally vaguely defined extension of British extraterritorial jurisdiction might bring other borderline cases of crime within its jurisdictional orbit. Whereas previously care had been taken to secure the consent of African rulers to an infringement of their jurisdictional powers, the law officers now advised the Colonial Office that an extension of British jurisdiction could take place on the basis of necessity instead of consent, as it was argued that the basic rules of international law did not apply to uncivilised states.[61]

The law officers' sweeping claims to jurisdiction represented a similar departure from the practice of proceeding on the basis of consent.[62] Consequently, doubts about its legality rose. However, the Colonial Office was less concerned about the possible violation of indigenous sovereignty through the neglect of consent than it was about the fact that the Act also claimed jurisdiction over subjects of civilised states, such as those of France, whose government would not be pleased with British jurisdictional pretensions.[63] As a result these objections were ignored. The new Act of 1871 applied not only to Sierra Leone but to the Gambia, Gold Coast, and Lagos. It explicitly recognised the legitimacy of Britain's claim to criminal jurisdiction on the basis of its having a superior and civilised justice system. In the light of these considerations the legislation empowered Britain to exercise criminal jurisdiction within twenty miles outside of the boundaries of its settlements over its own subjects and over anyone who was not a subject of a 'civilised power' as if the crime had been committed within British territory.[64] Furthermore, it applied to individuals resident in the settlements who strictly speaking were not British subjects, but who, by their residency, had acquired that character.[65] With the Act of 1871 consent as a legal ground was abandoned for the extension of extraterritorial jurisdiction in adjacent territories over British as well as African subjects. Furthermore, the 'uncivilised' nature of indigenous law as a justification for such extension was now put forward more strongly than ever.

Similar uncertainties with respect to the real extent of British extraterritorial jurisdiction existed on the Gold Coast. Here as well any new legal instrument widening the scope of extraterritorial jurisdiction gave rise to questions as to the limits of the actual authority Britain was already exercising. Several Orders in Council had been adopted in order to facilitate the exercise of Britain's adjudicatory jurisdiction in the protected territories, yet even the British government recognised that the actual exercise of jurisdiction was irregular as

it went well beyond the provisions of the orders. The British government contended that this had not attracted notice or caused any inconvenience.[66] This
might have been so but no one in the British government was exactly sure how
comprehensive British jurisdiction was in reality, which proved a problem
when it was decided in 1874 that a new Order in Council was to be drafted to
give the colonial administration greater extraterritorial legislative powers.

The legal basis for this extension of jurisdiction had formed the subject of
some debate within the Colonial Office. The Colonial Secretary was in favour
of a one-sided proclamation announcing a plan to extend jurisdiction to the
adjacent African territories without any negotiation. He argued that the most
recent international legal basis for extraterritorial jurisdiction on the Gold
Coast, namely the Bonds of 1844, which had only transferred limited powers of
jurisdiction, had become obsolete as the actual exercise of jurisdiction was
much broader than what was officially allowed.[67] This, he asserted, should not
be officially admitted to the African rulers, as it was not 'for Her Majesty to
take as a grant what was already claimed and held as a right' and it was better
not to wake any sleeping dogs.[68]

However, the problem remained that even in a proclamation some kind of a
public statement with regard to the extent of British jurisdiction would have to
be made. Eventually, it was decided simply to instruct the colonial governor
privately that his jurisdiction was not enlarged.[69] In other words, no clarifi-
cation was made as to the extent of British jurisdiction, not even within the
Colonial Office itself.

CONCLUSION

My analysis of the use of protection in Anglo-African relations on the Gold
Coast, Sierra Leone and the Niger delta has shown that during the first half
of the nineteenth century protection had already become entangled with
the increase of British extraterritorial powers. This stemmed from a desire to
extract British subjects from what was perceived to be a primitive and inhu-
mane native justice system. Equally, extraterritorial jurisdiction was both a
means to preserve peaceful relations between the British and native communities and an instrument for the development of favourable commercial
conditions. The growth of extraterritorial jurisdiction prompted the British
government to reexamine the relationship between Britain and the areas over
which it claimed extraterritoriality. By the 1860s, when a framework of British
governance had been established through the various legislative instruments
that created extraterritoriality, these areas were consistently referred to as
protectorates.

NOTES

1 W. David McIntyre, *The Imperial Frontier in the Tropics, 1865–1875*, Palgrave Macmillan, London, 1967, p. 15.

2 Robert B. Edgerton, *The Fall of the Asante Empire: The Hundred-Year War for Africa's Gold Coast*, Free Press, New York, 1995, p. 45; Graham W. Irwin, 'Precolonial African Diplomacy: The Example of Asante', *International Journal of African Historical Studies*, vol. 8, 1975, p. 85.

3 Harvey Feinberg, 'There was an Elmina Note, But . . .', *International Journal of African Historical Studies*, vol. 9, 1976, p. 618.

4 Larry Yarak, 'The "Elmina Note": Myth and Reality of Asante-Dutch Relations', *History in Africa*, vol. 13, 1986, p. 365.

5 Thomas E. Bowdich, *Mission from Cape Coast Castle to Ashantee*, J. Murray, London, 1819, p. 46.

6 Edgerton, p. 49.

7 Bowdich, p. 14.

8 Ibid., p. 92.

9 Colin W. Newbury, *Patrons, Clients, and Empire: Chieftaincy and Over-Rule in Asia, Africa, and the Pacific*, Oxford University Press, Oxford, 2003, pp. 101–02.

10 Article 2, Treaty Made and Entered into by Thomas Edward Bowdich, Esquire, in the Name of the Governor and Council at Cape Coast Castle, on the Gold Coast of Africa, and on Behalf of the British Government, with Saï Tootoo Quamina, King of Ashantee and Its Dependencies, and Boïtinnee Quama, King of Dwabin and Its Dependencies, in Bowdich, p. 124.

11 Sir Francis Fuller, *A Vanished Dynasty: Ashanti*, John Murray, London, 1921, pp. 58–61; Edgerton, pp. 72–73.

12 Ibid.

13 Deposition by the Officers and Gentlemen who Accompanied the Embassy Under Charge of Consul Dupuis, 11 March 1820, CO 267/57, National Archives of the United Kingdom (henceforth NA).

14 Article 5, Treaty Made and Entered into by Joseph Dupuis Esquire, his Britannic Majesty's Consul for the Kingdom of Ashantee in Africa, in the Name and on Behalf of the British Government, with Sai Tootoo Quamina, King of Ashantee and Its Dependencies, 23 March 1820, Colin W. Newbury (ed.), *British Policy Towards West Africa, Select Documents 1786–1874*, vol. 1, Clarendon Press, Oxford, 1971, p. 289.

15 McIntyre, p. 8.

16 Ibid.

17 Bernard Porter, *The Lion's Share: A History of British Imperialism, 1850–2011*, Routledge, London, 2013, p. 57.

18 William Ross Johnston, *Sovereignty and Protection: A Study of British Jurisdictional Imperialism in the Late Nineteenth Century*, Duke University Press, Durham, 1979, p. 11.

19 William W. Claridge, *A History of the Gold Coast and Ashanti*, vol. 1, John Murray, London, 1915, p. 415.

20 *British Parliamentary Papers* (henceforth *BPP*), 1842, Report of the Select Committee on the West Coast of Africa, Paper no. 551, p. v.

21 Ibid.

22 Joseph B. Danquah, 'The Historical Significance of the Bond of 1844', *Transactions of the Historical Society of Ghana*, vol. 3, no. 1, 1957, pp. 4–5.

23 William F. Ward, *A History of the Gold Coast*, George Allen & Unwin Ltd, London, 1948, p. 189. The text of the Bond is quoted in full here. Other full text versions can be found in Bond, 6 March 1844; Bond, 18 March 1844; Bond, 12 April 1844; Bond, 8 May 1844; Bond, 29 May 1844; Bond, 2 July 1844, CO 96/4, NA.

24 Mary McCarthy, *Social Change and the Growth of British Power in the Gold Coast*, University Press of America, New York, 1983, p. 145; Rebecca Shumway, 'Palavers and Treaty Making in the British Acquisition of the Gold Coast Colony (West Africa)', in Saliha Belmessous (ed.), *Empire by Treaty. Negotiating European Expansion, 1600–1900*, Oxford University Press, New York, 2015, p. 179.

25 Article 2, Bond, 6 March 1844, CO 96/4, NA.

26 Ibid., Article 3.

27 A.N. Allott, 'Native Tribunals in the Gold Coast, 1844–1927', *Journal of African Law*, vol. 1, no. 3, 1957, p. 165; Inez Sutton, 'Law, Chieftaincy and Conflict in Colonial Ghana: The Ada Case', *African Affairs*, vol. 83, no. 330, 1984, p. 44.

28 John D. Hargreaves, *Prelude to the Partition of West Africa*, Macmillan, London, p. 62; David Kimble, *A Political History of Ghana: The Rise of Gold Coast Nationalism, 1850–1928*, Oxford University Press, Oxford, 1963, p. 169.

29 Earl Grey to Lord John Russell, 27 December 1852, in Earl Grey, *The Colonial Policy of Lord John Russell's Administration*, vol. 2, R. Bentley, London, 1853, p. 284.

30 Governor Richard Hill to Grey, 23 April 1852, *BPP*, 1865, Report of the Select Committee on State of British Settlements on West Coast of Africa, Paper no. 412, p. 439; Grey to Hill, 26 January 1852, CO 96/23, NA.

31 Kimble, p. 173.

32 The Local Ordinance, commonly called the Poll Tax, 19 April 1852, *BPP*, 1854–55, Acts of Parliament, Orders in Council, Charters and Local Ordinances Defining Civil and Judicial Constitutions of British Settlements on the West Coast of Africa, Paper no. 383, p. 85.

33 Ward, p. 190.

34 Shumway, p. 181.

35 An Act for the prevention and punishment of offences, committed by Her Majesty's subjects, within certain territories adjacent to the Colony of Sierra Leone and Its Dependencies, and to declare that Liberated Africans are entitled to the rights, and subject to the liabilities of British subjects, 15 March 1841, CO 267/164, NA.

36 Ibid.

37 James Stephen, Minute, 22 September 1841, CO 267/164, NA.

38 Benjamin Pine to Grey, 23 October 1849, CO 267/208, NA.

39 Grey, Minute, 31 December 1849, CO 267/208, NA.

40 David Harris, *Sierra Leone: A Political History*, Oxford University Press, Oxford, 2014, pp. 20–24.

41 Johnston, p. 63.

42 See, for example, Treaty between Great Britain and Tangoh, Chief of Kykandy, 19 March 1851, *British and Foreign State Papers*, vol. 41, p. 731; Treaty of Peace, Friendship, Commerce and the Slave Trade between Great Britain and the Naloes, 21 March 1851, *British and Foreign State Papers*, vol. 50, p. 806; Treaty between Great Britain and the King or Chief of the Fouricaria Country, 2 August 1851, *British and Foreign State Papers*, vol. 45, p. 887.

43 Order in Council appointing Sierra Leone a Place for the Trial of Offenders brought there, under 6 & 7 Vict. c. 94, BPP, 1854–55, Acts of Parliament, Orders in Council, Charters and Local Ordinances Defining Civil and Judicial Constitutions of British Settlements on the West Coast of Africa, Paper no. 383, p. 37; Johnston, p. 63.

44 David Northrup, 'The Compatibility of the Slave and Palm Oil Trades in the Bight of Biafra', *Journal of African History*, vol. 17, no. 3, 1976, p. 354; Martin Lynn, *Commerce and Economic Change in West Africa*, Cambridge University Press, Cambridge, 2002, p. 15; Patrick Manning, 'Slaves, Palm Oil and Political Power in West Africa', *African Historical Studies*, vol. 2, no. 2, 1969, pp. 280; Susan M. Martin, *Palm Oil and Protest. An Economic History of the Ngwa Region, South-Eastern Nigeria, 1800–1980*, Cambridge University Press, Cambridge, 2006, p. 28.

45 Martin Lynn, 'Law and Imperial Expansion: the Niger Delta Courts of Equity, c. 1850–85', *Journal of Imperial and Commonwealth History*, vol. 23, no. 1, 1995, p. 56.

46 See, for example, Code of Commercial Regulations being deemed advisable for furthering the interests of commerce as well as for the better security of amicable connexion between the British supercargoes trading on the Rio Bento or Brass River and the natives of the Brass country, 17 November 1856, FO 84/1001, NA. For the Bonny court, see Gwilym Jones, *The Trading States of the Oil Rivers. A Study of Political Development in Eastern Nigeria*, James Currey, Oxford, 2000, p. 77.

47 Foreign Office to Thomas Hutchinson, 19 February 1857, FO 84/1030, NA.

48 Article 3, Bye-laws for the better regulation of trading matters, between the supercargoes and native traders of the river Cameroons passed at a meeting held on board HMS steam vessel 'Bloodhound', 14 January 1856, FO 84/1001, NA; Article 3, Bye-laws for the better regulation of trading matters between the supercargoes and native traders of Old Calabar, 19 September 1856, FO 84/1001, NA.

49 Article 6, 1856 Bye-laws of the Cameroons; Article 6, 1856 Bye-laws of Old Calabar.

50 Foreign Office to Hutchinson, 21 December 1857, FO 84/1030, NA; Cherry Gertzel, 'Relations between African and European Traders in the Niger Delta 1880–1896', *Journal of African History*, vol. 3, no. 2, 1962, p. 362.

51 Hutchinson to Earl Clarendon, 21 February 1857, FO 84/1030, NA.

52 Foreign Office to Hutchinson, 19 February 1857, FO 84/1030 NA; Foreign Office to Hutchinson, 23 April 1857, FO 84/1030, NA.

53 Foreign Office Memorandum by Charles Livingstone, 19 May 1871, FO 83/1343, NA.

54 Lynn, 'Law', p. 67.

55 Order in Council 1872, in Alan Burns, A *History of Nigeria*, Allen & Unwin, London, 1958, Appendix E.

56 Jones, p. 80; Lynn, 'Law', p. 67.

57 Robert Winniett to Grey, 31 January 1849, CO 96/15; Trevor R. Getz, *Slavery and Reform in West Africa: Toward Emancipation in Nineteenth-Century Senegal and the Gold Coast*, Ohio University Press, Athens, 2004, p. 85.

58 Johnston, p. 78.

59 See, for example, Consul Brand to Russell, 9 April 1860, *BPP*, 1862, Papers Relating to the Occupation of Lagos, Paper no. 339, p. 4; Duke of Newcastle to Consul Freeman, 22 August 1862, CO 147/1, NA; *BPP*, 1865, Report of the Select Committee on State of British Settlements on West Coast of Africa, Paper no. 412, p. 33.

60 See, for example, Stanley about Lagos: Foreign Office Minute, 26 August 1852, FO 84/895, NA; Robert Smith, 'The Lagos Consulate, 1851–1861: An Outline', *Journal of African History*, vol. 15, no. 3, 1974, p. 402.

61 Law Officers to Kimberley, 6 September 1870, CO 267/308, NA.

62 Johnston, p. 72.

63 Ibid.

64 An Act for Extending the Jurisdiction of the Courts of the West African Settlements to Certain Offences Committed out of Her Majesty's Dominions, 31 March 1871, 34 Vict. c. 8, Newbury, *British Policy*, p. 575.

65 Law Officers to Kimberley, 6 September 1870, CO 267/308, NA; Kenneth O. Dike, *Trade and Politics in the Niger Delta, 1830–1885*, Clarendon Press, Oxford, 1956, p. 13.

66 Colonial Office Confidential Memorandum, March 1874, CO 879/6, NA; Colonial Office Memorandum, 25 June 1874, CO 267/113, NA.

67 Colonial Office Confidential Memorandum, March 1874; Carnarvon to George Strahan, 20 August 1874, *BPP*, 1875, Correspondence Relating to Queen's Jurisdiction on the Gold Coast and Abolition of Slavery in the Protectorate, Paper no. C. — 1139, p. 318.

68 Colonial Office Confidential Memorandum, March 1874.

69 Ibid.; Johnston, p. 79.

PART V

Protection in an Inter-Imperial World

11

Between Imperial Subjects and Political Partners: Bedouin Borders and Protection in Ottoman Palestine, 1900–17

AHMAD AMARA

In May 1917, five months before the British occupied Beersheba, the southern region of Palestine, a group of Bedouin shaykhs participated in festivities in the Beersheba government house celebrating the Ottoman Sultan's commencement day. In a telegraph they sent to Istanbul six shaykhs expressed their loyalty, happiness, gratitude and deference to the Sultan, emphasising that they spoke on behalf of some 50,000 people of the Beersheba sub-district.[1] They commended the Sultan's efforts in spreading Islam and uniting all Muslims, and condemned anyone who deviated from the path of loyalty by supporting the religion's enemies.[2] In addition to being the protector of Islam, the shaykhs spoke of the Sultan as protecting 'our dear homeland', and added: 'We [shaykhs and Bedouin] are ready for its defence and support, and the expulsion of anyone who harms our sacred homeland, through the sacrifice of our money and souls to the very last drop of our blood.'[3] The Sultan made sure to respond to this telegraph and thank the Bedouin shaykhs.[4]

In the 1880s, as part of a major political and administrative reform concentrated in the imperial frontiers the Ottoman government had set about trying to enhance its rule over the Bedouin communities of Beersheba. In the eyes of Ottoman officials these communities were an unruly savage population that was a source of instability and threat to the empire, and one that had required several military campaigns to subdue and to enforce tax collection. By 1917, however, Ottoman reforming efforts seem to have paid dividends. The very unruly subjects from whom the empire was seeking protection had come to view the Sultan as their protector and the protector of their sacred homeland. At the same time, in addition to being the protected, they had themselves become protectors of the empire.

It is clear that protection came to occupy an important role in Ottoman domestic and foreign political relations in the second half of the nineteenth

century. The decaying power of the empire and various threats to its sovereignty had brought into question the legitimacy of both Ottoman rule and the
polity's ability to provide protection to its territory and subjects. In these circumstances the Ottoman ruling elite looked to establish its legitimacy and
centre its empire on protection. Indeed, the common epithet for the Ottoman
Empire among Ottomans – *memalik-i mahruse-i şahane*, the well-protected
domains of His Imperial Majesty – testifies to this imperative. However, since
the Ottoman domains were anything but well protected by this time, this
amounted to little more than a colossal irony. 'Every time the danger of the
disintegration of the state had to be mentioned', it has been remarked, 'it was
accompanied by *huda negerde* (may God forbid), almost as though to voice
the very words was to tempt providence'.[5] Consequently, alongside such calls
for divine intervention, the Ottoman government sought better ways to guarantee the protection of its land and interests.

Beginning in the 1830s, the Ottoman government began to introduce a
series of reforms that came to be known as the *Tanzimat*, which literally
meant 'ordering' and 'organisation'. Essential to this was the extension of the
reformed Ottoman administration and jurisdiction to territories that were
previously characterised by a limited state presence. Those territories included
eastern Anatolia, Yemen, Libya, and southern Syria, which comprised the
Hijaz, today's Jordan, and the Beersheba region of southern Palestine, known
today as the Negev. Scholarship on the Ottoman *Tanzimat* in relation to tribal
communities has largely focused on state imposition and discourses of modernity. There are no studies, to the best of my knowledge, that have utilised the
lens of protection in any comprehensive fashion in order to understand this
reform and the circumstances in which it was pursued.

In this chapter I consider the various discourses around protection as they
were configured within the Ottoman reform in Beersheba between 1900, the
foundation of the Beersheba sub-district for the Bedouin communities, and
1917, the end of the Ottoman rule. More particularly, I seek to examine the
role of the Bedouin in the wider Ottoman-British rivalry over Beersheba. The
Beersheba borderland evolved to become a site of inter-imperial competition over territory, sovereignty and Bedouin allegiance, all framed in terms of
historical, legal and national-religious claims. It became, in other words, a
zone of interaction where multiple polities collided. Within this zone an
important, but previously marginalised, political actor came into play, namely
the Beersheba Bedouin. In this chapter I foreground Bedouin input into the
reform in Beersheba and the making of the Ottoman-Egyptian border, which
allows us to understand better the political arrangements and inter-imperial
interactions around questions of protection, loyalty and sovereignty. The

interpolity competition over sovereignty or political dominance depended very much on the ability of each party to provide protection.

PROTECTION, INCORPORATION AND
BRITISH COMPETITION

I begin by focusing on protection in reference to the Ottoman reform between 1900 and 1917 in southern Syria, later southern Palestine, where the government founded the town of Beersheba and made it the centre of a new administrative sub-district, designed particularly for the Beersheba tribal communities, known today as the Bedouin. Prior to this time there were five large tribal confederations numbering some 70,000–80,000 Bedouin. These communities, together with seventy different towns and villages, belonged to the Gaza sub-district, which constituted part of the district of Jerusalem.

The Ottoman government held that these Bedouin tribes were in possession of a considerable amount of land, had increased their agricultural activity in recent years, and were inclined to civilisation, but that their territorial disputes were precluding further development. The government was concerned that intercommunal fighting was a source of both instability and a loss of revenue, due to non-cultivation. The central government also believed that the tribes' affairs and lands were barely administered due to their distance from the sub-district's centre and the fact that the Gaza administration was busy enough with its villages and towns. Thus, the government looked to expand its administration and jurisdiction to this frontier and bring its residents under the pale of law. Consequently, an 1899 Sultanic edict confirmed the foundation of a new sub-district that was designed exclusively for the Bedouin and the building of the town of *Birüssebi*, the Ottoman rendering of Beersheba.[6] This step constituted an important turn in Ottoman policies and politics from an emphasis on military force towards a new grammar of law, jurisdiction and permanent administration. The primary objective of forming the Beersheba sub-district was, according to the 1900 Council of State decision, 'to place the Bedouin on the road of civilisation, and to gradually have them settle down'.[7]

Clearly, the Ottoman government was seeking to expand its jurisdiction by establishing a relationship of tutelage or custodianship over the Bedouin. In doing so it cast itself as the best and sole protector of their interests. This work was done in large part by an act of conceptualisation: of itself as a modern state and of the Bedouin as savage and primitive, weak and ignorant. The law became essential for order and civilisation. This was, of course, typical of protective regimes that other imperial and colonial powers adopted towards native communities as they conquered or administered their territories.[8] At the same time, Ottoman policies in Beersheba were intertwined with political developments across the border.

Following the British occupation of Egypt in 1882, protection of the Beersheba frontier became a priority. The Ottoman Empire had sought to assert its political and territorial sovereignty in Beersheba against the British. Ottoman administrators repeatedly stressed the strategic location of Beersheba and the political value of establishing this new sub-district near the Egyptian border.[9] While evaluating Ottoman actions near the border, the Jerusalem governor argued in 1898 that 'there should be constant attention within the governorate (Jerusalem), particularly to the Gaza sub-district ... [and that] a number of steps should be taken as soon as possible, especially to identify and register the Gaza Bedouin ... and thus to enhance order and control'.[10] However, as the established relationships and structures around protection were not static, the Ottoman Empire was attempting to establish a political alliance with the Bedouin rather than securing their submission, and it was held that the reform had to adhere to existing political structures and avoid stark ruptures. Indeed, the central government treated the Bedouin through a lens of legal difference, and constantly needed to negotiate with local leaders and the provincial administration about any major steps it wanted to undertake.[11] This was because the Ottoman administration viewed the Bedouin as a special and different community, and at the same time held that Bedouin integration and co-operation were essential for the success of the reform and the defence of Ottoman territory and sovereignty. The role that the Bedouin could play in protecting the imperial frontiers meant that the Bedouin became not only the protected but also protectors and bearers of Ottoman sovereignty as well. The border dispute and its making in 1906 illustrate the various strands of protection as they were considered by the Ottoman centre.

PROTECTION ON BORDERLANDS

In 1906 a border question arose between the Ottoman and British-Egyptian government that demonstrates the threats to Ottoman sovereignty and territory, and encapsulates the domestic and inter-imperial politics of this period. The British aimed to push the border eastward in order to force the Ottomans further away from the Suez Canal, while the Ottoman government hoped to locate the border deep in the Sinai Peninsula close to Suez. Most of the available accounts of this matter, which have drawn mostly on British rather than Ottoman sources, have focused on the high politics of Ottoman-British border-making and the military and diplomatic exchanges.[12] Scholars have not examined the border question's entanglement with domestic politics and the Beersheba reform or investigated it from the Bedouin perspective.

The local Bedouin communities were active participants in border affairs as they sought to prevent the loss to British Egypt of what they deemed to be an important resource that was also 'Ottoman land'. The Bedouin not only presented strong claims to land and water but they served as the main source of knowledge and information to the Ottoman government. Ottoman officials continuously stressed the value of this information and the need to bring the Bedouin to testify in support of Ottoman claims against the British with regard to the actual border. Thus, in an inversion of the arrangement typically imagined by the state, the Bedouin were quite literally to serve as the protectors of Ottoman borders and interests. Further, Bedouin political loyalty was vital to the success of the claims of both sides. In the light of these political dynamics I discuss below the local Bedouin perspective on the border question and how they became important agents of protection.

The Ottoman and the Anglo-Egyptian authorities conducted intensive negotiations over the outline of the border between May and October 1906. The line with short dashes in Map 2 is the administrative line that was in force from 1840 until the negotiations, and it was generally known by the local communities as the 'separating line' because it divided the Beersheba and Egyptian tribes. The British insisted on having a straight line between Rafah and Aqaba (as indicated on the map), whereas Ottoman officials proposed a different line (marked by long dashes in the map) as a compromise, arguing that it would largely preserve the status quo and was close enough to the 'straight line'. The British government rejected this proposal. Despite objections by Ottoman officials and army officers to the proposed British border on the grounds that it was 'completely against the sacred interests of the Sultanate',[13] the Ottomans had to acquiesce in the end to the British proposal.

The Bedouin communities believed that the border demanded by the British government was not in their best interest. Consequently, during the negotiation Bedouin shaykhs and notables sent at least two petitions in protest to the Ottoman government, and claimed rights to lands lying on the Egyptian side of the border proposed by the British.[14] The shaykhs articulated their attachment to the lands that were being claimed by the British by deploying something very close to modern legal instruments. They framed their claims in terms of a system of private ownership of land and the fulfilment by the particular land owners of the legal obligation to pay tax. Further, they made clear that the owners held written contracts (*asnad*) and that the lands were registered under their names in the tribes' land distribution registries. Finally, the shaykhs claimed that the owners were from the Beersheba Bedouin, that

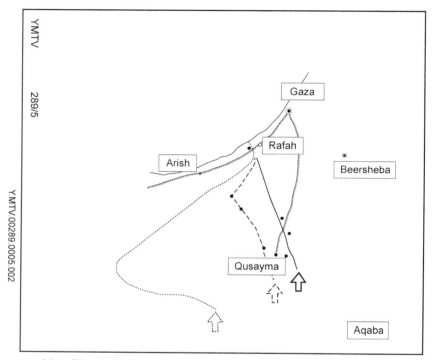

MAP 2: Map of Proposed Ottoman-Egyptian Border Schemes, July 1906
(The Başbakanlik [Government] Ottoman Archives, Y.MTV 289/05/02)

they belonged to the Beersheba sub-district, and that the water wells and
sites were named after the Beersheba Bedouin.[15] The Bedouin's intimate
knowledge of wells and other natural features helped bolster their claims,
but it was this use of written legal records and regular payment of taxes that
allowed them to call on the Ottoman state to protect their property. The basis
of Bedouin claims and the nature of property relations as described in the
petitions were practices of a kind that Ottoman officials had imagined the
Bedouin were incapable of when they had created Beersheba as a zone of
legal exception.

During the dispute the Bedouin generally displayed an understanding of
where sovereign authority lay that was different from the one the Ottoman
administrators held. The Bedouin understandably looked at this conflict as an
ancient territorial one that concerned them and the Egyptian Bedouin. In
their May 1906 petition the Bedouin shaykhs included an outline of what they
considered to be the 'real administrative line', to use an Ottoman term. They
described the 'line' by referring to local socio-spatial terms and listed dozens of

sites and Bedouin groups who lived near and across this line.[16] The Ottomans insisted that this was an administrative line, as they continued to view Egypt as part of its empire despite its special status under Mehmet Ali's rule. However, for the Bedouin this was in fact an intertribal boundary that was determined by mutual agreement between the Beersheba and Egyptian tribes following earlier boundary disputes, and which was formalised in 1890.[17] Since then each group had used their lands without interruption or disputes. The Beersheba shaykhs assured the Ottoman officials that the Egyptian Bedouin would not object to this border, and punctuated the assertion with a challenge that if they did object, 'let them show up and face us'.[18] In doing so not only did the shaykhs provide information to support Ottoman claims but they did so in a way that implied they would be willing to protect their lands and consequently the Ottoman borders.

The Bedouin communities were undoubtedly wary of the growing Ottoman imperial presence in their environs and the evolving interpolity tensions as they realised these could upset the existing territorial and political structure of what could be thought of as a 'Bedouin space'. Increased state presence would potentially lead to further taxation, conscription and border control. Nevertheless, the local Bedouin leaders sought to secure Ottoman protection and justify their claims by connecting them to broader Ottoman objectives in the region. Indeed, the Bedouin had in fact approached the Ottoman government because they recognised that they needed the latter's patronage in order to counter the British-Egyptian threat to their territories. They claimed that if their lands and water resources were lost as the result of the imposition of the border, the principal Ottoman objectives in the region would be undermined because 'cultivation and Bedouin settlement would be impossible', and Bedouin fighting would resume.[19] Such an evaluation of the situation may have been exaggerated, but such arguments demonstrate the shaykhs' shrewd comprehension of Ottoman jurisdictional project in their region and of their political objectives.

Although it was appropriate to regard the borderland region as a Bedouin space the shaykhs explicitly brought state borders into the discussion. Indeed, throughout their petitions the shaykhs drew a distinction between Beersheba and Egypt. They claimed that the landowners across the proposed border hailed from the Beersheba administration and thus the land should be considered as belonging to Beersheba. As discussed above, tax payments constituted one aspect of Bedouin claims to possession, but their connection to the land also involved something less tangible. As the Jerusalem governor testified, 'the Bedouin are much attached to their lands, thus, even if a small part is given to the Egyptian Bedouin, fighting will erupt and they may request for all their lands to be on that side'.[20] While the Bedouin were sometimes represented as aimless wanderers, it was in fact their profound connection to place that forced Ottoman officials to consider protecting their claims.

Despite its failure to provide the anticipated protection and save Bedouin lands, the Ottoman government still tried to protect the well-being of Bedouin communities. This is evident in the Ottoman decision regarding the location of the border and their guarantee of future water rights for the Beersheba Bedouin communities across the border. Some scholars who have studied the making of the Ottoman-Egyptian border have discussed the Ottoman insist-ence on having Taba as the original point of the border. Indeed, the border originated at Ras Taba at a distance of fourteen kilometres from Aqaba alongside the Gulf of Aqaba.[21] The Ottoman Special Council's decision confirming the final details of the British-Ottoman agreement (9 September 1906) indicated that the Ottoman government was to choose between two particular locations for the border. The first was Taba, which had military significance as a place from which to defend the Naqab al-Aqaba area; the second was the Qusayma, Qiddis Spring, and the Qdeirat Spring, which were sites that would ensure that the Ottomans gained further territory while also safeguarding Bedouin interests.[22] After studying the military and political value of each location, the officials chose Taba. They were concerned that if the British were granted Taba they would request further nearby lands to be part of Sinai.[23] In this case the Ottoman government favoured the military value of Naqab al-Aqaba for the protection of the empire over the economic or territorial value in protecting the lands claimed by the Bedouin. Yet, when the Sultan confirmed the decision of the council, he added that access to water should also be guaranteed for the police, the military and other Ottoman subjects, and this right should be stated clearly in the agreement. The Sultan furthermore required that funds be allocated for alternative water sources for Beersheba.[24]

Following the creation of the border, Bedouin mobility across the border began to gain different political meanings and raise administrative and secur-ity challenges in the eyes of both the Ottoman and the British authorities.[25] In addition, with the closing of the border question, the British threat and ambitions in the Holy Land became more real. Beersheba became the front line against this threat, and thus the new border and the imperial domain needed to be further protected.

PROTECTION AND POLITICAL ALLIANCE
OR ALLEGIANCE

The border marked a new limit to the empire and established a distinct political reality with which the British, the Ottomans and the Bedouin had to deal. The Ottoman government sought, after 1906, to consolidate its presence in the borderland against any British intervention by means of extending its rule and jurisdiction further south of Beersheba near the new border. The new judicio-administrative order needed the appropriate physical and human infrastructure for its success.[26] In 1907, since stability and social cohesion were essential in the eyes of the Ottoman government, the Jerusalem governor undertook efforts to reconcile two tribal confederations in Beersheba and expressed his intention of not allowing the possibility of even 'the smallest dispute' there.[27] In the same year border enhancement took place in Rafah as well.[28] Further, in 1908, the Ottoman administration founded the Ḥafir sub-district and the Maliḥa region (*nâhiye*) near the new border and promoted the administrative status of Beersheba.[29] In 1910, moreover, the Jerusalem governor discussed a five-year development plan for the Beersheba region involving the construction of schools, roads, a police station, an agricultural school and an agricultural bank. He stressed the need to support Bedouin cultivation and education as a way to transform the region for the benefit of the homeland and the welfare of the inhabitants, and as protection against the British in Egypt.[30] In other words, even, and perhaps especially, after the border was established the Ottoman effort of incorporating Bedouin into the Ottoman state through patronage and development assumed greater significance. For better protection, in addition to the greater Ottoman project of building new legal-bureaucratic subjects, it was important to create loyal Ottoman subjects.

Bedouin loyalty and political allegiance came to occupy an important place after the making of the border. Both the Ottoman and the British continuously observed the other side's activities across the border, collecting intelligence, expanding their knowledge of the region, and taking necessary preparations in light of the high likelihood of an upcoming military confrontation. The question of Bedouin loyalty was central to these dynamics, as both parties were aware of the role that Bedouin would play in protecting either side's interests in any fighting, political dispute, or border protection.

During the negotiation over the border Ottoman officials had expressed their concern to Istanbul about any British contact with the Bedouin, and noted that such contact should be avoided altogether.[31] The Jerusalem governor Ekrem Bey was aware of the threat of possible coalitions against the Ottomans from across the border, especially if the Beersheba Bedouin were brought to the side of the British.[32] Consequently, he was instructed by his superiors to pay special attention to the Beersheba Bedouins and 'convey to them the message of the sultan's benevolence'.[33] For example, in the course of a tour of Jaffa, Gaza and Beersheba in June 1907 to collect taxes, he distributed decorations, titles and robes of honour to the Bedouin on behalf of the Sultan to 'gain and strengthen the friendship of the frontier tribes'. The Sultan expressed satisfaction, through his first secretary, 'at the loyalty displayed by his distant subjects and has commanded his greeting to be communicated to them'.[34] Ottoman officials also utilised religious rhetoric in order to gain Bedouin political loyalty. They stressed the Islamic identity of the empire by distributing Qurans and conducting circumcision festivities at the Beersheba mosque. They also gave shaykhs robes and made donations to the poor.[35] In 1908 the Sultan took a further step by granting amnesty to forty-five Bedouin convicts.[36]

In addition to demonstrating beneficence, acquiring knowledge became vital to interpolity interaction. Guided by military and security considerations, the British administration worked on expanding its body of knowledge of the topography, human geography, and the daily affairs in Beersheba. In February 1913 it finished the preparation of detailed maps of Sinai and Beersheba, with site names, roads, inhabitants and water resources. Further, in December 1916 the British squadron began taking aerial photos of Sinai, Beersheba and Gaza that focused on roads and railways, bridges, water resources, towns and Ottoman military targets.[37] Likewise, the Ottoman ally, the Bavarian air force, took a large number of aerial photos for the Beersheba and the Sinai regions between September 1917 and September 1918.[38] Such information was a necessity given its connection to mapping and manipulation of local populations, both crucial for defining sovereignty.

The British, moreover, closely watched Bedouin-Ottoman relations across the border, often presenting the interventionist aspects of Ottoman rule as a potential spark for a Bedouin revolt. For example, in February 1913 the British consular agent in Gaza reported, on the basis of conversations he had had with the Beersheba governor among others, that there was unrest in the sub-district and claimed that the 'idea of an insurrection against Turkish rule [was] gaining ground'. He noted that the dominant Shaykh Hammad al-Sufi had reportedly warned the Ottoman authorities of a rising 'similar to that of Yemen'.[39] A month later, the British consulate in Jerusalem reported that there was an 'undeniable recrudescence of discontent among the Beersheba Bedouins on account of the general arbitrariness of the gendarmerie and Judicial Authorities with respect to the land and the tithe problem, the standing source of trouble in these regions'.[40] Seeking to justify their possible rule and political alliance with the Bedouin, the British consular agent of Gaza argued: 'it is evident that they [Bedouin] are thoroughly disgusted with the Turkish misrule and would welcome any regime which would allow of their leading their traditional existence in peace'.[41] Like in other British imperial cases, and similar to Ottoman politics of protection, local 'custom' and 'tradition' were perceived as key to establishing any future formal or informal political agreements. Indeed, in the post-Ottoman period, the British would resort to maintaining local custom in the local jurisdiction, adopting an approach that depicted the Bedouin as backward and unchanging communities.

Yet, despite the British claims that the Bedouin-Ottoman relationship was deteriorating, the vast majority of the Beersheba Bedouin remained loyal to the Ottoman government, which seems to have succeeded in its efforts to turn the Bedouin into loyal Ottoman subjects.[42] During the fighting the Bedouin took an active part in defending the borders and in the German-Ottoman efforts to cross the Suez Canal. At the same time, realising the changing power relations around them and their varying abilities to protect their interests, the Bedouin were beginning to shift loyalties towards the end of the Great War. It was reported that with the Ottoman retreat and the arrival of the Sharif's army, some Bedouin supported the advancing forces and made preparations to fight the Ottoman forces in Tafila (today's Jordan).[43]

For both the British and the Ottomans, the 'Egyptian frontiers' might have involved people described as 'distant subjects', but these same people were clearly at the forefront of the effort to establish sovereignty. By examining Beersheba we have seen that protection claims and discourses were frequently deployed by Ottoman officials and administrators and appeared at various interconnected levels, and that much of the time these were complementary rather than contradictory. The interpolity competition over sovereignty or political dominance depended very much on the ability of each party to provide protection. The Bedouin communities constituted an interesting challenge to imperial powers. However, the changing inter-imperial politics in the region and the making of the border transformed the Bedouin into an important political resource and agent of protection rather than a threat to Ottoman rule. Whereas a few decades before the border-making the Bedouin protected their lands against neighbouring Egyptian Bedouin tribes, they were now also involved in defending an Ottoman Muslim land against the British. At a time when empires were looking to establish subjecthood that was tied to fixedness, legibility and territorial demarcation, the Bedouin communities' mobile capabilities and intimate knowledge of their space qualified them to be providers of protection. Thus, imperial powers were working out a proper balance between treating the Bedouin as imperial subjects and as political allies.

CONCLUSION

Consideration of the Ottoman *Tanzimat* in general and the Beersheba Ottoman reform in particular cannot be separated from the phenomenon of protection. The Ottoman government had to uphold its claim to sovereignty both in regard to its own subjects and in respect of foreign political powers, especially apparent at the imperial frontiers. These requirements coincided with global changes in imperial rule and its components of territory, law and sovereignty, and took place within a legally and geographically variegated space.

Due to its crucial strategic location in 'the well protected domains of His Imperial Majesty', Beersheba was able to achieve meaningful administrative and socio-economic progress in its brief period under reformed Ottoman rule. And this had a significant impact on redefining Bedouin relationship with the central government as well as on the geography of modern Palestine, which would continue to unfold in subsequent decades. The Ottomans instituted political frameworks that aimed at constructing loyal imperial subjects that it had to treat also as partners in empire. The Ottoman exceptionalist policies, their aspiration for winning the hearts of the Bedouin, and the integration of proxy administration through the local shaykhs also characterised the British administration in Beersheba between 1917 and 1948. The British continued to allow so-called local custom to apply in the judicial realm by instituting official tribal courts that existed only in the Beersheba sub-district of Palestine. Further, shaykhs continued to play an important role in the local politics under official and semi-official positions. Concurrently, civilisational discourses of Bedouin primitivism, savagery and despotism were similarly used by the British in order to legitimise their political and legal authority. Thus, the politics of protection persisted, even as the identity of the central power changed.

NOTES

1 Bedouin Shaykhs to the Grand Vizier, 14 Mayıs 1333/14 May 1917, BEO 4469/335162, The Basbakanlik (Government) Ottoman Archives (henceforth BOA).

2 Probably referring to the Sharif of Mecca's decision to make an alliance with the British against the Ottoman Empire.

3 Bedouin Shaykhs to the Grand Vizier, 14 Mayıs 1333/14 May 1917, BEO 4469/ 335162, BOA.

4 Sultan's Chief Secretary to Ministry of Interior, 3 Haziran 1333/3 June 1917, İ.DUIT 12/93, BOA.

5 Selim Deringil, *The Well-Protected Domains: Ideology and the Legitimation of Power in the Ottoman Empire, 1876–1909*, Tauris, New York, 1998, p. 42.

6 Minister of the Interior to the Grand Vizier, 27 Mayıs 1315/8 June 1899, DH.TMİK-S 25/62, BOA. See Yasemin Avci, 'The Application of Tanzimat in the Desert: The Bedouins and the Creation of a New Town in Southern Palestine, 1860–1914', *Middle Eastern Studies*, vol. 45, no. 6, 2009, pp. 969–83.

7 Decision of the Council of State, 7 Teşrinisani 1316/20 November 1900, İ.DH 1380/1318.N/18, BOA.

8 See for example the chapter by Lisa Ford in this volume.

9 Minister of the Interior to the Grand Vizier, 27 Mayıs 1315/8 June 1899, DH.TMİK-S 25/62, BOA.

10 Jerusalem Governor to Vizierate, 16 Kanunusani 1313/28 January 1898, Y.A.HUS 381/21/2, BOA.

11 In the decision to found Beersheba in 1899 it was stressed that the institution of an Ottoman gendarmerie would only occur with Bedouin integration and service in it. Further, both the administrative and municipal councils were to be furnished entirely by Bedouin representatives (Minister of the Interior to the Grand Vizier, 27 Mayıs 1315/8 June 1899, DH.TMİK-S 25/62, BOA; Jerusalem Governor to Vizierate, 13 Haziran 1323/26 June 1907, BEO 3090/231705, BOA; 'Arif Al-'Arif, *Tarikh Bir al-Sab' wa Qaba 'iliha* [The History of Beersheba and Its Confederations], Madbuli Library, Cairo, 1934, p. 268).

12 British sources included the papers of Bramly and diaries of other surveyors as well as papers of the British Foreign Office. The diary account by Rushdi Bey who was the Ottoman Commander in Aqaba is a unique Ottoman source, titled 'The Problem of Aqaba'. See Nurit Kliot, 'The Evolution of the Egypt-Israel Boundary: From Colonial Foundations to Peaceful Borders', *Boundary and Territory Briefing*, vol. 1, no. 8, 1995, p. 4.

13 Commander of Fifth Army to General Command, 24 Haziran 1322/7 July 1906, Y.MTV 288/57, BOA.

14 The petition from July dated 28 July 1906 was sent by fourteen of the Bedouin notables and shaykhs. On petition writing particularly from Ottoman Palestine, see Yuval Ben-Bassat, *Petitioning the Sultan: Protests and Justice in Late Ottoman Palestine*, Tauris, London, 2013; and on Bedouin petitions in particular, see Yuval Ben-Bassat, 'Bedouin Petitions from Late Ottoman Palestine: Evaluating the Effects of Sedentarisation', *Journal of the Economic and Social History of the Orient*, vol. 58, nos 1–2, 2015, pp. 135–36.

15 Petition by Bedouin Shaykhs to General Command by the Jerusalem Governor, 15 Temmuz 1322/28 July 1906, Y.MTV 289/05/04, BOA; Commander of Fifth Army to General Command, 27 Temmuz 1322/9 August 1906, Y.MTV 289/168, BOA; Jerusalem Governor to Vizierate, 27 Ağustos 1322/9 September 1906, İ.DUIT 137/25/07, BOA.

16 Petition by Bedouin Shaykhs to General Command by the Jerusalem Governor, 15 Temmuz 1322/28 July 1906, Y.MTV 289/05/04, BOA.

17 In 1890 the Rmeilat Bedouin of the Arish area and the Beersheba Tarabin reached an agreement that was put on *asnad*, a copy with each party, which confirmed that Qusayma was the real border (Jerusalem Governor to Vizierate, 21 Temmuz 1322/3 August 1906, Y.MTV 289/150, BOA).

18 It could also be interpreted as an invitation for a battle.

19 Petition by Bedouin Shaykhs to General Command by the Jerusalem Governor, 15 Temmuz 1322/28 July 1906, Y.MTV 289/05/04, BOA.

20 Jerusalem Governor to the Vizierate, 21 Temmuz 1322/3 August 1906, Y.MTV 289/150, BOA.

21 Gideon Biger, *Boundaries of Modern Palestine, 1840–1947*, Routledge, New York, 2004, p. 32; Kliot.

22 Decision of the Special Council, 27 Ağustos 1322/9 September 1906, İ.DUIT 137/25, BOA.

23 The lands of the Ahiwat Bedouin near Mrashrash, known today as Eilat town in Israel.

24 Decision of the Special Council, 27 Ağustos 1322/9 September 1906, İ.DUIT 137/25, BOA; Patricia Toye (ed.), *Near & Middle East Titles: Palestine Boundaries 1833–1947*, vol. 1, Cambridge Archives Edition, Cambridge, 1989, pp. 548–630.

25 Jerusalem Governor to Ministry of the Interior, 15 Şubat 1333/27 February 1915, DH.ID 181/62, BOA.

26 Grand Vizier to the Sultan, 25 Kanunievvel 1323/7 January 1908, İ.DH 1463/27, BOA.

27 Jerusalem Governor to Vizierate, 13 Haziran 1323/26 June 1907, BEO 3090/231705, BOA.

28 Gil-Har, p. 562.

29 Grand Vizier to the Sultan, 25 Kanunievvel 1323/7 January 1908, İ.DH 1463/27, BOA; see also Yitzhak Gil-Har, 'The South-Eastern Limits of Palestine at the End of Ottoman Rule', *Middle Eastern Studies*, vol. 28, no. 3, 1992, p. 560.

30 Jerusalem Governor to the Ministry of the Interior, DH.ID 44–1/18, 6 Haziran 1326/19 June 1910, BOA.

31 Jerusalem Governor to Vizierate, 25 Temmuz 1322/7August 1906, Y.MTV 289/156, BOA.

32 David Kushner, 'The District of Jerusalem in the Eyes of Three Ottoman Governors at the End of the Hamidian Period', *Middle East Studies*, vol. 35, no. 2, 1999, p. 94.

33 David Kushner, 'Ali Ekrem bey, Governor of Jerusalem, 1906–1908', *International Journal of Middle East Studies*, vol. 28, no. 3, 1996, p. 355.

34 Gaza British Consular Agent to British Consul in Jerusalem, 24 June 1907, FO 195/2255, National Archives of the United Kingdom (henceforth TNA).

35 Vizierate to the Ministry of the Interior, 10 Mart 1322/23 March 1906, BEO 3018/226298, BOA. The total budget reached about 40,000 *kuruş*.

36 Sultan's advisor to the Sultan, 6 Mayıs 1324/19 May 1908, İ.HUS, BOA. These Bedouin were sentenced to terms of between one and three years.

37 WO 303/134–152, TNA, maps that are known as Newcombe maps; see also photographs taken by E. Indies and Egypt Seaplanes SQDN, 1916, AIR, 20/612, TNA.

38 Nada Atrash, 'Mapping Palestine: The Bavarian Air Force WWI Aerial Photography', *Jerusalem Quarterly*, no. 56, 2014, pp. 95–106.

39 British Consulate Jerusalem to British Consulate Constantinople, 14 March 1913, FO 195/2452/1153, TNA.

40 Ibid.

41 Ibid.

42 Bedouin Shaykhs to the Grand Vizier, 14 Mayıs 1333/14 May 1917, BEO 4469/335162, BOA.

43 Survey of Haksharat Hayishuv, 1920–21, CZA.L/18/127/2, The Central Zionist Archives.

12

Protection by Proxy: The Hausa-Fulani as Agents of British Colonial Rule in Northern Nigeria

MOSES E. OCHONU

In this chapter I consider protection not as a phenomenon made up simply of European protectors on the one hand and protected subalterns on the other, but rather as an enterprise that involved a range of actors and gradations of power. Protection in this frame was a process that required investment in hierarchies of authority, control and enforcement. These complex relations of power mirror the ambiguous and elastic nature of protection arrangements in other contexts examined in this volume. My analysis highlights a political arrangement in which British colonisers devolved authority upon a group of African enforcers who were regarded by the indigenous people as foreigners in the areas that the British government empowered them to govern on their behalf.

My focus is on northern Nigeria and in particular Adamawa Province, where an emirate named Adamawa had grown around the town of Yola. After the British conquest of Northern Nigeria (1900–03), British administrators made Yola the headquarters of the colonial province of Adamawa while the Lamido (or emir) of Adamawa became the pre-eminent British-protected protector, placed in nominal charge of the province's non-Muslim, non-Fulani ethnic groups under the protective supervision of British officials. In Northern Nigeria protection, narrowly understood, was the basis of a contract between two elites: British officials and Hausa-Fulani Muslim aristocrats. At the same time, however, protection turned out to be replicable in that the colonial government not only offered protection to this cadre of local rulers but authorised them to offer a derivative of it to other peoples who were not Hausa. In this way, I suggest that the Hausa-Fulani were empowered as proxy protectors and undertook the quotidian work of protection in rural districts. In this unorthodox and improvised system the existence of more than one protecting authority and protected party, and more than one set of claims to juridical authority at the grassroots, produced complication, tension and resentment.

The fact that the Hausa-Fulani elite assumed a role in these arrangements complicates conventional accounts of how protection worked. This has significance for two reasons. First, proxy chieftaincy undermined notions of indirect rule, as advanced by Frederick Lugard, the first British Governor of Northern Nigeria. Indirect rule relied on two underlining tenets: the notion that protected parties would only consider a protection arrangement legitimate and co-operate with it if its British-protected African executors and middlemen were indigenous to the protected ethnic groups, and the idea that Europeans were the sole civilising agents who were merely assisted by local auxiliaries. Second, such arrangements reveal the amorphous nature of protection even in an age that is conventionally regarded as the high water mark of imperialism, when colonisation supposedly followed formulas informed by centuries of colonial experience and a deep repository of knowledge about African groups.

THE EMERGENCE OF THE HAUSA-FULANI AS PREFERRED ALLIES

By way of starting it is necessary to provide the brief intellectual and political history that helped to produce and legitimise British officialdom's alliance with the Hausa-Fulani elite. The Hausa inhabited the savannah grasslands of West Africa, hemmed between the Songhai and Bornu Empires. Hausaland was largely defined by the linguistic primacy of various dialects of the Hausa language. Prior to the beginning of the British encounter with Northern Nigeria, Hausaland hosted a steady traffic of Fulani migrants who settled in the region, sometimes establishing peripheral communities, sometimes integrating into Hausa communities. A Fulani-led Islamic movement that swept through the region between 1804 and 1808 saw a new ethno-religious category of Hausa-Fulani emerge and Islamic solidarity supersede other affinities,[1] except in the Middle Belt communities, which were predominantly non-Muslim areas of Northern Nigeria that were neither significantly affected by the reform movement nor dominated by the Sokoto caliphate that it spawned.

Acting on behalf of the British government, Frederick Lugard declared a protectorate over Northern Nigeria on 1 January 1900 and thereafter commenced a process of conquest that culminated in the defeat of the Sokoto caliphate in 1903. However, even before the British conquest, the Hausa-Fulani elite had emerged as the preferred colonial allies of the British government. There was a long preconquest process that was marked above all else by the production of a sophisticated script that differentiated between the peoples of northern Nigeria on what was held to be ethno-religious grounds. This conceived of the Hausa-Fulani as potential allies deserving privileged protection status and non-Muslim ethnic groups as their subordinates in the emerging colonial hierarchy.

In 1823 British explorer Hugh Clapperton reached Sokoto, the seat of a Sokoto caliphate, where he interacted extensively with its ruler, Mohammed Bello. As a result Clapperton was seduced by the political astuteness of the Sokoto hierarchy and thereafter recommended the caliphate's personnel and culture as candidates for use in any future British administration. Moreover, he later wrote accounts and created maps that essentially endorsed Mohammed Bello's discursive efforts to delineate a Hausa-Islamic political and geographic entity.[2] This would define the trajectory of British colonial policy in Northern Nigeria in the decades that followed.

Clapperton himself confessed that the map he drew and published in his travel account was based on outlines and claims provided to him by Sultan Bello and members of his household.[3] This map was the first to be introduced to British metropolitan society on the territorial span and power of the Sokoto caliphate, and it established a baseline from which subsequent British travellers to Northern Nigeria constructed their maps and narratives about the caliphate, its territorial and political reach, and the control they assumed it had over non-Muslim groups. Yet we know that Clapperton's map and the accompanying narrative of caliphal power grossly exaggerated both the caliphate's territorial sovereignty and its foray into several non-Muslim territories of what would later be designated colonial Northern Nigeria. Indeed, the map and the political claims Clapperton wove around it reflected nothing more than the imperial fantasy of Sultan Mohammed Bello,[4] since the caliphate was struggling to pacify and incorporate the Alela and Zamfara polities less than two hundred miles from its headquarters in Sokoto, and was helpless in the face of consistent harassing raids from the kingdom of Ningi on its northwestern and northeastern frontiers.[5] Nonetheless, the narrative of precolonial caliphal imperial rights over non-Muslim peoples and of Middle Belt peoples being historically subordinate to caliphate influence came to shape British views on Northern Nigeria, enabling British colonial interlocutors to imagine the Hausa as protected British partners and the non-Muslim peoples of the Middle Belt as the protected, and as civilisational pupils of the former.

However, it was another British explorer, William Baikie, who drew a line between a Muslim caliphate that he viewed as deserving of the British government's protection and patronage, and a vast Middle Belt non-Muslim region that he suggested comprised a collection of backward non-Muslim peoples suitable for protection and tutelage to be offered by subordinate Hausa Muslim agents whom the British government would supervise. In an 1856 account of a voyage of exploration he had undertaken up the Niger and Tsádda Rivers,

Baikie wrote: 'I believe that for the promotion of commerce and of civilisation ... it is essential to cultivate the friendship of the Pulo [Fulani] nation
as being exceedingly powerful and influential, and therefore likely, under
good management, to be useful [to us].' More specifically, Baikie recommended the signing of a commercial treaty between Britain and the Sultan
of Sokoto, arguing that 'such a step gained would be of infinite importance,
and would greatly facilitate future progress'.[6]

Over time Baikie would emerge as a committed believer in the Hausa-
Fulani as potential allies and protected agents of future British colonisers. In
1863 he gave an address to the House of Commons in which he presented a set
of sixteen rules, designed to deal with indigenous peoples along the River
Niger, in which he made this distinction: 'If obliged, always give preference to
a Mohammedan, as the worshipper of God, to an idolater.'[7] This helped to
establish a notion of Hausa-Fulani Muslims as fairly civilised 'worshipper[s]
of God' and of non-Muslim of Northern Nigeria peoples as uncivilised ido-
laters or so-called pagans. This valuation of the caliphate and the concomitant
devaluation of the Middle Belt persisted throughout the remainder of the
nineteenth century and acquired a utilitarian character as the British colonial
project began to evolve in the first decade of the twentieth century.

LUGARD AND THE HAUSA-FULANI

If Clapperton, Baikie and other British travellers established the formula
for designating the Hausa-Fulani as cultural and political superiors of non-
Muslim ethnic groups who would benefit from the delegated protection of
the former, it was Frederick Lugard who turned the formula into a theory and
manual of colonial administration in Northern Nigeria. Lugard's *The Dual
Mandate in British Tropical Africa* is regarded as the canonical manual of
British colonial administrative practice in Africa. The book's prescriptions were
informed by Lugard's two stints in Nigeria, first as Lieutenant Governor of
Northern Nigeria and then as Governor of Nigeria, and most of them applied
specifically to circumstances in Northern Nigeria. Equally important, Lugard's
manual provides invaluable insights into how the British administration conceived of Hausa-Fulani rule in Northern Nigeria because its author was the last
British Governor of the Northern Nigeria protectorate (between 1912 and 1914)
and the first Governor-General of Nigeria (between 1914 and 1919).

In *The Dual Mandate* Lugard argued that continuity and decentralisa-
tion were the cardinal principles that should guide administrative policy in
Northern Nigeria: continuity with old political traditions and arrangements,
and a decentralised delegated rule of native African subordinates. Lugard thus

espoused a colonial system in which the traditions and customs of a people would be respected and adapted for the purpose of administering them through the agency of indigenous elites familiar to them. The overarching goal was the same, he argued, for 'conservative Moslem[s]' and the 'primitive pagan[s]', namely to instil British-borne civilisation in Africans by reconciling their pre-existing institutions and ways of life with the markers of civilisation as defined by the colonisers.[8]

In making the case for the administrative system he called indirect rule Lugard was critical of the British government's administrative practices in India that had in his view privileged 'the narrowest of oligarchies' and so were unrepresentative of those they presided over. Consequently, he stressed the value of native rulers whom he argued were unlike what he called an 'alien usurper' since they were inured from xenophobic demagoguery that might result from a 'crisis of legitimacy'.[9] Yet, despite railing against 'alien usurpers', Lugard endorsed what amounted to the alien rule of British-supervised Fulani chiefs in Northern Nigeria's Middle Belt.

In the eyes of Lugard and his peers in the Northern Nigerian colonial bureaucracy the Fulani were racially different from those they saw as the negroid autochthons of the Middle Belt. Islam was, they believed, an important marker of this difference. Lugard held that the non-Muslim polities had not 'produced so definitive a code of law, or such advanced methods of dispensing justice, as the Koran ha[d] introduced, and they lack[ed] the indigenous educational advantages which the use of Arabic and religious schools ha[d] conferred on the Moslem'.[10] Consequently he argued that the Muslim emirates were better prepared for indirect rule than the non-Muslim groups. Indeed, he argued that the imposition of such methods of colonial statecraft on 'the conditions of primitive tribes would be to foist upon them a system foreign to their conceptions'.[11]

At the same time, however, Lugard held that Muslim elites from the more advanced, more indirect rule-ready Hausa-Fulani polities could help prepare the so-called primitive institutions and societies of the Middle Belt for a fully fledged implementation of indirect rule there. This was the premise of Lugard's vision of protection and it was a striking departure from his own principles of indirect rule. British colonisers would appoint Hausa-Fulani officials to oversee and protect non-Muslim communities and prepare some of the latter's members for the role of protectors among their own people in the future. There was thus a contradiction at the heart of this scheme. Lugard's philosophy of indirect rule hinged on the British-protected mediatory role of local, legitimate indigenes. However, colonial rule in the Middle Belt moved instead in the direction of centralisation and homogenisation as colonisers sought to bring Middle Belt non-Muslims they regarded as backward relative to the Muslim Hausa-Fulani into some sort of civilisational uniformity with the latter through the protection work of imported, non-indigenous Hausa-Fulani officials who would prepare the ground for their own replacement by protectors indigenous to the Middle Belt. The contradiction of promoting indigenous protection under the indirect rule precept and implementing a policy that privileged non-indigenous Hausa-Fulani protectors would later haunt colonial administration in Northern Nigeria.

How did Lugard attempt to resolve this contradiction? He admitted that empowering the Hausa-Fulani over the peoples of the Middle Belt was an unequivocal violation of his principle of delegating colonial duties to indigenous proxies since the proxy rule of Hausa-Fulani officials would 'deny self-government' to the people [of the Middle Belt] over whom they rule[d]'.[12] However, for Lugard, this problem was offset by the fact that the British government considered this 'alien race' to be 'more capable of rule than the indigenous [Middle Belt] races'.[13]

Lugard endorsed the subordination of indigenous chiefs to the Muslim Hausa-Fulani chiefs by highlighting the stance that the Lamido (emir) of Adamawa took toward ruling his non-Muslim sphere: 'If they [non-Muslims] think you are trying to make them Fulani or Moslems they resent it. I would not put a Fulani headman to live in their country, but he should constantly tour amongst them, and advise the pagan chief, and tell all the people that they may appeal to him, but he should not go behind his back.'[14] The Lamido's approach highlighted the fact that those whom the British protected could extend that protection to others. What is clear from the way Lugard received the Lamido's conception of paternal proxy rule is that the British were largely comfortable with the sub-colonial initiatives of Hausa-Fulani chiefs and agents among Middle Belt peoples and that they saw the former as invaluable civilisers and protectors.

Lugard's positive reception of the Lamido's protection prescription is hardly surprising given the fact that the Muslim ruler gave succinct expression to this idiom of protection in the following words: 'as the British govern us through ourselves, so we must govern the pagans through their own chiefs'.[15] The British and their Hausa-Fulani partners appreciated that protection was a diffuse, malleable phenomenon in the quotidian grind of colonial administration. Furthermore, both the British and the Hausa-Fulani understood the complementary roles they were to play in the task of civilising the peoples of the Middle Belt: the British setting the terms and obligations of colonial subjecthood and the Hausa-Fulani protectors ensuring that the protected non-Muslims fulfilled their colonial obligations while internalising the rationale behind those obligations.

FULANI RULE IN ADAMAWA

Once the concept of Hausa-Fulani political primacy was established, the formulation of a colonial administrative policy around it took its course, and the new policy subjected the peoples of the Middle Belt to the ensuing administrative paradigm. British officials believed that the administrative ideal was an arrangement in which Fulani Resident Heads presided over the affairs of non-Muslim districts with the assistance of so-called 'Pagan Heads' whom the former would supervise and guide.[16] This was a system in which a non-Muslim would rule under the supervision and guidance of a Fulani official as a transition to the eventual rule of indigenous protectors.[17] The formulation of a Hausa-Fulani imaginary in the Northern Nigerian colonial system had a utilitarian purpose to it. The most important component was the desire for paternal patrons or protectors, who would address the quotidian concerns of their clients while imparting to them the ethos of colonial obligations and respect for constituted authority. In Adamawa Province, all these imperatives were visible and were tested against the messy quotidian realities of colonial life.

During the first few years of the British administration Adamawa Province was partitioned into several divisions. Each of them fell under the authority of the Fulani Lamido of Adamawa, whom the British recognised as possessing a right to rule the vast Adamawa non-Muslim hinterland. Reconciling Fulani overlordship to the Lugardian principles of indirect rule proved to be a considerable challenge. Colonial officials sought to legitimise Fulani rule, combat its excesses as it unfolded, and assuage opposition to it. Fulani rule was then gradually and haphazardly extended to the various non-Muslim communities through Fulani polities like Muri, Goila and Song. All of these states were satellites of Adamawa emirate in Yola, and their rulers were beholden to the Lamido of Adamawa.

In 1920 Ronald MacAlister, the colonial District Officer of Muri District of Adamawa Province, sought to justify the system the British government had created and to explain the rationale for it. He did so believing that the non-Fulani, non-Muslim communities could be said to be in need of protection from the Fulani Muslim rulers given that for many years before the advent of British rule the former had been raided and enslaved by the latter.[18] In other words, some British officials believed that empowering Fulani rulers over the non-Muslim communities of the Province would amount to reestablishing an old Fulani suzerainty that had been supplanted by British military conquest and rule.

MacAlister justified this arrangement in two ways. First, he argued that the agents of 'native' administration should be recruited from what he deemed to be African groups, such as the Fulani, who were 'nearest in sympathy and type to the people to be governed'.[19] In other words, MacAlister held that while the non-Muslims were wary of Fulani control the Fulani were more familiar to them than the British could ever be, and that this would make the Fulani more effective, albeit still imperfect, colonial agents than British officials. 'The personnel of such Native Administration may be foreign in race to the pagans concerned', he remarked, 'but they will be African and very much nearer to them in ideas, instincts, and way of thinking, than any European could be'.[20] Here, we see a recognition that the protected non-Muslim peoples could resent their Hausa-Fulani protectors, but we also see a forceful, counterbalancing statement of the Fulani's value to the British colonial administration.

Second, MacAlister predicted that, through intermarriage, Fulani and non-Muslims 'would weld into one nation' that was 'self-governed under British supervision'.[21] As for the possibility of non-Muslim communities rebelling against the imposed rule of Fulani agents, MacAlister surmised that this could be diminished by the Fulani rulers involving the non-Muslim communities in their own administration.[22] To achieve this, he recommended the recruitment of 'intelligent non-Muhamadans' as understudies. This, he claimed, would 'avoid the appearance of bringing the pagan under his hereditary enemy'.[23]

If in British eyes the question of how Hausa-Fulani rule was to be implemented over areas such as Muri proved difficult, this was even more the case with what they called 'no. 2 Division', which comprised the Bura, Hona, Kilba and Lala ethnic groups. The British found that the Bura had never been conquered by the Fulani, and so the argument for subjecting them to the authority of the nearby Fulani district of Song was weak at best. Nevertheless they proceeded in 1912 to place the Bura under a Fulani chief from Song on the basis of some tenuous ethnographic references to reciprocal tributary contacts between Song and the Bura in precolonial times.[24] They also crafted a similar scheme of Fulani chieftaincy for the Lala people when they approved Yerima Iyawa, a Fulani from Song, becoming ruler and protector over the Lala.[25] The Hona, Marghi and Uba peoples similarly came under the authority of Fulani protector-chiefs appointed by the Fulani sub-emirate of Goila or Yola directly.

The British government's consideration of the aforementioned appointments skirted the question of whether the imposition of Fulani rule on non-Muslim ethnic groups with or without histories of subservience to Fulani

power was appropriate. Their discussion instead focused on whether the
Fulani entities of Song and Goila should have the symbolic right to control
the Bura, Lala and Hona on the Lamido's behalf or whether these Fulani
Muslim chiefs should be directly controlled and supervised by the Lamido
himself, who was accountable to the British Resident. Officials considered the
merits of the Fulani chiefs paying symbolic tribute to Song and Goila or
directly to Yola, and whether or not they should remit their taxes as 'sub-
districts' of Song and Goila or directly to the Lamido as his appointed agents.
These questions were ultimately resolved on a case-by-case basis.

Attempts to compel Fulani rulers to reside among their non-Muslim subjects floundered even though British officials bemoaned 'the evil effects of a
[Fulani] District Chief who is non resident, and the abuses that occur when
he merely visits the tribe for the purpose of tax collection'.[26] This problem
increased as the Fulani chief's distant residency accentuated his foreignness to
his non-Muslim subjects, making the implementation of colonial instructions
contentious. The British administration proposed a compassionate, more
humane residential Fulani chieftaincy as the solution to this problem. This
remedy would prove elusive, yet pursuit of it would result in two blueprints for
governing the non-Muslim communities of the Adamawa. These in turn
produced a new administrative configuration founded on the utility of Fulani
chiefs being resident among those they purported to protect and rule. It is hard
to date this shift precisely, but it seems to have occurred between 1925 and
1928; this new thinking contrasted sharply with the notion of a Fulani chief
remaining in Song, Goila, Mubi or Yola and paying occasional visits to the
non-Muslim communities for purposes of tax collection, judicial enforcement
and other colonial tasks. British authorities needed Fulani rule to be close to
the subjects of such rule. After all, Fulani Muslim chiefs were expected to
civilise the non-Muslim peoples and it was believed that this could only occur
if they were in physical proximity to them.

In the late 1920s this new residential Fulani rule would begin to replace the
model of the touring Fulani chief in several districts. It led to a system in
which resident Fulani chiefs would mentor a cadre of non-Muslim quasi-
chiefs in the art of political protection, paternal compassion and problem
solving. This was a further expansion of the colonial system as the chain
of protection would now comprise several steps, flowing from Lieutenant
Governor to Resident to Lamido to lesser Fulani chiefs and, finally, to non-
Muslim apprentices.

The transition from non-resident to resident Fulani chieftaincy preserved
the control that the Lamido, through his appointees in Song and Goila,
exercised over the Bura, Hona and Lala peoples. The Lamido's control

extended to several other non-Muslim communities, even those that comprised the so-called Pagan Independent Division consisting of Kanakuru, Lunguda, Chamba, Mumuye, Waka, Bachama, Bata, Mbula, Yundam, Yakoko, Zinna and Piri. For these groups, British officials articulated prior familiarity with political centralisation and strong chieftaincy as reasons for subjecting them to British-mandated Fulani supervisory rule.

PROTECTION IN PRACTICE

The full range of the protective rule of Fulani officials is difficult to capture. However, a scattered body of evidence allows us to make a fairly accurate assessment of Fulani officials' operations in non-Muslim districts, the resentment of non-Muslim subject communities, and the efforts made by the British administration to address this problem. Fulani proxy rulers had a clear administrative remit: they collected taxes and tolls on behalf of the government, settled disputes in local courts, assessed farms and assets, appointed petty officials to oversee small constituents, and kept the peace in their non-Muslim domains by deploying a vast infrastructure of policemen, enforcers, court officers, scribes and messengers.

The British had hoped that the supervision of European officers would provide a layer of administrative oversight and mitigate excess. However, as early as 1921, it became apparent that this expectation was not being realised. British officials observing a range of interactions from close quarters began to comment regularly on the frequent crises in the relationship between the Fulani and non-Muslim communities. Fulani officials were placing multiple arbitrary levies on non-Muslim traders and farmers, a practice that was described in some British memoranda as extortion.[27] Furthermore, Fulani herdsmen were provoking non-Muslim farmers by encroaching on their land. 'In nine of ten [cases] the Fulani are to blame; they leave small children to act as herdsmen and the cattle get into the farms', the District Officer of Numan Division claimed in 1926.[28] Once this complex regime of protection began to unfold at the grassroots, the British colonisers seemed to have become concerned about the fate of the protected non-Muslim communities under the rule of Fulani protectors that they themselves had installed.

Complaints poured in from non-Muslims who felt that Fulani rule had overstepped its mandate and had become a parallel bureaucracy of colonial exploitation. British officials increasingly began to take the side of non-Muslim groups in these disputes. They condemned excessive tolls that the Fulani rulers imposed on their non-Muslim subjects as well as a tendency for the Fulani elites to dispossess non-Muslim farmers of their crops or force them to sell their wares below the going market prices.²⁹ Such condemnation of incidents of Fulani oppression of non-Muslims was anything but disinterested. British officials wanted agricultural produce delivered steadily to the European-owned Niger Company stores in order to protect the economic mainstay of the colonial state. They also resented a system of arbitrary tolls imposed by Fulani rulers that discouraged many non-Muslim farmers from producing for the market or making the dangerous journey to the produce-buying.³⁰ Such taxation threatened the project of civilising non-Muslims, for which the Fulani administrative presence was deemed necessary. For all these reasons the excesses of Fulani rule had to be confronted by the British government.

Oppressive practices by Fulani rulers and the complaints they provoked among non-Muslim people allowed the British to reposition themselves as compassionate mediators seeking to protect weak non-Muslims from powerful, oppressive Fulani rulers. In a sense the ultimate protector and enabler stepped aside and assumed the position of neutral, empathetic arbiter capable of holding its protected proxies accountable. This new posture, regardless of whether it was genuine or merely strategic, represented a dramatic contortion for officials who previously saw non-Muslim colonial subjects as the historically ordained subordinates of Hausa-Fulani elites. Put another way, the colonial overlord was now intervening against its own protected proxies in order to protect non-Muslim populations against Fulani impositions. With the subordinated protectees of an imperially designated protector becoming the object of protective interventions by the coloniser, the seemingly well-ordered protectionist regime of indirect rule was revealed as unstable, malleable, and inherently negotiable.

In some cases officials even went so far as to valorise the non-Muslim and to devalue the Fulani. The District Officer of Numan Division exemplified this tendency when he stated: 'the pagan is the greatest productive asset of the province in contrast with the non-productive Fulani.'³¹ In several cases British officials began to act to protect non-Muslims. As a result of intense pressure by the Resident and other British officials the Lamido had reluctantly abolished the much-abused market dues in all non-Muslim districts under his jurisdiction in 1926, though tensions mounted sporadically and complaints of Fulani exactions continued to trickle in. It was a token gesture but it proved the merit of non-Muslim grievance against Fulani rule.

The Lamido's decision to abolish the much-hated market tolls of the Fulani agents had been a culmination of a steady if unheralded decline in the fortunes of Fulani rule among the Adamawa non-Muslim communities, which looked increasingly to the British colonisers, the ultimate protectors, as a counterweight against the excesses of Fulani rule. During the heyday of

British preoccupation with Fulani rule, British officials fantasised about compassionate and good-tempered Fulani administrators 'civilising' the Adamawa non-Muslim communities.[32] Many years of Fulani rule later, officials seemed to be less sure about the attitude and temperament of Fulani colonial agents in regard to the non-Muslim peoples of the province. They now feared that they might have helped consolidate a conceited Fulani disposition towards the non-Muslim groups of the Adamawa area. 'It is quite obvious in Adamawa Division that the Fulani view of the pagan is that he is a person whom half a brick should always be heaved on sight', one official stated.[33]

British officials also wondered whether they were complicit in Fulani excesses. In 1937 and 1938 they acted on this anxiety, initiating a reform of Fulani rule among the largest non-Muslim ethnic group of Adamawa, the Chamba. This reform had many aims. Devolution of administrative power and initiative from Fulani to Chamba and other non-Muslim groups was one of them. By 1950, however, many of these goals remained unrealised, as many of the proposed components of non-Muslim administrative self-determination were ignored in favour of the Fulani-centred status quo. As part of the reform Haman Tukur, the Yola-appointed District Head of Nassarawo, had been installed as the President of the Chamba Subordinate Native Authority. By British declaration his mandate was 'to demonstrate [to the Chamba Chiefs] efficient and honest District administration'.[34] The thrust of the reform was for Tukur to 'help the Chamba to reach these goals, and when they had he would retire from the scene'.[35] The premise of paternal Fulani authority over the Chamba people was clear and finite in this vision. Under the terms of the reform, paternal protection was imagined as a terminal pedagogical intervention.

However, in the period between 1938 and 1951 no progress, as far as can be made out from British memoirs and reports, seems to have been made towards the avowed purposes of the reform.[36] One of the starkest indicators of this failure to advance towards the stated goals of devolution and self-determination was the fact that Haman Tukur not only retained his position as President of the Chamba Council but also that of the Chief of Nassarawo District, a clear departure from one of the cardinal goals of the 1937 reform, which was that these districts should in due course have either a non-Muslim head or a non-Muslim council.[37]

In the same period several developments occurred to stoke Chamba grievances against Fulani rule. Haman Tukur had consolidated his position, transmuting to a de facto paramount ruler over the Chamba. He now had the final say, save for British review, over all judicial and administrative matters among the Chamba. The British attributed this unexpected consolidation of Fulani control to the absence of British administrative touring for twelve years.[38] It was clear even to British observers that 'there was now less administration of the Chamba by the Chamba than there was before [the] 1938 [reform]'.[39]

Since the reorganisation established a Chamba Native Authority subordinate to the Lamido's Native Authority in Yola, the titular protocols and political symbols of the Yola Emirate found their way into the Chamba Council. The Lamido formalised this reality by renaming the office of the President of the Chamba Council (subordinate NA) the *Wakilin* (Emir's representative for) Chamba, with all the trappings and obligations of that office as prescribed by the rules of the defunct Sokoto caliphate. For his part Haman Tukur worked insidiously to entrench and institutionalise Fulani rule among the Chamba people. With Yola's blessing, he appointed more Fulani District Scribes for all the Chamba chieftaincies, swelling the existing number of Fulani officials, and undercutting Chamba apprentice chiefs. The District Scribes in turn appointed other Fulani subordinate colonial auxiliaries: tax and fee collectors, messengers, enforcers, judicial personnel and policemen. Together, these cadres of Fulani personnel ran the colonial bureaucracy, and the Chamba encountered many more Fulani officials than they did Chamba ones in their relationship with and obligations to the colonial state.

Resentment against Fulani rule among the Chamba grew in the 1940s, with a few individual petitions making their way up the chain of the colonial bureaucracy. In 1950, there seemed to have been a tactical shift in the Chamba struggle against Fulani rule, with agitators seeking direct meetings with supervisory British officials rather than submitting petitions to the Fulani. In December that year the first of several face-to-face confrontations occurred. A delegation comprising five Chamba youths sought and obtained a meeting with the Assistant Divisional Officer, a Mr Phelps, to inquire about the implications of the ongoing constitutional debates for the Chamba area.[40] The delegation, composed of a group of mission-educated young men, wanted to know the government's plans concerning the old question of Chamba separation from Fulani rule represented by Yola and the Lamido. After listening to the delegation, Phelps promised to tour the Chamba communities and discuss the government's plans. However, no official response came regarding the substantive issue of constitutional guarantees of Chamba self-rule.

One month later, the delegation, now expanded, wrote a joint letter to the Resident referring to their earlier meeting with Phelps about the Chamba's place and rights in the unfolding constitutional order. This new missive explicitly demanded that the Chamba be granted independence from Fulani rule, which the office of the Wakilin Chamba symbolised. The petitioners labelled the office and its occupant symbols of their subjugation by the Fulani.[41] The Chamba delegation travelled to Yola a few days later to meet with the Resident and elaborate on their demands. They moderated their earlier demand for outright separation from the administrative ambit of the Lamido's authority, stating that they would now be content with the modest change of having a Chamba in the position of Wakilin Chamba instead of a Fulani.[42]

In February 1951 a mission-educated Chamba Christian known as Simon penned a petition to the District Head of Yebbi. He railed against what he termed the betrayal of Chamba apprentice chiefs, who would rather keep their positions than confront Fulani rule and its most powerful symbol, the Lamido, and argued that those chiefs were oblivious to the political import of their flirtation with Fulani rule. Their decision to side with the Fulani was the result of fear, he argued.[43] In making these declarations, Simon, rather than attacking the Fulani and the British that empowered them, sought to target the Fulani's allies in Chamba society.

British sensitivity to the problem of hardening Fulani rule was slow to emerge. But when it did it was surprisingly candid. In September 1951, the District Officer of Chamba wrote in a confidential memorandum to the Resident: 'I have discussed the matter on several occasions with the Waziri, and more recently with the Wakilin Chamba himself. All of us are agreed that no progress whatsoever is being made towards the obvious and correct goal of the administration of the Chamba by the Chamba and that the office of Wakilin Chamba is redundant, having long outlived its usefulness.' In another section of the same document the District Officer stated pointedly that 'Haman Tukur should go'.[44] It was clear, as officials would later acknowledge in a secret memorandum, that they believed that the Yola Native Authority led by the Lamido had to delegate power sooner or later.[45] But events and time were no longer on the side of the Fulani or the British. Anti-Fulani agitation continued until independence was granted in 1960.

CONCLUSION

The production of a paradigmatic colonial script that simultaneously posited Hausa-Fulani Muslim superiority and non-Muslim Middle Belt inferiority authorised an unorthodox colonial system of proxy rule that enabled protection to be reproduced in more than one form. This chapter has outlined the process that produced the socio-political categories upon which the rule of

Muslim aristocrats in non-Muslim communities was constructed, and has demonstrated the messy nature of Fulani rule in the non-Muslim communities of Adamawa Province.

As this case reveals, protection was seldom straightforward, even in a period often viewed as a high water mark of colonial control. Instead, it could be reproduced across more than one political and cultural platform. Equally, protection was as much about power as it was about constructing and maintaining civilisational and political hierarchies. Furthermore, this example indicates the diffusion of the ethos of colonial protection. Fulani officials in Adamawa Province had such expansive administrative leeway that they were able to constitute and reconstitute new political hierarchies, adding further layers and parties to the business of colonial rule and thereby replicating and deepening protection across more than one realm.

NOTES

1 John Edward Philips, *Spurious Arabic: Hausa and Colonial Northern Nigeria*, African Studies Center, University of Wisconsin, Madison, 2000, p. v.

2 Hugh Clapperton, *Into the Interior of Africa: Records of the Second Expedition, 1825–1827*, edited Jamie Bruce-Lockhart and Paul E. Lovejoy, Brill, Leiden, 2005. See Appendix V–VI, pp. 485–86, 493. Sultan Mohammed Bello himself would go on to make the same outlandish imperial claims in his own text, the *Infakul Maisuri*. See E.J. Arnett, *The Rise of the Sokoto Fulani: Being a Paraphrase and in Some Parts a Translation of the Infaku'l Maisuri of Sultan Mohammed Bello*, School of Oriental and African Studies, University of London, London, 1922.

3 Clapperton, preface.

4 For a full discussion of Mohammed Bello's imperial claims, see Moses Ochonu, 'Caliphate Expansion and Sociopolitical Change in Nineteenth Century Lower Benue Hinterlands', *Journal of West African History*, vol. 1, no. 1, 2015, pp. 144–45.

5 Adell Patton Jr, 'An Islamic Frontier Polity: The Ningi Mountains of Northern Nigeria, 1846–1902', in Igor Kopytoff (ed.), *The African Frontier: The Reproduction of Traditional African Societies*, Indiana University Press, Bloomington, 1987, pp. 195–213; Samuel Peter Umaru, 'Incorporation and Resistance: A Study of the Relationship between Alela and the Sokoto Caliphate to the British Occupation c. 1804–1910' (MA thesis, Ahmadu Bello University, Zaria, 1992).

6 William Balfour Baikie, *Narrative of an Exploring Voyage up the Rivers Kwóra and Bínue (Commonly Known as the Niger and Tsádda) in 1854*, J. Murray, London, 1856, p. 393.

7 William Balfour Baikie, 'Inclosure No. 74 (General Rules for Dealing with the Natives along the River Niger), Rule 14, in *Accounts and Papers of the House of Commons*, vol. 43, Harrison and Sons, London, 1863, p. 91.

8 Frederick Lugard, *The Dual Mandate in British Tropical Africa*, William Blackwell and Sons, Edinburgh, 1922, pp. 193–94.

9 Ibid., p. 196.

10 Ibid., p. 204

11 Ibid., p. 214.

12 Ibid., p. 198.

13 Ibid.

14 Cited ibid., p. 220.

15 Ibid.

16 Assistant Resident No. 2 Division to Resident, Yola Province, 1 October 1912, and Resident, Yola Province to The Resident Touring Pagan Emirate, 12 September 1912, Pagan Administration Collected Papers, YolaProf/F3, National Archives of Nigeria, Kaduna (henceforth NAK).

17 Assistant Resident No. 2 Division to Resident, Yola Province, 9 December 1912, and Resident, Yola Province to the District Officer I/C.E.P Division, 1 October 1912, Pagan Administration Collected Papers, YolaProf/F3, NAK.

18 Ronald MacAlister, D.O in charge of Muri Division, to Resident, Yola Province, 5 August 1920, Notes on Taxation of Backward Tribes and Direct Versus Indirect Administration of Pagan Communities, Pagan Administration Collected Papers, YolaProf/F3, NAK.

19 Ibid.

20 Ibid.

21 Ibid.

22 Ibid.

23 Ibid.

24 Assistant Resident No. 2 Division to Resident, Yola Province, 12 September 1912.

25 Assistant Resident No. 2 Division to Resident, Yola Province (Fulani District Head Lala Tribe), 17 September 1912, Pagan Administration Collected Papers, YolaProf/F3, NAK.

26 Chiefs of Pagan Districts, Pagan Administration Collected Papers, YolaProf/F3, NAK.

27 DO Numan Division to Resident, Yola Province, Notes on the Treatment of Raw Pagans in Districts Not Yet Under Control, 16 March 1921, Pagan Administration, Collected Papers, YolaProf/F3, NAK.

28 Ibid.

29 Ibid.

30 Ibid.

31 Ibid.

32 Ibid. See also Resident, Yola Province, to Chief Secretary of Northern Nigeria, 9 October 1912, Chiefs of Pagan Districts, Pagan Administration Collected Papers, YolaProf/F3, NAK.

33 DO Numan Division, to Resident, Yola Province, Notes on the Treatment of Raw Pagans in Districts Not Yet Under Control.

34 DO Yola Division to the Resident, Adamawa Province, 22 February 1951, Camba (sic) and Bata Movements, Chamba Federation Separatist Movement, YolaProf/C778, NAK.

35 Ibid.

36 Ibid.

37 Ibid.

38 Ibid.

39 Ibid.

40 Senior DO Yola Division to Resident, Adamawa Province, 22 February 1951, Chamba Federation, Chamba Federation Separatist Movement, YolaProf/C778, NAK.

41 Ibid.

42 Ibid.

43 Simon of N.T.S. Numan to Chief of Yebbi, 19 February 1951, Original in Hausa, translated by the Office of the DO Yola Division, Chamba Federation, Chamba Federation Separatist Movement, YolaProf/C778, NAK.

44 Ibid.

45 Ibid.; Provincial Official Office, Yola, to the Permanent Secretary, Ministry of Local Government, Kaduna, 30 September 1955, Chamba Districts, Adamawa Emirate, Chamba Federation Separatist Movement, YolaProf/C778, NAK.

13

The Problem of Protectorates in an Age of
Decolonisation: Britain and West Africa, 1955–60

BARNABY CROWCROFT

It is by now a commonplace that the history of Britain's global empire bore little resemblance to the monochrome shading of early twentieth-century world maps. A decade of scholarship on imperial politics, law and political thought has provided us with an understanding of European empires which over the course of some five centuries created globe-spanning systems of profound political fragmentation, legal differentiation, and divided and shared sovereignty, even while under the banner of some national imperial project.[1] The historiography of the end of empire, however, has remained largely unaffected by the concepts and categories with which we have reconceived its rise and ascendance. In its most popular form this history reverts to a story of the irrepressible rise of anti-colonial nationalism against largely undifferentiated foreign empires, a setting in which 'fight or flight' can ultimately account for the extent of available imperial options.[2] Growing recognition of the intricacy of European empires seems to have simply presented a greater number of anachronisms to be swept aside, deepening the achievement of nationalist movements in creating the dozens of 'new nations' throughout Africa and Asia that would forever transform the map of the world. This consensus has deep roots. We would now be strongly inclined to challenge the famous claim by the 'father of African nationalism', Kwame Nkrumah, that 'imperialism knows no law'. But Nkrumah's corollary assertion could still stand as a summary of the decolonisation field: that whatever legal 'camouflage' or other 'sham gestures' European empires deployed to acquire or maintain their overseas dominion, these would ultimately prove irrelevant when confronted by the overriding desire of colonial peoples everywhere to achieve their national independence and freedom.[3]

The historical reality, however, increasingly seems to have been rather different. Recent scholarship on the end of the French empire, for example, has revealed how reformist imperial visions of a multinational empire-state

moved metropolitan and colonial actors after 1945, and that it was only the
failure of this project that resulted in the reluctant retreat to the independent
nation-states of today.[4] Even in the British empire, long renowned for its
traditional scepticism toward grand reforming projects, recent works have
revealed the range of and following for bold plans for reconfiguring the
imperial order in the early twentieth century, which endured to find expression in the visionary though short-lived colonial projects of the post-war
Labour government.[5] The next decade of scholarship is likely to show that
the conventional nationalist account of Britain's end of empire is flawed from
the micro as well as the macro side. Not, that is, that the colonial populations of Britain's empire aspired, as in the French experience, to some greater
supra-nationalism, but rather to smaller sub ones. The receding of the
imperial tide in the middle of the twentieth century revealed beneath it a
patchwork-quilt of political compromises that its uneven legal geographies
had preserved and created. These would show far greater reluctance to duck
under the nationalist tide than is conventionally assumed, and a far greater
sense of plausible alternatives.

The greatest of the legal constructs of Britain's late empire lay in the
practice of imperial protection. By the eve of decolonisation, its major vehicle,
the protectorate, constituted a majority of Britain's overseas territories. In an
age of empire, the fictions of protection offered a versatile rhetorical gloss
to cover many kinds of imperial expansion. In an age of decolonisation,
however, those same fictions and the complex legal structures in which they
had been incorporated could suddenly offer a range of oppositional possibilities for protected populations suddenly caught up in the passage from
empire to independence. This chapter introduces the story of one such
protected imperial enclave in the British West African territory of the Gold
Coast and its struggle in the late 1950s to use its protectorate status to derail
Britain's planned transfer power to the new nation that would emerge in
1957 as Ghana. This local challenge to British decolonisation erupted into
a wider debate about Britain's vast protected empire, when the lawyers and
historians of the Colonial Office took a remarkable stand on behalf of the
successors of West Africa's historic treaty-states against a British imperialism
ready to disregard the law in its dealings with colonised populations. This
largely forgotten crisis in Britain's end of empire offers a glimpse into some
of the unique legal and political challenges caused by decolonisation throughout its empire of protectorates after 1945. The episode's ultimate resolution by
the end of the 1950s, in the face of a fresh challenge from Nigeria, Britain's
largest remaining dependency, would reveal some of the persistent ironies
of the fabled 'return to sovereignty' that authors have since perceived in

decolonisation, and of the fate of Britain's old protected empire in the new
era of colonial freedom and national independence.

THE BRITISH EMPIRE OF PROTECTORATES

For a lawyer surveying the British empire at the end of the Second World War
there would have been little prospect of widespread *decolonisation* taking
place, simply because only a minority of the empire was made up of colonies.
Beyond British India and the old Atlantic empire in the Caribbean, colonial
provinces were relatively few. The remainder of the empire's vast population lived instead under an array of constitutional oddities within the British
imperial orbit.[6] Legally, this other imperial real estate could be categorised as
colonial protectorates, protected states, native states, trucial states, mandates,
trust territories, dominions, condominiums and a company-state.[7] Politically,
its inhabitants, though under the paramount power of Britain's constitutional
monarchy and parliament, were governed by an assortment of kingdoms,
princedoms, sultanates, sheikhdoms, emirates, nazirates, chieftaincies, tribes
and even a board of directors, each with widely varying degrees of practical
British intervention. It was an empire, as the long-serving minister and minor
philosopher Arthur Balfour reflected with some pride at the end of the
nineteenth century, which 'embraced almost every form of government which
the mind of man can conceive'.[8] A more precise legal term, however, for what
exactly would happen when this other British empire came to end was
unclear. While imperial politicians found inspiration in this diverse system,
colonial lawyers found its very existence a cause for considerable concern.
'In layman's language', as one serving in the Colonial Office reflected, when
the imperial deluge had already begun, 'it may ... be said that we have built a
very large edifice on a slender footing'.[9]

The practice of imperial protection was at the heart of this other British
empire. Its major vehicle, the protectorate, had been transformed by the
early twentieth century from an obscure device in continental European
diplomacy to become the most widespread imperial status of convenience
in its extra-European empires.[10] But in the course of this growth the designation had come to conceal a wide variety of constitutional forms. In its
classical form the protectorate was an arrangement in which the protected
state surrendered control over its foreign relations to a larger power in return
for a guarantee of protection against external aggression. Protectorate relationships were based on treaties, allowing considerable scope for individual
variation in founding agreements, but in the theory that found expression in
the works of Grotius, Wolff and Vattel protected states retained control over

their internal government and were thereby considered to have maintained their sovereignty, though not their external independence.[11] For the protecting power the protected country remained foreign territory and therefore not subject to its municipal laws or courts. The status was more than an alliance, but less than the full sovereignty that would later characterise a formal colony or any conquered, settled or annexed territory.

The earliest extra-European protected provinces of Britain's empire, such as India's princely states, Nepal, Zanzibar and the Malay sultanates, initially approximated to this model. Founding agreements provided recognition to local government structures, gave some acknowledgement of the kind of society and civilisation that functioned there, and permitted the appointment of a British Resident or Adviser to the protected state, rather than a High Commissioner or Governor.[12] Later acquisitions toward the last quarter of the nineteenth century were also acquired along these lines, generally if the state in question was considered to have a high degree of organised statehood, such as the kingdom of Tonga, or was ruled by Europeans, such as the states of Sarawak or North Borneo.[13] These protected states could entertain widely varying understandings of what many styled as their sovereign independence under imperial protection, and suffered varying degrees of practical British interference. Often protection proved to be a mere preface to empire. But they were nonetheless considered to have retained some separate legal status apart from the imperial power, which was often expressed in treaties as sovereignty. It was not until the post-war period that international lawyers and commentators came regularly to deny outright any state character to these dependencies, as it became customary to treat sovereignty as interchangeable with external independence.[14]

Innovation in international doctrine and practice in the last decade of the nineteenth century considerably muddied the situation for these classical protectorates and protected states, crystallised in the invention of the colonial protectorate in the course of the European colonisation of Africa. The colonial protectorate presented two profound departures from the existing practice. First, the colonial protectorate eradicated most practical distinctions between annexation and protection on the basis of a claim about the perceived level of civilisation in a non-European territory. Protectorates in so-called uncivilised countries required the exercise of authority and jurisdiction almost akin to sovereignty, either on purely normative grounds or on the practical ones that their political organisations could not carry out the reciprocal requirements necessitated in the conventional protectorate relationship.[15] In Great Britain, the Foreign Jurisdiction Act of 1890, which placed the powers of the British Crown on a statutory basis in what were known as

foreign protected territories, thus stated in its preamble that '[w]hether jurisdiction acquired is based on treaty, capitulation, grant, usage, sufferance or
other lawful means, it can be held and exercised in as ample a manner as
if acquired by cession or conquest of territory'. This appeared to eradicate
any distinction between how territories had been acquired or the basis upon
which they were held, and through such jurisdictional imperialism the British
government could ultimately assume full powers in these putatively foreign
colonial protectorates, which international convention increasingly expected
it to exercise.[16]

Second, the colonial protectorate was not created to follow or even
resemble the boundaries of existing states. Their borders were the product
of inter-European agreement, usually announced locally by proclamation,
and created new units with no natural indigenous rulers, though these
were often preserved as sub-polities or 'native authorities'. This facilitated
the infamous carving up of precolonial Africa into arbitrary international
units. In British Africa, where a colonial presence reached back centuries,
these new colonial protectorates became parts of composite states, attached as
the vast hinterland provinces of older colonial enclaves. These were multiple
dependencies: Nigeria, Gambia, Sierra Leone, Kenya and Aden, all bore the
formal title of 'Colony and Protectorate'; following the invention of mandates
under the League of Nations, Nigeria and the Gold Coast became 'three-
decker' dependencies, combining crown colony, protectorate and mandate.[17]
Through the first four decades of the new century these legal distinctions were
increasingly dismissed as irrelevant to more practical demands of imperial
administration. But practical distinctions between protected and colonial
provinces were broadly maintained; protected populations were governed
differently from neighbouring colonies, 'in accordance', as the interwar doyen
of imperial constitutional law put it, 'with the barbarism of their people'.[18]
Almost all the British territories that would go on to become independent
nation-states were therefore made up of amalgamations of different provinces,
acquired at different times, under different legal bases, and often governed
according to very different principles.

Following the Second World War, when colonial nation-building became
the declared objective of the British empire, there was fresh imperative to
treat the colonial protectorates, protected states and crown colonies as single
'national' units. This only encouraged growing popular and scholarly dismissals of the whole concept of the protectorate empire as a mere cloak for the
untrammelled exercise of imperial power, one which had little place in the
new world order enshrined in the principles of the United Nations.[19] In an
intervention which would come to serve as an epitaph on the protectorate as

it disappeared from the international scene in the 1960s, the lawyer-historian Charles Alexandrowicz wrote that the conversion of the protectorate into an 'instrument of absorption' in the name of superior civilisation constituted Europe's greatest breach of faith with the extra-European world. The protectorate, he said, could have played a constructive role in facilitating the entry of the African continent into the family of nations. Instead, it was used to eradicate the polities of precolonial Africa so that the redemptive 'return to sovereignty' by the extra-European world, which Alexandrowicz saw in decolonisation, had to be achieved by new nations rather than old states.[20]

DECOLONISING PROTECTORATES:
THE CHALLENGE FROM THE GOLD COAST

A story of decolonisation in Britain's empire of protectorates, however, runs along in the shadow of the larger and better known epic of the end of empire after 1945. This also began in Asia and the Middle East, where the first terminal challenges to British rule were successfully mounted. This first wave of protectorate decolonisation involved struggles over the older and the more sophisticated protected states of the empire: of India's more-than-six-hundred Princely States, of the protected Malay sultanates and the Borneo states of Sarawak and North Borneo in Southeast Asia, and the Anglo-Egyptian Condominium over the Sudan, in the Middle East. These early struggles were framed in the language of the sovereignty of the older protected states, legally reserved to them in founding agreements with the British empire, and which could even find itself placed in opposition to the newer understanding of 'national sovereignty' which would come to characterise the dawning age of decolonisation.[21] It was only in the second wave of decolonisation, when the colonial protectorates came to be decolonised, that, having no recourse to that of sovereignty, the language of protection came to the forefront of these anti-colonial struggles. And it was the colonial protectorate that made up the northern province of the Gold Coast in West Africa which would precipitate one of the most decisive episodes in the ending of Britain's protected empire in Africa.

The Protectorate of the Northern Territories, the hinterland of the annexed Ashanti territory and the Gold Coast Colony to its south, had been acquired through some sixty-three treaties reached with the kings and chiefs of the region during the European incursions of the 1890s. The protectorate contrasted sharply with the tropical coastal provinces of the Gold Coast, and the heavily forested hill-country of Ashanti, made up of undulating savannah, sparsely populated and with a culture marked by the influences of the Sudanic and Islamic societies to the north. These differences had been used to justify the creation of an entirely different British administration in the north, which resulted in a profoundly different relationship to those modern forces that would transform the Gold Coast's southern regions in the 1940s. The post-war efforts to prepare for self-government and a transfer of power in the Gold Coast only fully included the Northern Territories as late as 1951. But early experience of progressive self-government from Accra under the nationalist administration of Kwame Nkrumah revealed little inclination among the rulers and educated elites of the Northern Territories to cast aside their anachronistic and parochial politics to join up with the new national struggle. Post-war politics in the Northern Territories instead revolved around affirmation of the region's separateness from the remainder of the newly united Gold Coast state, in their languages, history, society and religion, an affirmation which was increasingly framed in reference to the idea of the protectorate.[22]

Through the course of the most active years of the struggle for independence in the Gold Coast, between 1951 and 1955, the Northern Territories found themselves unable to slow the pace of the British administration's concessions to the relentless march of the Gold Coast towards full self-government. As the prospect of national independence suddenly dawned upon the region's leaders, and in the increasing fear that they were being handed over to a government which they had plenty of reasons to distrust, and perhaps even despise, they set out to use their protected status to derail the course of British decolonisation in the Gold Coast. As in the struggles over protectorate decolonisation in Asia, the case made by the Northern Territories centred upon an appeal to the treaties which underpinned British presence in the protectorate. The first argument was a historical one about the origins of the treaties. Contrary to popular myth, it was argued, the North's rulers had not been the African rulers of popular stereotype who had suffered treaties being 'thrust up their noses'.[23] Rather, the treaties were the result of African agency, sought at a time when internecine warfare and European encroachment had made it entirely logical for many of the chiefdoms of the savannah territories to the north of Ashanti to accept outside protection. The nonagenarian ruler of the northern Gonja chiefdom, Isanwurfo III, had as a young man spent six months travelling south to Accra to meet British officials and was locally reputed to have risked his life in order to get the treaty of protection signed, a story with which he continued to regale his European visitors in the 1950s.[24] There was nothing in the origins of these treaties, therefore, that could vitiate their status as legally valid agreements.

The second argument was a legal one about the application of these treaties. Not only had the protectorate's chiefs not abrogated the treaties

between them and Great Britain but they had also repeatedly based their
co-operation in each phase of constitutional advance toward self-government
on the treaties not being compromised by the changes. Since the consent of
both parties was required for proper abrogation of any bilateral agreement, the
treaties must still therefore be valid and binding agreements. Finally, antici-
pating a common British counterthrust, the chiefs contended that modern
conditions had not made the terms of the treaties obsolete. On the contrary,
conditions in the 1890s resembled conditions at the present time since the
disruptive nationalist struggle had, as one Northern chief lamented, recreated
'the very conditions ... which the treaties were originally signed to avoid'.[25]
As political organisers for a new Northern People's Party warned populations
throughout the protectorate, Nkrumah's 'black imperialist government' would
seek in an independent Ghana to use the peoples of the North as the infamous
slave-raiders of the late-nineteenth century, Samory and Babatu, had used 'our
forefathers in the olden days'.[26]

The leaders of the Northern Territories therefore set out two options for
Britain over its ongoing responsibility to the protectorate. It could either continue protection and prevent the amalgamation into a new national Gold Coast
under Nkrumah's leadership; or it could return the powers it had assumed to
the original signatories of the agreements. This latter was the logical implication of any bilateral agreement. But it was also a legal obligation for Britain
because the treaties of protection explicitly bound the protecting power not
to hand over protected subjects to another government. The peoples of the
Northern Territories, their leaders explained, were not against self-government;
they were simply against the kind of self-government that Britain was trying
to force upon them. 'Who, we would ask, governed Mamprusi before the
coming of the white-man?' one prominent councillor from this major northern kingdom challenged the Gold Coast's governor in a public meeting;
'It was the Mamprusi themselves'. The same applied in other parts of the
Northern Territories. If there was going to be a return to sovereignty in British
Africa, he said, 'We want to revert to this.'[27]

The Gold Coast colonial administration tried hard to dislodge the leaders
of the protectorate from this position. But with Kwame Nkrumah adamantly
committed to creating a unitary nation-state in the Gold Coast, and his Convention People's Party administration considerably distrusted in the Northern
Territories, this was to no avail. The chiefs and people of the Northern Territories, the governor of the Gold Coast, Sir Charles Arden-Clarke, concluded,
were unshakeable. '[T]hey must be allowed either to retain Her Majesty's
protection, or return to pre-treaty independence from the rest of the country'.[28] Either way, they demanded from the British government an immediate

statement as to whether it still honoured the treaties of protection and its responsibility as a protecting power. Increasingly distrustful of British good faith, the leaders of the Northern Territories joined their appeals to the Gold Coast's governor and British colonial secretary with a petition to the United Nations Trusteeship Council.

For its part, the British administration in the Gold Coast was little moved by this apparently reactionary challenge against national independence by a group of elites threatened with the loss of their historic privileges. But the potential danger of an accusation that Britain was in breach of its treaty commitments was very real in an empire still made up overwhelmingly of protectorates. Arden-Clarke therefore set his staff to work to prepare a rebuttal of the Northern Territories' case. In the summer of 1955 Gold Coast colonial officials gathered together scattered copies of the sixty-three treaties of protection that had been made in two successive phases of late-nineteenth century colonial expansion. In the official review of the legal position, however, it was concluded that the existence of these treaties was a red herring. As the Gold Coast's Attorney General Sir George Paterson put it, bilateral treaties with historic African chiefdoms in general, irrespective of their particular detail, had had 'no real validity for more than 50 years'. The treaties had been merely 'bargaining counters in the arguments going on in Europe over the division of this terri-tory'. Consequently, following their early use in the acquisition of territory, they had all been superseded by British acts of state applied under the Foreign Jurisdiction Act. On its proclamation of the Protectorate of the Northern Terri-tories in 1901, which had defined the region's boundaries, Britain had therefore assumed as 'absolute a power' as if the area had 'been acquired by cession or conquest', making the precise conditions of its acquisition irrelevant.[29]

The Gold Coast administration took a similarly hard stand on the protect-orate itself as a constitutional form. All the enduring legal distinctions between the four political units of the Gold Coast were mere 'fictitious matters' con-jured up by the Colonial Office's lawyers and far removed from the reality of the present day. There was thus no need to get caught up on the meaning of protectorates or Britain's obligations regarding its protected subjects. The answer to the question of how to end these constitutional oddities was simply that there was no such requirement; they were already defunct.[30] Finally, it was concluded that whatever the treaties of protection may have said about not transferring protected subjects to a foreign power, Britain, in subsequent international boundary negotiations in the 1890s, had ceded the territories of a number of its new treaty-allies to French and German colonial administrations without regard to the wishes of the inhabitants.[31] It was surely quite possible, Paterson observed, simply to do so once again.

This Gold Coast administration's analysis was in line with the prevailing dismissals of the colonial protectorate as a mere fig leaf for imperial rule. This echoed in sentiment the verdict of the great Victorian parliamentary draughtsman, Sir Henry Jenkyns, who considered it absurd that Britain's presence in its African territories could be legally grounded in 'a convention with a half-savage tribe' or in 'so-called treaties' with 'some naked chief living in the country'.[32] And, on the basis of this historical and legal analysis, Arden-Clarke prepared a statement to inform the chiefs and political leaders of the Northern Territories of the position they were really in: the Northern Territories, as he put it privately in a letter home, were 'going to have [independence] whether they like it or not!'[33]

THE COLONIAL OFFICE AGAINST EMPIRE

The British Colonial Office, however, had also been busy studying late nineteenth-century treaties through the course of 1955, and the news from the Gold Coast arrived at a particularly unfortunate moment. A scandal over the treatment of Britain's Somaliland Protectorate had been precipitated by the arrival of a delegation of aggrieved Somali Sultans and their entourages in London protesting at the handing over of their lands to Ethiopia, embarrassing the Colonial Secretary and even catching the attention of the Prime Minister, amidst widespread press criticism of the government's shameful betrayal of its 'loyal subjects'.[34] The mistake was not to be repeated. In the aftermath of this episode the head of the Colonial Office's International Relations Department circulated a note insisting that, from now on, 'Her Majesty's Government' must 'show deference to the protectorate treaties', given the risk of 'very serious difficulties with the International Court of Justice or the United Nations, or both, if we disregard [them]'.[35]

The new policy of deference made Arden-Clarke's proposals particularly jarring. The Colonial Office, moreover, was itself wrong-footed when it was discovered that it did not even possess copies of the Northern Territories' treaties of protection, and had to promptly despatch an official to the Public Record Office to find them and prepare a historical study of their status that could inform the Legal Department's official response.[36] Louis Branney, the man appointed to this considerable task, had already prepared a series of trenchant investigations of the legal structure of Britain's African empire to resolve disputes over land tenure and property rights which had arisen in the early 1950s. He was now a principal officer in the Colonial Office's African Studies Branch, where he had in the late 1940s been the colleague of the historian Ronald Robinson, and the two remained close after Robinson moved up to Cambridge to work with Jack Gallagher on their own re-writing of the origins of Britain's African empire, *Africa and the Victorians*. The two studies Branney prepared over 1955–57 present the most sophisticated defence of the protectorate empire in the post-war period, and laid the basis for the official policy that was initially followed. Both set out to demolish the Gold Coast's attempt to discredit the treaties and dismiss Britain's historic pursuit of a protectorate empire.

From the outset Branney's historical reconstruction of the origins of the treaties of protection and the meaning of Britain's empire of protectorates came down firmly on the side of the Northern Territories. The principal historical misconceptions over the empire by treaty, he reflected, resulted from confusion between the activity of commercial companies in Africa before the period of full British engagement, where treaties were 'imposed on ... chiefs ... for the proverbial bottle of gin or roll of calico', and that of official agents of the British government at the end of the nineteenth century. There were well over 500 treaties of protection concluded on behalf of the British government, Branney calculated, which still underpinned Britain's African territories. They had been made for a very clear and appreciable reason: to bring territory under British influence which the government had had 'no desire to govern' but wished to prevent falling into the hands of other European powers then advancing into Africa. The protected African empire was designed, therefore, as an alternative to a policy of territorial aggrandisement or extension of imperial jurisdiction rather than a case of some 'alleged unscrupulous policy of imperialism'. And it was an imperial practice that showed a respect for African political organisation at a time when such respect was in woefully short supply.[37]

Branney set the Northern Territories' treaties of protection of the 1890s in the context of a longer shift in the meaning of the 'protection' promised in the several hundred Anglo-African treaties over the course of the century. In the first three-quarters of the nineteenth century obligations to protect contained in these treaties were defined in positive terms toward the achievement of an internal end, enjoining their African parties to change their own 'uncivilised habits', such as slavery and human sacrifice. After the 1870s, however, and in the acquisitions of the age of 'new imperialism', the obligations contained in British treaties of protection were increasingly defined in terms of an external end, in defence against other European colonial powers, and by the 1890s this had been extended to include individual Europeans, such as unscrupulous traders, concession-hunters and criminals. Coincident with the rising physical demands placed upon African polities by the increasing numbers of Europeans encroaching into their territories, the ideological demands treaties

made of them declined. The appearance of guarantees committing Britain
to respecting native rulers in their 'place and dignity', maintaining 'traditional power and authority', and even guaranteeing a succession became a
staple feature of British treaties of protection.[38] The empire of protectorates
constructed in the late nineteenth century, Branney concluded, had therefore sought not to eradicate the African states with which it had signed
agreements – in the name of civilisation or otherwise – but to protect their
existence. The leaders of the Northern Territories were, then, quite right in
their present reading.

As to whether the treaties of protection had been mere fictions of no present
consequence, as the Gold Coast administration wished to inform their holders
in the Northern Territories, Branney's analysis was similarly scathing. Here, he
said, the Gold Coast administration had piled 'bad logic' upon 'bad history'.
The idea that these treaties were simply 'bargaining counters' in diplomatic
contests played out in European chancelleries was irrelevant to the matter of
the treaties themselves: since 'even if the immediate object of one's concluding a treaty was unworthy, one's attitude to it thereafter [could not] be properly
be inferred a priori from that ... it could only be inferred from the facts'. And
the facts revealed successive British secretaries of state affirming that treaties of
protection concluded with African chiefs and their polities were 'valid engagements' that could 'not be repudiated or annulled by only one of the parties'.
The proclamation of territorially defined protectorates, which the Gold Coast
administration alleged had superseded any treaties, was merely one side of a
two-sided process designed to exclude foreign powers; the other was to create
bonds between tribal populations and Great Britain. It was 'simply false', he
reflected, to assert that the treaties were 'merely the instruments of political
expediency or convenience'. They were, on the contrary, 'at the time and
afterwards regarded by the Crown as serious engagements to be seriously
honoured'.[39]

Britain's subsequent vast expansion of its jurisdiction in protectorates,
ending with the de facto exercise of sovereignty, likewise had no bearing on
the treaties' status as valid bilateral agreements. Britain had been compelled,
Branney argued, to overreach the limited legal jurisdiction it had initially
acquired in its African protectorates by force of facts 'rather than theories or
policy designed to promote her authority', due both to the imperatives of its
anti-slavery efforts and the desire to prevent its protected subjects falling victim
to unscrupulous European concessionaries. This signalled neither a disregard
nor an implicit abrogation of the treaties of protection but rather a reasonable,
and legally sanctioned, interpretation of their intent.[40] The 1895 ruling by
Britain's Law Officers had established that in colonial protectorates the Crown

might rightly 'assume such authority and jurisdiction ... as are required for the due discharge of the Protectorate'. All authority was thus legal if directed toward this purpose. This gave potentially limitless possibilities for imperial rule but it also had several major implications for the present-day meaning of these protectorates. First, in legal terms, it would be clearly absurd 'to suppose that the authority to abandon its Protectorate function was one of the rights required by the due discharge of that function'.[41] Therefore, in spite of its ultimate political authority in its protectorates, Britain's legal jurisdiction could not be held to include the right unilaterally to abrogate any individual protectorate. Second, in practical terms, British authority in the Northern Territories Protectorate had been exercised toward a distinctly different, and more limited, end than it had in the Gold Coast Colony, on areas ranging from education, training and economic development, demonstrating that the legal position had been historically recognised, even if unwittingly, by successive governments. And, third, as Branney concluded in a final rhetorical flourish, even if Britain's treaties of protectorate with the Northern Territories chiefs had been exceeded or even completely disregarded in the past, 'it would surely be the depths of Machiavellianism ... for us now to repudiate them *on that ground*, thus merely invoking our own (alleged) unscrupulousness to justify another'.[42] In short, there was simply no historical, legal, or moral case to be made to suggest that Britain's treaties of protection with the Northern Territories were not valid and meaningful agreements.

The position set out in Branney's note provided the basis of the opinion supplied by the Colonial Office's lawyers. They reiterated the overriding principle that the treaties of protection had been, and remained, meaningful and binding agreements upon Great Britain. As the Colonial Office's chief legal adviser Sir Kenneth Roberts-Wray summed it up, 'British jurisdiction flows from the treaties ... and its exercise is not inconsistent with them'.[43] Since the Northern Territories was still a protectorate in law, and the protectorate flowed from the treaties, the treaties could therefore not have been abrogated. There was 'no room for doubt', the legal advice supplied to the Colonial Secretary concluded, that the treaties with the Northern Territories remained operative. Even worse, as officials noted glumly to each other, it would not even be possible to cover the whole thing up, since the documents in question were in the open section of the Public Records Office and could be examined by anyone, including any lawyers who might be retained by the Northern chiefs. Protection was owed to the successors of the signatories of the treaties, and they were now demanding it of Great Britain and against the new nationalist-run Gold Coast administration. The obligation must be satisfactorily discharged or else resolved through agreement.

The Colonial Office's decision was a revolutionary judgement on the significance of the late Victorian Anglo-African treaty-making, set out in the twilight of empire. Branney's historical review was deemed of such importance that his entire fifty-page study was sent to Arden-Clarke in the Gold Coast, where a copy, covered in sarcastic marginalia written in the governor's distinctive red pencil, remains today in the archives in the Protectorate's former capital, Tamale.[44] It suddenly changed the game for British management of decolonisation in the Gold Coast. The Northern Territories now seemed to have full legal right to demand separate treatment and even separate independence from the rest of the newly created country. And so some eighteen months before the Gold Coast's independence the British Colonial Secretary, Alan Lennox-Boyd, gave Arden-Clarke some new instructions: 'In these circumstances', he wrote, 'it will be necessary to approach the successors of the signatories of the original treaties to persuade them that it would be to their advantage that the treaties should be abrogated'.[45] This was, one official noted as the letter went out, going to 'throw . . . a very considerable spanner in the works' of Gold Coast decolonisation and would 'come as a rude shock to the Governor'.[46] Those suggesting that Britain's empire of protectorates was a mere fiction had decisively lost the argument. Those 'scraps of paper' gathered at the height of the 'Scramble for Africa' could only be abrogated, almost sixty years later, through mutual consent.

THE CHALLENGE FROM NIGERIA AND THE RETURN OF 'CIVILISATION'

Following this verdict, decolonisation in colonial protectorates assumed a far more complicated prospect for Great Britain in the years to follow. The stance taken by the Colonial Office on the relevance of nineteenth-century treaties of protection in the changed world of the 1950s salvaged Britain's public international stance against the unilateral abrogation of treaty commitments and allowed it to uphold the notion of British respect for agreements with African states at a time when anti-colonial denunciations of imperialism sought to discredit the European presence in the continent. But the corollary was to affirm that the many hundreds of treaties that underlay Britain's remaining dependencies in Africa, 'except insofar as they have been properly annulled or abrogated by agreement', as Branney's subsequent policy conclusions document set out, remained valid and binding engagements.[47] This created a potentially endless array of challenges for the years ahead and a significant burden upon colonial officials and British ministers in a policy grounded in the principle of consent, however dubiously this would go on to be obtained in the Northern Territories by the Gold Coast authorities.

The passage of a few tumultuous years between 1955 and 1958 would see the Colonial Office's lawyers take a remarkable stand on behalf of historic African kingdoms and chiefdoms and their bilateral agreements with Great Britain, and then beat a gradual and eventually total retreat. Through a combination of persuasion, pageantry and, when all else failed, simple duplicity, the Gold Coast's governor Sir Charles Arden-Clarke was able to gain the verisimilitude of consent from the Northern Territories in late 1956, enabling London to claim that legal principle had been upheld.[48] But in 1957 the Colonial Office found itself confronted with treaties of protection with the states of the Niger River Delta region in Nigeria, Britain's largest remaining dependency. The chiefs of the Rivers region, moreover, had taken the precaution of retaining London-based lawyers to advance their cause against the Colonial Office, making a policy of obfuscation no longer possible. Louis Branney, somewhat disillusioned by the course of events in the Gold Coast, wrote another truculent paper detailing the historical and legal merit of the Nigerian petitioners' position, insisting that this challenge could not be brushed off so easily.[49] The price demanded by the holders of the treaties in return for consenting to their abrogation, however, was more than Britain was prepared to pay.

The result was a final shift in the interpretation of the meaning of imperial protection and the obligations contained in its protectorate treaties. The Colonial Secretary had passed on the details of the legal challenge from the chiefs of Nigeria's Niger Delta to Britain's Law Officers and the head of the judiciary in Cabinet, the Lord Chancellor. Lennox-Boyd had asked for an opinion able to resolve the paradox that Britain needed both to recognise that the treaties of protection were still legally in force and obviate the obligations they contained.[50] The Lord Chancellor, Viscount Kilmuir, found the answer in the treaties of protection themselves. Almost all of these treaties contained statements to the effect that British protection would be carried out toward the goal of furthering the 'general progress of civilisation'. The return of sovereignty to the dozens of states that had originally possessed it, as these Nigerian chiefs and their lawyers now seemed to be demanding, would 'tend toward anarchy' and thus be contrary both to the purposes of civilisation and the commitment to protection.[51] Britain was, therefore, merely pursuing the policy of protection to 'its logical conclusion', as Lennox-Boyd set it out in a final declaration to the Nigerian Rivers Chiefs, by relinquishing its protection and awarding *national* self-government to a united Nigeria in the interests of 'peace, order and good government, and the general progress of civilisation'.[52] The language of civilisation was thus revived at this other end of empire, once again to exclude African polities from recourse to the law in their struggles against empire, and now against nation-states.

CONCLUSION

One might ultimately conclude that this whole intellectual-come-political episode in the five years after 1955 changed precisely nothing at all. The legal anachronisms of Britain's old colonial empire were swiftly swept aside, and Ghana and Nigeria emerged as independent, sovereign states along borders determined in the chancelleries of Europe in the late-nineteenth century, as we have always surmised. But uncovering the detail of how this happened reveals a number of ironies about the epoch-making shift from empire to independence, and hints at how the wider process of decolonising Britain's African empire might one day be reconceived.

For followers of the redemptive version of the end of empire and return to sovereignty, the retrieval of the language of the requirements of civilisation at this other side of Britain's empire in West Africa presents the paradoxical situation that the same kinds of legal artifices that Alexandrowicz was denouncing as characteristic of late-nineteenth century imperialism were again being deployed in the process of decolonisation in order to deliver an outcome that he was also celebrating as proof of their supersession. So it rather seems, to stand Alexandrowicz's own conception of protectorates on its head, that in the empire's end was its beginning. The episode also challenges Kwame Nkrumah's and later nationalist-inspired accounts of the legal edifice of Britain's empire being forced aside in the face of surging popular demands for colonial freedom and national independence. By contrast, decolonisation in Ghana's protected northern province reveals those same legal fictions scorned by Nkrumah being placed in the service of his nationalist movement and against prevailing popular sentiment. In March 1957, Britain finally annexed the Protectorate and legally transferred it to the new national government in Accra, while rising popular political consciousness in the villages and towns of the Northern Territories clamoured for the continuation of a protected status.

The bitterest of ironies, however, was probably that left for Britain's former protected populations themselves. With this coupling of protection and civilisation at the close of the 1950s, the meaning of protection in Britain's protected African empire had come full circle. As Louis Branney's work revealed, while mid-nineteenth century treaties of protection had often been directed toward civilising reform of African societies, the mass of the treaties that had underpinned the creation of the empire of protectorates in the last quarter of that century were concerned with external protection of native polities from outside infiltration, implicitly, and increasingly explicitly, too, giving guarantees of protection as preservation. The protectorate mode of government that took shape in this empire seemed designed to appeal to a generation 'less confident than its predecessors of the possibility or the advantages of the rapid Westernisation of non-Europeans'.[53] It emphasised the protection of traditional rulers from obsolescence, of traditional forms of justice from modern legal systems, of rural communities from urbanisation, and of protected populations from mass and especially Western education. If the legal empire of protectorates had proved to be something of a fiction in the end, the political empire of protection had been very real; its consequences by the end of the 1940s were clear and could not be quickly remedied. Protected populations throughout British Africa, now out of favour for their undeveloped societies, were left at the mercy of the colonial enclaves which formed the nucleuses of the new national states that were rapidly emerging throughout the continent. Branney's aim was to suggest that this long middle-period, when protection meant preservation, was the aberration, while protection as the progress of civilisation was the true British tradition to which, in decolonisation, it was returning. It was the misfortune of Africa's colonial protectorates that the aberration endured as long as the empire did.

NOTES

1 For example, Jane Burbank and Frederick Cooper, *Empires in World History: Power and the Politics of Difference*, Princeton University Press, Princeton, 2013; Lauren Benton, *A Search for Sovereignty: Law and Geography in European Empires, 1400–1900*, Cambridge University Press, New York, 2010; Lauren Benton and Richard Ross (eds), *Legal Pluralism and Empires, 1500–1850*, New York University Press, New York, 2013; Sankar Muthu (ed.), *Empire and Modern Political Thought*, Cambridge University Press, New York, 2012; David Armitage, *Foundations of Modern International Thought*, Cambridge University Press, New York, 2013; Duncan Bell, *Reordering the World: Essays on Liberalism and Empire*, Princeton University Press, Princeton, 2016.

2 Martin Thomas, *Fight or Flight: Britain, France and their Roads from Empire*, Oxford University Press, London, 2014.

3 Kwame Nkrumah, *Towards Colonial Freedom: Africa in the Struggle Against World Imperialism*, Heinemann, London, 1962, pp. x–xviii; epithet from David Birmingham, *Kwame Nkrumah: The Father of African Nationalism*, Ohio University Press, Athens, 1998.

4 See, for example, Frederick Cooper, *Citizenship between Empire and Nation: Remaking France and French Africa, 1945–1960*, Princeton University Press, Princeton, 2014, and Gary Wilder, *Freedom Time: Negritude, Decolonization, and the Future of the World*, Duke University Press, Durham, 2015.

5 For example, Karuna Mantena, 'Popular Sovereignty and Anti-Colonialism', in Richard Bourke and Quentin Skinner (eds), *Popular Sovereignty in Historical Perspective*, Cambridge University Press, Cambridge, 2016, pp. 297–319; Daniel Gorman, *Imperial Citizenship: Empire and the Question of Belonging*, Manchester University Press, Manchester, 2006; W. David McIntyre, *The Britannic Vision: Historians and the Making of the British Commonwealth of Nations, 1907–1948*, Pan Macmillan, London, 2009; and Harshan Kumarasingham, 'The "Tropical Dominions": The Appeal of Dominion Status in the Decolonisation of India, Pakistan and Ceylon', *Transactions of the Royal Historical Society*, vol. 23, 2013, pp. 223–45. For early post-war reform, see, for example, Randall Hansen, *Citizenship and Immigration in Post-War Britain: The Institutional Origins of a Multicultural Nation*, Oxford University Press, London, 2000; and Ronald Hyam (ed.), *The Labour Government and the End of Empire 1945–1951*, 4 vols, HMSO, London, 1992.

6 Phrase from Memorandum by Lord Hailey on the Proposals for Malaya, A.J. Stockwell (ed.), *Malaya*, HMSO, London, 1995, vol. 1, p. 44.

7 'Scheme of the Political Organisation of the Empire', in A.B. Keith, *The Constitution, Administration and Laws of the British Empire*, Collins Sons & Co., London, 1924, pp. 319–24; and discussion in Martin Wight, *British Colonial Constitutions, 1947*, Oxford University Press, London, 1952, pp. 1–95.

8 Jason Tomes, *Balfour and Foreign Policy: The International Thought of a Conservative Statesman*, Cambridge University Press, Cambridge, 2010, p. 60.

9 Note by S. Gordon Smith for the Colonial Office Protectorate Working Group, n.d. [1955], CO 536/390, National Archives of the United Kingdom (henceforth NA).

10 Alfred Kamanda, *A Study of the Legal Status of Protectorates in Public International Law*, University of Geneva Press, Geneva, 1961, pp. 17–25, 34.

11 See Arthur Weststeijn, 'Treaties in Seventeenth-Century Dutch Colonial Expansion', in Saliha Belmessous (ed.), *Empire by Treaty: Negotiating European Expansion, 1600–1900*, Oxford University Press, New York, 2015, pp. 19–44.

12 W. Ross Johnston, *Sovereignty and Protection: A Study of British Jurisdictional Imperialism in the Late Nineteenth Century*, Duke University Press, Durham, 1973, pp. vi, 81.

13 Henry Jenkyns, *British Rule and Jurisdiction Beyond the Seas*, Clarendon Press, Oxford, 1902, pp. 170–71; Wight, p.10.

14 Kamanda, pp. 37–39, 179–87.

15 Johnston, pp. 189–263, Wight, p. 8. For wider context, see Marti Koskenniemi, *The Gentle Civilizer of Nations: The Rise and Fall of International Law, 1870–1960*, Cambridge University Press, Cambridge, 2001.

16 Wight, pp. 7, 68–87; Jenkyns, pp. 165–67; Johnston, pp. 310–25.

17 Wight, pp. 68–87.

18 Keith, pp. 265–67.

19 Kamanda, p. 17; Wight, p. 14.

20 C.H. Alexandrowicz, *The European African Confrontation: A Study in Treaty Making*, Sijthoff A.W., Leiden, 1973, pp. 78–80, 128; and see Alexandrowicz, 'New and Original States: The Issue of Reversion to Sovereignty', reprinted with a new editorial introduction in David Armitage and Jennifer Pitts (eds), *The Law of Nations in Global History: C.H. Alexandrowicz*, Oxford University Press, Oxford, 2017, Chapter 28.

21 For these struggles in the Indian States see, for example, Yaqoob Khan Bangash, *A Princely Affair: The Accession and Integration of the Princely States of Pakistan, 1947–1955*, Oxford University Press, Karachi, 2015; A.G. Noorani, *The Destruction of Hyderabad*, Hurst & Co., London, 2014. The post-war struggle over the Malayan Union has generated an extensive literature; see, for example, A.J. Stockwell, *British Policy and Malay Politics during the Malayan Union Experiment*, JMBRAS Monograph, Singapore, 1979; Albert Lau, *The Malayan Union Controversy, 1942–1948*, Oxford University Press, Singapore, 1991. For the Anglo-Egyptian Sudan, see especially W. Travis Hanes III, *Imperial Diplomacy in the Era of Decolonization: The Sudan and Anglo-Egyptian Relations, 1945–1956*, Praeger, New York, 1995.

22 A comprehensive account of the Northern Territories and Gold Coast decolonisation is provided in Martin Staniland, *The Lions of Dagbon: Political Change in Northern Ghana*, Cambridge University Press, Cambridge, 1975, and Paul Ladouceur, *Chiefs and Politicians: The Politics of Regionalism in Northern Ghana*, Longman, London, 1979.

23 The phrase was Maurice Smith's, one for which he was much criticised. In 'Minute for T.B. Williamson on the Treaties of Friendship and Protection with the Northern Territories', 7 April 1953, CO 554/254, NA.

24 J. A. Braimah and Jack Goody, *Salaga: The Struggle for Power*, Longmans, London, 1967, pp. 50–59, 83–84, 91.

25 Letter from Sulemana, Kpembewura of Gonja, to the Yabumwura of Gonja, 2 October 1954, FCO 141/5142, NA; 'Transcript of a Meeting between the Governor and the Chiefs of the Northern Territories Held at the Tamale Social & Cultural Institute', 30 May 1956, FCO 141/5143, NA.

26 Cited in Dennis Austin, 'Elections in an African Rural Area', in his *Ghana Observed: Essays on the Politics of a West African Republic*, Manchester University Press, Manchester, 1976, p. 83.

27 'Transcript of a Meeting ... at the Tamale Social & Cultural Institute', 30 May 1956, FCO 141/5143, NA.

28 Sir Charles Arden-Clarke to Alan Lennox-Boyd, 16 December 1955, FCO 141/5142, NA.

29 'Protectorate Status of the Northern Territories', paper contained in Arden-Clarke to Lennox-Boyd, 15 August 1955, FCO 141/5142, NA.

30 Sydney MacDonald-Smith to Arden-Clarke, 11 February 1956, FCO 141/5143, NA.

31 George Paterson to Arden-Clarke, 16 September 1955, FCO 141/5142, NA.

32 Jenkyns, pp. 179–94.

33 Draft-statement in Arden-Clarke to Lennox-Boyd, 15 August 1955, FCO 141/5142, NA; phrase from Arden-Clarke letter cited in David Rooney, *Sir Charles Arden Clarke*, Rex Collings, London, 1982, pp. 188–89.

34 The case is summarised in 'Somaliland Petition to the United Nations Organization: Note on the Historical Background of the 1897 Treaty & Legal Aspects of the Petition', n.d. [1955], CO 1015/868, NA.

35 Harry Bourdillon minute, 11 January 1956, CO 554/812, NA.

36 Note on Maurice Smith's visit to the PRO, CO 554/254, NA, and the recruitment of Louis Branney, CO 554/812, NA.

37 Louis Branney, 'A Survey of the Protectorate Treaties in the British African Territories: Covering their Origin, Terms and Import, and their Subsequent History and Attitude of HMG to Them', CO 959/11, ff. 1–2, NA.

38 Ibid., ff. 30–35, 59–60.

39 Branney, 'Historical Note on the Northern Territories Treaties, the Treaty-Policy, and Its Background of Constitutional Principles, 1890–1901', CO 554/812, ff. 4–5, NA.

40 Branney, 'Survey', ff. 34–35.

41 Ibid., f.7.

42 Ibid., f. 4, his emphasis.

43 'Note by Legal Advisers on the Treaties of Protection with Chiefs of the Northern Territories of the Gold Coast', Annex A in Lennox-Boyd to Arden-Clarke, 28 January 1956, FCO 141/5143, NA; and minute by Sir Kenneth Roberts-Wray, 21 December 1955, CO 554/812, NA.

44 In 'Protectorate Status of the Northern Territories: Governor's File', NRG 8-5-127, National Archives of Ghana, Tamale Branch.

45 Lennox-Boyd to Arden-Clarke, 28 January 1956, FCO 141/5143, NA.

46 Eastwood to Lloyd, 21 December 1955, CO 554/812, NA; Note by John Hare for the Secretary of State, 25 January 1956, CO 554/812, NA.

47 Branney, 'Summary of the Legal and Policy Conclusions of 1955/56 from the Gold Coast Protection Treaties', CO 554/1808, NA.

48 A fuller account of this episode will be provided in my forthcoming PhD dissertation on decolonisation in Britain's empire of protectorates.

49 Branney, 'Memorandum on the Protection Treaties with the Chiefdoms of the Rivers Province and Adjacent Areas of Nigeria in Connection with the Petition of those Chiefs', December, 1956, FCO 141/13645, NA.

50 Lennox-Boyd to Viscount Kilmuir, 8 October 1958, CO 554/1809, NA.

51 Kilmuir to Lennox-Boyd, 13 October 1958, LCO 2/695, NA.

52 Lennox-Boyd, 'Statement by the Secretary of State for the Colonies on the Treaties between the Crown and the Oil Rivers Chiefs', CO 554/1809, NA.

53 Martin Wight, *The Development of the Legislative Council*, Oxford University Press, Oxford, 1947, p. 64.

Index